Networking Smart

Networking
Smart

How to Build Relationships for Personal and Organizational Success

Wayne E. Baker

McGraw-Hill, Inc.

New York   San Francisco   Washington, D.C.   Auckland   Bogotá
Caracas   Lisbon   London   Madrid   Mexico City   Milan
Montreal   New Delhi   San Juan   Singapore
Sydney   Tokyo   Toronto

Library of Congress Cataloging-in-Publication Data

Baker, Wayne E.
    Networking smart : how to build relationships for personal and
organizational success / Wayne E. Baker.
        p.   cm.
    Includes index.
    ISBN 0-07-005092-9:
    1. Communication in management.   2. Communication in
organizations.   3. Public relations.   4. Interpersonal relations.
5. Information networks.   I. Title.
HD30.3.B364   1994
658.4'5—dc20   93-22704
                                                                          CIP

1 2 3 4 5 6 7 8 9 0   DOC/DOC   9 9 8 7 6 5 4 3

ISBN 0-07-005092-9

*The sponsoring editor for this book was Philip Ruppel, the editing supervisor
was Jane Palmieri, and the production supervisor was Suzanne Babeuf. It was
set in Palatino by McGraw-Hill's Professional Book Group composition unit.*

Printed and bound by R. R. Donnelley & Sons Company.

 This book is printed on recycled, acid-free paper con-
taining a minimum of 50% recycled de-inked fiber.

To Cheryl

Contents

Part 3. Managing Relationships and Networks outside the Organization

9. Finding Good People (or Changing Jobs)   185

10. Building Relationships with Customers and Clients   197

Part 4. Conclusion

Preface

*Power in organizations is the capacity
generated by relationships.*
                    MARGARET J. WHEATLEY
          Leadership and the New Science[1]

Networking smart is meant to be a provocative idea. The term *networking* elicits strong feelings, positive and negative; some people swear by it, others swear at it. *Smart*, too, can go two ways; it can mean intelligent, resourceful, and knowledgeable, or just crafty and cunning. By combining these two terms, I wish to engage your interest in a powerful idea that goes far beyond the usual definitions and preconceived notions. It's an idea at the heart of excellence in business.

Networking, as I use it here, is the active process of building and managing productive relationships—a vast network of personal and organizational relationships. The process embraces everyone you work with—your superiors, peers, team members, subordinates, and many others. The process includes relationships within and between organizational units—departments, teams, functions, offices, divisions, subsidiaries. And it includes external ties—relationships with customers, suppliers, competitors, investors, and communities.

Networking smart means building and managing this vast network in intelligent, resourceful, and ethical ways. Networking smart means learning how to network well and applying the knowledge responsibly. Businessmen and businesswomen who network smart see themselves, their people, and their organizations as members of a complex web of connections. These businesspeople forge and manage this complex web in ways that are positive, constructive, and beneficial for all involved. Networking smart means developing relationships that are good for you and your career, good for the people you work with, good for your organization, and good for your customers. Networking smart is the key to your personal and organizational success.

The Power of Relationships

The foundation of *Networking Smart* is hard evidence, not just my personal experience as a general manager, researcher, and professor of business. I've based this book on scientific research that I and others have conducted over the years on relationships and networks in business, personal, and social life.

Just how important are relationships? You might be surprised. Most people are astonished at the variety of personal and organizational benefits. Consider a few of the facts we've learned about the benefits of managing business relationships well:

- Managers with large personal networks get higher-paying positions than managers with small networks.[2]

- Managers with large, well-diversified networks get promoted faster and at younger ages compared with their peers with underdeveloped networks.[3]

- Professionals who find jobs through personal contacts (instead of classified advertisements or other impersonal means) find better, more satisfying jobs that they stay with longer.[4]

- Building good working relationships is the main cause of success for managers who take charge of a new situation.[5]

- Close relationships with customers save money. It costs three to five times as much to get a new customer as it does to keep an old one.[6]

- Strong partnerships with suppliers yield lower costs and higher-quality products and services.[7]

- Business effectiveness, in general, depends more on "human-related activities," such as building relationships, interpersonal skills, and communication, than on technical skills and abilities.[8]

Relationships are vitally important in all spheres of life. Here are a few facts about the importance of social relationships:

- People with strong social support networks enjoy better physical and mental health than those without such networks. Not only are people with good support networks less likely to become ill, but when they do, they recover faster.[9]

- People with large personal networks tend to live longer than those with small networks.[10]

- Personal happiness and satisfaction depend in large part on the quality of relationships with other people.[11]

- Social rejection and isolation in childhood cause serious and persistent problems of adjustment later in life.[12]

- Homelessness is caused by poverty coupled with a lack of "network resources" such as family, kin, church, friends, and neighbors.[13]

People who network smart recognize the vast power of relationships in business, social, and personal life. They empower themselves, their associates, and their organizations by working hard to develop positive relationships in all areas. In this book, I show you how to build the relationships you need for personal and organizational success. No matter where you are in your career, this book will help you develop and use the networking skills you need to survive and thrive in the 1990s and beyond.

Networking smart isn't an option anymore. Not if you want you and your organization to flourish in the emerging business order. Managing relationships has always been an important part of a businessperson's job. *But it's more critical today than ever before.* The world of business is changing so fundamentally that your success depends more than ever on how well you manage relationships.[14]

Downsizing and restructuring force you to contend with much wider spans of management, much heavier work loads, more and broader responsibilities. You need a new way to manage, a better way to work with and get things done through others.

The implicit employer-employee contract of lifelong employment is quickly vanishing. Personal contacts can help you find new jobs, but you have to build your network before you need it. When you change jobs, you carry important network assets with you—your contacts and relationships. Networks are portable. Managing your career well means building networks that help you get your job done now *and* position you for the future.

Multifunctional teams are now a popular way to spur innovation and cut time to market. Working in team-based organizations isn't easy. It means everyone has to develop better relationship skills. Peer-to-peer relationships, for example, are more important than ever before, but you don't have formal authority over peers. And you have to develop the entrepreneurial ability to assemble teams, secure the resources they need, and coordinate their efforts with other teams and groups.

External alliances and partnerships with customers, competitors, and suppliers are increasingly important. This trend presents unprecedented challenges. It means you have to abandon the traditional go-it-alone, adversarial mindset. You have to become comfortable with and adept at building all sorts of external networks.

Globalization means it's not enough to be proficient at managing domestic relationships. To be successful in the emerging business order, you must become a global manager with a viable network of worldwide relationships as well.

Network organizations are replacing traditional hierarchies. These new organizational forms knock down walls between departments, functions, and divisions; network organizations remove external barriers, building partnerships with customers, suppliers, competitors, and investors. Learning to thrive in network organizations is the biggest challenge of all. You can't rely on formal rank, position, and authority. Instead, you have to become an expert at building all sorts of cooperative, mutually beneficial relationships that span traditional boundaries, inside the company and out. You have to learn how to network smart.

Overall, we're moving from *high-volume* enterprises—where profits come from scale and volume, says Harvard political economist Robert Reich (Secretary of Labor in the Clinton administration)—to *high-value* enterprises—where profits come "from continuous discovery of new linkages between solutions and needs."[15] High-value enterprises demand a new core role—the *strategic broker*. This relationship builder links problem identifiers and problem solvers, gets them the resources they need, and sets them free to get the job done. That's networking smart.

And Tom Peters recognizes the urgent need for networking in the new business order.[16] He advises everyone to develop network-building skills, to hire people who have them, to train people who don't, to reward those who network well. That, too, is networking smart.

Four Objectives

I have four key objectives for this book. My first objective is consciousness-raising: increasing *awareness* of the importance of relationships and networks in business. Most people, I've found, underestimate the importance of networking. Even those who are already adept at managing relationships, I've learned, don't always realize the diversity and range of business areas in which relationships and networks are now so important. This lack of awareness presents enormous opportunities to those who learn how to network smart. As Northern Trust Company vice president John N. Iwanicki puts it, "...most people place such a low priority on internal [and external!] networking that a very modest effort creates a big payoff. A modest effort really makes you stand out."[17]

My second objective is to short-circuit the arduous, inefficient ways in which most managers are forced to learn relationship skills. Most managers learn the hard way: They teach themselves, just like those who learn to swim by being thrown into the deep end of a pool. The sink-or-swim method works, but the casualty rate is too high. And all the mistakes and sins committed along the way are visited upon the organization.

My third objective is to increase the legitimacy of the idea of managing networks of relationships. Concepts such as networking, managing relationships, and making connections come with a lot of negative baggage. Such negative associations are more than unfortunate—*they threaten your ability to succeed in the new business order*. Networking smart isn't optional. The swift-changing business world creates an urgent need to be better, faster, and smarter at building relationships. Those who network smart actively build productive relationships in responsible and ethical ways.

My fourth objective is to help practicing managers, entrepreneurs, and businesspeople at all levels learn how to *do* things better. I devote each chapter to a specific business topic, and I conclude each one with concrete advice on how you can use what you've learned: what you can do now, what you can do soon, what you can do in the long run. You can immediately put into practice what you learn in each chapter, and you'll have plenty to think about for the future as well.

The World Is a Network

Sometimes it helps to have an image in mind as you read a book. Let me close this preface with an image I invite you to consider as you read this book: the world as a network of relationships. Every person is a nexus of relationships; everyone is the center of a vast circle of contacts and connections. The circle encompasses old and new friends, family and relatives, business colleagues and associates, professional contacts, acquaintances, neighborhood and community ties, on and on and on. The circle includes old ties that lay dormant and forgotten now but would be recalled the instant you encountered a person. The circle includes endless chains of indirect links—a friend of a friend of a friend, etc. Each of us is more than an individual; each is an individual with a wide network of relationships.

Your personal network is a great resource. When you work with someone, you're joining two personal networks, creating even greater potential. Put together a team, and you've assembled a vast and powerful network, a complex set of internal and external relationships. Your organization is a "node" in a network of relationships made up of customers, suppliers, competitors, communities, regulatory agencies, on and on. You can even think of the global economy as a vast network of trade flows. The world *is* a network.

It's important to appreciate how much the network image conflicts with deeply ingrained ways of thinking about success. We're more accustomed to thinking of the world as an assortment of disconnected individuals—a collection of free-floating, independent "atoms." Personal success, for example, is viewed as an *individual* matter: Each person is in charge of his or her own fate. That's true, but only in part. The first lesson we need to *un*learn, says Stanford Business School's Jeffrey Pfeffer in *Managing with Power*, "...is that life is a matter of individual effort, ability, and achievement." But "[i]ndividual success in organizations is quite frequently a matter of working with and through other people, and organizational success is often a function of how successfully individuals can coordinate their activities."[18]

The network concept is one of the most powerful ways of understanding the world. If you see the world as a network, you're traveling in august company. Charles Darwin, for example, describes in *The Origin of Species* the complex interconnections among all animals and plants.[19] The idea of the interconnectedness of all things is as old as Eastern mysticism and as new as modern physics. The parallels are striking and exciting, as physicist Fritjof Capra describes.[20] Eastern thought emphasizes the basic unity of all things, the universe as an organic interconnected whole. Quantum physics sees the world the same way, rejecting the older Newtonian view of the world as a giant machine that could be disassembled and studied part by part. "Gradually," says Capra, "physicists began to realize that nature, at the atomic level, does not appear as a mechanical universe composed of fundamental building blocks, but rather as a *network of relations....*" Some of the legendary physicists of our time—Julius Robert Oppenheimer, Niels Bohr, Werner Heisenberg—found inspiration in the harmony of modern physics and Eastern mysticism.

The same powerful ideas apply in organizations. In our outdated Newtonian view of organizations, says organizational consultant and business professor Margaret Wheatley in *Leadership and the New*

Science, we think of organizations as collections of parts—jobs, roles, unconnected individuals. But we're in the quantum age—the age of connections—in physics and business. And we need to adopt the network view for managing. "Now," says Wheatley, "I look carefully at how a workplace organizes its relationships; not its tasks, functions, and hierarchies, but the patterns of relationships and the capacities available to form them." And, she says, "I cannot describe a person's role, or his or her potential contribution, without understanding the network of relationships and the energy that is required to create the work transformations that I am asking from that person."[21]

Wheatley's not alone. Tom Peters, too, calls on us to reject the Newtonian view of organizations and put into practice the insights of quantum physics.[22] Indeed, the quantum view is the powerful logic behind the movement to rebuild the corporation around *processes*—as Michael Hammer and James Champy illuminate in *Reengineering the Corporation.*[23] In the new business world, networking smart—making connections and building relationships—is the key to personal and organizational success.

A Suggestion for Reading This Book

I think of this book as a guide for action. In it I tell you where, why, and how you can become more successful by building relationships. I've written it so you can turn right now to any chapter. You'll learn immediately why networks are so important in a given area and what you can do now to start building the relationships you need. I recommend, however, that you read first the Introduction for an overview of key themes and a chapter-by-chapter preview of the rest of the book.

After the Introduction, I've divided the book into three main parts. The three chapters in Part 1 describe the networking perspective. Chapters 1 and 2 are more "theoretical" than the rest of the book, and you may be tempted to skip them. But I suggest that you read (or at least skim) both chapters. To understand networking, it helps to know its opposite. Chapter 1, "The Cult of the Deal: Old Attitudes in a New Business World," describes the prevailing antithesis of networking. The cult is your main obstacle to learning how to network smart.

Chapter 2 is important because it explains why networking "works." Networking smart is more than common sense; it works for real scientific reasons, which I explain in this chapter. Be sure to complete the Management Style Questionnaire near the end of Chapter 2. It's a short, self-administered instrument that helps you evaluate your own management orientation. It's the first of dozens of exercises, hands-on tools, and checklists I put in the book to help you learn and use the lessons of networking smart. If you wish, you can turn right now to the questionnaire and fill it out.

Parts 2 and 3 cover *internal* and *external* networking, respectively. After you read Part 1, you can turn next to either Part 2 or Part 3, depending on your interests and needs. (The last chapter in Part 1, Chapter 3, "Building Intelligence Networks," addresses both internal and external networking, so I suggest you read it before turning to Part 2 or 3.)

Wayne E. Baker

Acknowledgments

Friends and colleagues helped me in many ways. Mark Shanley, Harry Davis, and Steve Persanti commented on a very early draft. Their constructive comments helped to reshape the book at a critical formative stage. Both Linda Ginzel and John Deighton provided a level of suggestions and insights well beyond the call of collegial duty. Howard Haas, Chip Heath, and Shantanu Dutta provided input on various chapters that helped improve the book considerably. Chapter 6 owes a great deal to the many conversations I've had with Ananth Iyer about serendipity. Sheila Taylor provided able research assistance throughout the research and writing process as well as helpful comments on Chapter 7. Don Schwartz provided insights, counsel, and moral support.

Rob Faulkner aided this endeavor in many ways. Sometimes it was commenting on written material; sometimes it was a key article that arrived in the mail at just the right time. Often it was his enthusiasm for the project, along with his patience in waiting for me to finish so we could continue our several collaborations.

I thank my agent, Ken Shelton of Executive Excellence Literary Agency, for sound editorial and business advice throughout the various stages of bringing a book idea to fruition. I thank Meg McKay of Executive Excellence for her wisdom and advice. I thank Roger Terry, formerly of Executive Excellence, for his help as well. My appreciation to Allan Cox for putting me in touch with Ken and his agency.

I thank the many MBA students at the University of Chicago Graduate School of Business who have taken my course "Managing Organizations through Networks." They may not know it, but I worked out many ideas about business networking while teaching this course over the years. I owe a special debt of gratitude to two cohorts of Executive MBA students who took my course "Role of the General Manager." My students in XP 62 suffered through a rough draft of the book; their comments and applications of the ideas were essential for rewriting the book. My students in XP 63 read the next-to-last version; their input was vital for testing and improving the final version. To both cohorts, I give a special note of appreciation for their excitement about networking in business.

I thank Eleanore Law for faithful reading of the page proofs, and Martha Krause for expert indexing services. I am grateful to the professionals at McGraw-Hill, who have helped in countless ways to make this book a reality. Among them, I thank especially Philip Ruppel, editor and publisher; Allyson Arias; Jane Palmieri; and Laura Friedman.

It's customary to place last the most important acknowledgment, and I don't break tradition. My wife, Cheryl, helped in ways I can only begin to recount. She supported the project from its earliest stage with enthusiasm and encouragement. She read every word of every draft; the clarity of the ideas owes much to her careful review. She knows better than anyone about the ups and downs of producing a book from start to finish. I dedicate this book to her.

Introduction

Relationships determine success.
PHILIP B. CROSBY
The Eternally Successful Organization[1]

People can be taught how networks operate, how to establish new networks, what networks already exist, how to improve existing networks, what kinds of relationships are desirable or undesirable.
NOEL M. TICHY
The University of Michigan[2]

Bill Hansen was delighted. In May 1992, he was named general manager of the new Philadelphia facility of StorageAmerica, one of the fastest growing national companies in the $8 billion public and contract warehousing industry.[3] The Philadelphia unit opened to high expectations and visibility. StorageAmerica is a major player in the midwest and northwest, but the 500,000-square-foot Philadelphia unit is the company's beachhead in the eastern region. If this first move is successful, the company plans to advance aggressively into New England and the Atlantic seaboard and build several more warehousing facilities.

StorageAmerica ranks in the top 15 of about 700 companies operating in the industry. Companies like StorageAmerica provide storage, spot market logistical support, and distribution services to major consumer products companies and industrial materials suppliers. Each facility accumulates and stores products shipped by its clients. These products are routed and delivered to local supermarkets, department stores, drug stores, purchasing clubs, and other retailers. Public warehousing lets manufacturers focus on their core competencies, avoiding the expense and hassle of owning and operating warehouse space in many different local markets. It's often much more economical to use

1

third-party warehouse services. Candy companies, for example, use public warehouses to accommodate seasonal needs for storage and distribution. Most candy is made and stored in the summer months for delivery and sale in the short September–December season. And it's cheaper for just about any manufacturer to ship large loads to a few central warehouses than it is to make thousands of small shipments directly to local retailers.

Bill was looking forward to taking charge of the Philadelphia facility. It was a big challenge, but he felt he was ready. He had just completed three years as assistant manager of customer service and operations at the Milwaukee facility, where he played a major role in the unit's turnaround. (The Milwaukee facility had always been a mediocre unit in the StorageAmerica system.) In the process, he acquired quite a reputation for his ability to "move the most product for the least money." He developed a real knack for calculating storage and handling rates in ways that minimized costs yet kept customers happy. His success at Milwaukee figured prominently in his appointment as general manager of the Philadelphia unit.

In addition to his track record at StorageAmerica, Bill had a lot going for him. He had four years of leadership experience as a junior officer in the U.S. Navy. Recently, he completed an MBA with an emphasis on logistics and production. Overall, StorageAmerica's top managers felt Bill had all the right stuff: smart, experienced, energetic, mature.

Bill worked long and hard in his new job, but things just weren't going right. He had troubles everywhere he looked. For one, he suffered from a nagging lack of communication with the corporate office in Chicago. He waited and waited for decisions on his requests for staff and resources. Often, he found out too late about decisions made at the corporate level. Several times, for example, the corporate sales and marketing department had quoted warehousing rates for national customers who were already storing in his facility. These quotes often undercut his own rates, and left him with a lot of explaining to do to his customers.

Bill had other troubles with his major national accounts. National accounts require coordination across facilities to ensure uniform levels of service. It was always an embarrassment for the company—and a source of irritation to clients—when clients discovered that one facility was delivering one level of service while another was delivering a lower level. Each facility developed its own billing practices, and national clients often complained because they had to deal with several billing methods. StorageAmerica was a decentralized organization, however, and it lacked formal mechanisms for coordination across facilities.

Bill's assistant manager of operations, George Bennett, was a never-ending source of problems. George began his career as a warehouseman, working his way up to become assistant manager. It soon became clear that George was causing significant delays and added expense because he lacked the right training in logistics. Bill would have liked to replace George, but the corporate office had a policy of promoting from within, and StorageAmerica (like most companies in this quick-growing industry) lacked people with solid logistics backgrounds. As a result, Bill spent an inordinate amount of time working with George to train him and get him up to speed.

Bill had even more problems with operations. He was in the process of negotiating a contract with the local Teamster's union (which represented warehouse and dock personnel and material handlers), but it wasn't going well. Union leaders weren't pleased with his first offer, and now the workers (who were working without a contract) appeared to be conducting a deliberate slowdown. Just recently, Bill heard a rumor that the union steward was drumming up support for a possible strike. The work slowdown itself was interfering with Bill's efforts to build a customer base and get his facility up to efficient operating capacity, and a strike at this time would be disastrous.

And Bill was also running into problems with the local zoning commission. Soon after he arrived in Philadelphia, Bill saw the need to add a "high-cube" or high-density storage facility. A high-cube facility minimizes handling costs by stacking products in vertical racks instead of storing products on the floor. Such facilities were very efficient for high-volume customers who stock hundreds of different products requiring lots of handling. A high-cube facility can be four stories high, however, and proximity of the unit to the Philadelphia airport would require a zoning variance. Bill had applied for one, but three months later, the commission still hadn't acted on his application, and it didn't seem likely that they would any time soon. Without the high-cube facility, however, Bill wouldn't be able to service some of his major consumer products clients.

Bill wasn't going to make it.

Why was Bill having so much trouble? It wasn't because he lacked *technical* skills. He had those. But he was unaware of his *relationship* responsibilities: The need to build solid working relationships, inside and outside his organization. Had he known how to manage upwards, he could have improved communication with headquarters and solved the rate-cutting problem with sales and marketing. Good relationships with peers at other StorageAmerica facilities could have supplied him with vital information, good advice, and moral support. Bill had rotated through several of these units during his management training period (he had even studied some detail), but he failed to seize these opportunities and cultivate budding relationships with his peers. As a result, he never became part of the informal network among general managers that compensated for the lack of a formal coordination mechanism.

Bill didn't have the right set of relationships. When StorageAmerica vice president of warehousing Hank Wagner came from Chicago to help Bill, he quickly tapped his relationships around the company. When he saw the problem with George Bennett, for example, he negotiated with the general manager of the Minneapolis facility (whom Hank had trained himself) to get his logistics manager "on loan." In a month, the Minneapolis logistics manager was in Philadelphia working with George.

Bill never discovered key networks, but Hank quickly found connections and contacts that were useful in negotiations. It turned out, for example, that a key labor leader in Philadelphia was a close friend of a Chicago labor leader that Hank had worked with for years. Hank also discovered contacts that helped move the building variance through the zoning commission. An influential commission member, Hank learned, had been a classmate of StorageAmerica's CEO at the University of Illinois. Bill couldn't help but admire how Hank tapped relationships and networks to get things done.

Bill, like many managers who fail, suffered from *management myopia,* a sort of shortsightedness that restricted his field of vision to the technical part of the job. He didn't know that his ability to get the job done hinged on his success in cultivating, maintaining, and mobilizing a vast array of relationships.[4] He didn't realize that his success depended so much on people he didn't yet know. Because he didn't build relationships and get hooked into the network, Bill wasn't able to discover critical information, influence key decision makers, negotiate successfully, or implement his strategy. He didn't see the world as a network of relationships. Bill, like many who fail, wasn't networking smart.

Oh, yes. You're probably wondering what happened to Bill. Well, he was fired.

Why Building Relationships Is More Important Than Ever Before

To some degree, Bill Hansen's problem is everyone's problem. As most of us advance in our careers, we face an impending personal and professional crisis. We discover a growing mismatch between the skills that got us where we are and the skills we need to continue progress. At first, *technical* skills are enough. Early jobs are technical in nature, and success is based on individual achievement. When we took our first managerial jobs, good technical skills could still carry the day. But, as we move up, technical skills just aren't enough. Success depends more and more on *relationship* skills: how well we build good relationships with peers, superiors, subordinates, groups, teams, customers, suppliers, investors, and a multitude of others. Indeed, the main cause of failure for managers who take charge of a new situation—like Bill—is the failure to develop good relationships.[5] Study after study shows that success as a manager hinges on the ability to cultivate, maintain, and mobilize a vast array of relationships inside and outside the organization.[6] And network-building skills become more and more important the higher up you go.[7]

Building relationships has always been an important part of the manager's job. But it's absolutely crucial today. The world of business is changing so fundamentally that new ways of managing are required—demanded—and your success depends more than ever on how well you build and manage networks of relationships. A new business order is emerging. You can see it in several widespread trends that are creating the urgent need to be better, faster, and smarter at building relationships.

Restructuring

During the past decade, many companies have delayered and downsized, slashing huge numbers of jobs. For example, since 1980, the *Fortune* 500 companies have cut an estimated 4.4 million net jobs.[8] The trend is far from over. In the same month the 1992 recession was declared officially "over," IBM announced plans to cut 25,000 jobs; General Motors was closing plants and making deep cuts; Boeing announced massive layoffs; Sears planned to close 113 stores, close the Big Catalog, and cut 50,000 jobs; the U.S. Post Office planned to slash 30,000 jobs; and the employer of last resort—the U.S. military—was downsizing dramatically.[9] And these are only the most sensational examples; thousands of smaller companies are doing the same. Restructuring is far from over, and we'll be feeling the aftershocks for years to come.

Cost cutting is the main reason for downsizing, but restructuring yields an organizational advantage: It flattens organizations and enables them to respond more quickly to changing competitive and market conditions. People in the restructured organizations of the

1990s can't rely on old ways of managing. Restructuring brings new challenges and pressures—vastly wider spans of control, much heavier work loads, more and broader responsibilities. Managers have to let go. They don't have the time or energy to micromanage. "An overburdened, overstretched executive is the best executive," said General Electric chairman and CEO Jack Welch in a *Harvard Business Review* interview. "He [or she] doesn't have time to meddle, to deal in trivia."[10] Restructuring means you must *reconceive* your job. It's more productive, for example, to think of span of *coordination* than span of *control.* The only way you can get your job done is to put much more emphasis on empowering and enabling others, much less on formal top-down authority and intrusive micromanagement.

The New Employer-Employee Contract

The days of lifelong employment are over. Nowhere is this more evident than in the recent restructurings at Sears, GM, and IBM—just a few of the well-known companies that once gave employees the implicit promise of lifelong employment. Job security has been eliminated as a clause in the new implicit employer-employee contract.

The good news is your networks are portable. You take your contacts and relationships with you wherever you may go. Your challenge is to build the right networks, inside the organization and out, before you want to leave. Or have to leave. Managing your career well means building relationships that help you get your job done now *and* position you for future career moves.[11]

New Information and Communication Technologies

Electronic information and communication technologies are turning traditional organizations upside down and inside out.[12] The new technologies break barriers between groups and get more people involved in problem solving and innovation. Linked to customers' systems, the new technologies provide rapid-response capability. By giving users unprecedented access to almost limitless information, the new technologies decentralize power and loosen hierarchical control; they level and democratize the workplace. And these advances are making obsolete the manager's traditional role as a collector, analyzer, and relayer of information. Control of information is no longer a source of managerial power.[13]

Multifunctional Teams and Groups

Multifunctional teams and groups are now commonplace. "Indeed," writes University of California, Berkeley, business professor Homa Bahrami, "during the last decade 'teams' and 'groups' have become part of our managerial vocabulary and are now viewed as a central organizational building block."[14] Quality is a big reason. TQM (total quality management), for example, uses teams to break traditional barriers between departments. And the results are stupendous: high-quality products, cost-saving work processes, satisfied customers. Speed is another big reason for teams and groups. Multifunctional teams help to shorten the new-product development cycle, bringing new products and services to market faster than ever before.

The widespread use of teams and groups demands different management skills. A manager's effectiveness was once judged by the ability to navigate the bureaucratic maze of formal channels and vertical lines of authority. Now effectiveness is judged on the manager's entrepreneurial ability to *create:* to put together and run individual teams and networks of teams; to initiate and manage horizontal (peer) relationships; to find and secure resources from around the organization.

External Partnerships

The traditional arm's-length, go-it-alone frontier mentality is becoming more and more obsolete. Many companies are discovering that long-term partnerships with suppliers produce a wonderful paradox: higher quality, lower costs. Alliances with competitors yield yet another productive paradox: Competitors compete more effectively by joining forces via joint ventures, technology sharing, joint marketing, manufacturing, R&D, and so on. But the explosive growth of partnerships and alliances presents new challenges. You must develop a new mindset, one that sees suppliers, customers, and competitors as allies and partners, not adversaries or enemies. You must become adept at building external as well as internal networks. You have to learn how to cultivate and manage a complex array of relationships that cross organizational—and national—boundaries.

Globalization

Globalization means more than the reduction of trade barriers. It means the pace of business is increasingly set by foreign competition. For many companies, globalization means "foreign" markets are more important than "domestic" markets. Some major U.S. firms, for example, make more profits outside the United States than in. More and more firms use parts and components made by suppliers outside the United States, especially in high-tech industries. And more and more companies export unit headquarters abroad to be closer to key markets, suppliers, and competitors. In 1992, for example, AT&T moved its corded telephone headquarters from New Jersey to the French Riviera, and Hyundai Electronics Industries shifted its personal computer headquarters from South Korea to San Jose, California.[15]

Globalization means managers must change how they think about their jobs. It's not enough to be adept at managing domestic relationships, you must also become a global manager with a viable network of worldwide relationships. No matter where you call home, your internal and external relationships must span places, cultures, nations, and time zones. A successful career path now includes significant stints abroad, with the double challenge of learning to work in new places and coping with the problem of reintegration upon return.

The Rise of Network Organizations

Traditional organizations are too rigid, slow, and lumbering to survive in what GE's Jack Welch calls the "white-knuckle decade" and Tom Peters calls the "nanosecond nineties."[16] Accelerating change everywhere—new technologies, new products, shifting markets, the rise of knowledge-based economies, geopolitical upheaval, globalization—makes hierarchy as unfit as the dinosaurs were when their environment changed. To win in the 1990s and beyond, companies must dismantle the hierarchy and replace it with fast, flexible, innovative network organizations. Digital Equipment consultant Charles Savage calls this the shift to "fifth-generation management." It's "the transition from steep hierarchies to flatter networking organizations."[17] Fifth-generation companies, says Savage, are those run by "human networking."

Companies in industries such as professional services, high-tech Silicon Valley, and Hollywood filmmaking have used the network design for years, as I and others have documented in detail.[18] Tom Peters hails these firms as role models for the future.[19] Now, more than ever, companies in all industries desperately need the same flexibility and versatility. They need the same fire and spirit.

We see traditional companies experimenting with the network design. The most daring of them all is GE. Jack Welch is now attempting an extraordinary transformation of the century-old giant, turning the company into the ultimate network organization: the *boundaryless organization.*[20] A boundaryless company is a seamless network of relationships. The walls that separate people inside the company are torn down; departments and functions are replaced with multidisciplinary project-based teams that form, disband, and reform again in a continual process of change and renewal. The walls between "domestic" and "foreign" are knocked down, producing a genuinely global company. And the barriers separating inside and outside are broken, bonding the organization and its suppliers, customers, investors, and communities in common purpose.

Making it as a manager in the network organization means throwing out the old management rule book. The old ways don't work in the new organizations. In the traditional hierarchy, formal position and authority were the power behind the manager's command.[21] But today's manager must learn to live in a brave new world of "influence without authority."[22] This calls for a "new kind of business hero," says Harvard Business School's Rosabeth Moss Kanter. "[They] must learn to operate without the might of the hierarchy behind them. The crutch of authority must be thrown away and replaced by their own ability to make relationships, use influence, and work with others to achieve results."[23] The new manager rejects the old roles of controller, boss, intimidator; in the 1990s and beyond, the effective businessperson is an inspirer, coach, enabler.

Management Philosophies, Old and New

In many ways, we're at a turning point. Organizations and their leaders are searching for new and better ways of surviving and thriving in the new business order. But the search is far from over. "Although much has been written about the act of leadership," says Charles Fombrun in *Turning Points,* "our firms continue to be managed more like autocracies and fiefdoms than like inspired hotbeds of innovation...."[24] Progressive companies like GE are pioneering new ways of managing and leading, but most companies continue to struggle with old-line bureaucracies and top-down management styles that are increasingly out of step with today's business world.

I see signs of the turning point in the clash of fundamental management philosophies, old and new—the philosophy of *control* versus the philosophy of *empowerment.* Control is the heart of hierarchy; empowerment is the essence of networking. How the clash of control versus empowerment plays out in your company determines in large measure how competitive—and how exciting!—it will be in the years to come.

The key difference in these competing philosophies revolves around how they deal with a central problem, what I call the *dilemma of indirect management.* This dilemma means your success depends on how well *other* people do their jobs, but you can only manage others *indirectly.* The dilemma of indirect management arises, in part, because most of the work you're responsible for is done beyond your direct supervision and observation. Do you *really* know what your people do? What your salespeople tell customers? How your engineers work together? How your managers are managing? The dilemma also arises because everyone in an organization is interdependent—you rely on so many others outside your realm of responsibility to get their jobs done. In a large or decentralized organization, you don't know—and may have never even met—those on whom you depend to perform faithfully. And yet you're responsible for getting results anyway.

The new business order exacerbates the dilemma of indirect management. Wider spans of management and broader responsibilities stretch you thinner and thinner. You have a finite amount of time to spread among more and more people. If your direct reports have doubled or tripled or quadrupled, you have much less time to spend with anyone. And the erosion of formal authority means you can't just order people about and hope to get good results. Making multifunctional teams work means building more and better peer relationships—yet with peers you *only* have influence, no direct authority at all. The growth of external partnerships extends the dilemma of indirect management well beyond your organization's boundaries—your success hangs in the balance of how well suppliers do their jobs, how well joint ventures work, how loyal customers are.

Whips and Chains: Philosophy of Control

The old way to resolve the dilemma of indirect management is to *control people,* or at least try to. Over the years, managers have tried a host of techniques. One traditional method is what I call *ultra-control:* the attempt to specify everything in advance and make people behave like parts of a machine. Based on the assumption that those "above" can prespecify what those "below" ought to do, higher-ups try to preprogram workers by specifying tasks, activities, and jobs in excruciating detail. Work processes are formalized into rules, regulations, procedures, instructions, job descriptions. Good employees are those who do things "by the book." Those who don't are penalized and disciplined. At GE—before the big cultural revolution—this was known as the "whips and chains environment."[25] Ultra-control.

The shortcomings of ultra-control weren't obvious when U.S. companies dominated a domestic economy. But globalization brought new competitors, especially the Japanese, who produced better-quality products at lower costs. Then the defects and inefficiencies caused by ultra-control became painfully clear. Worst of all, the whips-and-chains environment wastes the tremendous talents, energy, and creativity of those who are "controlled." As GE general manager of manufacturing told Robert Slater in *The New GE*, "All you got was what you specified and nothing else. None of the heart or inspiration of the person."[26]

Another traditional control method—managing by the numbers—is just as bad. In this approach, you're just given performance targets, usually sales or profit objectives. You're on your own to figure out what to do to meet your targets. Pay is tied to performance, so the theory says you're motivated to do things right. The hope is you'll also do the right things—use resources wisely, be efficient and productive, satisfy customers. The concept works better on the drawing board than it does in practice.

Managing by the numbers fails in several ways. The best known is the sacrifice of long-term viability for short-term results. Because performance targets are often short-term, managers focus on immediate results. But what's good in the short run often isn't good for the long. You could raise prices to boost immediate profits and meet short-term objectives, for example, but you risk alienating customers in the long run.

A more serious defect is overreliance on pay as a motivator. Now don't get me wrong. Pay *is* a powerful motivator. Linking pay and performance is a sound idea, basically. The trouble is that pay is a tricky motivator. Psychologists know, for example, that pay can take some of the joy out of enjoyable work and make people *less* motivated.[27] The reasons are complex, but the main idea is working for pay can detract from the pleasure of doing work for its own sake. That doesn't mean pay is unimportant, nor that you can get away with neglecting to reward your superior performers with money. What it does mean is this: *Most people work for more than money.* This is a basic fact psychologist Douglas McGregor and others pointed out long ago.[28] If you use only money to motivate, you miss the opportunity to tap other powerful motivating forces: the needs for social approval, acceptance, achievement, self-esteem, self-fulfillment.

Not providing the means to meet these needs may be a cause of the turmoil we see in organizations today. We need "organizational models that are more congruent with human nature," says Hanover Insurance president Bill O'Brien in Peter Senge's wonderful book on the learning organization. "When the industrial age began, people worked 6 days a week to earn enough for food and shelter. Today, most of us have these handled by Tuesday afternoon. Our traditional hierarchical organizations are not designed to provide for people's higher order needs, self-respect and self-actualization. The ferment in management will continue until organizations begin to address these needs, for all employees."[29]

Tapping people's higher-order needs as motivators doesn't have to cost extra. "For 25 years," said a middle-aged GE worker in *The New GE*, "you've paid for my hands when you could have had my brain— for nothing."[30] In fact, the argument could be made that it costs *less*. If people get more than money from work, they may not demand additional pay as compensation for frustrating and unfulfilling work. Leaders who inspire high performance know how to motivate by creating conditions that help their people meet their higher-order needs on the job.

Managing by the numbers is whips and chains of a different sort; you suffer the lash if you don't meet performance targets and you're chained to the same old processes of work. Managing by the numbers is a deception: It only *appears* to grant freedom to act. The freedom is empty, empty because it doesn't really change anything fundamental about the way people work.

Let me illustrate. I've been working with a large law firm that's exploring new ways to be competitive. When we talk about marketing, it's clear that most senior partners see the problem simply as one of incentives: How do we "incentivize" our attorneys, they ask, so they'll bring in new business? That is, how do we link pay and performance—manage by the numbers—to get them to generate and keep new customers? The problem, I said, is that incentives aren't enough. Taking people who are motivated already and motivating them even more is an exercise in futility. Unless you provide them with tools, skills training, and education—unless you help them learn how to work differently—added incentives will only generate frustration and disappointment.

Both ultra-control and managing by the numbers suffer the same fatal flaw: failure to change the fundamental processes of work. We know from total quality management (TQM) experts that "[t]he main source of quality defects is problems in the process."[31] This powerful insight applies everywhere and anywhere in the organization. TQM also supplies us with hard evidence that the philosophy of control doesn't work: "*exhortation, incentives, and discipline of workers are unlikely to improve quality.*"[32] You have to change the process. Indeed, the most productive companies in the world have this in common: They all concentrate on managing processes—how well the parts work together—not on how well each part works alone.[33] This is a revolutionary turn of perspective. If you observe low productivity, you shouldn't go hunting for unproductive people; you investigate the culprits of poor processes and faulty systems. Unless you change the way people interact and work, you really haven't made any changes at all.

Soft Values for a Hard Decade: Philosophy of Empowerment

Today, forward-looking companies are learning they can't be competitive by prespecifying and preprogamming or managing by the numbers. Instead, they're finding competitiveness though *empowerment*. As GE's Jack Welch puts it: "We know where competitiveness comes from. It comes from people, but only from people who are free to dream, to risk, free to act."[34] The source of productivity, Welch argues, is people, values, and culture: "That's where we have to turn in the '90s—to the *software* of our companies—to the culture that drives them." What we need, he says, are "soft values for a hard decade."[35] The philosophy of empowerment.

Empowerment and control are polar opposites. Control philosophy, in its heart of hearts, holds a bleak view of human nature: People dislike work and seek to avoid it, so they must be controlled, coerced, and threatened to put forth in the interests of the organization.[36] Empowerment begins with a different set of assumptions about motivation and managing. It assumes work is natural. People desire fulfilling and rewarding work. Under the right conditions, people flourish on the job; under the right conditions, externally imposed "control" isn't necessary—people will exercise self-control and self-direction in the service of the enterprise.

"Under the right conditions" is the operative phrase. To empower, you must create the right conditions. Hierarchy doesn't work because it creates the *wrong* conditions. By design, hierarchy is *dis*empowering. It treats adults like children.[37] It presumes, for example, that people "above" are always superior; they know more and are more mature and capable than those "below." People "above" command and expect obedience; they judge those people "below" and mete out rewards and punishments. The truth is those above *don't* know better. Those closest to the customer know best what the customer wants. Those who work on the production line know best what the production problems and solutions are. Not those in the corporate office. "This method [empowerment] works because of the energy and brains of people who are working on a specific job," says Champion International chairman and CEO Andrew C. Stigler in a *Milwaukee Journal* article. "When they want to, they can find better ways of doing it and becoming more productive."[38] It's a lesson the Japanese have known for years.

The manager's central task is creating the right conditions, the right circumstances in which people will flourish on behalf of the enterprise. It's everyone's job, not just those at the "top." It's essential to your success wherever you are in the organization and wherever you want to go. You need to create a climate, a context that empowers you and your people to build and maintain the networks all of you need to get your jobs done. Datatrack president Richard Papolis put it well: "I order no one to do anything....I don't make big product or market decisions. I create the right conditions under which those decisions are made. I think of myself as a gardener, as an arranger, as a creator of climate."[39]

"Human networking," says Charles Savage, is "self-empowering."[40] You empower people by helping them network smart. "Top management's job," writes *Business Month* contributing editor Fred Guterl, "is to put in place mechanisms that promote the interactions—not to control them but to create the proper conditions for them to work."[41] It can be as simple as putting people from diverse specialties in the same location as a way to spur innovation. Or using multifunctional teams to break functional boundaries. Or investing in new information technologies that encourage peer-to-peer networking. Or inviting key suppliers and customers to join your in-house teams.

It's important to know from the start what "empowering" *doesn't* mean. It doesn't mean abrogating responsibility or failing to intervene in basic structural changes. Empowerment through networking recognizes the dilemma of indirect management (people can't be controlled) but it doesn't mean you should adopt an extreme hands-off policy. I've seen several companies make this mistake. Some create teams and give them resources but never set goals, guidelines, or overall parameters of the job. Others don't even do that much. They inform their people "you're empowered" but don't do anything to change basic processes—no teams, no resources, no education, training, or skills development—just empty rhetoric.

Some sort of balance is needed. You have to set the mission. This must be loose, of course, so it doesn't stifle creativity and initiative, but you still need broad guidelines and goals. General Norman Schwarzkopf (retired) offers us a good model. During the Persian Gulf War, he issued statements of "Commander's Intent" to his line officers. These conveyed the general mission and military objectives but allowed lots of room for local commanders to improvise and adapt to local exigencies and surprises. The concept of Commander's Intent puts into practice an important lesson Schwarzkopf says he had learned: "...staying flexible enough on the battlefield to react to unexpected enemy actions."[42]

GE's Jack Welch recognizes the value of flexible strategy in the 1990s. Welch was inspired by Kevin Peppard's letter to the editor of *Fortune* about Karl von Clausewitz, the nineteenth-century Prussian general and military strategist.[43] In his famous military tract, *On War*, von Clausewitz argued that strategy has to leave ample room for unexpected events, surprises, and chance opportunities.[44] The most detailed battle plan can't enumerate and take into account all possible scenarios. It's impossible. Like the game of chess—which is a lot simpler than war or business—it's impossible to work out in advance all moves and countermoves. As a result, one unexpected move by the enemy, or one element of strategy that doesn't unfold as planned, and the whole strategy begins to fall apart. The best strategies, argued von Clausewitz and his many disciples since, set only broad goals and objectives—like Schwarzkopf's Commander's Intent—and encourage flexibility and improvisation to fit changing circumstances. Welch conveys Commander's Intent—broad goals and mission—and he's pushed strategy making down to the business unit level where it can evolve, adapt, and change. It empowers—and it improves strategy.

But you have to do more than just convey Commander's Intent to empower your people. The proper balance also includes intervention in basic processes of work. That begins with education, training, and skills development. Most organizations suffer serious learning disabilities when it comes to networking. Hierarchy is toxic to flexible networking, and networking skills atrophy without exercise and nourishment. This book will help you and your people learn and develop the skills you need for networking, team building, and relationship management. For now, I invite you to consider a powerful metaphor for empowering people and strengthening the organization via relationship building.

The Company of the Table: A Metaphor for Relationship Building

The military is an old metaphor for organizations. It evokes an image of top-down management, absolute authority, unthinking obedience. This image is an increasingly inaccurate picture of today's organizations, and it's a prescription for disaster as a role model for the 1990s. But there's another military metaphor, a little known and well-kept secret, that *is* appropriate for the manager who empowers by managing conditions. It's called "The Company of the Table,"[45] and it's based on the scientific principle that powerful groups and teams are built on relationships that grow out of the natural interests of the people involved. Once you understand the principle of The Company of the Table, you can use it to create conditions that help people build powerful relationships.

The Company of the Table was the basic military unit of the Syssitians of ancient Sparta. Here's how it worked. Men sat 15 to a table, all by free choice. One could join a table only by unanimous consent. So who sat at the table? As you might expect, The Company of the Table was composed of men with common kinship bonds and neighborhood ties. The army harnessed the natural loyalties and common interests of The Company of the Table by using it as the basic military unit. The Company of the Table was the sturdy building block of Sparta's military might.

Just ancient Greece, you say? Jump ahead about 2500 years to Europe in the 1940s. After the defeat of Germany, the U.S. Army brought in social scientists from the University of Chicago and asked them to figure out why the German army had been such a powerful fighting force.[46] Some people thought it was ideological brainwashing—abstract allegiance to the fatherland and all that. The real reason, it turned out, was the German army used its own version of The Company of the Table. The basic units of the *Wehrmacht* were formed in boot camp and kept intact throughout the war. Each unit developed extremely strong, durable, cohesive ties. Soldiers didn't fight so hard because they were defending the fatherland; they were so tough because they were defending their dearest friends.

Fast-forward 25 years. The Vietnam War. Here The Company of the Table was overturned. The U.S. military created fragile and unstable units.[47] Each basic unit had a shaky and unhealthy mixture of green recruits, others in the middle of tours of duty, and veterans who were about to rotate out. Units were never kept intact. This strategy was a prescription for organizational disintegration and disaster. The groundwork for cohesive relations never formed. Instead of all for one and one for all, it was every man for himself. As one Vietnam veteran told me, "Our motto was, 'Look out for number one.'"

Why does The Company of the Table work? It works because it taps and releases natural human energy. It permits those involved to realize their fundamental social needs. These, said organizational psychologist Douglas McGregor, are the needs "for belonging, for association, for acceptance by one's fellows, for giving and receiving friendship and love."[48] The Company of the Table helps people realize their needs for self-esteem, achievement, recognition, and respect. Many managers know about these human needs. But, as McGregor says, "it is often assumed quite wrongly that they represent a threat to the organization....[M]anagement, fearing group hostility to its own objectives, often goes to considerable lengths to control and direct human efforts in ways that are inimical to the natural 'groupiness' of human beings." Those who recognize the vast power of The Company of the Table, however, go to considerable lengths to *encourage* the formation of relationships and cohesive groups. That's networking smart.

Many don't realize it, but the principle of The Company of the Table lies behind every high-performance organization. Every effective leader knows it, at least intuitively. Effective leaders marshal, harness, and direct natural human energies in service of organizational goals. Effective leaders don't fight human tendencies; they go with them. They transform raw human energies for a higher purpose as they help people help themselves. That's what The Company of the Table is all about. It was *The Soul of a New Machine* chronicled by Tracy Kidder.[49] Data General (DG) group manager Tom West *had* to create a cohesive group of computer scientists if he wanted to design DG's new minicomputer in record time. He did so by creating conditions that focused their natural energies and produced the powerful teams known as the "Hardy Boys" (hardware designers) and "Micro Kids" (encoders of software microinstructions). Tom Furey, director of the IBM Rochester Development Laboratory, did the same thing with the fabulous Silverlake Project—producer of Big Blue's best-selling AS/400.[50] He led a concerted effort to abolish IBM's traditionally *dis*empowering ways of doing business. He empowered his people by giving them the right resources, tools, and incentives; he empowered them by creating the right conditions—those that harnessed and focused creative energies and enabled his people to forge the cohesive relationships they needed. The results were spectacular. Not only did the Silverlake team create a computer that strengthened IBM's hand in the midsize computer market, but the team won the Malcolm Baldrige National Quality Award as well.

Preview of the Book

I've organized the book in three main parts. Part 1 presents the networking perspective. In Chapter 1, "The Cult of the Deal: Old Attitudes in a New Business World," I describe one of the biggest obstacles to networking smart: the prevailing deal mentality. It reached its dark glory in the decade of the 1980s. Instead of utilizing the power of relationships, deal-obsessed managers treat everyone and everything as impersonal transactions. They ignore the relationship-building power of The Company of the Table.

In Chapter 2, "The Networking Leader," I introduce the solution to the cult of the deal: building relationships and networks. This chapter tells you *why* and *how* networks work. I describe three levels of relationship management and the spectrum of relationships. I present five basic networking principles that help you build networks and tap the power of The Company of the Table. The chapter concludes with advice on how to evaluate your own networking style.

Managing information is so critical and so fundamental that I devote an entire chapter to it. Our information problem is severe. "A weekday edition of *The New York Times*," notes Richard Saul Wurman in *Information Anxiety*, "contains more information than the average person was likely to come across in a lifetime in seventeenth-century England."[51] Not only is there a prodigious increase in the production of information but fast-changing markets soon turn new information into old news. Chapter 3, "Building Intelligence Networks," tells you how to manage the information problem. Those who network smart build independent intelligence networks to scan the environment, double-check information, and monitor key people, events, and decision situations. They help their people build their own intelligence networks. They turn the organization into a vast information-processing machine.

In Part 2 of the book, I look *inside* the organization, focusing on managing internal relationships and networks. Chapter 4, "Managing Up, Down, and Sideways," focuses on managing one-on-one relationships, your direct ties with your superiors, team leaders, subordinates, team members, and peers. I describe how good personal relationships are built on the combination of mutual understanding and mutual benefit and tell you how to diagnose and improve your relationships.

Chapter 5, "Bottlenecks and Bridges," focuses on one of the most important and widespread problems in organizations today: degeneration into isolated groups, functions, and departments. The result goes by different names in different companies—silos, turf, stovepipes, fiefdoms, walls, empires, and so on. Whatever you call it, it spells trouble for the organization, particularly in the new business environment. I summarize the problem as one of *bottlenecks.* In this chapter, I explore the reasons that groups erect walls, and tell you how to spot bottlenecks. I then introduce the concept of *bridges*—the pathways across group boundaries. I conclude Chapter 5 by telling you how you can build bridges in your organization.

Chapter 6, "Managing Serendipity," addresses the creative process. The chapter's title may strike you as a contradiction or a vain hope:

Creativity is so mysterious that many managers give up all hope of influencing it. Yet, as I show in this chapter, it *is* possible to improve the odds of serendipity—the essential role of chance in problem solving, creativity, and discovery. By managing conditions—facility design, group composition, and information gatekeepers—you can indirectly boost innovation in your creative group. I conclude Chapter 6 with concrete advice on what you can do to improve the odds of serendipity.

Chapter 7, "Tapping the Power of Diversity," helps you manage and reap the power of an increasingly diverse work force. Diversity can benefit an organization by bringing in new information, fresh viewpoints, new knowledge. The benefits of diversity don't occur easily, however, due to the glass ceiling, stereotyping, and the natural tendency for relationships to form between *similar* people (a basic networking principle I describe in Chapter 2). In this chapter, I tell you how to overcome such obstacles through education and training, job and career management, organizational redesign, and other interventions. By integrating men, women, and minorities in your company, you can boost both personal and organizational performance.

Chapter 8, "Networking through the Organizational Life Cycle," examines the organization over time. I describe the natural sequence of developmental stages that most organizations go through, as well as the typical crises that arise as an organization makes the transition from one stage to the next. I discuss the networking challenges common to each stage. I tell you how you can personally cope with each transition, and how you can strengthen your organization's ability to handle crisis by building bridges. These bridges help the organization survive crisis by improving information exchange, breaking down stereotypes, building allegiances, and promoting a common world view.

In Part 3 of the book, I look *outside* the organization: how to manage external relationships and networks. Chapter 9, "Finding Good People (or Changing Jobs)," focuses on the key role of personal networks in the matching of good jobs and good people. With the new career realities—the elimination of job security as a clause in the new employer-employee contract—it's more important than ever that you learn how to network well. The same is true for employers. The increased rate of job hopping makes it imperative for employers to learn how to use networking to find good people. In this chapter, I tell you how to build your networking base and use personal contacts to find good jobs or to find good people for jobs.

Chapter 10, "Building Relationships with Customers and Clients," is based on a powerful marketing principle: Profitable transactions follow relationships. I describe the rise of relationship marketing, present a practical framework for diagnosing customer relationships, and show you how to build strong customer relationships via information links, fast feedback channels, and multilevel business and social ties. And I describe what it takes to create a real relationship-building infrastructure.

Chapter 11, "Word-of-Mouth Marketing," presents a powerful but neglected technique for increasing sales and launching new products and services, word-of-mouth communications. Though most sales of products and services come via word of mouth, few companies make word of mouth systematic. In this chapter, I describe why word of mouth is so powerful and how it works, and I tell you how you can tap its tremendous power by developing explicit word-of-mouth marketing programs.

Chapter 12, "Building Supplier Partnerships," shows how close relationships with suppliers can lower costs and increase product quality. I begin this chapter by describing how word-of-mouth networks can be used to find good suppliers of products and services. I discuss the growing trend toward supplier partnerships, and I disclose the key differences between managing suppliers of products versus suppliers of professional services. I end the chapter with practical advice on how you can build win-win supplier partnerships.

Organized networking clubs are such a growing nationwide phenomenon that I devote an entire chapter to them. In Chapter 13, "Networking Clubs," I describe how executives and managers utilize networking clubs to swap leads, contacts, information, and ideas. This chapter tells you how to find, join, and participate in networking clubs.

Chapter 14, "Cooperating with Competitors," describes how and why leading companies are abandoning the adversarial go-it-alone mentality and cooperating with competitors via strategic alliances. In this chapter, I illustrate the various mechanisms competitors use to cooperate—joint ventures, research consortia, common manufacturing and marketing arrangements, and technology sharing—and reveal the two underlying rationales for cooperation. I tell you what makes alliances succeed (and fail) and what you can do to initiate, build, and maintain cooperative alliances with competitors.

The book's conclusion is Chapter 15, "The Boundaryless Organization: Role Model for the 1990s and Beyond." In this final chapter, I bring together the ideas of previous chapters and integrate them into the model of the ultimate network organization: the boundaryless company. I use Jack Welch's vision of General Electric as a boundaryless company as the key role model and describe four revolutionary management techniques—work-out, process managing, best practices, education and training—that he's using to turn a traditional hierarchy into a fast and flexible network organization. By applying the lessons from this book, you can prepare your company for the "nanosecond nineties" by transforming it into the dynamic network model of the future.

PART 1

The Networking Perspective

1

The Cult of the Deal: Old Attitudes in a New Business World

Everything becomes a transaction....
KEN AULETTA
Greed and Glory on Wall Street[1]

Something strange was afoot at Playco. Before the 1980s, this *Fortune* 500 manufacturer of computers and electronic learning aids, games, and toys was a typical staid, laid-back, buttoned-down company.[2] Executives had disputes and disagreements, of course, but these were handled with decorum and discretion. "We used to have conflicts between departments," a long-time executive told sociologist Calvin Morrill, "[like] engineering and design. In those days, the president always settled them when the two department VPs [vice presidents] couldn't get a grip on it. But it was all done very quietly, behind closed doors....It was a different world then. There was also a lot more discipline within the departments."[3]

All this changed in the 1980s, which Morrill observed in his intensive study of Playco. Instead of settling their differences behind closed doors, executives now engaged in what they called "shoot-outs" over business decisions. One combatant would "call out" the other, just like in the Old West, and they staged a public "duel." Opponents and their allies would wear "flak vests" (three-piece suits) to deflect "bullets" shot by foes. The victors "put some notches in their guns," adding to their reputations and gaining power in the firm, while the vanquished lost face and influence. Honorable executives—"white knights"—would fight fair (indeed, they often "rescued" executives "in distress"). "Black knights," however, played dirty, "ambushing" and "bushwhacking" adversaries in all sorts of overt and covert actions. At times, conflict erupted in outright violence among executives, "meltdowns" as they called them—shoving and pushing, ripping clothes, fist fighting—until security guards would step in and break it up. Playco was at war.

What happened to Playco? What turned a placid corporate climate into a battleground of hostility, aggression, and violence? Around this time, corporate America was in the throes of a major revolution: merger mania. Along with this mania, the hostile takeover—once considered a maverick technique used only by the lunatic fringe of business—became a legitimate part of mainstream business culture.[4] Shoot-outs, white knights, greenmail, ambushes, poison pills, shark repellent, golden parachutes—the merger culture of the 1980s had its own colorful vernacular. And it was this corrosive culture that had worked its way into the heart of Playco, as Calvin Morrill so clearly documents.

Playco executives knew all about merger mania. They made several friendly takeovers, adding publishing houses, movie studios, and chemical companies to Playco's portfolio. They repulsed two hostile takeover attempts and rejected a few friendly offers as well. Now they internalized the symbols, language, and mentality of the deal-oriented takeover culture. "Everyone seemed to be talking about [hostile] takeovers," an executive said, "white knights this and black knights that; how some takeover players played the game dirty....The art of the takeover became big conversation at parties and at the office....We began talking about the 'art'...of the meeting, getting promoted, dealing with each other; especially fighting with each other. Now it consumes us."[5]

Playco had succumbed to the cult of the deal.

A Good Idea Taken Too Far

The cult of the deal is a good idea taken too far. It happens when the right to make and break business relationships—the right to make deals—is taken to its extreme and worshipped as the solution to everything. At Playco, the impersonal, deal-oriented takeover mentality was used as a philosophy for human relations. The deal mentality may have its place in mergers and takeovers, but it is a bleak substitute for proper conduct between people.

As long as it doesn't get out of control, however, our right to make and break relationships can be a good and beneficial idea. If you're underpaid, for example, you can seek a better offer from another company. If you're unhappy with your employer, you're free to quit and seek better opportunities. Even if you signed an employment contract, you cannot be forced to work against your will; slavery—an unbreakable relationship—was outlawed long ago. And you're free to dispose of private property as you see fit. If you're dissatisfied with the return on your investment in a company, for example, you can sell stock and reinvest elsewhere.

And you're not imprisoned by the circumstances of your birth. People born in medieval times were locked into a predetermined station in life, a fixed point in a rigid social hierarchy. Serfs, for example, were bound forever to labor for a local lord. Talent, effort, and luck could not raise them above their station of birth.

The right to make deals is a new idea, historically speaking. Only 500 years ago, says sociologist James Coleman, did individuals and corporations begin to be recognized as having rights we take for granted today: "rights of ownership, rights of transaction, [and] particularly rights to act under their own will, to establish and break relationships, to make contracts."[6] This new freedom of action—the right to engage in transactions, to buy, sell, and hold property—revolutionized what had always been static and stable societies. It shattered predetermined, tradition-bound relationships, and introduced unprecedented flexibility, mobility, and change. By doing so, the right to make and break relationships became a powerful engine of economic growth and development. This right released great creative energy; the potential to better one's station in life is a great motivator.

The problem occurs when we fall in love with our right to make deals and become blind to the alternatives or the consequences of our actions. Some hostile takeovers are healthy and productive; they drive out inefficient managers and rekindle the company's competitive spirit. The problem crops up when takeovers become a mania: when takeovers are made only for short-term gains, or to break labor contracts; when good managers are cast out with the bad, and those who remain are consumed with insecurity about their jobs; when valued customers and suppliers are slighted and ignored; when takeover candidates are hounded by raiders who have no interest in a company beyond its immediate breakup value.

The consequences of takeover mania are so severe that some economists—who on the whole love the idea of takeovers—call hostile takeovers *breaches of trust:* violations of implicit agreements with managers, workers, and communities.[7] Hostile new owners exploit their newly acquired companies by breaking the implicit contracts employees had with the previous owners. For example, employees may have agreed informally to a voluntary wage freeze in exchange for the (unwritten) promise of future benefits. The new owners haven't made such commitments and don't feel bound by them. So they ignore the implicit agreements, and employees get stuck. Worse, the new owners may unilaterally impose a new wage or benefits cut, knowing full well that it isn't easy for workers and managers to pick up and find new jobs, particularly comparable ones.

The glorification of deals and deal-making blinds us to the importance and power of relationships. Now, it is true that the deal mentality *is* the best strategy in certain situations. If you can't get your employer to raise your salary, for example, your last resort might be to secure an offer from a competitor. In many situations, however, there are better ways. I describe plenty of them in this book. For now, consider this scenario. Let's say you need blood for surgery. Would you rather have blood that was purchased from a paid donor or obtained free from an unpaid donor? In other words, would you rather have blood that was treated as a commodity, subject to the laws of the marketplace, or would you prefer blood that was given as a gift? The quality of blood purchased as a commodity is generally lower.[8] To those who sell blood for money, blood donation is an impersonal transaction, a deal; the incentive to give is purely monetary. The quality of blood is higher from donors who don't need or want the money. They give blood out of a sense of civic duty, altruism, or the hope of reciprocity in the future, all of which imply a stronger, longer-lasting relationship to society than can be purchased for the moment. In many situations, relationships are superior to deals.

The cult of the deal makes it difficult to learn and adopt better ways. For years Detroit auto makers have ignored the quality lessons available from the Japanese.[9] (Recall that U.S. manufacturers shunned W. Edwards Deming's quality control ideas while the Japanese embraced them!) Instead, the auto makers used the whips-and-chains approach they know so well. Suppliers were viewed with distrust and held at arm's length. Contracts lasted less than a year. Price competition was intense, with suppliers dropped for minuscule price differences. Each auto maker maintained a huge pool of suppliers. Not so long ago General Motors had a staggering 3500 suppliers, not counting material suppliers! Such excessive numbers make it impossible for the auto company's engineers to know personally their supplier counterparts. Personal ties are viewed with great suspicion. (Recall McGregor's observation that many managers fear such affiliations!) But without personal ties, quality must be managed clumsily by impersonal specifications, blueprints, and contracts.

Big companies still throw their weight around. GM, for example, still has a lot to learn and a long way to go. GM has made some improvements, but by the end of 1992 suppliers still accused the ailing auto maker of roughshod treatment.[10] Old attitudes die hard. The cult of the deal is so deeply ingrained in companies like GM that it's uncertain whether they'll change in time to save themselves from extinction.

The Japanese, in contrast, know how to manage suppliers. Even though Japanese firms buy *more* parts than their U.S. counterparts, they deal directly with a much smaller number of parts suppliers. Small numbers mean they can build the personalized relationships necessary for high quality. Whereas U.S. auto makers specify everything in detailed blueprints and brook little deviation, Japanese auto makers build partnerships with suppliers and tap their expertise and insights by including them in planning and design. Close ties yield quality, flexibility, and innovation. Strong manufacturer-supplier ties have an added benefit: They are formidable "nontariff barriers" for outsiders—such as American companies.

It's not that Japanese practices don't work here. Japanese auto assembly plants and their suppliers in the United States have successfully transplanted Japanese practices in the U.S. business environment.[11] The real obstacle is philosophical. The cult of the deal—the enchantment with transactions over relationships—makes it tough for U.S. managers to learn how to network smart.

A Pervasive Problem

The hostile takeover symbolizes the cult of the deal, but the problem goes far beyond. The takeover battles of the 1980s are part of a larger war. "At issue," says sociologist and organizational expert Paul Hirsch, "is who gets to define the very purpose of the corporation."[12] On one side are traditional corporate stakeholders—executives, managers, employees, and their communities—with customers and suppliers as keen allies. These groups have a vested interest in the long-term viability and stability of their companies. Short-term profitability is important, but in their view the company's mission includes long-range projects, investment in research and development, and contributions in the community.

On the other side are the champions of the cult of the deal. Chief among them are investment bankers, financiers, and takeover artists, who all benefit from takeover mania and have little interest in the long-term future of their corporate victims. "Their hostile attack," says Hirsch, "challenges the value, competence, and credibility of companies and their managers."[13] Most of the battles in the 1980s were won by the champions of the deal. And it's still not clear who's going to win the war. The new business order is still in a larval state.

Look at who runs U.S. companies today. CEOs used to come from engineering, sales, and marketing. Now they come from finance. And to many finance types, a firm is little more than a bundle of assets deployed to maximize short-term earnings.[14] Shareholder value, not product quality or customer satisfaction, has become the modern grail.

Global competition intensifies the deal mentality. Cheap labor alternatives in Mexico, Korea, and Taiwan tempt U.S. manufacturers to shift production abroad rather than seek solutions at home. The latest trend is to migrate data processing and other back office jobs overseas to Ireland, Barbados, Jamaica, the Philippines, and other cheap English-speaking labor sources.[15] I've noticed this trend in publishing, for example. When a manuscript is accepted for publication, the publisher always has it copy edited before it reaches print. Many publishers perform copy editing in-house, but others contract out to third parties. Lately I've received copy-edited manuscript pages and galley proofs from contract services in Ireland, Hong Kong, or other non-U.S. sources, even though the final articles are published in U.S. journals and magazines.

Such trends illustrate the larger problem, what Tom Peters calls the "minimization of labor's role."[16] Rooted in the traditional adversarial relationship between managers and workers and driven by economic pressures, companies seek cheap labor abroad or in low-cost states, outsource work by hiring back exemployees as freelance "consultants" (i.e., no benefits), automate and eliminate jobs altogether, and diversify into capital- (versus labor-) intensive businesses, rather than exploring and developing long-term partnerships with labor.

No industry is free from the sway of the deal mentality. The deal mentality runs rampant in the making of films, music, books, and newspapers. Formerly independent newspapers, for example, are now under tight corporate control with fierce attention paid to short-term profits, argues former *Chicago Tribune* editor James D. Squires.[17] As a result, he says, editorial policy has passed from the "editor" to business managers who base newspaper content on what "sells," not on what readers need to know. Rob Faulkner and I traced the rise of deal making and commercial control in the Hollywood film industry.[18] The industry always struggled with its famous dilemma—Is film business or art? In the 1970s, however, business interests gained the upper hand as film making was reoriented to pursue the blockbuster—the big-budget, big-revenue film. In this new environment, says film critic Pauline Kael, film making moved "...into the control of conglomerates, financiers, and managers who treat them as ordinary commodities."[19] "Deal-making," concludes Hollywood observer Mark Litwak, "has replaced film-making as the principal activity of Hollywood."[20]

Service industries, some of the few bright stars left in the U.S. economic firmament, are also succumbing to the cult of the deal. In a 1986 article in *Harvard Business Review,* James Brian Quinn and Christopher Gagnon asked, "Will Service Follow Manufacturing into Decline?" Their answer is not optimistic. "It will take hard and dedicated work not to dissipate our broad-based lead in services, as we did in manufacturing. Many of the same causes of lost position are beginning to appear. Daily we encounter the same inattention to quality, emphasis on scale economies rather than customers' concerns and short-term financial orientation that injured manufacturing."[21]

Evidence of the decline of relationships and the ascendancy of the deal mentality is everywhere: the increasingly litigious nature of our society, the sharp rise in medical malpractice claims, the dissolution of the traditional family, and the erosion of trust in social and public institutions of all kinds. The decline of relationships is so pervasive that philosophers ask whether it is possible for us to sustain commitments to others in personal, business, or public life.[22]

The Networking Solution

The deal orientation has its place. It's a good idea in certain situations, but too often it's taken too far. Building relationships is often a more appropriate and more powerful alternative. Given the way the business world is changing, networking smart—making connections and building relationships—is more important than ever before.

In this book I present the alternative to the cult of the deal: building relationships and networks instead of cutting deals. I don't expect you to accept my argument as an article of faith. This book contains the evidence. In the next chapter, I describe the perspective and working principles of the networking leader. In Part 2 of the book, I demon-strate the power of relationships and networks *inside* the organization. In Part 3, I demonstrate the power of relationships and networks *out-side* the organization. Every chapter offers hard evidence about rela-tionships and networks in a specific business area. And each chapter tells you *how* to reap the power of relationships. With this knowledge, you can learn to network smart—a leader who builds relationships and networks—and thrive in the changing business world of the 1990s and beyond.

2

The Networking Leader

Think networks.

ROBERT K. MUELLER
Director, A.D. Little International
Corporate Networking[1]

People who network smart see relationships as the essential way to get their jobs done. "The point is you can't separate the problem of influencing the organization from the question of influencing individuals," said an executive in John Gabarro's *The Dynamics of Taking Charge.* "My interpersonal relationships are how I influence the company."[2] Leaders manage by getting things done through others.[3]

Too often, I've found, people view their jobs mainly as a set of impersonal and technical tasks: setting policy, budgeting and planning, acquiring and allocating resources. Technical tasks are important, of course, but they're only a fraction of your job. And this fraction shrinks over time as your career develops. You can always compensate for a lack of technical knowledge by hiring experts, but you can't delegate the most important part of your job: the task of building networks of relationships.[4] Once you appreciate the power of relationships, you won't want to delegate—because building and managing networks is your key to personal and organizational success.

33

	Inside	**Outside**
Personal	superiors peers subordinates team members directors etc.	customers suppliers investors union leaders gov't officials etc.
Group	work units teams departments divisions subsidiaries offices etc.	organizations of: clients suppliers investors communities etc.

Figure 2-1. The networking territory.

The Networking Territory

People who network smart build a broad and diverse range of relationships. The networking territory covers relationships inside and outside the organization, at both the personal and the group levels (see Figure 2-1). Inside, effective leaders develop good relationships with a wide range of people—superiors, board directors, peers, team members, subordinates, subordinates of subordinates, and many others. Beyond one-on-one relationships, effective leaders foster good relations between work groups, teams, departments, functions, divisions, and other organizational units. Outside, good leaders cultivate strong ties with suppliers and vendors, customers and clients, competitors, investors, the capital markets, regulatory agencies, local communities, the press, trade associations, and various other publics and outside constituencies. Only with a well-developed network that covers the entire territory can you get your job done.

The networking vision includes relationships that *are* and that *can be*. Think back, for example, to your first days on the job. Your initial task was "sizing up" the situation, figuring out what relationships exist.

"One of the first things newcomers typically pick up," says Stanford University's Jane Hannaway in *Managers Managing*, "is *who* is important and to *whom* they should pay particular attention."[5] Later, you forged and built your own relationships, probably in an intuitive and not-always-conscious way. You cultivated relationships upward, downward, and sideways as you worked with bosses, subordinates, and peers. You met and learned to work with people from around the company through teams, task forces, and other groups. You created new relationships, strengthened or weakened existing ones. And at times you severed relationships, knowingly or not, as you moved, transferred, or fired people.

Managing Relationships Is a Tough Job

Managing relationships is a tough job because it demands high levels of intellectual and emotional development. Every relationship involves what psychologist Donald Schwartz calls *interpersonal problems*, "where an individual feels a mismatch between his [or her] own expectations and the behavior, feelings or motives of another."[6] Interpersonal problems are part of the intrinsic nature of relationships. Problems arise in relationships all the time; if they didn't, your job would be simple—or simply unnecessary.

People experience and understand interpersonal problems differently, and that's where the difficulty comes in. Let's say, for example, that your superiors ask you to relocate. It's a good position but the move would uproot you and your family from friends, school, and community. All things considered, you'd rather stay, and you say so. How do your bosses understand your decision?

- Your decision is not a valid answer. You're not a team player. You don't know how to play the game. You don't have what it takes.

- Your decision is accepted as legitimate, but your bosses really don't understand the reasons behind it. You may not have what it takes (and you may not be considered next time).

- Your decision is accepted, and your bosses understand your reasons. Your bosses may explain it in terms of prior experiences ("We've learned that it doesn't help anyone to move someone who doesn't want to go"), external conditions ("He/she can't move because the kids are finishing high school"), or with full empathy and understanding of all your reasons.

The first reaction is what Dr. Schwartz calls a *low-level response* to interpersonal problems. A person stuck at this level feels irritation, resentment, exasperation, even rage over an interpersonal problem. He or she finds it difficult to separate the problem from the person, to view the other's behavior as valid, or to appreciate reasons for the behavior. The other person is dismissed as a "jerk," "pain," "asshole," "troublemaker," "not a team player," and so on. The second response indicates an *intermediate level* of understanding. The other person's behavior is accepted as legitimate, even though the reasons for the behavior are not understood. The person operating at this level might blame him or herself ("Maybe it's all my fault") or experience internal conflict about causes of the behavior. The last response illustrates a *high level* of understanding. The person understands the reasons that the other acts in a particular way and accepts the behavior as legitimate and authentic, despite the tension or inconvenience it might cause. The person operating at a high level easily separates the problem from the other person, understands the other's motives and feelings, and can take the role of the other with great empathy.

Low-level responses are much too common in business. I'm sure you have plenty of examples. Consider this one. I know of a department head at a professional association in Chicago who suffered from a peculiar problem: She just couldn't find "good people." Every few months her administrative assistants would quit. This happened six times in two years. In fact, it was hard to find "good people" for the whole department: This unit had the highest turnover of all departments at the association! This excessive turnover was related, in large measure, to the department head's inability to move beyond low-level responses to interpersonal problems. She blamed others for her interpersonal problems, identifying the "cause" of all personnel troubles as lack of "good people."

Low-level responses to interpersonal problems epitomize the cult of the deal. Instead of understanding interpersonal problems at higher levels, the other person or company is dehumanized, stereotyped, treated as a commodity.[7] For example, corporate takeover artists—masters of the cult of the deal—depersonalize corporate victims by referring to vulnerable takeover targets as "pigeons." They use all sorts of sports and courtship/marriage metaphors to make takeover activity seem more respectable and legitimate.[8]

Those who network smart strive to operate at *intermediate* and *high* levels. It's not easy. GE CEO and chair Jack Welch demonstrates a high level of understanding as he recognizes how difficult it is to put yourself in another's shoes. "Most of our people have never been acquired," he said in a recent employee roundtable discussion, "and they don't know what it's like to be acquired. They don't know that your family roots have all been torn apart. Your children's education's in doubt. Everything is gone. Your relationships with your boss are now over, [ones] that you've built for 15 years. Your pension plan. The first doubt is, is it real? Enormous trauma goes through these companies. And GE people come in right away, a lot of the time, with their heels dug in and say, 'Here's how we do it,' without any appreciation of the enormous personal and emotional trauma that people who've just been sold—I mean, just been sold—feel. So, we've got to get better at that."[9] It's much easier to depersonalize, stereotype, or simply "write off" another person (or company) than to really understand an interpersonal problem and its causes. But the hard way is the only way to develop healthy and productive relationships.

The Five Networking Principles

I hesitate to talk about principles. Most managers do not suffer theory gladly, and for good reason—what flies on the drawing board often crashes and burns in practice. But it's also true, as the saying goes, that there's nothing as practical as a good theory.[10] A good theory lets you see the forest and the trees; it helps you organize and integrate your thinking. Networking smart is based on five fundamental principles. People who network smart apply all five to build and manage relationships. An overview of the five now gives you a framework to keep in mind as you think, reflect, and act on the facts and advice I offer in this book.

Principle 1: Relationships Are a Fundamental Human Need

People create relationships for all sorts of reasons. The most basic reason is we need to. We like to think of ourselves as independent and self-reliant, but there are no Robinson Crusoes in modern society; each of us is a point in a vast network of interdependent relationships. We also create relationships to multiply our efforts: We can do more together than apart. Sometimes relationships emerge from a common focus of interest. We find our friends at work, place of worship, next door, the health club—any place or activity where common interests bring people together. And we form relationships because we are told to by the voices of authority and tradition.

Beyond these, however, we create relationships because we're social by nature and value relationships as ends in themselves. Sociologist

Georg Simmel coined the term *sociation* for the universal desire for human interaction.[11] We seek relationships for social approval, for defining ourselves and our place in the world. We find meaning in life through relationships. Mihaly Csikszentmihalyi, a psychologist at the University of Chicago, has spent a quarter of a century studying *flow*, the psychology of optimal human experience. "Studies on flow," he reports, "have demonstrated repeatedly that more than anything else, the quality of life depends on two factors: how we experience work, and *our relations with other people*" [my emphasis].[12]

Relationships are good for you. The benefits can be scientifically measured. All of the benefits I listed in the Preface are backed by solid evidence. Both mental and physical health, for example, are related to social networks. People with good social support networks are healthier, happier, and better able to cope with stress and life's crises.[13] Patients with positive, long-term relationships with their physicians are more satisfied with their health care and are more likely to stay with their prescribed regimens.[14] Managers with large, well-developed networks are more effective; they earn more and get promoted faster.[15] Supplier partnerships yield higher-quality products and services at lower costs.[16] The list of documented benefits goes on and on.

Principle 1 is the key to effective management. The human need for relationships is potential energy you can tap and direct to generate high performance and productivity. "The need to belong is a powerful human force," says Allan Cox in *Straight Talk for Monday Morning*, "that finds expression in teamwork."[17] By creating the right conditions—like multifunctional teams—you turn potential energy into a powerful realized force. By helping people build and manage relationships, you are helping them fulfill very human desires.

Principle 2: People Tend to Do What Is Expected of Them

Expectations are self-fulfilling prophesies. What we expect of people is often what we get. I think of it as the Pygmalion principle. Remember the story of Professor Higgins and Eliza Doolittle, the flower girl, in George Bernard Shaw's *Pygmalion*? It illustrates Principle 2. "You see, really and truly," Eliza said, "apart from the things anyone can pick up (the dressing and the proper way of speaking, and so on), the difference between a lady and a flower girl is not how she behaves, but how she's treated. I shall always be a flower girl to Professor Higgins, because he always treats me as a flower girl, and always will; but I know I can be a lady to you, because you always treat me as a lady, and always will."[18]

Expect the worst from people and you'll bemoan the low state of human nature. But expect the best and you'll be singing the praises of your fellow men and women. Sounds naive, doesn't it? Well, Principle 2 is based on scientific evidence. Consider the original discovery of the "Pygmalion Effect." Robert Rosenthal and Lenore Jacobson conducted an experiment on expectations and reported the results in *Pygmalion in the Classroom*.[19] They told teachers in an elementary school that 20 percent of their children showed "unusual potential for intellectual growth" and gave them a list of their names. Unbeknownst to the teachers, the names of "unusual" children had been drawn at random. Even so, eight months later the "unusual" children exhibited significantly greater increases in IQ than the other children. Why? The "unusual" children blossomed because their teachers expected them to. But it wasn't magic. Their high expectations led them to subtly and unintentionally treat their "bright" charges in different ways—more attention, closer observation, faster positive reinforcement. A "bright" student was allowed to give wandering answers that eventually got on track, for example, while an "average" student giving the same answers (and heading in the same direction) was cut off early. Prophesy became reality.[20]

A classic example of the self-fulfilling prophesy is the 1932 run on banks that precipitated the Great Depression. Banks failed because depositors expected them to. When enough depositors lost faith in a bank and expected it to fail—even though "in reality" it was solvent—they lined up and withdrew funds until the bank actually failed.[21] The world is full of similar stories:

- Victims of civilian and military disasters respond to the expectations of rescue workers. The U.S. Army discovered that psychiatric casualties of war who are treated as such are less able to return to active duty.[22] (The issue of psychiatric casualties and their treatment was discussed during the Persian Gulf War.)

- Insurance agents grouped in the same office and informally labeled "superstaff" outperformed the most optimistic projections.[23]

- When a line supervisor was told that some workers had scored higher than others on intelligence and dexterity tests (when, like the "unusual" schoolchildren in Rosenthal and Jacobson's study, those workers' names were drawn at random), the "better" workers actually outperformed the others.[24]

- When manufacturers and suppliers expect their relationship to continue in the long run, they make investments in the relationship that actually sustain and strengthen it.[25] The Pygmalion principle isn't limited to personal relationships. It applies to company-to-company relationships as well.

Why are expectations self-fulfilling? It has to do with subtle differences in the quality of interaction. "[E]xpectancies cause one to act in ways that elicit behavior interpretable as confirming those expectancies," says psychologist Edward E. Jones, "even when the expectancies might have been mistaken."[26] Let's say you're Bob's manager.[27] You're not sure, but you think he's lazy, lacks initiative, and needs to be carefully supervised, so you tell him exactly what to do. You check up frequently, stopping by his office; you look over his shoulder and convey concern. Bob, who's taking this all in, wonders why you treat him so. He perceives you as a police officer, always watching and checking up. Your behavior makes him nervous and undermines his composure. He interprets your behavior to mean you don't expect him to do anything on his own, so he waits for you to tell him what to do. His responses confirm your initial assumptions—he's lazy, lacks initiative, needs supervision.

As Bob's story illustrates, managers' expectations profoundly influence the performance of their subordinates. Productivity, says business professor and consultant Dov Eden in *Pygmalion Management*, is a self-fulfilling prophesy.[28] Unfortunately, Bob's story is the rule, not the exception; many managers expect poor performance and get it. Most theories of management are based on *negative expectations*, what Douglas McGregor called "Theory X" assumptions: People are lazy, hate work, and avoid responsibility; therefore, they must be coerced and threatened to put forth in the interests of the organization.[29] Theory X assumptions are still with us. These negative expectations reside at the heart of the management philosophy of control, whips and chains (see Introduction).

The new management philosophy—*empowerment*—activates the strong positive effects of the Pygmalion principle by setting high expectations. "A unique characteristic of superior managers," says J. Sterling Livingston, who wrote in the *Harvard Business Review* about Pygmalion management, "is the ability to create high performance expectations that subordinates fulfill."[30] Eden describes four ways Pygmalion leaders explicitly and implicitly communicate high performance expectations[31]:

- *Socioemotional climate.* Climate includes all nonverbal behaviors that effective managers use to create a supportive interpersonal environment: "looking subordinates in the eye, nodding affirmatively and approvingly, smiling, drawing near to the subordinate physically, voicing warm, supportive intonation, and holding one's body in an erect, attentive posture during conversation with the subordinate."

- *Feedback.* Good managers give continuous feedback. Lots of positive feedback communicates trust and confidence. Negative feedback is necessary, too, but it must convey encouragement and confidence that the subordinate can and will improve.

- *Input.* Good managers invest in their relationships with subordinates. This investment includes time, energy, training, and mentoring. Good managers provide the *tools* their people need.

- *Output.* Good managers provide challenging, fulfilling assignments. They give their people ample opportunities to demonstrate their competence and ability. Good managers provide opportunities to risk, take chances, succeed, and fail.

Principle 3: People Tend to Associate with Others Like Themselves

This principle, in shorthand, is called the "similarity principle." It is one of the best-documented facts in social science research.[32] And it's common sense; as the saying goes, "Birds of a feather flock together." There are so many examples of Principle 3 that it's difficult to know which one to use. Consider one close to home: Are you free to marry anyone you want? In theory, yes. But in practice people tend to marry people like themselves. Social class, religion, and ethnicity matter a lot in many societies. These are less important in U.S. society, but that doesn't mean we've escaped the similarity principle. We've just replaced the traditional selection rules with another one: Americans with *similar educations* tend to marry.[33]

The similarity principle is a powerful force in organizations. It drives relationships everywhere. Like the first principle, you can activate it to create desired relationships. For example, putting people with common interests in close physical proximity germinates new connections.[34] Bringing scientists and engineers together under one roof encourages the exchange of ideas and stimulates serendipity (see Chapter 6). The Company of the Table was built on similarity (kinship and common neighborhood) within each military unit.

But the similarity principle can cause problems. It is well known that senior executives and managers become isolated because they prefer the company of other senior people.[35] They get out of touch and lose the ability to operate at a high level of understanding of problems with their subordinates. Without sufficient contact with subordinates, a manager can suffer from what's known in psychology as the *actor-observer bias.*[36] When a subordinate (the actor) has a problem of, let's say, low productivity, the manager (the observer) will attribute it to personal factors like stupidity, sloth, or laziness. The superior is much less likely to consider situational factors. The subordinate's low productivity could be caused by poor materials, failure of just-in-time delivery, or even reluctant compliance with informal norms restricting output. Different interpretations lead to different solutions. The out-of-touch manager, who attributes low performance to personal factors, will fire the "lazy bum" (only to be surprised later by the "lazy" behavior of new hires). The in-touch manager, one who has overcome the actor-observer bias caused by the similarity principle, will investigate situational factors and fix them if they're the real culprits.

You must also overcome the similarity principle to find good people for jobs in your organization; good people often reside in different business circles, and you have to jump the similarity obstacle to get to them (Chapter 9). Bottlenecks in organizations occur because people from different departments have trouble sustaining a dialogue and building cooperative ties (Chapter 5). And the similarity principle makes it difficult to tap the power of diversity (Chapter 7). Managers who operate at high levels of understanding when they share the same background as their subordinates often drop to a lower level when managing people from different backgrounds. Differences in slang, custom, and styles of interaction make it difficult to "take the role of the other" and walk a mile in another's shoes.

Principle 4: Repeated Interaction Encourages Cooperation

Familiarity breeds contempt sometimes, but as a rule people who interact repeatedly tend to cooperate and develop positive relationships.[37] Why? There are many reasons. Some social scientists explain cooperation as the result of simple self-interest. So-called game theorists, for example, who view the social world as a giant chess board, believe you cooperate when it's in your self-interest to do so.[38] If you want customers to make repeat purchases, they say, you'll treat them fairly; you don't cheat customers because they won't come back, and they'll say nasty things to ruin your reputation.

Sounds pretty good, right? But here "cooperation" is viewed as a cold self-interested calculation. Once the gains from cooperation fall below the gains from cheating (and you don't think you'll be caught), game theorists predict you'll cheat. This is too cynical for my taste—and it doesn't fit my experience. I can think of examples of such brutal logic, but it can't account for a lot of the cooperation I see. Just as relationships are a basic human need (Principle 1), it is natural for people to take each other's welfare into account. Indeed, dozens of psychological experiments show that people have a strong tendency to cooperate, even in experiments designed to elicit cold, rational, self-interested behavior.[39] It's not a simple matter of costs and benefits. You wouldn't cheat friends even if you were certain they would never find out.[40]

You can make Principle 4 work even better by setting goals that encourage *cooperation* rather than competition.[41] A multifunctional team, for example, brings together people from different functions and compels them to interact repeatedly over time. By itself, repeated interaction will encourage cooperation. It's important, however, that you boost this process by giving the team a *common goal* that induces its members to rely on each other for success. Group-level rewards for achieving this common goal can also help the team pull together.

Principle 4 makes your job easier in many ways. Repeated interaction, for example, provides the information about others you need to operate at a high level of understanding. By helping others interact, you activate the natural human tendency to cooperate. Continued interaction is a way to overcome the dark side of the similarity principle, the tendency for people to *avoid* others who are different. As I describe in later chapters, repeated interaction builds bridges between diverse groups, helps tap the power of diversity, reduces conflict, and helps build cooperative ties with customers, suppliers, and competitors.

Principle 5: It's a Small World

This is the typical response when we experience what is called the small-world phenomenon: the seemingly unlikely discovery of a shared acquaintance.[42] Though it always amazes us, the small-world phenomenon is the result of simple arithmetic. Here's how it works. Everyone's network is comprised of zones of contacts. Your "first-order zone" contains your direct contacts.[43] Your "second-order zone" contains the contacts of your direct contacts, your indirect contacts, those once-removed. An average professional's first-order zone contains 3500 contacts.[44] If each direct contact also has 3500 contacts, the second-order zone could contain as many as 12,250,000 contacts! (Assuming no overlaps, of course.) If acquaintanceship were random, the average number of links between any two people in the United States would be less than two.[45] It's a small world.

The small-world phenomenon means you're closer to critical information, resources, and people than you think. You have an enormous number of second-order contacts. Every time you add a single direct contact to your personal network, you expand your indirect contacts. The small-world principle is the networking leader's ally. So-called lucky people, says Max Gunther in *The Luck Factor*, create "luck" by forming a large network of contacts—a "spiderweb" structure that catches lots of information from diverse sources.[46] As I describe in later chapters, the small-world principle helps you find good people for jobs in your organization and expand your personal intelligence network. It's the power behind word-of-mouth marketing. And the power of the small-world principle is exploited productively in organized networking clubs.

The Spectrum of Relationships

So far I've talked about relationships as if they were all the same. There is, of course, a spectrum of relationships. Relationships can range, for example, from life-long friendships to very narrow, short-lived contacts, with lots of variations between the two extremes. The terms *strong ties* and *weak ties* are used to describe the two ends of the spectrum[47]:

Strong Ties <- ->Weak Ties

A strong tie means lots of interaction and high emotional intensity. A strong tie has a history and a mutual commitment to continue the relationship. There are many levels to a strong tie ("I work with my brother-in-law who is also my best friend" implies three levels: work associate, family relative, friendship). A weak tie lacks these features. At the extreme, it's a one-shot transaction with low emotional intensity; no history, no future commitment. Such weak ties are glorified in the cult of the deal.

People who network smart recognize the full spectrum of relationships and work to fit the relationship to the situation. Sometimes strong ties are best, sometimes not. For years, Detroit auto makers thought that weak ties were the best way to manage parts suppliers. Suppliers were held at arms' length: short contracts, no commitment, no personal ties. Detroit has since discovered what Japanese auto makers have always known: Strong ties yield better quality and lower costs. Detroit auto makers now cultivate long-term partnerships with a small number of suppliers. They've moved from the weak end of the spectrum toward the strong end.[48]

Like every story, every relationship has two sides. The relationship grid (Figure 2-2) is a handy general-purpose tool for mapping both sides of a relationship. I use it in several chapters of this book. You can

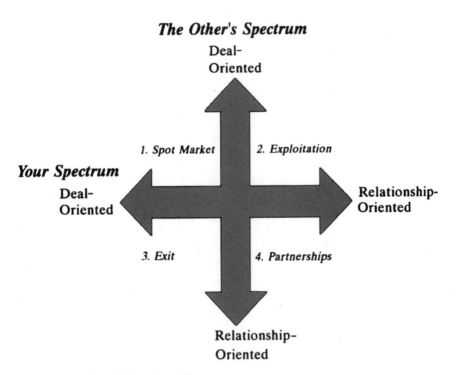

Figure 2-2. The relationship grid.

apply the grid to diagnose and understand many different types of relationships: how you relate to subordinates, peers, or superiors, and how they relate to you; your company's marketing strategy versus customer buying behavior; your company's purchasing strategy compared with your supplier's marketing strategy.

The relationship grid arrays the spectrum of relationships along two dimensions. The horizontal dimension is your spectrum; the vertical dimension represents the other's spectrum. The "other" could be a peer, subordinate, supplier, customer, etc.[49] The two dimensions create four quadrants, each representing a match or mismatch of the two sides of a relationship.

1. *Spot market.* In the first quadrant, both sides are deal-oriented. I call this a "spot market" because it typifies an economic arena in which "relationships" are short-term, fleeting transactions. There's no history and no expectation of or commitment to future interactions.

Relationships in quadrant 1 are sustainable because orientations match. Spot-market transactions can be appropriate in many situations. I believe, however, that the appropriateness has been greatly exaggerated by the cult of the deal. Given the fundamental changes in the business world, the number of situations is shrinking in which the spot-market approach is appropriate.

2. *Exploitation.* In the second quadrant, you're relationship-oriented, but the other side is deal-oriented. I call this "exploitation," because that's exactly what happens to you: You get exploited by others who don't make investments in the relationship and who take advantage of the investments you make.

Relationships in quadrant 2 are *not* sustainable because orientations are *mis*matched. Eventually, you protect yourself and withdraw from the exchange, or you convince the other side of the merits of the relationship orientation.

3. *Exit.* In the third quadrant, you're deal-oriented, but the other side is relationship-oriented. From your perspective, this is the opposite of "exploitation" because the other is willing to make investments but you're not. I call this "exit" because that's what the other side will do, sooner or later.

Relationships in quadrant 3 are *not* sustainable; the orientations don't match. Usually, the best option is to change your orientation to better match the relationship expectations of the other side.

4. *Partnerships.* The fourth quadrant represents loyal, mutually beneficial, long-term relationships. I call these "partnerships." Partnerships are the opposite of spot-market relationships.

Relationships in quadrant 4 are sustainable and desirable, given the personal and organizational benefits of relationships. In many, many situations, this quadrant represents the ideal: It's the state in which most people and organizations achieve their highest performance.

I've used the relationship grid for many years in consulting engagements and executive education. I find that it reveals for the first time why people and their companies experience so much trouble in certain relationships. They discover a basic mismatch. Employees who seek long-term employment relationships, for example, become frustrated with a company that refuses to provide training, career development, or long-term benefits; these employees leave when they get the opportunity to take jobs with more suitable employers. Deal-oriented customers try to maximize the benefits of each individual transaction; with such customers, a relationship-based, loss-leader strategy just leads to losses, not repeat business. As I describe in later chapters, however, you can turn mismatches into matches. Airline carriers, for example, use frequent flyer programs to convert deal-oriented customers into repeat purchasers. These programs increase value (upgrades, free tickets) and improve the odds customers will use the same airline again.

Ethics and Responsibility

By now you've probably asked yourself a question about the ethics of managing relationships. One of my Executive MBA students, who read an early version of this book when he took my course "Role of the General Manager" at the University of Chicago, put it this way: "Doesn't the theory of utilizing relationships to achieve an end goal actually become a transaction-oriented philosophy in itself? In other words, if I perceive that you are trying to be my friend simply because you see me as a means to achieving an end, won't I respond by being more suspicious of not just you but all people?"[50]

This question is very important. But the problem isn't that relationships help you achieve some goal. Good working relationships were, are, and always will be the chief way to get things done.[51] As long as the relationship is authentic and genuine (more on that in a moment), both parties benefit. Think of friendship. Friends help out friends everywhere. A friend who won't help you is not much of a friend. Indeed, anthropologists tell us that material exchange and economic assistance is the most common function of friendship in all cultures.[52]

The real problem arises when trust (or what might be called "pseudo-trust") is cultivated for purposes of exploitation. Remember *The Sting* with Paul Newman and Robert Redford? This classic film is an exquisite portrayal of the classic confidence game: The con artist wins the mark's trust to set him up for the sting. In everyday life we often encounter a legal form of the sting, what might be called the "super-salesperson problem": the salesperson who is very adept at developing rapport, understanding what makes a customer tick, and then pushing the right psychological buttons to close the sale, even when it's not in the customer's best interest.

Here's the troubling issue. Con artists and supersalespeople understand interpersonal problems at high levels.[53] They have to. But they're operating without an essential ingredient: mutuality. In an authentic relationship, each person takes the other's welfare into account. Both parties cooperate to attain mutual benefits. No one is conned. Those who network smart build this kind of trust relationship. It is the only way to be successful over time. "If there is little or no trust," says Stephen R. Covey, author of the business best-sellers *The Seven Habits of Highly Effective People* and *Principle-Centered Leadership,* "there is no foundation for permanent success."[54]

One more essential ingredient: ethics. Ethical conduct is mandatory because trust relationships can be created for base or noble purposes. I just read, for example, a riveting account of a professional "fence," a broker of stolen goods.[55] A fence employs the same techniques used by legitimate business: word-of-mouth marketing, third-party referrals, recruitment of a stable network of suppliers (thieves), buyers (store merchants, wholesalers), and competitors (other fences). The fence's relationships involve trust, mutual benefit, and support. Similarly, the Wall Street scandals of the 1980s were founded on trust relationships among bankers, raiders, and speculators, as Pulitzer-prize winning reporter James Stewart describes in *Den of Thieves*.[56] Most price-fixing conspiracies, as Rob Faulkner and I learned in our research on conspiracy networks, are based on stable trust relationships.[57]

So this is my answer to my Executive MBA student's excellent question: *Trust, mutuality, and ethics are essential.* The networking leader couples a high level of understanding of interpersonal problems with mutuality and ethics. The high road to success lies in cultivating authentic, win-win relationships, inside the organization and out, while operating at the highest standards of ethics.

What You Can Do *Now*

What you can do *now* is candidly assess your own managerial style. Where are you on the spectrum of relationships? What kind of relationships do you build? Are you someone who networks smart? You could answer these questions for each of your relationships, any and all throughout the entire networking territory (Figure 2-1). For now, I recommend that you focus on your close interpersonal relationships, those with direct subordinates, peers, and superiors. In many ways, the best insights into managerial style come from examining relationships with *subordinates*. Begin with these relationships. Later, you can return and examine your management style in relationships with peers and superiors.

On the next page is a short quiz designed to assess your general management style with subordinates. The following questionnaire contains eight statements. Read each statement and indicate the extent to which you *agree* or *disagree* with it by circling the number above the response that best fits your feeling. Be objective and honest. Indicate what you *really* feel, not what you think you should feel or what someone expects of you. Answer on the basis of your *first reaction* to a statement.

What does your score mean? Your total score is a general indicator of your management tendencies, the philosophy or principles you use as a guide to managing others. The principles behind a person's style

Management Style Questionnaire

1. The average human being prefers to be directed, wishes to avoid responsibility, and has relatively little ambition.

(5)	(4)	(3)	(2)	(1)
Strongly Agree	Agree	Undecided	Disagree	Strongly Disagree

2. Leadership depends on having the right inborn traits and abilities.

(5)	(4)	(3)	(2)	(1)
Strongly Agree	Agree	Undecided	Disagree	Strongly Disagree

3. The use of rewards (for example, pay and promotion) and punishment (for example, failure to promote) is the best way to get subordinates to do their work.

(5)	(4)	(3)	(2)	(1)
Strongly Agree	Agree	Undecided	Disagree	Strongly Disagree

4. In a work situation, if your subordinates can influence you, you lose some of your influence over them.

(5)	(4)	(3)	(2)	(1)
Strongly Agree	Agree	Undecided	Disagree	Strongly Disagree

5. A good leader gives detailed and complete instructions to subordinates rather than giving them general directions and depending on their initiative to work out the details.

(5)	(4)	(3)	(2)	(1)
Strongly Agree	Agree	Undecided	Disagree	Strongly Disagree

6. Individual goal setting is superior to group goal setting.

(5)	(4)	(3)	(2)	(1)
Strongly Agree	Agree	Undecided	Disagree	Strongly Disagree

7. A superior should give subordinates only the information necessary for them to do their immediate tasks.

(5)	(4)	(3)	(2)	(1)
Strongly Agree	Agree	Undecided	Disagree	Strongly Disagree

8. A superior's influence over subordinates in an organization is primarily economic.

(5)	(4)	(3)	(2)	(1)
Strongly Agree	Agree	Undecided	Disagree	Strongly Disagree

(Continued)

Scoring the questionnaire: Each number above a response indicates the point value associated with a particular answer. For example, the "(5)" above "Strongly Agree" is worth five points. Determine your total score by adding together the points for all eight statements.

_____ Your Total Score

SOURCE: Adapted from M. Haire, E. Ghiselli, and L. Porter, *Managerial Thinking: An International Study*, Appendix A (New York: John Wiley & Sons, Inc., 1966). Used with permission.

are often implicit, which is why this exercise is valuable. Here's how to interpret your score. A score of greater than 30 points indicates a tendency to manage subordinates according to the *philosophy of control* I described in the Introduction. A score of fewer than 16 points indicates a tendency to manage subordinates according to the *philosophy of empowerment.* A score between 16 and 30 indicates a mixed management style; if your management style is changing, it could also indicate a transition point in your movement from one philosophy to the other.

No matter what your score is, this book will help you become a better, more effective, more successful leader. If your current management style tends toward control, this book will help you learn how to manage via empowerment. I strongly recommend developing in this direction. The philosophy of empowerment is a much more suitable and effective style in the emerging business order. The control approach might have been appropriate in the past; now, it's a prescription for failure. Today, the key to success is found in empowering others to do their jobs.

If your current management style tends toward empowerment, this book will help you learn how to *practice* the new philosophy. In each chapter, I give you concrete advice on *what to do*—how you can build empowering networks of relationships in a vital business area. I offer advice on three levels: what you can do *now,* what you can do *soon,* and what you can do in the *long run.* Many people talk empowerment; this book helps you do it.

What You Can Do Soon

Here's a big twist on the exercise you just completed. How do *others* see you and your management style? Is your self-image consistent with how others experience their relationships with you? Sometimes a boss thinks he or she has an empowering management style, but subordinates see it quite a different way. This next exercise isn't comfortable—it isn't meant to be—but it will help you to get important information you need to develop as a leader. What you can do *soon* is pick one of your trusted subordinates and ask him or her to rate you according to your management style.

Give your subordinate the management style questionnaire. Describe what you're doing and why. Ask your subordinate to read each statement and answer it according to how he or she actually experiences your management style. This shouldn't be a test of what your subordinate thinks *you* think but an indicator of how he or she sees your management style.

Once you have this feedback, compare and contrast your assessment against your subordinate's. Are there differences? What are they? How big is each difference? Why does the difference occur?

In most cases, managers discover big differences. Their subordinates see them differently than they see themselves. It's a well-documented fact in research on superiors and subordinates.[58] For now, the comparison is useful for getting a more accurate assessment of your managerial style, pinpointing areas for improvement, and motivating you to pursue your professional and personal development.

As something else you can do soon, encourage your subordinates to use the management style questionnaire to assess their own styles. Are your people relationship or technical types? Do they have good interpersonal skills? Do they work well in teams? Remember the dilemma of indirect management: You depend on others to network smart when you're not there. This book will help your people learn how to build and manage the relationships they need. Encourage them to read and use it. By empowering your people, you empower yourself.

What You Can Do in the *Long Run*

There are, of course, many things you can do in the long run. The process of learning how to manage well—of how to network smart—never ends. And you really have to teach yourself. Others can show the way, but you do the learning. Consider what the famous psychologist Carl Rogers said: "The only learning which significantly influences behavior is self-discovered, self-appropriated learning."[59] This book will help you in your journey of self-discovery and self-learning. What you can do for *long-run* success is to read and apply the lessons from this book. After you've given yourself sufficient time to experiment, come back and repeat the management style questionnaire. Compare the results and see how far you've come.

3
Building Intelligence Networks

*To manage a business well is to manage its
future; and to manage the future is to manage
information.*

MARION HARPER[1]

Former President George Bush was much better off without John Sununu. When Sununu was Bush's chief of staff, he would indulge in a favorite pastime of subordinates: intercepting information before it could get to the big boss.[2] Helpful John, it seems, would stop letters sent by the president's longtime advisors and keep them from ever reaching the Oval Office. He simply answered the letters himself or referred George's advisors to junior aides. George was the last to know. To get around his chief of staff, George had to establish a back channel—a private post office box in Maine—to which his advisors could send letters directly.

Bush's problem wasn't unusual. And it's not limited to the chief executive; people at all levels suffer from it. The problem just gets worse and worse the higher up you go or the farther away you move from the company's actual operations. The dilemma of indirect management means you rely more and more on information fed to you by others. You get out of touch. And you make poor decisions.

Managers can be their own worst enemies. As they move up, many fall for the management folklore that says they should withdraw from operational affairs and contemplate the big picture. "If he [or she] follows the advice to free himself from operations," warns Ed Wrapp in his famous *Harvard Business Review* article, "he [or she] may soon find himself subsisting on a diet of abstractions, leaving the choice of what he [or she] eats in the hands of his [or her] subordinates."[3]

What can you do? You can't rely on the formal organization to help you out. "The very purpose of a hierarchy," says Kenneth Boulding, "is to prevent information from reaching top layers. It operates as an information filter, and there are little wastebaskets all along the way."[4] Information is garbled as it wends its way through formal channels; often it arrives too late to do any good. Conflicting and ambiguous messages create a dull buzz of confusion. Critical details are lost in aggregated summaries. At worst, reports are sanitized, numbers massaged; information is hoarded and withheld, even fabricated.

To get the information you need, you have to take matters into your own hands. Richard Neustadt discovered an important lesson for managers everywhere when he studied the information-collecting habits of Presidents Roosevelt, Truman, and Eisenhower: "It is not information of a general sort that helps a President see personal stakes; not summaries, not surveys, not the bland amalgams. Rather...it is the odds and ends of tangible detail that pieced together in his mind illuminate the underside of issues put before him. To help himself he must reach out as widely as he can for every scrap of fact, opinion, gossip, bearing on his interests and relationships as President. He must become his own director of his own central intelligence."[5]

That's what you can do. To get the information you need, you have to build your own intelligence network. Good managers and executives have always done so, but it's more important today than ever, no matter where you are in the organization. Knowledge, says futurist Alvin Toffler, is now the basis of power and wealth creation.[6] We are in the information age. By the mid-1980s, for example, more than half of the U.S. work force already held jobs that were information-related.[7] There's a prodigious increase in the production of information; fast markets and rapid technological change make today's information more perishable than ice at the equator.

This information explosion aggravates the manager's intelligence problem. The information explosion is really the *data* explosion, says Richard Saul Wurman in *Information Anxiety,* and you have to sort and process data to get anything useful.[8] Just getting more data won't help. In fact, psychologists have learned that more data actually hinders good decision making because it makes decision makers feel overconfident.[9] What you need is the *right* information, not more data.

In this chapter, we look at how effective leaders at all levels get the information they need. I describe how personal intelligence systems work and tell you how to build them. Even if you're a seasoned and successful businessperson, there are many things to learn. And, as you'll see, the information theme of this chapter is woven throughout the topics covered in the rest of the book. Managing information well is an essential part of managing relationships and networks in all business areas.

Your Internal Intelligence Network

Effective leaders develop their own independent intelligence networks to keep informed about a wide range of decisions, activities, people, and events. Their personal networks help them to monitor ongoing activities and to spot incipient problems and opportunities. "[E]ach of my heroes," says Ed Wrapp, "has a special talent for keeping himself [or herself] informed about a wide range of operating decisions being made at different levels in the company. As he [or she] moves up the ladder, he [or she] develops a network of information sources in many different departments. He [or she] cultivates these sources and keeps them open no matter how high he [or she] climbs in the organization. When the need arises, he [or she] bypasses the lines on the organization chart to seek more than one version of a situation."[10]

Consider Walter Wriston, the corporate leader who transformed First National Citibank into Citicorp—one of the preeminent financial institutions in the world.[11] Wriston was a master builder of informal intelligence networks. As a fellow executive described in Harry Levinson and Stuart Rosenthal's chapter on Wriston in *CEO:*

> He relies very heavily on information that comes to him from different parts of the organization. He gets and absorbs the feelings of people who are not only department and group heads but always has a wary ear open to be alert to situations, circumstances within the shop that might not surface in the ordinary routine of management information flows....He's got a very acute sense...of the ideas as they float around the organization....

Wriston understood very well how easy it is to get out of touch. When Jack Welch took the top job at GE, he reports in an interview with

Financial World that Wriston warned him of this common problem: "Jack, remember one thing, you're always going to be the last one to know the critical things that need to be done in your organization. Everyone else already knows." "He was right," says Welch.[12] Wriston's advice applies to any one, not just those at the top. Without intelligence networks, you're always out of touch, out of the swim of things, out of the loop.

Personal contacts are your direct lines of communication with the various parts of the organization. Building your intelligence network means initiating, cultivating, and maintaining these contacts. You have plenty of opportunities to do so in the course of day-to-day activities. "Managing by Wandering Around"—Tom Peters and Robert Waterman's MBWA principle—offers chance encounters that yield vital information.[13] Merck CEO Roy Vagelos, for example, often takes lunch in the company cafeteria so he can talk informally with scientists.[14] It's a great way to get informed of the latest developments and discoveries. In a similar fashion but a different content, then-governor Bill Clinton regularly visited a local Little Rock McDonald's to sit and chat with people and hear their concerns.[15]

Mobility and movement offer you chances to make personal contacts. Any move you make inside the company—promotions, transfers, temporary details, special projects, committee assignments, relocations, stints in foreign offices—provides great opportunities to develop new information contacts. A pending relocation or reassignment might look brighter if you consider its network-building potential. It might be just the right move if it enables you to meet different people, make new contacts, and build new relationships that'll be helpful down the road.

As a rule, diverse contacts are better than similar or redundant contacts. A large, diverse network of contacts, argues network expert Ronald Burt, gives you the best access to information.[16] You can't stay in the know with a few or a narrow set of contacts. With a diverse set, however, you're better able to quickly discover new opportunities. And broader access to information has its rewards. Burt shows in his impressive study of managers in a high-tech *Fortune* 500 company that those who bridge lots of diverse groups get promoted faster and at younger ages than their peers.

Zigzag career paths are better than linear paths for building the diverse set of connections you need. Vertical paths—moving up rung by rung within the same function—help you build contacts in the same business area. These contacts are useful, of course, but your intelligence network is a mile deep and an inch wide. Zigzag job changes—moving laterally, jumping functions, going abroad—provide the breadth you need. The Japanese have known for a long time about the network-building benefits of zigzagging. That's why Japanese managers have what look to us like inefficient, meandering career paths. All the changes you make, however, are just *opportunities* to build information contacts. You must seize them and actively cultivate contacts. Remember the lesson of Bill Hansen (Introduction). He had visited his peers at other StorageAmerica facilities, but he failed to capitalize on these contact-building opportunities.

When I talk to businesspeople about building personal intelligence networks, many raise an objection. You ought to have more respect for the formal hierarchy, they tell me; you shouldn't advise people to go around their subordinates to get to the bottom of a story. When I press them for details, they usually tell me about superiors who circumvent *them* and go straight to the source. They feel undermined, frustrated, caught in the middle. All too often their feelings are justified—many managers throw their weight around and gather intelligence in cavalier and callous ways. If you use your personal intelligence network this way, you're asking for trouble. Your aggrieved subordinates will search for some way to thwart you, and your intelligence network will crumble.

Managing information relationships, just like any sort of relationship, entails ethics and responsibilities. You may need to go around people to get information, but those you go around need to be taken into account. Sometimes just explaining *why* you go directly to an information source is all you need to do. When appropriate, share what you find out. Information dissemination is part of your job. Sharing includes confidential information, though you have to do so judiciously. "The manager is challenged," says management expert Henry Mintzberg, "to find systematic ways to share privileged information."[17] With your diverse set of contacts, you're in a great position to piece together information that can help others do their jobs. Remember that sharing information *empowers* people. A person's power—the ability to get the job done—depends directly on his or her access to information.[18] You empower your people—and yourself—by collecting and sharing information.

Your responsibility to share information extends to your information sources. Reciprocity, the natural give-and-take between people, is one of the basic rules in all cultures and societies.[19] It's essential for building information relationships (or any other kind of relationship for that matter). The reciprocity rule links a future action (repayment) with a present action (a favor, gift, etc.). By linking the present and the future, it activates the fourth networking principle: Repeated interaction encourages cooperation (see Chapter 2). If you sponge information and never give, your sources will dry up. But give and you shall receive. This doesn't mean you should be an inveterate gossip. Be a tactful, judicious supplier of information and a trustworthy, responsible user of information.

Above all, take what you learn from your personal intelligence system with a grain of salt. You must work hard to gather every tidbit of data, gossip, rumor, and innuendo. Some tidbits are the most timely and accurate pieces of genuine information you'll ever get.[20] A few help you peer into the future. But many pieces of information are irrelevant, others are innocent errors, and more than a few are deliberate disinformation and malicious lies. All, however, are parts of some larger story. You're faced with a balancing act. If you wait until you get the whole story, it'll be too late to act; but if you don't get enough of the story before you act, you'll make bad decisions, alienate your people, and let your organization be ruled by the tyranny of rumor and gossip.

Donuts with Ditch

Donuts with Ditch? OK, here's a more formal-sounding title: information-exchange forum. Donuts with Ditch is the informal communication sessions Allan Ditchfield created ten years ago at AT&T.[21] It was so effective and popular that he imported the practice to MCI when he became chief information officer (CIO) of the long-distance communications company, and then imported it once again when he became CIO of Progressive Corporation, the Ohio-based national auto insurance company. "I do it to break down the hierarchical barriers," he told me. "It's basically a communications meeting." Allan uses these informal meetings to hear everyone's concerns, get and give information, and keep everyone in touch. It's a great way to get at the real issues, the real problems. It gives people a voice and a forum, many of whom have no other means to communicate with or hear from upper-level managers.

Allan holds a Donuts-with-Ditch session at Progressive every two weeks. (He would hold weekly sessions at MCI because the department was much bigger.) The typical meeting lasts about 2 or 3 hours. Attendance is limited to a small number of people. "I have no more than 10 people at a time," he says. "If you have more than 10, people don't like to talk." People are chosen on a random basis for Donuts with Ditch, "but some people ask to be invited, especially if they have a burning issue to discuss." Trust is the most important ingredient for success. "I have a rule—it's a sacred open door—that there will be no retaliation, no one's going to be hurt by [what they say]. I don't tell management."

How has Donuts with Ditch changed over the years? "I have a lot more fruit these days," he says.

Donuts with Ditch is a great example of creating conditions that encourage information flow. Donuts with Ditch comes in all shapes and sizes:

- American Airlines CEO Robert Crandall holds conferences around the country to talk directly with employees.[22]

- Federal Express uses its Open Door policy to encourage employees to communicate directly to management their ideas, questions, or comments about the industry or company; the express courier's Guaranteed Fair Treatment policy makes sure employees can get a fair hearing for any concern or complaint about fair treatment (e.g., questions about a performance review or other personnel matter).[23]

- Royal Bank of Canada establishes conferences to help area managers share expertise, data, and intelligence.[24]

- GE uses its Corporate Executive Council as a forum for leaders from GE's various businesses to get together, exchange information and advice, and to integrate what could be disparate units.[25]

- The U.S. State Department uses the secretary's open forum to encourage "differences of opinion by publishing papers, sponsoring discussions, and inviting critics to speak."[26] State also has a "dissent channel" that lower-level managers can use to send messages directly to the secretary, bypassing the Sununu-type blockade I described earlier.

- Donuts with Ditch, Japanese style, is the regular Friday meeting (*kinyo-kai*) of the presidents of the member companies in the Mitsubishi *keiretsu,* one of Japan's vast and close-knit groups of companies. The Friday meeting has taken place every month for over forty years![27]

Regular operational meetings are another effective variation on the Donuts with Ditch theme. Such meetings are common at Silicon Valley firms, which are role models of the new network organization. Zap Computers, for example, Kathleen Eisenhardt's code name for the large computer maker she studied, relies on frequent operational meetings—two or three a week—to share, relay, and discuss information about sales, inventory, backlog, engineering schedules, new releases, product introductions by competitors, technical developments in the industry, and so on.[28] Zap's top managers use these meetings to relay information they glean from constant phone calls, travel, and business and university contacts.

Lots of meetings, face-to-face interaction—all the variations of Donuts with Ditch—create real-time intelligence networks. Real-time networks help managers accelerate decision making, says Eisenhardt, which is essential wherever the pace of change is fast and furious.[29]

Can Computer Networking Help?

Computers are often heralded as the technological cure to the information problem. In a computer-networked company, for example, you *can* find the proverbial needle in a haystack. With electronic mail or an electronic bulletin board, you can query hundreds or even thousands of people all at once. You'd get a few wrong answers, but the odds of getting the right one are tremendous when compared with the luck you'd have with the telephone.

Searching the haystack is just one example of the many ways in which computer technology is revolutionizing communication.[30] Computer technologies free us from the friction of time and space. In 1991, for example, more than 5.5 million people worked as "telecommuters," commuting to work via phone and modem instead of a car. This is a 38 percent increase over the previous year, according to Link Resources National Work at Home Survey.[31] The new advances in networking technologies can help transform and redesign traditional organizations, yielding quicker, more responsive, more effective decision making.[32] Flexible computer networking is often used to support the new network organizations.

But there are serious limitations. Despite great advantages, electronic communication cannot become the cornerstone of your independent intelligence system. To see why, let's begin by looking at the older computer technologies, management information systems (MIS). Part of the folklore about managers, argues Henry Mintzberg, is that senior managers need aggregated information like that produced by MIS. The fact is good managers eschew formal systems that spew forth abstracts and stylized facts.[33] Instead, they obtain and transmit information via all sorts of *verbal* media: face-to-face conversations, phone calls, traveling, meetings, spontaneous and impromptu discussions. "I was struck during my study," Mintzberg said, "by the fact that the executives I was observing—all very competent—are fundamentally indistinguishable from their counterparts of a hundred years ago (or a thousand years ago). The information they need differs, but they seek it in the same way—by word of mouth."[34]

Why do managers prefer word of mouth? MIS provides only aggregated information and old news. Word-of-mouth networks are on-line, real-time systems that give you live, rich, quick, timely information about what's going on. You need this kind of information to get news as it happens, to spot opportunities and problems early. "Every bit of evidence," says Mintzberg, "suggests that the manager identifies decision situations and builds models [mental maps of the organization] not with the aggregated abstractions an MIS provides, but with specific tidbits of data."[35]

Is computer networking better? In some ways, yes. Greater efficiency is one of the benefits companies find when they establish electronic networks: shorter elapsed time for transactions, quicker turnaround, faster group communication.[36] Saving time is important, of course, but electronic networks aren't the appropriate medium for the complex, rich, nuanced communication essential for intelligence gathering. "Proponents of the efficiency benefits of computer-based communication often assume that it delivers the same message as any other medium but simply does so more rapidly," write networking experts Lee Sproull and Sara Kielser in *Connections*. "That view is misleading because a message—even the same `message'—changes its meaning depending on the forum within which people convey it." Compared with face-to-face interaction, they say, "today's electronic technology is impoverished in social cues and shared experience."[37]

Consider the results of a study by James McKenney and associates at Harvard Business School on how managers use electronic mail versus face-to-face communication.[38] They discovered conspicuous differences in how managers use these media:

- Managers use *electronic mail* for efficient communication in well-defined contexts—monitoring task status, coordinating efforts, exchanging factual information, sending alerts, and broadcasting information.

- Managers use *face-to-face interaction* for defining and discussing problems and solutions, building a shared understanding of the situation, discussing shifting priorities and external pressures, interpreting ambiguous signals, and socialization of members.

Electronic communication is efficient, but only face-to-face interaction provides the richness, interactivity, immediacy of feedback, and social context needed for complex problem solving and fostering a shared set of values, beliefs, and meanings. Former ITT CEO Harold Geneen recognized the difference: "In New York, I might read a request and say no. But in Europe, I could see that an answer to the same question might be yes...it became our policy to deal with problems on the spot, face-to-face."[39] Even Allan Ditchfield, who as chief information officer is a champion of electronic communication, relies on informal, face-to-face sessions via his regular Donuts with Ditch.

It is difficult (if not impossible) to initiate or nurture meaningful relationships via electronic interaction. (It's true that some people who meet electronically become friends and even marry, but these are exceptions.) The ritual and ceremonial value of group meetings cannot be simulated with electronic communication.[40] Group meetings, says Stanford University professor Jane Hannaway, "keep a sense of community alive in the organization...[and] affirm the place of the individual and others in that community...."[41]

Computer networking can save you a lot of time communicating routine information. But such networking is ill-suited to the rich, sensitive, live, private information you need to be an effective manager. For that, you must build an independent intelligence network based on personal contacts.

Your External Intelligence Network

Along with internal intelligence networks, effective managers build *external networks* of personal contacts. External contacts help you stay informed about what's going on "out there"—changing customer preferences, a competitor's plans and actions, social and economic trends, pending regulations, emergent technologies, and so forth. One reason Ned Tanen of Paramount Pictures was so effective as president of production, for example, was his "dozen Rolodexes of contacts."[42] A colleague who studies the publishing business told me a story about an editor who returned to his office to find his desk taped shut. It seems the publishing house had been taken over abruptly, and the new owners were feeling a touch protective about their new assets. He spotted his rolodex on the desk, snatched it, and walked away saying, "That's all I need."[43]

External intelligence networks help you manage the information problem, the problem of too much data and not enough real information. A few years ago, I was talking with the treasurer of a global high-tech firm about his relationships with investment banks. I commented on the foot-high pile of proposals and brochures on his desk. "It's a problem coping with it all," he said. "I'll look at it eventually; there may be a nugget buried in there. But I don't have time to go through it now." He then told me how he finds out what he really needs to know: the company's senior vice president of finance. "He's talking with

Goldman Sachs, Salomon Brothers, Merrill Lynch, Morgan Stanley, and who all else," the treasurer said. "That's what he's paid for—his network of contacts." External contacts provide the right information.

"External networks are reality checks," explains Howard Haas, who was CEO of Sealy Inc. for 19 years. "How do you know the numbers you've got in your own company are correct? You don't know unless you have some way to prove it. Or, I know how my business is, but I don't know how my business is in relation to somebody else's business. How do I find out about that? I say to a competitor, `How's your business?' He says, `Terrific! We're 35 percent ahead!' I know the guy's lying through his teeth. So I go out and I call a bunch of dealers and talk to a lot of people. And finally I put together a consensus of the information and say, well, ours is up 5 percent so we're doing a lot better. That's a reality check."[44]

People throughout your organization have special access to the outside world—and it pays to link up with them. "The MIS professional," says Tom Peters, "will be the first to hear that a competitor is developing a sweeping new electronic linkup with hundreds of major customers."[45] Your people in finance have contacts throughout the financial world. Your sales representatives meet your competitor's sales reps every day in customer waiting rooms or at trade shows. They swap stories and gossip (and a few fibs, no doubt!) about you, each other, customers, other competitors, the industry, and so on. Do you have a way of learning what they know? Your scientists and engineers have innumerable contacts in professional and learned societies; they always know what's going on, what's hot, what's new. Do *you* talk with *them?* Remember that *everyone* in your organization has a life outside the company; everyone can be the company's eyes and ears. Recruit them into your external intelligence system.

Just as the daily rounds of business help you make internal contacts, your everyday work life offers plenty of opportunities to make external contacts. Most people think Peters and Waterman's MBWA principle applies only inside the company. But it's just as useful for making outside contacts. Peters advises marketers, for example, to spend more time "hanging out" in the marketplace.[46] It's an idea that Japanese companies have practiced for years. The invention of the Sony Walkman is a great example.[47] The original idea came right from Sony CEO and chairman Akio Morita. But he didn't dream it up sitting in his office. Morita spent lots of time hanging out, observing young people and getting to know their lifestyles and tastes in music. And what he saw was a huge untapped demand for a personal, compact, portable tape player. That's what he conveyed back to Sony designers. The result, as you know, was a smashing success.

Recently, GE instituted the hanging-out principle in its QMI—quick market intelligence technique.[48] QMI is an excellent way to get fast market intelligence and make quick decisions in response. As GE describes in its 1992 Annual Report, "Quick Market Intelligence is our term for the magnificent boundary-busting technique pioneered by Wal-Mart that allows the entire Company to understand, to sense, to touch the changing desires of the customer and to act on them in almost real time."[49] QMI taps the knowledge and insights of people in the field, those who see, touch, and listen to the market daily. Once a week, GE salespeople and managers come in from the field and report what they've learned. "It is a process that gives every salesperson direct access, every Friday, to the key managers and the CEO of the business, to lay out customer problems and needs. The product of the meeting is not deep or strategic in nature, but action—a response to the customer right away."[50] That's networking smart.

Virtually any outside event or gathering—professional meetings, trade conferences and shows, business roundtables, civic activities, charitable work, and so on—provide tremendous network-building opportunities. Michael Mach, CEO of Capital Partners, a very success-ful commercial real estate development firm, put it this way: "I involve myself in a number of things. Most of them are directly or indirectly related to our business. One reaches the point where one does not deliberately go out and search for things that help one's busi-ness. But the important factor is the networking that we all do when you take on one of these other challenges. I take on civic challenges in order to get some form of extra edge in our business, since they are interrelated in some way."

Customers and Suppliers as Eyes and Ears

Customers and suppliers are some of your best contacts in the out-side world. Their networks reach into different nooks and crannies; they have different perspectives; they're steps closer to vital news as it breaks. Your customers, for example, are called on regularly by your competitors. Competitors offer them all sorts of enticements to woo them away from you—new and innovative ideas, special promo-tions, new marketing strategies. As a result, your customers almost always know before you do what your competitors are up to. Of course, finding out what your customers know is a delicate matter. There are no easy rules. You don't want to put them in an uncomfort-able or compromising position; you need to respect their other relationships.* Your customers can't always tell you everything you want to know, but they often can let you know what's in the wind.

Using your customers' eyes and ears is critical if you don't deal directly with the final consumer. If your customers are a link in the chain leading to the final consumer, they are closer than you to information you need. In the soft drink industry, for example, Pepsi, Coca Cola, and other concentrate producers sell most of their output to the bottlers. Bottlers sell to retail stores, who in turn sell to you and me. Because the bottlers stock local retail shelves, they know the nitty gritty details about local markets. Is a competitor making special deals to grab more shelf space? Is there a last-second change in a competitor's marketing policy? Is a new brand or flavor appearing on the shelves?

Your suppliers are also excellent sources of outside information. Former Sealy CEO Howard Haas, for example, tapped advertising and media types to garner information about competitors. "The people [who] sell us space in the trade papers," he told me, "are the greatest contact people in the world. I would pump them as to what was happening with my competitors."[51] A Midwestern auto dealer uses suppliers' eyes and ears in a very creative way to get customer feedback.[52] He provides free taxicab service for customers who need a ride after dropping off their cars. The cab drivers (his suppliers) converse with riders about their car troubles and the auto dealer's service. The drivers relay this critical information back to the auto dealer.

Lawyers, accountants, bankers, management consultants, advertising agencies, architects, and engineers are all prime information sources. These people sit at the crossroads of complex information flows. By virtue of a diverse client base, they are vast repositories of data. They can provide invaluable information and insights about ongoing developments, events, and business trends. Such informational benefits add a new twist to outsourcing decisions. Many companies try to save money by dropping outside service suppliers and doing it themselves. You can save money this way. The cost of in-house lawyers, for example, is 40 percent lower than the cost of using an outside law firm for the same work.[53] What is not included in these cost calculations, however, is the opportunity cost of lost information: the value of information received from outside suppliers. The lost information can be critical and irreplaceable. Cutting relationships severs information links with the outside world.

---

*You also don't want to solicit price lists or other pricing information which could be construed as attempted price fixing.

You can also incorporate professional intelligence suppliers into your external intelligence system. Chicago-based CombsMoorhead Associates, Inc., for example, is a professional intelligence-gathering service that produces analyses for its clients on such subjects as product trends, environmental issues, sales projections, competitor information, and patents.* The firm systematically combs an array of information sources—industry and government contacts, trade associations, the media, computerized databases, and so on. Companies like this specialize in building information networks, and you tap their extensive networks when you employ them.

High-Level Eyes and Ears

Your company's board of directors is a set of high-level links to the outside world. One of the best-documented findings in organizational research is that top executives and managers use corporate boards to collect critical information from the company's environment. In my study of 1530 companies and their investment banks, for example, I found that many companies invite investment bankers on their boards to gain access to financial advice, ideas, new product developments, investor attitudes, and market intelligence.[54] Northwestern Business School professor Gerald Davis discovered that executives learn the ins and outs of poison pills, golden parachutes, and other tricks from their outside directors.[55] In fact, he learned, if your outside directors already have experience with these tactics, then your company is much more likely to use them as well. It's easy to see why. Your outside directors have direct experience and can tell you exactly how and when to use them.

Because directors are used as high-level eyes and ears, the composition of a company's board can tell you a lot about the kind of environment the company operates in and what information executives feel is important to get. Hospitals, for example, put local community and civic leaders on their boards because they operate in highly politicized environments. Community and civic leaders help them gather the specific kind of political intelligence they need. If financing is especially important, companies populate their boards with commercial bankers, investment bankers, and insurance executives (insurance companies are big lenders).

---

*The principals of the firm, Richard E. Combs and John D. Moorhead, have written *The Competitive Intelligence Handbook* (Metuchen, N.J., Scarecrow Press, 1992) which describes competitive intelligence techniques.

Some companies invite executives from key customers or suppliers to sit as board directors.* These high-level links can provide information about the outside director's company that helps coordinate and improve the relationship (see also Chapters 10 and 12). Other companies invite executives from critical *industries* to serve on their boards. This kind of link provides unbiased information about events, trends, and happenings in the industry.[56]

Trade associations and lobbying organizations can also be your high-level eyes and ears. Sociologists Edward Laumann and David Knoke report a great story about how this can work.[57] When the executive director of a petroleum-industry trade association spotted a *Federal Register* announcement by the Federal Aviation Administration (FAA), he immediately realized the danger to his member firms. The FAA wanted to require the filing of detailed flight plans of noncommercial aircraft as a way to help find downed planes. Under the Freedom of Information Act, however, companies could obtain competitors' flight plans and learn where they were exploring for natural resources. The executive director quickly alerted the membership and mobilized efforts to exempt member organizations.

What You Can Do *Now*

What you can do now is assess the current state of your personal intelligence system. Are you in the know, or are you the last to know? Do you get news in time to act? Or are you surprised time and time again when decisions are made that affect you and your group? In short, are you the director of your own intelligence network?

The following short quiz will help you assess the current state of your intelligence system. Answer each question yes or no depending on which answer best describes your situation. To score the quiz, simply circle the number of each question to which you answer yes. Count the number of questions that you answered yes. If you answered yes to 15 or more questions, your personal intelligence system's in good shape (though there's always room for improvement!). If you answered yes to 10 or more but fewer than 15, you have substantial room for improvement. And if you answered yes to fewer than 10 questions, well, you've some work to do.

---

*Of course, one must be careful to avoid so-called tying arrangements, wherein the sale of one product or service is tied to the sale of another. A tying arrangement would occur, for example, if a computer maker hired an investment bank *on the condition* that the bank agrees to buy the computer maker's products.

Evaluating Your Intelligence System

1. Do you feel that you're generally "in the know" and typically find out about key decisions, events, and activities inside the organization?

2. Have you stayed in touch with operations as you've moved up?

3. Have you maintained your contacts in other groups or departments as you've moved around the company?

4. Do you regularly supplement reports from management information systems (MIS) with informal word-of-mouth information?

5. Do you prefer to talk face-to-face to define and discuss complex problems and shifting priorities?

6. Do you usually accept contact-building opportunities—transfers, temporary details, committee assignments, relocations?

7. Have you (or would you) accept an assignment abroad?

8. Do you have personal contacts in a wide range of different groups (as opposed to contacts concentrated within the same group)?

9. Do you share actively information with your subordinates, peers, and superiors?

10. Do you provide information *to* your sources? Do you reciprocate?

11. Have you developed real-time intelligence networks, such as your own version of Donuts with Ditch?

12. Do you know people in other groups or departments that have special access to external information that would be useful to you?

13. Do you maintain contacts with lawyers, accountants, bankers, consultants, advertising agencies, and other outside sources?

14. Do you use professional information suppliers?

15. Do you stay in close touch with your customers (including final consumers)?

16. Do you tap suppliers as sources of information?

17. Have you developed fast internal channels to transmit information gathered from outside sources?

18. Do you regularly "wander around" in the outside world, attending trade shows, meetings, civic and charitable events, and so on?

19. Do you know and talk with your peers in other organizations?

20. Do you use board directors, lobbying organizations, and trade associations as high-level eyes and ears?

What You Can Do *Soon*

What you can do soon is figure out how you can improve your personal intelligence network. Even if your personal network's in good shape, still work on it: The best time to build your intelligence network is before you really need it. Times and situations change, and you never really know where the next piece of critical information will come from. By continually augmenting your network, you improve the odds that you'll get the news you need when it breaks. If you wait until you need information, it's too late to develop your network.

The key to creating your personal network is knowing *where* to build contacts, not just *how*. You must figure out *what* critical information you need and *where* it's produced before investing in the establishment of an information network infrastructure. First, look inward and consider your internal information needs:

- What kinds of information do you need? What information is critical to your ability to do your job? What's critical to your group's ability to do its job?

- Where are you (and your group) in the flow of internal information? Who are your internal customers? Who are your internal suppliers?

- Where are your key information uncertainties and threats?[58] Who makes decisions that affect your fate or the fate of your group? Where is information generated that you *really* need to know?

Now look outward and consider the types and sources of information you need from the organization's wider environment:

- What kind of information do you need? What information is critical to your success, your group's, and your organization's?

- Where's your organization located in the production-consumption chain? How far are you from the ultimate consumer?

- Where are your critical uncertainties and threats—customers, suppliers, competitors, regulatory actions, emergent technologies, and so on?

You may find that you can't pin down precisely all the types and sources of information you need. That's OK, because you never really know where the next piece of critical information will come from. You may not even know that a bit of information *is* critical until some time after you get it. People who network smart report that chance encounters, free-ranging and seemingly aimless conversations, tidbits dropped and overheard are frequently the sources of what, in retrospect, was vital information. There's a healthy element of chance in intelligence gathering. That's why a diverse set of information contacts is necessary. Your objective is to be in the right place at the right time—wherever and whenever that is—and you must cast a broad net to make sure you are.

Once you have some idea of the critical types and sources of information, your task is to build contacts. Remember the fifth networking principle: It's a small world (Chapter 2). It's your ally in the network-building process. The small-world phenomenon means you're never that far from the information you need. Every time you increase your network of direct contacts by a single person, you tap into a vast network of indirect contacts. This principle may help you see massive restructurings as blessings in disguise. Why? Restructuring means much wider spans of management, and wider spans augment your information network: You get more direct information sources (your additional direct contacts) *and* many more indirect sources (the personal networks your direct contacts bring with them).

Look back at your answers to the 20-question quiz. Is there a pattern to your yes and no answers? If you tended to answer no to questions 2 through 12, then your internal intelligence system is deficient and you should start there. Here are three suggestions for getting started:

- Start your own version of Donuts with Ditch. You don't have to make a big deal about it by making formal announcements. Just extend a casual invitation to chat about "things." Keep it open and free-wheeling. (Be sure to bring your favorite nosh—food is always hard to resist!)

- Reactivate one or two old contacts in groups or departments in which you once worked. Pick up the phone and extend an invitation to coffee or lunch. Or just stop by.

- Share information with a subordinate or team member; let him or her know something that you know. Remember that sharing information empowers people. A subordinate's or team member's power—the ability to get the job done—depends directly on his or her access to information.[59]

If you tended to answer no to questions 13 through 20, then your external intelligence system is deficient and you should concentrate there. (If your no answers appear in both sections, start building your internal network first and then proceed to work on external networks.) Here are three suggestions that can help you begin the process of building your external intelligence system:

- Think of who inside the organization is a natural bridge to a part of the outside world you want more information about. The bridger could be a salesperson, scientist, district manager, computer person, secretary, and so on. Invite that person to your next Donuts with Ditch session.

- Identify an outside supplier who might be a good source of information. It could be your company's law firm, ad agency, banker, and so on. Call them and invite them to lunch.

- Take a trip to an outside conference or trade show. It could be directly related to your business but it doesn't have to be. Attend the sessions, go to cocktail parties, don't eat alone if you can help it. Volunteer to do something at the next meeting.

What You Can Do in the *Long Run*

What you can do in the long term is manage *conditions:* create the right context that will help you and your organization develop and refine the overall intelligence system. Remember, the more you help others build their personal intelligence networks, the more you multiply your own.

Develop a reward system that encourages network building. Establish a travel budget that lets people attend trade shows, conferences, professional meetings, learned societies, educational seminars, and so on. In fact, make it a formal requirement that *everyone* goes to one such event at least every six months. If you can't afford to send everyone out of town, have them attend local events during the day, evenings, or weekends. And give everyone this chapter to read before they go.

Develop fast internal channels for processing information and getting it to the right people. Internal channels at Tennant Company are a good example. This leading manufacturer of floor maintenance equipment uses the sales force as "quality eyes and ears" in the company's total quality improvement program. "Every time a machine is delivered," say CEO Roger L. Hale and associates, "the salesperson fills out an installation report. If any defects are present, each one is the subject of a separate report. These reports are sent to the warranty and quality departments at company headquarters."[60]

When hiring, ascertain each candidate's *network assets* (the contacts a candidate brings with him or her) and *networking capabilities* (a candidate's motivation and ability to make new contacts). Everyone's personal network is portable. Every time you hire a well-connected person you annex a new network of direct and indirect contacts, new sources of information. (This is one reason behind the federal government's so-called revolving door restriction: a one-year waiting period after leaving a government post before an ex-federal employee can return and lobby for private interests.) When firing, or thinking about it, be sure to consider a person's network. If you don't, you might unwittingly sever important links to the outside.

When accounts are up for review, don't forget that your suppliers have network assets and networking capabilities as well. Are you getting the information you need from your lawyers, bankers, consultants, engineers, advertising agencies, and other professional service suppliers? Because these are easier to change than suppliers of goods (see Chapter 12 for why), you may want to consider adding or switching suppliers to boost your intelligence networks.

Establish a long-term intelligence trajectory—the directions into which you want to expand the organization's intelligence system. Pick a key uncertainty and establish a plan to build networks in that direction. If you're in an industry noted for fast technological change, for example, work to build information networks of scientists, engineers, university contacts, and so on. If you're in a highly regulated and politicized environment, think of adding political and regulatory contacts to your network. If supply of critical raw materials is a recurrent problem, build networks that will help you monitor supplies, substitutes, and suppliers.

Physical location can be used to create the right intelligence conditions. Edison Electric Institute didn't relocate from New York to Washington, D.C., because real estate was cheaper in the nation's capital.[61] It relocated as a way to become more central in political communication networks. As the major trade association for the electrical utility industry, the Institute had to enlarge its information-collecting and processing capabilities in response to the increasing politicization of energy policy making. Companies locate in close proximity to facilitate the face-to-face exchange of information too ambiguous or sensitive to transmit via electronic media.[62] General Motors' long-time advertising agency, McCann Erickson (now part of The Interpublic Group of Companies), has offices located right in GM's Detroit office building. Similarly, Capital Partners' main architectural firm has its headquarters in Capital Partners' home office.

A few final words. You'll never really be done building your personal intelligence network. Times and situations change. Always look for ways to supplement your intelligence contacts. From time to time, reread this chapter, reassess your situation, and work to become the director of your own intelligence network.

PART 2

Managing Relationships and Networks inside the Organization

4

Managing Up, Down, and Sideways

*I am less inclined to protest,
"Why don't you see it the way I do?"
and more inclined to say,
"You see it that way? Holy cow! How
amazing!"*

ROBERT FULGHUM
It Was on Fire When I Lay Down on It[1]

Recently I had the pleasure of working with a great Chicago law firm. By any standard, they're very successful. Most Chicago law firms are cutting back—some are even firing partners!—but this one is growing and hiring. Yet the firm's leaders saw a problem looming on the horizon. They founded the firm a decade ago as an alternative to the traditional large and impersonal law firm. They had split away in frustration from just such a firm and vowed to never recreate it. Ten years later, however, they saw some worrisome symptoms and feared they might be in danger of becoming that which they abhorred.

I met three senior partners for lunch at the Standard Club, and we talked about the firm. They all felt that relationships between partners and associates were strained. Some partners, they said, were dissatisfied with the performance of associates. Many associates complained of lack of communication, training, and guidance. Some had expressed the feeling that their firm was becoming "just another law firm." To better understand the problems, the senior partners and I agreed that I would interview a sample of partners and associates and design a scientific survey to investigate relationship issues. I would reveal the results of my study at the upcoming attorneys' retreat.[2]

What I learned from the survey is that lawyers aren't so different. They suffer from the same relationship problems that plague organizations everywhere. Specifics vary, of course, but the overriding principle is the same: No two people see the world in exactly the same way. And this difference is the root of the problem of managing relationships.

Consider some of the survey results. I designed a number of questions to elicit perceptions from both sides of the great partner-associate divide. For example, I wanted to know what partners and associates feel about the *quality of work* produced by associates. Figure 4-1 illustrates the big gulf in perceptions: Over 50 percent of all associates feel that most of the time they deliver the quality of work partners expect, but only 19 percent of all partners feel the same way! When I revealed these findings at the retreat, partners and associates alike were shocked. The contrast in perceptions astounded them. But now that they saw the differences, they were on the road to bridging the gulf.

People are often surprised to discover such systematic differences in perceptions, but those differences are not a real shock. A real shock would be the *absence* of differences. All sorts of obstacles stand in the way of mutual understanding. Differences in position, education, gender, seniority, age, and countless other factors are formidable barriers. Even identical twins don't see the world in quite the same way. Big differences in perception are the rule, not the exception.[3] That's why managing relationships is difficult. Mutual understanding doesn't come naturally; you have to work at it. Now that the attorneys at the law firm see their differences, they can work toward better mutual understanding and improved partner-associate relationships.

In this chapter I focus on managing one-on-one relationships in three directions: managing up (superiors), managing down (subordinates), and managing sideways (peers). I reveal the "secret formula" for developing good relationships and apply it to managing in all three directions. By thinking and working along these lines, you can improve your daily relationships with those around you. The chapter ends with concrete advice on what you can do now, what you can do soon, what you can do in the long run.

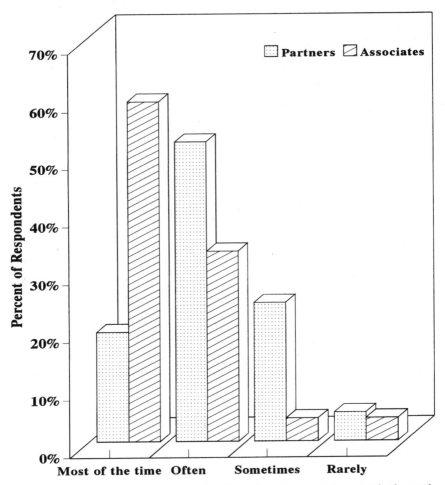

Figure 4-1. Partners versus associates: How often do associates provide the quality of work partners expect? (*Used with permission.*)

The Secret Formula

Yes, there *is* a secret formula for managing relationships. But the secret isn't the formula itself. The formula is simple. The secret is that it's very hard to implement. Managing relationships is tough work. It takes time, energy, and effort. Both parties must be mature and capable. In fact, neglecting your relationship duties—epitomized by the cult of the deal—has one advantage going for it: Neglect doesn't take much time, energy, or effort. But the fallout and unintended consequences are so terrible that learning to manage relationships is a far better strategy in the long run. Even if you're the most hard-nosed, bottom-line kind of person, managing relationships is the way to go. It's good business.

The formula for managing any relationship—up, down, sideways— involves the same basic elements: *mutual understanding* and *mutual benefit*. When there's mutual understanding, each person understands the reasons that the other acts in a particular way and accepts the other's behavior as legitimate and authentic, despite the tension or inconvenience it might cause. Each person understands the other's motives and feelings; each can take the role of the other with great empathy. When there's mutual benefit, both parties get what they need from the relationship. Each helps the other. It's win-win.

Mutual Understanding

How well do you understand your significant other? Two of my colleagues at the University of Chicago's Graduate School of Business, Harry Davis and Steve Hoch, interviewed husband-wife couples and asked each spouse to predict the other's preferences for a number of new consumer products.[4] Husbands and wives were confident that their predictions would be accurate. Not so. The average spouse was right only 2 times out of 10! Not only were most spouses very inaccurate, but they based their predictions on what *they* liked.[5] Each projected his or her feelings and desires on the other. Spouses really didn't understand each other's preferences at all.

The inaccuracy of these spousal predictions illustrates the crux of the problem of managing relationships: Mutual understanding is harder than we think. Like perfection, such understanding may not be attainable on this earthly plane, so consider it a stretch objective: Reaching for mutual understanding gets us closer to better relationships.

It's important to know *why* true mutual understanding is difficult. It's difficult because both people must be operating at advanced levels of psychological development. Both, as I described in Chapter 2, must be able to understand interpersonal problems at a high level.[6] Many people, however, operate at a low level. We all know these people. Everything's a personal insult. Nothing's ever their fault. It's always the other person. People operating at a low level get irritated, resentful, and angry over problems with others. They can't separate the problem from the person, view the other's behavior as valid, or appreciate reasons for the behavior.

Sometimes people operate at a low level because they lack the right interpersonal tools—they would like to achieve better understanding but they just don't know how. Smart leaders seize such opportunities and arrange for training and education—observation and listening skills, giving and getting feedback, group dynamics and team building—so their people can acquire and develop their interpersonal abilities. Far too often, however, the budget for such "soft skills" is one of the first items slashed when companies go on cost-cutting rampages. Given the importance of relationships, this training should be the *last* budget item to go.

Too often, the organization makes it difficult (if not impossible) for even the most capable people to operate at high levels of interpersonal relations. Mutual understanding takes time, but the pace of business can be so swift that it's hard to find the time. It takes effort, but just getting your job done can be taxing enough. The fundamental changes sweeping the business world make it harder to build relationships. Fast downsizing, for example, changes the players so quickly that you need a scorecard just to keep track of who's who. A shrinking organization disrupts the existing network of relationships. It plays havoc with attempts to manage relationships. It's hard to invest in relationships that may end suddenly; instead of building relationships, people retreat into a mad scramble for self-preservation.

The third networking principle, the similarity principle (Chapter 2), can stand in the way of mutual understanding. Because people tend to associate with others like themselves, they get too much feedback that simply reinforces their self-image. They miss the kind of feedback they *really* need to understand how others perceive them. Missing feedback is a universal problem for senior managers. Because they prefer the company of their peers, they become isolated from the rest of the organization.[7] These managers don't get enough feedback from subordinates, especially the negative kind. Prejudice is the offspring of isolation and uncritical reinforcement of self-image. "Hang out at most corporate headquarters," says Tom Peters in *Thriving on Chaos*, "and you soon come to believe that in most firms everyone on the line is considered a 'bozo.' As one (line) friend put it to me, 'They've never met a dumb marketing staffer or a smart sales manager in their lives.'"[8]

Let's look again at the law firm. As you might expect, partners didn't get the feedback they needed, especially from associates. Lack of feedback showed up in their responses to a question I posed to partners about how associates viewed them. Suppose all associates, I asked, were given the opportunity to rank you against all partners according to how desirable it would be to work with you. Would they rank you in the upper third, the middle third, or the lower third of all partners? Look at the results in Figure 4-2. Just like Garrison Keillor's Lake Wobegon—where all the women are strong, all the men good looking, and all the children above average—90 percent of all partners ranked themselves in the upper third. Why? Partners don't get the feedback from associates that would enable them to accurately rank themselves. They especially don't get *negative* feedback. And the partners who need negative feedback the most are the least likely to get it.

What about the associates? They did a better job of ranking themselves. I asked them the same sort of question: Suppose partners had the opportunity to rank you against all associates according to your contribution to the firm. As shown in Figure 4-3, a little over half put themselves in the upper third, just about a third put themselves in the middle third, and a few put themselves in the lower third. Some distortion, sure, but the associates are not as far off as their bosses. The reason is better feedback. Associates know where they stand because they get positive *and* negative feedback from their superiors. They used this feedback to rank themselves. Further analysis showed that associates who put themselves in the upper third report receiving from partners lots of positive feedback and little negative feedback. Those who put themselves in the bottom third report they get much more negative than positive feedback.

The differences between partners and associates illustrate an important principle: Feedback is like water—it flows downward, not upward. Because feedback flows down, associates know where they stand, but partners don't. Mutual understanding is possible, however, only when feedback flows in both directions. Leading companies know this, so they institute a system of upward appraisals as a corrective to this natural tendency.

So that you and I achieve greater understanding, let me anticipate and address an issue that often comes up when I talk about the importance of mutual understanding. "Do you mean," some ask, "that I should just 'turn the other cheek' when someone's behavior causes me problems?" Not at all. It doesn't mean you let others take advantage of you. Look back at the relationship grid (Chapter 2). Mutuality takes place in two quadrants: when both sides are deal-oriented and when both are relationship-oriented. When there's a mismatch, trouble's brewing. If you try to build a long-term relationship with a disciple of the cult of the deal, you'll be abused. You have to protect yourself in these situations. But maybe, just maybe, you can convert the mismatch into a match.

Operating at a high level of understanding of interpersonal problems means you accept the other's behavior as legitimate and try to understand the reasons for it, but it doesn't mean you have to like it— or live with it. People have different needs, and they're often in conflict. Mutual understanding is the vehicle for arriving at a common view of such needs and working out a mutual accommodation.

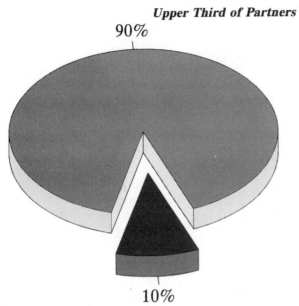

Upper Third of Partners

90%

10%

Middle Third of Partners

Figure 4-2. How partners think associates rank partners. (*Used with permission.*)

Sometimes it's a real struggle. A genuine relationship isn't easy. It can mean a fight now and then, just as long as it's a productive fight.

Mutual Benefit

Both parties win in an authentic relationship. Each person takes the other's welfare into account; each helps the other meet his or her needs. In *Influence without Authority*, Allan Cohen and David Bradford express this as *mutual exchange*.[9] Organizational consultant Robert Kaplan calls it *trade*.[10] You might be a little uncomfortable with terms like *exchange* or *trade* because they sound too cold and calculating. The norm of reciprocity in social exchange, for example, sometimes works best when it's implicit. People can be offended by talking frankly about formal exchanges.[11] But terms like *exchange* and *trade* contain a great truth: People give and get something in every relationship. This great truth is so much a part of human relationships that it's the basis of social exchange theory—one of the best known and accepted theories in sociology and psychology.[12] As far as I'm concerned, there's nothing wrong—and a lot right—with exchange or trade as long as it's ethical and both parties benefit.

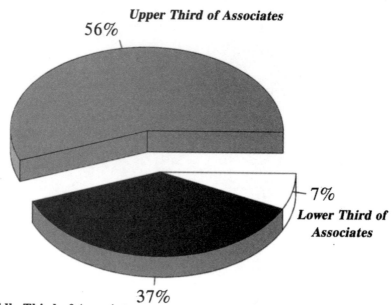

Figure 4-3. How associates think partners rank associates. (*Used with permission.*)

Subtle exchanges take place in interpersonal relationships, which sociologist Peter Blau was one of the first to document in organizations.[13] When you give advice, for example, you get something valuable in return: recognition of your superior knowledge and expertise. And the person who comes to you gives something in the exchange—public admission that he or she doesn't know something. That can make it hard to go to others, especially in macho organizations. Some people exact a high price for giving advice, forcing advisees to grovel or advertise their lack of knowledge. Going to others for advice is construed as a sign of weakness. That's why I try to be sensitive to new professors who come to me for teaching advice. I know it's hard to do, especially at a university where you're supposed to know everything. It's hard to do in your business, too.

People value lots of things in relationships, far more than generally believed. Remember the first networking principle? *Relationships are a fundamental human need.* There are many reasons. At work, for example, we interact with others because jobs are interdependent. "Beyond the people in the most routine functions," says Harvard's Rosabeth Moss Kanter, "no one has within a small domain all of the things he or she needs to carry out his or her job."[14] But we also create relationships because we're social by nature and value relationships as ends in themselves. Social interaction is a universal human desire. As illustrated by the principle of The Company of the Table, the human desire to belong is a source of great motivation and energy. Disciples of the cult of the deal look at it as only a simple matter of money: People are motivated to get paid. But those who network smart—those who empower rather than control—recognize mightier motivating forces: the higher needs for social approval, acceptance, achievement, self-fulfillment. They help themselves and their people attain these higher-order benefits on the job.

Cohen and Bradford provide a helpful catalog of the many different types of benefits (which they call currencies) that can be attained or exchanged in relationships.[15] What I really like about their catalog is that it goes far beyond the list of standard items, including both basic and higher-order needs. *Task-related* benefits include the technical and human resources usually associated with getting a job done, such as access to raw materials, financing or budgets, people, information, and help and assistance. *Relationship-related* benefits are based on the fundamental human need for relationships, the first networking principle (see Chapter 2). These benefits include understanding, empathy, social approval, friendship, and emotional support. *Inspiration-related* benefits appeal to a person's search for meaning and the desire to be involved in significant activities, such as being part of a lofty vision or doing the right thing. In my view, inspiration-related benefits also include the psychic rewards of achievement and satisfaction, as well as fulfillment of the human needs to be creative and productive.[16]

Most people are surprised at the wide range and variety of benefits that can be attained or exchanged through relationships. Smart leaders learn how to obtain and provide all of them. Self-understanding is critical: Do *you* understand what *you* want in a relationship? You can get what you seek, but do you know what it is? What about your partners? Do they understand the benefits they seek? Finally, is there *mutual* understanding? Have you exchanged your self-understandings? Does each partner recognize his or her own needs and the needs of the other? When you work toward mutual understanding of benefits desired, you're a big step closer to helping each other attain them.

The Relationship Contract

It's helpful to think of a relationship as an *implicit contract*, an unwritten agreement or understanding between two parties. The two parties can be two people (which I emphasize in this chapter), but implicit contracts also arise in relationships between groups, departments, and organizations.[17] When it comes to the implicit agreement between two people, the terms *psychological contract* or *interpersonal contract* are often used. For example, Harvard Business School's John Gabarro defines the *interpersonal contract* as "...a tacit, but agreed upon, set of mutual expectations concerning performance, roles, trust, and influence. This interpersonal contract develops and grows, for better or worse, as two people work together."[18] The same could be said for the implicit agreements that emerge between organizations, such as that between a company and a supplier. To cover all situations, I prefer the term *relationship contract.* (In later chapters, I use the idea of relationship contracts at the interorganizational level.)

Your relationship contracts up, down, and sideways evolve in stages. When two people begin working together, each forms initial impressions of the other. This mutual sizing-up, says Gabarro, lays the groundwork for the relationship.[19] Later, expectations are worked out in more detail, tested, refined, and reformulated. Finally, the relationship contract is stabilized and established. Yet the process is never really over. Changes in the business or personal needs and aspirations eventually destabilize the relationship, and the implicit contract must be renegotiated.

Keep in mind the concept of relationship contracts as you read and think about the rest of this chapter. What kind of implicit contract have you negotiated with your boss? With your subordinates? With your peers? Are these contracts mutually beneficial? Can they be improved? Is it time to renegotiate?

Managing Up: Working Well with Your Superiors

Managing up—"bossing the boss" as former Sealy CEO Howard Haas puts it—may sound peculiar, even suspicious. It's an automatic reaction. When most of us think of "managing," what comes to mind immediately is managing *downward*—directing and coaching one's *subordinates*—not the other way around. And when we do think of the upward direction, what often comes to mind is all the distasteful behaviors for which we have many expressions, such as politicking, currying favors, buttering up, and so on.

The concept of managing up sounded suspicious to me when I first heard of it. Now, however, I wish I had heard of it much earlier in my career—it would have enabled me to have built better relationships with my superiors in days gone by. (And I would have been a better boss, too, realizing that my team had to manage me as well.)

If you feel uncomfortable with the idea of managing up, as I did, you should know that your feelings are natural. It's important to understand the source of discomfort so you won't let it interfere with managing up. The source lies in the traditional (and now outdated) relationship contract. David McClelland calls it "the patriarchal contract" between the organization and its employees.[20] "The traditional contract is patriarchal," says Peter Block in *The Empowered Manager*, "in its emphasis on a top-down, high-control orientation."[21] This implicit agreement, which is inherent in the philosophy of control (see Introduction), actively *discourages* (and often punishes) the practice of managing up.

In the patriarchal contract, the subordinate agrees to *submit to authority:* obey, comply, conform.[22] Because the boss is assumed to be wiser, smarter, and more knowledgeable, the subordinate is not supposed to question or negotiate, much less *manage* the boss. The patriarchal contract is a formidable barrier to managing up. If you buy into it (or the organization strictly enforces it), learning how to manage up is almost impossible. But if you reject the passive role inherent in the patriarchal contract and embrace your right to manage up, you can begin to learn how to build better relationships with your bosses.

Know that managing upward relationships is ethical and responsible behavior. It's good for you, your boss, your organization. As Harvard Business School's John Gabarro and John Kotter put it in their famous *Harvard Business Review* article, "by using the expression *managing your boss*, we…mean the process of consciously working with your superior to obtain the best possible results for you, your boss, and the company."[23] It makes good sense to work with your superiors to improve effectiveness all around. *Not* managing up will do more than just limit your effectiveness, it'll threaten your job—even your career. Remember the plight of Bill Hansen: a chief cause of his downfall was his failure to manage up.

Mutual Understanding

The secret to managing up (like any relationship) is to apply the generic "secret formula." The first half of the formula, we know, is mutual understanding. And we know that mutual understanding is naturally difficult. The associates and partners in the law firm, for example, are bright, well educated, sociable people—yet they didn't really understand each other very well. That's the rule, not the exception.

Unfortunately, when it comes to achieving mutual understanding with the boss, there's an additional complication: attitudes toward those in positions of authority.[24] Some people, I've observed, operate at high levels of understanding when they deal with subordinates and peers, but drop to lower levels when it comes to their bosses. This drop happens when the superior-subordinate relationship arouses psychological remnants of parent-child relationships.[25] Patriarchal organizations (which treat adults like children[26]) aggravate this psychological tendency.

When the parent-child relationship is aroused, the subordinate casts the boss in the role of father or mother. In some cases, the boss-as-parent is expected to be all-powerful, all-knowing, flawless, and infallible. The subordinate assumes a passive, dependent, even powerless stance, and looks to the parental figure for nurturance, protection, recognition, and fulfillment of all needs. This situation, of course, is doomed to fail. "A boss in a corporation," says Abraham Zaleznik in *The Managerial Mystique*, "cannot deliver the promise of nurturance embedded in the image of the father [or mother]."[27]

In other cases, the boss-as-parent becomes the object of anger, derision, resentment—even hatred. Such subordinates don't trust anyone in a position of authority. They resist, challenge, disobey, question. Of course, there's some appeal to the practice of questioning authority. Challenges to authority can invigorate an organization.[28] And challenging authority is part of the fabric of American culture. I'm reminded, for example, of the film *Sweet Liberty* with Alan Alda and Michelle Pfeiffer. Alda plays a history professor whose book about the American Revolution is being turned into a Hollywood film. In one scene, the director instructs the professor about the formula for a commercially successful film. The director's first rule—"defy authority."

Defying authority, like submitting to it, is a problem if you do it as an automatic reaction rather than as a conscious choice. If you defy or submit as a reaction to parent-child relationships, you'll have trouble developing genuine, productive relationships with your superiors. But, if you defy or submit by choice (such as knowing which battles are worth fighting and which are not) you can be more effective and influential. It's important, therefore, to recognize your natural proclivities and how they may get in the way of real mutual understanding. If you think all bosses are jerks, for example, you'll distort your boss's true motives and intentions. You'll dismiss decisions out of hand without trying to really understand them. You'll never look beyond the immediate situation to appreciate the conflicting pressures any boss must accommodate. Or, if you feel bosses should be obeyed unquestioningly, you won't clarify objectives or instructions, which always leads to gross misunderstandings.

The most productive attitude is what psychologists call *interdependence* or *mutual dependence*.[29] It's the recognition that you and your boss need each other, that your fates and fortunes are intertwined. It's the recognition that people get things done through and with others. Your boss relies on you to get your job done, without constant supervision, and to get it done in a way that furthers his or her objectives. You also rely on your boss to get his or her job done, and to do it in a way that takes you into account. Mutual help and cooperation are vitally important. Each of you is a critical node in the other's intelligence network, for example, and each depends on the other to collect and relay critical information.

Don't confuse *inter*dependence with *in*dependence. Independence is a prized value, but it becomes a liability in the extreme. Overly independent people act as if they're not dependent on the boss (or anyone else, for that matter). They get the job done, but that's it. Such people are often quite good *technically*—that's all they care about—but they're not good at building relationships. They don't appreciate the importance or the power of cooperation, collaboration, shared responsibility, and teamwork. They certainly don't see the world as a network. While the interdependent person knows that no one is an island, the overly independent person believes he or she *is* an island. This go-it-alone attitude gets back to basic attitudes I talked about in the Preface. We're more accustomed to thinking of the world as an assortment of disconnected individuals, free-floating atoms. But, says Jeffrey Pfeffer in *Managing with Power,* success depends on getting things done with and through others.[30] As James Newman and Roy Alexander put it, "Lone wolves belong on the prairie."[31]

So, how can you improve mutual understanding with your bosses? Your objective is to operate at a *high level* of understanding of interpersonal issues and problems. To begin, consider your attitudes toward those in positions of authority. What is your main tendency? Defiance? Submission? Independence? It's hard to change one's attitude, but a giant first step is recognizing what your attitude is. You can then begin to understand how your attitude might get in the way of mutual understanding, and how you may have to compensate. If you know that you have trouble questioning authority, for example, you have to muster the courage to ask questions.

Once you have a better understanding of your role in your relationship with the boss, you are better prepared to "take the role of the other" with empathy, understanding the boss's situation, motives, and feelings. Begin with objectives. Do you really understand your superior's objectives? What's he or she trying to accomplish? In what time frame? What's your boss's strategy for your group? How does it fit in with larger objectives and strategies for the organization? How do *your* objectives and strategies fit in? Too often, subordinates don't know the answers to these basic questions. It's partly the boss's responsibility to inform you, but don't wait. Ask. Find out for yourself. If your boss holds a version of the Donuts-with-Ditch idea, use this forum to clarify and communicate objectives. If not, interview your boss on a regular basis.

What is your superior's preferred mode of operation, interaction, and communication—what some call "managerial style"?[32] In her insightful study of new managers, Harvard Business School's Linda Hill observed three dimensions of managerial style: "task- versus people-oriented; authoritative versus participative; and less often, informal versus formal."[33] Where is your boss on these three dimensions? Do you know? Where are *you* on these three? Do your preferred styles mesh or clash? If styles clash, can you adjust?

By itself, style doesn't matter. An informal boss can be as effective as a formal boss. But style does matter when it gets in the way of mutual understanding. Some people are put off by a formal boss, for example, inferring that the boss's reserved style means he or she doesn't care about them. Some people have trouble with an authoritative boss because it triggers old issues about people in authority. If you're operating at a high level of understanding, however, you can tolerate such uncomfortable feelings and keep them from getting in the way of working out the relationship. A healthy response is to take stylistic differences for what they are—distinctions without substance—and work to accommodate them. Management expert Peter Drucker provides an excellent example, which Gabarro and Kotter summarize.[34] Managers, Drucker says, are either "readers" or "listeners." His advice: Give written materials to readers, and later discuss your findings and conclusions in person; give oral reports to listeners, and later send along a written version. Communication and understanding are improved in both cases.

Mutual Benefit

The second half of the secret formula is mutual benefit. With improved mutual understanding, you should have a clearer sense of what benefits your boss seeks, and he or she should have a clearer sense of what benefits you seek. The task now is to help each other obtain valued benefits. Remember that exchange is part and parcel of every human relationship, in and out of business. (For now, I focus on your role in obtaining mutual benefits. In the next section, I focus on your boss's role.)

What *really* motivates your boss? Money? Social approval? Achievement? Self-fulfillment? All of the above? What really motivates *you?* How can you help both of you obtain these? When I was a manager, for example, I sought interesting, creative tasks; I worked best when I was really intrigued by what we were doing. My team helped me obtain this valued benefit when we marketed interesting work for us to do. In contrast, one of my peers didn't care as much about the nature of the work; what mattered most was effective teamwork, even if the task was (in my view) dull and boring. In this case, the team helped the most when it pulled together and got the job done.

At the most basic level, your boss needs resources of many kinds. These include raw materials, information, ideas, personnel, financial resources, access to networks, even legitimacy and social support.[35] Information, for example, is a key resource you can be sure your boss needs. Every manager is more or less out of touch (as I described in Chapter 3). It's a perennial problem for just about everyone. By building your intelligence network (Chapter 3), you can collect and transmit information the boss needs. If you're talking with your boss on a regular basis, you'll know what kind of information he or she seeks. And in reverse: Does your boss know what kind of information you need? This could be information directly from your boss, such as timely updates on policies or procedures, or information you need from other parts of the organization or from outside the organization itself.

Every boss faces the tough task of finding good people for jobs in the organization. You can be a hero by finding the right person. And it may be easier than you think. By virtue of your unique position in internal and external networks, you can help find suitable internal or external candidates (see Chapter 9, "Finding Good People"). You can also use your networks to find other essential resources: suppliers, new customers, investors, strategic allies, and so on (see Chapters 10–14).

No one is good at everything; everyone has strengths and weaknesses. What is your boss good at? Not so good at? One of the most valuable benefits you can offer your boss is compensation for his or her weaknesses. If your boss is a finance whiz but weak on marketing, for example, you can compensate by building marketing strengths. If your boss doesn't stay in touch with operations, you can—and then relay what you learn. If your boss has good internal networks but weak external networks, you can compensate by building external ties. If your boss is more task-oriented than people-oriented, you can help by handling the relationship tasks.

Of course, all of this works in reverse as well. Does your boss have a good understanding of *your* strengths and weaknesses? Do you have the same ones as the boss? The similarity principle can be a problem (see Chapter 2). Because people prefer to associate with others like themselves, bosses sometimes hire subordinates who are just like them. A numbers person hires another numbers person, for example. Is this true in your case? Are you and your boss too similar? If so, you have to help the boss hire people with *complementary* strengths.

Managing Down:
Subordinates as Partners

Managing down is the traditional direction, but don't think of it traditionally. The days of command-and-obey are long over. Effective people get things done through others. You're dependent on subordinates, just like they're dependent on you. Empower them to do their jobs better, and they help you do yours better. Think of them less as subordinates and more as partners and allies in your quest for personal and organizational success.

Thinking of your subordinates as partners and allies might be harder to do than you realize. Many superior-subordinate relationships are founded, implicitly, on the control-oriented patriarchal contract. Often, superiors buy into this traditional relationship contract, even when subordinates are able to avoid doing the same. This old-fashioned attitude can plague anyone, but Linda Hill found that new managers are particularly susceptible.[36] Many new managers adopt an autocratic style, attempting to use their new formal authority to direct and control their people. They soon discover that control doesn't work. Part of becoming a true manager, says Hill, is learning to lead by persuasion, not by command. Effective leader-managers learn how to treat their subordinates as partners and allies. That's networking smart.

Mutual Understanding

It might surprise you to know that the remnants of parent-child relationships can interfere with mutual understanding even when you're the boss. The reaction simply works in reverse: The superior casts subordinates in the role of children. If the subordinate colludes in this reaction, the superior and subordinate become locked in an unhealthy relationship. The relationship might appear to work, at least for a while, but it's not an effective arrangement for the organization or for the people involved. The first step toward mutual understanding, therefore, is to examine your attitudes toward subordinates: Do you treat them like adults or like children?

To really understand your subordinates, you need to "take the role of the other." You need to put yourself in your people's shoes and understand their world. If you came up the ranks, you may think you already do. But the world has changed since you were in it; their pressures and concerns are different now. You can't project what you thought and felt onto your subordinates.

Getting into the world of your subordinates isn't easy, particularly if your organization is a traditional straight-up-and-down hierarchy. But you have plenty of mechanisms at your disposal. Think back to the previous chapter on building your own personal intelligence system (Chapter 3). You can use your version of Donuts with Ditch to encourage give-and-take with your subordinates and learn what their problems and concerns are. Merck CEO Roy Vagelos's habit of eating lunch in the company cafeteria is another way.[37] Or consider a version of Federal Express's Open Door policy, which encourages employees to communicate directly to management their ideas, questions, or comments.[38] And, you can simply *talk* with your subordinates one on one. As they learn that you won't use information against them, they'll open up more and more. Remember the fourth networking principle: Repeated interaction facilitates cooperative relationships.

Sometimes it's hard to understand your subordinates, especially if they're different from you. It's not just rank that stands in the way. If your people come from diverse backgrounds, for example, differences in language, slang, custom, and styles of interaction make it difficult to really understand them. Even good managers who operate at high levels of understanding when they share the same background as their subordinates can drop to a lower level when managing people from different backgrounds. But if you recognize this as a *natural* problem, you're less likely to blame your subordinate for difficulty in mutual understanding and more likely to seek ways around the problem. Most differences like these are differences in *style*, not *substance*.

I bet some of you bosses are chafing at my advice about managing down. Why should I work so hard to understand my subordinates? Is the whole burden on my shoulders? Not at all. At the same time you're working to understand them, they're working to understand you. Help them. Help them understand you, your world, your pressures and concerns. It's a two-way street. When both sides try, it's not as hard.

Getting feedback from your subordinates is critical. This doesn't happen naturally in most organizations. Feedback, especially negative feedback, is often a one-way street. In general, most people are reluctant to transmit bad news.[39] Subordinates often consider giving negative feedback to the boss as too risky. And in many cases they're right.

History is littered with the corpses of shot messengers. To develop as a professional, however, you need feedback, positive *and* negative. You need feedback to keep in touch. Because you're the boss, you can do something about getting more feedback. Establish feedback-boosting mechanisms. Your Donuts with Ditch, for example, is a forum for continuous feedback. You can institute a system of upward appraisals. This can be as simple as a suggestion box for anonymous messages. Or, like such leading companies as GE, Ford, and First National Bank of Chicago, you can establish a formalized system of upward and team appraisals to provide everyone with feedback on a regular and systematic basis. If used correctly, upward appraisals provide useful feedback, reinforce productive behavior, identify areas for personal development, and improve one-on-one relationships. In the "What to do" section at chapter's end, I offer some concrete advice on how to institute a system of upward and team appraisals.

Building mutual understanding also means giving subordinates the feedback they need to reinforce good deeds and correct mistakes. In the best of circumstances, this happens on a daily basis; you don't wait for the scheduled six-month or annual performance review. Positive *and* negative feedback are necessary, what Allan Cox calls "pokes and strokes" in *Straight Talk for Monday Morning*.[40] Most bosses, Allan says, give too many pokes and too few strokes. Consider a simple statistic he reports from Dr. Mark Tager's work as a corporate consultant with companies on health and fitness programs: "The ratio of pokes to strokes is about 4 to 1."

The 4-to-1 ratio means something worse than you think, because one negative comment far outweighs one positive comment. When my students formally evaluate my courses, for example, one negative remark stings so much that it cancels 10 positive ones. My friends on the faculty tell me they experience the same effect, and it's a documented fact in scientific research on interpersonal interaction in general.[41] It may have something to do with how the brain functions. Recent psychological studies, for example, show that the brain's mental accounting system pays more attention to negative stimuli than positive stimuli.[42]

This effect is magnified when the negative comment comes from above. Subordinates always take a remark made by a superior more seriously than the superior does. If your objective ratio of negative to positive comments is 4 to 1, your subordinates feel it as if it were 20 to 1. You have to go out of your way to correct the balance. One good way is to take to heart Ken Blanchard's advice in *The One-Minute Manager:* Catch your subordinate in "the act of doing something right."

Mutual Benefit

As the boss, you're in an advantageous position to help you and your subordinates obtain mutual benefits. You control or have access to many resources subordinates need. These include, of course, the basic resources to get the job done—raw materials, access to people, financing, political support, and so on. Part of your job is to make sure your people have what they need to perform their jobs. Another part of your job is letting your people know what resources you need from them.

Keeping subordinates informed is one of the most important benefits of all. Here's why. What characteristic do subordinates value the most in their superiors? Far and away, it's this: *Honesty*. Eighty-three percent of 2615 managers surveyed by James Kouzes and Barry Posner ranked honesty number one.[43] Kouzes and Posner have conducted other surveys of managers in both business and government and they've found the same answer. The overwhelming importance of honesty reveals the benefit subordinates value the most—the truth. GE CEO and chairman Jack Welch, for example, knows the importance and significance of the truth. It's institutionalized in several key GE values—candor, reality, openness, and honesty.

I believe superiors value honesty in their subordinates just as much as subordinates value it in their leaders. Gabarro and Kotter, for example, argue that honesty is one of the most important characteristics a subordinate can have.[44] Both superiors and subordinates need hard, factual, honest information. No one benefits if one holds back. But it's often difficult for subordinates to supply information, especially negative information. To get the benefit of mutual exchange, either you learn how to accept negative information without reprisals, or establish impersonal devices that boost the upward flow of information, such as upward appraisals.

Learning is another shared benefit. What are your subordinates' strengths and weaknesses? Can you find ways to turn weaknesses into strengths? As the boss, you can assign tasks and jobs that will help your people grow, professionally and personally. You can provide training and education to improve both technical and relationship skills. As your people become more effective, they make you more effective. And, you learn from your subordinates as much as they learn from you. Teaching, for example, is thought of traditionally as a one-way process: Students are empty vessels waiting to be filled with knowledge. I've discovered, however, that students are a great source of learning for me. The classroom is a great testing ground for ideas, as well as a source of new ideas and knowledge. Physicist Richard P. Feynman, Nobel laureate and raconteur, said that he would never give up teaching for a research-only position.[45] Teaching and students, he said, were great sources of new research ideas. They kept life going. So, too, with your subordinates. They can teach you a lot; they're allies in the learning process.

Do you invoke the power of The Company of the Table? Do you provide the means for your subordinates to fulfill their basic needs for belonging, acceptance, and social approval? Do you encourage them to work in teams, build and solidify good working relationships? And do you provide inspiration-related benefits, a grand vision, a larger-than-life sense of mission and purpose? In the process of doing so, you'll inspire and motivate yourself.

A final word. You've got good people; let them do their job. One of the best benefits you can bestow on your people is to give them the room to do their jobs. Remember the Pygmalion principle—people tend to do what's expected of them, positive or negative. Expect the best and let them do it.

Managing Sideways: The Power of Peers

Old images die slowly. We still tend to think of organizations as pyramids with an overemphasis on up-down relationships. This vertical image is obsolete. Modern organizations are changing in ways that make *lateral* relationships more important than ever. Almost every person I talk with these days tells me that success depends more and more on managing *peer* relationships. The fundamental changes I talked about in the Introduction—restructuring, new communication technologies, multifunctional teams, the rise of flexible network organizations—have made peer relationships essential to your success, now more than ever before.

Peers hold the keys to critical services and resources. Organizational consultant Robert Kaplan notes that peers control all sorts of services—technical expertise, information, advice, political backing, and moral support.[46] Entrepreneurial managers, says Rosabeth Moss Kanter, reach beyond the boundaries of their formal positions to secure the information, resources, and support they need.[47] Putting together multifunctional teams, for example, means you must become adept at negotiating with peers from different groups and functions to secure the people and resources you need. Without peer support, your career will stall, even though your individual accomplishments may be rewarded.[48] Peers make powerful friends and dangerous enemies. You need their support and they need yours.

The power of peers isn't easy to tap because peer relationships are officially undefined. Organizational charts and job descriptions only define and officially sanction our *vertical* relationships: who we report to and who reports to us. The charts are silent on peer relationships. You don't have formal authority over peers, even though they're critical to your success. Working with peers involves persuasion and influence, not command. To some, that makes managing sideways seem, well, so *political*. Political or not, it's essential. And, it's worth the effort. Peer relationships are an underutilized and neglected source of power and influence. Building peer networks is critical for both personal and organizational success.

Mutual Understanding

Just like managing up and down, mutual understanding is one of two keys to managing sideways. Before we consider how to improve mutual understanding, let me ask what might seem like an odd question. Who are your peers? Most people, I've observed, think too narrowly about whom they include on the list of peers. Your immediate peers are obvious—those of similar rank or level in your team, group, function, or department. But peers also include people from different teams, groups, and departments. And, peer relationships can even span different levels in the organization, such as what Robert Kaplan calls "lateral superiors" or "lateral subordinates."[49]

As in any relationship, your objective is to operate at a high level of understanding of peer relationships. This is difficult, however, because unique obstacles stand in the way. (Kaplan calls these obstacles "trade barriers" because they interfere with exchange among peers.[50]) Peer relationships can be problematic because peers are rivals for resources and promotions. Associates in the law firm, for example, compete to become partners. Associates know that only a select few will become partners. The similarity principle is another barrier between peers (Chapter 2). Peers from different functions have different objectives, interests, and subcultures. These differences make it difficult to attain mutual understanding. Picture, for example, the classic strained relationships between people from engineering versus people from sales. (See Chapter 5 for more on "bottlenecks" between groups.)

Despite these natural barriers, peers need one another. Peers are interdependent. Peers depend on each other to do their jobs; they must cooperate to achieve results. Interdependence is the impetus for mutual understanding. One way to think about interdependence among peers is to trace the flow of work inside the organization. Tracing the flow helps identify key peers and key resources. Consider your inputs—raw materials, information, personnel, funding, even political support and legitimacy. Who are your internal suppliers? What resources do you get from them? Who are your suppliers' suppliers? What do they need from each other? Then consider your outputs. Who are your internal customers? What do they need from you? And who are your customers' customers?

The concept of relationship contracts applies to peers, just like any interpersonal tie. In some ways, it's easier to be explicit about contracts between peers than it is between superiors and subordinates. The reason, I think, is the peer relationship is so undefined that it's wide open for explicit horse trading and negotiation. What kind of relationship contract do you want to negotiate with each of your peers? What understandings do you have (or want to have) about terms, conditions, promises, and expectations?

Mutual Benefit

Mutual benefits are attained via exchange. That's true in most relationships, but it's particularly important in peer relationships: Exchange is the *only* way to influence peers because you don't have formal authority over them. You can't fall back on the power of your formal position.

Exchange among peers takes all sorts of forms. "Peer alliances often worked through direct exchange of favors," says Rosabeth Moss Kanter in *Men and Women of the Corporation.* "On lower levels information was traded; on higher levels bargaining and trade often took place around good performers and job openings."[51] Managers trade political support by uniting against a common external threat. A friendly peer finds funds in his or her budget to support your project, or speaks up on your behalf in meetings and one-on-one with important people.

Exchange depends on reciprocity. Because exchange is your primary means of influence with peers, reciprocity is vitally important. Indeed, it's so important that Kaplan calls reciprocity the *first principle of trade* among peers.[52] Reciprocity is a universal social rule.[53] In politics, for example, allies reciprocate by swapping votes for each other's bills, a practice called "logrolling" (originally the custom of neighbors helping neighbors to clear land by rolling logs into a common spot for burning). Reciprocity is a kind of organizational "glue." "Many organizations," says Charles Savage, "are actually held together by an intricate web of accommodations and IOUs."[54] Mutual aid, anthropologists tell us, is the most common function of friendship in cultures around the world.[55]

Reciprocity can be simultaneous or delayed. When it's simultaneous, you give something to a peer at the same time you get something, such as swapping gossip, information, and ideas. To a degree, exchange *always* involves simultaneous reciprocity because so many intangibles are traded in interpersonal relationships. When you get advice, for example, you simultaneously acknowledge that your advisor is smart, knowledgeable, wise, and a good person for helping you out. When reciprocity is delayed, repayment is made at some later date. If you help me, for example, I've incurred an obligation to help you at some point in the future. What is given immediately is an implied promise to return the favor.

Over time, peers build up an unwritten system of debits and credits.[56] Payment and repayment are implicit and unspecified, but accounts must balance in the long run for relationships to work. Those who try to maximize their benefits on each exchange lose in the long run. Remember the fourth networking principle: repeated interaction encourages cooperation (Chapter 2). By engaging in exchanges over time, repeated cycles of give and take, you build a solid foundation of trust and cooperation.

Sometimes, however, you lack the resources a peer needs, and you don't have anything to exchange. In such cases, you acquire and accumulate what the other wants (or build alternate pathways to the resources you need). Information is always a valued commodity. At the very least, you are (or can become) a member of your peer's personal intelligence networks (Chapter 3). You can collect and provide critical information about what's going on inside and outside the organization. The better your intelligence network is, the more likely you'll come across information newsworthy to your peers. The new electronic networking technologies can help. Many companies are now shifting from the old client-server approach to the new peer-to-peer electronic networks.[57] In the old model, you can't communicate directly with your peers (other clients). In the new peer-to-peer systems, you can be a client *and* a server. You can freely talk with peers throughout the organization.

What You Can Do *Now*

What you can do now is figure out your *critical contacts* and *critical gaps. Critical contacts* are those interpersonal relationships that are particularly important to your effectiveness and success. These could include people up, down, sideways, or any combination thereof. *Critical gaps* are interpersonal relationships that *should* exist but don't. These involve key people who are critical to your success but with whom you don't have working relationships. Your ultimate objective here is to bridge critical gaps by converting should-be relationships into actual relationships.

Your first step is to *catalog* existing critical relationships—up, down, and sideways. You might think you can do this from memory. If you're like most people, however, you interact with many more people than you think. As I mentioned in Chapter 2, the typical professional has 3500 contacts. Only a few of these are *critical* relationships, of course, but you have more than you're able to recall in the abstract. Recall must be triggered by specific events, encounters, or probes. So, keep a running log of whom you interact with. It can be as simple as jotting on your day timer the people you see throughout the day. Note basic facts: who, what, where, why. Keep this running log for at least two weeks.

At the end of the two weeks, you've collected the raw data for inventorying your relationships. Now you need to organize the data. I suggest you do this at home, rather than at work. Observers may misconstrue your motives. Follow these steps:

- Write the who, what, and where on a set of index cards (or on your computer with a database, indexing, or contact/sales call program). Use one card per person.

- Organize the index by categorizing them by *type* of relationship: up, down, and sideways. Don't forget your lateral superiors and lateral subordinates.

- Within each category, rank-order the cards from *most critical* to *least critical*. Which are vital for your success? On whom do you depend the most? How unequal is that dependence?

- Make special note of the most critical relationships that are especially problematic. Which cause you the most trouble? Which are the most difficult? Which are in the worst shape?

Now that you've organized your relationships, prioritize them into categories: invest, hold, divest. Prioritizing relationships may seem a little cold and impersonal, but it just makes explicit what most of us do intuitively. Effective managers, for example, invest most heavily in their most critical relationships.[58] The hard truth is you can't be everywhere at once, you can't be all things to all people. Unless you never sleep and enjoy boundless energy and infinite time, you can't have strong relationships with everyone. Time and energy are scarce resources; husband and allocate them wisely.

- *Invest* is your strategy for critical relationships that are especially important for getting your job done. These could be good working relationships that you want to maintain, problematic relationships that are so vital you need to give them special attention, or relationships with people on whom you are very dependent.

- *Hold* is your strategy for critical relationships that are fine and don't need special attention or effort at this time. This doesn't mean they're unimportant, just that they're clicking along fine and you don't have to invest additional resources in them now.

- *Divest* is your strategy for relationships that aren't so critical or important. You may spend less time, less energy, or withdraw resources. Warning: Be careful. It's usually better to adopt the hold strategy than to burn bridges. Burning bridges can be appropriate, however, in cases where an associate behaves unprofessionally with customers or fellow workers or engages in unethical or illegal behaviors.

Once you've identified critical contacts, your next main task is to identify critical gaps. This is a tougher task. It's one thing to catalog existing relationships; it's quite another to catalog ones that don't exist but ought to. Here's a few ways to probe and prompt yourself:

- Look at your list of critical relationships. Does the list for any type of relationship—up, down, sideways—appear to be a little too sparse? Any obvious gaps? A common gap is peer relationships, especially in companies adopting the network organization model.

- Do you have any new direct reports that you just haven't found the time to get to know? These are critical gaps that should be converted into real relationships.

- Do you have a new boss—or a new lateral superior—whom you haven't gotten to know yet? It's easy to put it off and wait for the boss to come to you. Take the initiative instead.

- Do you have good working relationships with peers who work at other locations? Bill Hansen never nurtured budding relationships with his peers at other StorageAmerica facilities and so he couldn't get information or advice from them when he really needed to.

- List the functions, departments, teams, and groups that are important to you. These could be important for any number of reasons—information, money, political support, and so on. Now look back at your list of critical relationships. Do you have them in these critical functions?

- Take a long look at the organization chart. Are there people whom you know by name only (or don't know at all) who work in departments, teams, or functions that are critical to your success? Are there informal groups or coalitions that don't appear on the chart that are critical to your success?

What You Can Do *Soon*

Effective managers, observes John Kotter in *The General Managers,* invest most heavily in their most critical relationships.[59] You've already figured out your most critical relationships, as well as your most critical gaps. What you can do soon is work to improve these relationships and fill these gaps.

Improving relationships means applying the "secret" formula: better relationships equal mutual understanding plus mutual benefit. Begin with mutual understanding. With greater understanding, mutual benefits will follow: You'll be able to better understand what other people want, and they will be able to better understand what you want. The main barrier to mutual understanding is feedback. To surmount it, make feedback a two-way street: Institute your own informal feedback and appraisal system. This system can provide regular, accurate, two-way feedback. The system will help both of you understand each other, appreciate each other's concerns and pressures, develop agreed-upon expectations, and foster the spirit of trust and cooperation.

Now I don't mean anything elaborate by an informal feedback and appraisal system. In the long run (as I talk about in a moment) you may want to institute a formalized system, but for now keep it informal and simple. Here's some of the steps you can take:

- Initiate a series of informal away-from-the-office lunches with the person. These are great opportunities to talk about a wide range of topics and get to know a person.

- Simply set up an appointment to clarify expectations, objectives, assignments, and so forth. Most people will respond well to your initiative. After all, by taking these steps you're acknowledging how important they are to you.

- Conduct an informal "reverse role play." Before you meet with the person, put yourself in his or her shoes and imagine his or her world—the pressures, concerns, objectives. When you meet, test the accuracy of your mental exercise by playing back what you thought.

- Invite a trusted peer, subordinate, or superior to give you a candid assessment of your performance. Don't retaliate for negative feedback; you may be tempted to, but resist the urge. Negative feedback is a gift you can use to learn, adjust, change, and grow.

Filling critical gaps is tougher to do. In an existing relationship, even a troubled one, you've gotten over the first hurdle, the introductory phase. You're not strangers. For critical gaps, however, you haven't been "formally introduced," so to speak. Your task, therefore, is to *initiate* the relationship. Expect it to be uncomfortable; if it's not, you're an unusual person or you're not doing it right. Remember that your ultimate goal is mutual benefit: You're going to help the other person as he or she helps you.

- Put yourself in circumstances that will enable you to meet the person on a natural and casual basis. Such circumstances include company outings and events, lunch in the company cafeteria, and so on.

- Volunteer for a temporary assignment that puts you in the person's department, function, or team.

- Find a third party who can introduce you. Remember the fifth networking principle: It's a small world. Once you look, you'll find plenty of third parties you have in common.

- Do something as direct as simply introducing yourself, explaining that you thought you both should know each other.

What You Can Do in the *Long Run*

What you can do in the long run is expand and formalize the informal feedback and appraisal system you've already started. Doing so creates the right conditions for encouraging and spreading feedback throughout your group. It's one of the best ways to improve your own effectiveness as well as the solidarity and performance of the group itself.

Before we talk specifics, it's important to recognize that formal performance appraisals are used for two purposes: *development* and *evaluation*. The difference is critical. When appraisals are used for development, people get feedback that helps them improve their performance, managerial skills, and interpersonal relationships. When used for evaluation, people get grades or ratings that are linked to their compensation (e.g., share of bonus pool). Linking ratings and compensation is a way to motivate people to accept feedback and change behaviors. This might be necessary to motivate a few stubborn people, but I think it's important to keep in mind that the *real* purpose of appraisals is *personal and professional development.*

Hard incentives may not be enough to make some people improve simply because they don't know *how* to change. Incentives motivate, but you also need to supply people with the *tools* to improve. The philosophy of empowerment is based on the recognition that you have to change the underlying *processes* of work; you have to help people change the fundamental ways they relate to one another in the workplace. Education, training, and counseling are often necessary to help people develop better interpersonal skills—active listening, observation, giving and getting feedback, taking the role of the other, time management, group dynamics, team building, and so on. Provide the *means* to improve along with the motivation.

As a long-term goal, plan to develop a broad-based, multiple-rater system of feedback and appraisals. Digital Equipment Corporation, for example, uses *team appraisals* to make sure employees get feedback from every member of their groups.[60] Team appraisals make sense for a number of reasons. "Traditional performance appraisals," says *Training* staff editor Brad Lee Thompson, "are often trashed for being too subjective, too easy to manipulate, too hard to conduct and too burdened with fear of confrontation."[61] Team appraisals, however, are more valid than ratings done by superiors. Team members have more (and often better) information than superiors do. This is particularly true, notes Thompson, as an organization is delayered and spans of management increase.[62] With more and more direct reports, it's harder to get to know each one well enough to conduct an accurate evaluation by yourself.

Conceive of the "team" in a broad sense and expand your formal feedback and appraisal system to include both inside people and outside people. Some call this a *360-degree appraisal system,* as illustrated in Figure 4-4. In addition to internal sources (superiors, peers, and subordinates), a 360-degree system includes customers, suppliers, and outside peers (e.g., others in your profession) as sources of feedback about individual and organizational performance. Remember that "customers" and "suppliers" include internal clients and suppliers as well as outside organizations.

How should you begin to develop a 360-degree system? It's perilous to jump abruptly from a traditional (downward) appraisal system to a 360-degree system. The shock to the organization would be too great. To make the change work, your people have to participate in the development of the system and buy into it. Their active participation improves the validity, accuracy, and relevance of the appraisal system. Move toward the 360-degree system in a series of steps or stages, informing and involving your people all along the way.

It often helps to use an outside expert. Because 360-degree systems are new, many companies lack in-house experience and expertise. An outsider can also provide confidential processing of information. (One

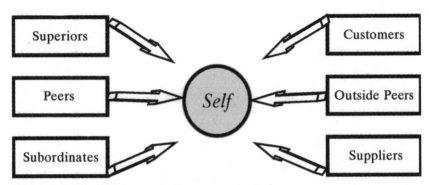

Figure 4-4. The 360-degree performance appraisal.

company I know considered using internal computer systems to collect, record, store, and feed back appraisal data. Several people object-
ed, arguing that "hackers" could breach confidentiality. They decided
to use an outside service.) For example, management expert Harry
Levinson recommends using an outsider for upward appraisals.[63] A
third party acts as a buffer, counselor, and interpreter. At least in the
beginning, subordinates are more likely to provide *specific* information
(especially negative information) to a third party than to their bosses
directly. This information can be packaged, summarized, and fed back
to the bosses as part of their personal and professional development.

Analytic Research Associates (ARA), a Chicago-area consulting firm
that helps companies develop and implement multiple rater systems,
has developed a helpful approach. As ARA implements a performance
appraisal system for a client, they consider different *natural groups* of
evaluators, both inside and outside. Inside, several groups are natural
evaluators—superiors, peers, and subordinates. Each of these is aware
of different aspects of an evaluee's behavior and performance.
Outside, customers, suppliers, and external peers continuously gauge
your employees' performance, even though they typically don't provide formal feedback. By incorporating these natural groups of evaluators, employees can get valuable concrete feedback for both personal
and professional development.

ARA considers seven natural groups of evaluators. Picking the right
groups is one of the most important questions ARA answers before
designing a performance appraisal system. Group 1 is the traditional

top-down appraisal; from this base, companies usually add groups 2 and 3 before incorporating additional groups of evaluators.

1. Downward: Supervisors rate subordinates.
2. Upward: Peers rate supervisor.
3. Peer: Peers rate other peers.
4. Client: Clients rate company contact.
5. Supplier: Suppliers rate company contact.
6. Outside peers: Outside peers rate peers within your company.
7. Self: You rate yourself.

ARA uses a unique method to identify appropriate evaluators. A qualified evaluator is one who interacts significantly with the evaluee over a period of time. To identify these evaluators, ARA conducts a formal network survey. In the survey, employees are asked to describe three types of interaction: "workflow networks" (whom they work with to get their jobs done), "communication networks" (whom they talk with to get work done), and "friendship networks" (whom they socialize with on an informal basis). By analyzing each network, ARA identifies objectively those who are the most qualified to rate particular evaluees.

Using an approach like ARA's can help you move from traditional top-down performance appraisals to the 360-degree approach. Remember, however, that the 360-degree approach isn't an end in itself; it's the means that gets you where you really want to go: improved working relationships, up, down, and sideways.

5

Bottlenecks and Bridges

After successfully completing a temporary assignment as planning manager at a subsidiary of Post Chemical Company, Bill Foxx had just been named the new Business Development manager and given his biggest challenge yet.[2] His new assignment: Take charge of an exciting R&D pilot project and do whatever it takes to bring it to full commercial production.

The exciting R&D project involves the breakthrough development of a product with an unexciting name—polyimide, PIM for short. PIM is a specialty electronic polymer used to coat and insulate printed circuit boards. That might sound dull at first, but electronic polymers are big business. They're used in computers, television and video equipment, military and space applications. Electronic polymers make up one of the fastest growing segments in the chemical industry. The global market in 1992 was estimated to be bigger than $5 billion.

Post Chemical has staked its future on the successful commercialization of PIM. If Bill Foxx pulls it off, PIM will put Post Chemical over the top—and make Foxx a hero.

It won't be easy. No one knows if PIM can be produced in commercial quantities. R&D pilot production is only 2000 pounds per year, but commercial volume means 200,000 pounds or more per year. The commercialization effort has run into a number of snags. The project is already behind schedule and over budget. Post's customers think PIM is a great product; it's performed superbly in customer tests. But customers are frustrated by delays and broken promises about availability. Customers are so frustrated, in fact, that they're threatening to stop waiting and go to Post's competitors instead.

Foxx also faces serious organizational problems. The previous Business Development manager, Frank Mills, tried but failed to wrest control of the pilot project from R&D. Insiders said Mills was a poor leader and had let R&D director Paul Nelson dominate the project. Indeed, Nelson referred to the PIM project as "my baby" and told Mills that R&D had to retain full control to make sure commercialization was successful.

R&D and Business Development reached an impasse on several critical issues. R&D wants to keep PIM feedstock production in-house, but Business Development wants to use an outside supplier. R&D wants to mass-produce PIM at ultra-high purity levels, but Business Development has opted for the purity customers find acceptable. Overall, R&D wants to continue its free-wheeling research mission, but Business Development wants R&D to concentrate on less glamorous polymer work, purification, engineering, and design. Their unsettled differences have devolved into antagonism, competition, and suspicion.

Bill Foxx's problem might sound familiar to you. It's one of the all-time classic organizational problems: lack of cooperation between departments, functions, or groups. It's a well-known fact of organizational life that different units have trouble working out cooperative relationships. The result is what I call "bottlenecks." A bottleneck is a narrowing or constriction of relationships between groups. "Bridges" are used to overcome bottlenecks. Bridges open the free flow of traffic between groups. Bridges unite disparate groups in concerted effort. Without bridges, all sorts of problems crop up—marketing makes impossible promises, R&D invents products customers don't want and production can't make, and research breakthroughs never make it to the market. Networking smart means *anticipating* natural bottlenecks and *building* bridges to overcome them. In this chapter, I tell you how to spot bottlenecks and what you can do about them.

It's important to recognize that Bill Foxx's problem is greater than the problem of managing up, down, and sideways I discussed in Chapter 4. Foxx has to manage relationships between *groups*. In

Chapter 4, I focused our attention on managing *personal* relation-ships—direct one-to-one ties between people. The subject of this chap-ter—managing *group-to-group* relationships—widens the focus and moves us up an entire level of analysis. In a sense, it's the subject of Chapter 4 writ large.

I wish I could tell you that Bill Foxx was successful. He wasn't. He wasn't able to pull it off. Foxx suffered from the Bill Hansen problem. Post's top managers thought they needed a Business Development manager with strong *technical* skills. Foxx was their man. He definitely had superior technical skills, including a Ph.D. in chemical engineer-ing and an MBA from a leading business school. But he didn't have good *relationship* skills. He viewed the tension between R&D and Business Development as a technical problem, not a relationship prob-lem. Let me give you one telling example. When Foxx assembled his team, he brought in organic chemist David Smith from Post Chemical's R&D headquarters. Smith has a Ph.D. from Stanford University and is considered one of the best technical types. But he's also a confirmed loner. He can't work in teams, and he's so protective of his research that he's immediately threatened when colleagues show any interest in his work. Not exactly the kind of person you want to help solve a *relationship* problem between R&D and Business Development.

Even though Foxx couldn't pull it off, the story has a happy ending. Post's top execs decided to intervene and "jump-start" the project. What they did represents the best lessons of networking smart. They transferred Foxx abroad and prodded R&D director Paul Nelson into early retirement. They replaced them with two managers who had successfully worked together before and already had a solid relation-ship. Smith (the recluse) was retained for technical continuity, but an R&D person with good relationship skills was made the formal liaison between R&D and Business Development.

The changes worked. The PIM project moved ahead rapidly, and Post soon broke ground for its new PIM production plant.

Differentiation: First Principle of Organization

The root of problems like Post Chemical's is the division of the organi-zation into specialized groups. This is called *differentiation*, and it's the first great principle of organization.[3] Organizations are split and divid-ed in several ways. Division into ranks, layers, and levels is called *ver-tical* differentiation. Separation of functions, like the segregation of

R&D and Business Development at Post Chemical, is *horizontal* differentiation. And the division of an organization into multiple geographic locations, such as branch or foreign offices, is called *spatial* differentiation.

Differentiation is the root of Post Chemical's problems, but it's important to appreciate that organizations are split into specialized groups for a very good reason: We aren't superhuman. No one can do everything, know everything, be everywhere. Specialization helps solve the problem. The division of labor—breaking jobs into simpler, repetitive tasks—yields greater speed, efficiency, and productivity. Workers learn how to perform their specialized tasks with alacrity and skill, and multiple tasks are performed in parallel rather than in sequence. The benefits of the division of labor are stunning. During World War II, for example, Henry J. Kaiser used it to revolutionize wartime ship building.[4] In 1940 it took six months to build a 10,400-ton Liberty Ship, using traditional job-shop construction methods. By introducing the division of labor and other mass production techniques, Henry J. cut production time to just 36 days!

Differentiation also yields relationship benefits. Specialized groups almost always develop internal strength and cohesion. Members of the same group share common interests, objectives, and a unifying culture. The Company of the Table is a great example (see Introduction). Sparta's basic military unit was founded on natural differentiation: common kinship and neighborhood bonds. Sparta's leaders understood the fundamental principle that powerful groups are built on relationships that grow out of the natural interests of the people involved.

So far, so good. Differentiation yields technical and relationship benefits. But it simultaneously creates its own problems. Paul Lawrence and Jay Lorsch of Harvard Business School were among the first organizational researchers to document the ways in which segmenting an organization into departments and functions influences how individuals think, work, and feel.[5] They observed that members of disparate groups differ along four important dimensions:

1. *Orientation toward different goals.* Sales managers, for example, may focus on sales volume, production managers focus on low manufacturing costs and process efficiency, and R&D types focus on new scientific discoveries.

2. *Orientation toward time.* Individuals may have a short-, medium-, or long-term orientation toward time. Salespeople, for example, are typically short-term oriented, because they have to focus on the next sale. Researchers are usually more long-term oriented. The

new employer-employee contract, which no longer guarantees life-long employment, forces people to be more short-term oriented on the job.

3. *Orientation toward people.* Some people are very task-oriented, whereas others tend to be relationship-oriented. This dimension hits foresquare the main theme of this book. The need to be relationship-oriented does vary by functional group, but I argue that *all* groups should be more relationship-oriented than they are.

4. *Formality of structure.* Different units develop all sorts of different structures: different reporting requirements, incentive systems, career ladders, performance standards, control mechanisms, amount of flexibility, and so on.

Differences in thinking and working make it very difficult for people from different departments or functions to communicate, cooperate, or just get along. Without some sort of intervention, a differentiated organization degenerates into isolated groups, distant islands of independent activity. Group members become unabashed chauvinists for their own groups and champion their group's interests, often to the detriment of the organization itself.

The problems caused by differentiation go by different names in different companies—silos, turf, chimneys, stovepipes, Balkanized states, fiefdoms, factions, empires, and so on. I summarize it all as *bottlenecks.* Whatever you call it, it spells trouble for you and your organization. Given how the business world is changing, it's become one of the most pressing problems in organizations today. To be competitive in the new business order, organizations must learn how to overcome their bottleneck problems.

To gain insight into the root of the problem, consider how the two departments at Post Chemical—R&D and Business Development—differ along the four dimensions. R&D is an uncertain game in which serendipity plays a big role (see Chapter 6). As a result, R&D goals are hazy and long-term, revolving around the unpredictable process of scientific discovery. Business Development's goals, however, are much more concrete and short-term—there are time tables, schedules, and budgets for bringing the new product to market. R&D types tend to be more task-oriented than people-oriented (witness loner David Smith at Post!). Business Development types, in contrast, tend to be more people-oriented than task-oriented. This wasn't true for Bill Foxx (who failed), but it was true for his replacement (who succeeded). R&D thrives on informality; anything too stiff and formal would stifle imagination and creativity. Business Development is quite different. More formalized structures, with specific measurement, control, and reward systems, tend to work better.

Now that you see these sharp differences, it's no wonder people from different departments have so much trouble getting along. I wasn't surprised to learn of the friction between Business Development and R&D at Post Chemical. Their differences are natural and expected. Only a *lack* of tension would have been a surprise! Like Post Chemical, most companies struggle with discordant and strained relationships between units.

Integration: Second Principle of Organization

Duality is a universal property of nature, and so we find it in organizations. If differentiation is the organizational *yang*, then integration is the organizational *yin*. Integration, the second great principle of organization, brings together what differentiation splits apart. The two principles are opposite and complementary forces; they always exist together in every organization. The key difference between organizations is the relative *balance* of opposing forces. In traditional hierarchies, differentiation is the strong force; in the new network organizations, integration is the strong force. Organizations between these two poles are based on varying balances of the two forces.

In a hierarchy, integration refers to the type and quality of coordination among distinct organizational units.[6] A hierarchy is well-integrated when its various departments and functions work well together. This definition of integration presumes, as Charles Savage puts it, that "...materials and information are passed *serially* from one department or function to the next."[7] An organization is well-integrated if the "series of sequential handoffs"[8] from department to department go smoothly and efficiently. I call this *level-one integration* because it presumes the continuing existence of separate departments and functions. Post Chemical, for example, suffered from a level-one integration problem. This level is the highest attainable in organizations built from the blueprint of the traditional hierarchy. Even organizations that are computer-networked are still integrated at level one if they haven't evolved beyond separate departments and functions.[9]

In the network organization, integration means something far more. The principle of integration takes precedence over the principle of differentiation. Integration is the strong force. The multidisciplinary, multifunctional team is the primary organizational unit, not the department or function. An organization integrated at level one is a static structure of fixed lines and boxes; an organization integrated at level two is a fluid, flowing pattern of project-based teams coming together, accomplishing tasks, and disbanding afterward, only to be drawn together again in different combinations as new tasks arise. Multiple teams work concurrently, yielding the tremendous power of *parallel* processing of tasks, not sequential handoffs.[10]

In a well-functioning network organization, multidisciplinary teams are assembled easily, get the resources they need, go about their work without undue outside interference, and disband gracefully after their missions are accomplished. In addition, the efforts of multiple teams are coordinated via an overarching *network of teams*. I call this *level-two integration*. This level is attainable only in organizations based on free and flexible networking. The organization of Hollywood filmmaking is one of the best examples I know.[11] A virtual army of freelance producers, directors, screenwriters, actors, actresses, music composers, cinematographers, and others come together, make a film, disband. The entire industry ebbs and flows with this rhythm. In the context of a giant corporation, Jack Welch's image of GE as a boundaryless organization is a good example of level two integration.

Techniques for Level-One Integration

Today, many companies are experimenting with the network organization design. Most, however, like Post Chemical Company, still struggle with problems of level-one integration. I'm repeatedly astonished that so many U.S. companies still cling desperately to the traditional organizational blueprint. Problems like Post Chemical's are still the rule.

Integrating traditional organizations is easier said than done. The force of differentiation is very powerful. Integration doesn't come easily because differentiation ceaselessly reinforces the *differences* between people from various units. It creates a natural tendency for the organization to fragment and fly apart. The problem is this: People in a differentiated hierarchy work primarily with people like themselves. This designed-in segregation aggravates the similarity principle, the tendency for people to prefer others like themselves (Chapter 2). Members of the same unit develop similar ways of working, thinking, and feeling; they become inbred and fall into the Us-versus-Them syndrome. Whenever differentiation is the strong force in an organization, integration is like sailing a small boat into the wind.

Given these obstacles, integration must be a constant and continuous effort. Good managers use a number of techniques, *formal* and *informal,* to overcome the bottlenecks formed by differentiation. Well-integrated organizations incorporate a healthy mix of both types. Regardless of the techniques used, the overall objective is the same: creating good working relationships between groups by building bridges.

Designate People as Official Bridges. Good managers overcome bottlenecks by designating individuals as official bridges. A production engineer, for example, has one foot in production and the other foot in R&D. The integrator should be rewarded for the joint performance of both groups, rather than for the performance of a single group.

Boost Information Exchange. Encourage groups to exchange information and participate in each other's intelligence networks. Information exchange can help to develop better personal relationships between groups.

Invest in Peer-to-Peer Computer Networking. Computer networking, especially peer-to-peer networking, such as Artisoft's Lantastic, can facilitate communication between groups. It's not suitable, however, for initiating *new* intergroup relationships. By itself, computer networking can't transform an organization if it's just grafted onto a traditional departmentalized hierarchy.[12]

Rotate Personnel. Rotation of people among groups builds bridges. A marketing person, for example, could be put on temporary assignment in R&D, production, or another department. Rotation helps people take the "role of the other" and develop a broader world view.

Get Staff Members into the Field. So says Tom Peters in *Thriving on Chaos*—"encourage them to be 'business team members' rather than narrow functional specialists."[13] This breaks the natural bottleneck between staff and field, staff and line.

Make Middle Managers "Functional-Boundary Smashers." According to Peters, these managers do more than just "coordinate," they "aggressively...force activity that involves multiple functions to occur faster."[14]

Pool Rewards. Develop pooled bonuses and other rewards based on successful joint efforts. Investment banks, for example, induce cooperation between product specialists and account executives by using a pooled bonus system.

Use Facility Design to Induce Interaction. Creating mixed-use, mixed-group facilities increases the odds of interaction between members of different groups. Unlike most business schools, at the University of Chicago and Stanford University, the offices of faculty from various disciplines—finance, marketing, statistics, organizational behavior, and so on—are mixed. This creates chance encounters that lead to multidisciplinary exchanges and collaborations (see also Chapter 6).

Techniques for Level-Two Integration

Level-one integration gets you just so far. It's a band-aid approach, one that patches together organizational pieces. That may suffice for a long time, but eventually you have to move beyond and attempt level-two integration. The move is a quantum leap, however, not an incremental improvement over past efforts. The move means establishing *multifunctional, project-based teams* as the primary building blocks of the organization. Such teams are self-integrators, natural bridge builders. Where traditional organizations suffer the built-in tendency to fly apart, team-based organizations enjoy the natural tendency to hold together.

General manager Jerome Simpson made the team his basic building block as he revitalized Navigation Devices, a division of Fairweather Corporation.[15] Every team he forms is composed of people from multiple functions and areas. His 20-person *planning team,* for example, includes workers, managers, and union representatives, who collaborated to develop and implement a plan for mobilizing the division. Multilevel, cross-functional teams are organized around specific tasks: a *business management team* sets broad strategy, *product management teams* develop new products, *production process teams* solve quality and cost problems in the plant, and *engineering process teams* address methods and equipment. To aid the integration of multiple teams, Simpson uses *team-leader teams.* Simpson, his staff, and key stakeholders (union steward, finance manager, human resources facilitator) are members of a so-called *bridge team* that monitors the entire effort. This may seem like a lot of teams, but Simpson's change effort is a great success story: Quality, profits, and all other measures of performance are way up. Employee morale is the highest of any division in the company.

Organizational consultant Charles Savage proposes the useful concept of *virtual teams.*[16] A virtual team is a self-organizing, self-managing, multitasking, cross-disciplinary group. It forms around tasks broadly defined by top management but works out the details on its own ("task-focusing"). Members of a virtual team employ peer-to-peer computer networking, so they don't have to be located in the same place. Most important, a virtual team is *outward-oriented*, directed toward its internal and/or external customers and suppliers. An organization composed of virtual teams is a *virtual enterprise.* "Virtual enterprises," says Savage, "are built upon their ability to define and redefine multiple cross-functional teams as needed. These teams may include not only members of the company, but also persons from vendor or client companies."[17]

Every solution contains the seeds of a new problem. As a company becomes an organization of teams, it must face the need to coordinate teams. That's the new challenge of integration in the network organization. In the drive to create multifunctional teams, many leaders fail to recognize the need for cross-team integration. To get closer to customers, for example, some companies decentralize and create multiple customer-focused teams but then forget to integrate by building a *network of teams.*

StorageAmerica, the company I featured in the Introduction, is one of many examples I could describe. StorageAmerica is a decentralized organization, running each of its facilities as an independent operation. Without coordination across units, however, relationships with national customers suffer. For example, the corporate sales and marketing department would quote rates at one facility for customers who were already paying different (usually higher) rates at another facility. Different facilities provided different levels of service. Different facilities developed different billing and invoicing practices, which sometimes confused and always aggravated national clients.

In the past, StorageAmerica's integration problem was partly solved through informal networks created by the general managers (you may recall that Bill Hansen failed to do this). Today, the company is experimenting with more deliberate coordination methods. The general managers are now charged with developing a "superstructure" or "network" that unites facilities. For example, general managers now have a mandatory monthly meeting at corporate headquarters to coordinate their activities. And a new organizational role has emerged— informally dubbed "the orchestrator," a general manager who is responsible for linking together the various facilities.

Large, global companies use similar integrating devices. Such devices go by many names—network, superteam, network of teams, team of teams. Management consultant Ram Charan calls them simply "networks" in his *Harvard Business Review* article because they're designed to transcend group boundaries. "The members," says Charan, "are drawn from across the company's functions, business units, and geography, and from different levels in the hierarchy."[18]

He's observed these superteam-networks in companies as diverse as Royal Bank of Canada, Conrail, and Dun & Bradstreet Europe.

GE's Jack Welch uses the network concept with his Corporate Executive Council (CEC).[19] GE faces a potentially drastic integration problem. The company is made up of more than a dozen global businesses, each number one or number two in its respective markets—everything from appliances and light bulbs to aircraft engines, sophisticated medical equipment, and financial services. The CEC helps solve the integration problem. The CEC is a high-level network composed of senior people from all the businesses who convene on a regular basis at GE's management center in Crotonville, New York. There, they exchange information, advice, and ideas. "In practice," says Noel Tichy and Stratford Sherman in *Control Your Own Destiny or Someone Else Will*, "the CEC is a high-level think tank, where the company's best informed (and presumably most talented) people work together on issues of common concern."[20] More important, the CEC is a place where executives from around GE forge a unifying community—strong bonds, loyalties, and a common set of values.

Overall, a network of teams yields many important benefits. A network can help avoid wasteful duplication of effort, such as the independent development of redundant systems, methods, and procedures. A network aids learning and diffusion of knowledge; what one team learns can be transferred to others. A network can unite a diverse company by building strong bonds and a common set of core values. And a network can help coordinate external relationships with customers, suppliers, competitors, regulatory and governmental agencies, and so on.

Capital Partners: A Case of Successful Level-Two Integration

A few years ago I was introduced to a fascinating company, Capital Partners, a very successful commercial real estate development firm.[21] I say fascinating because the firm's organized in a special way that encourages active bridge building. The great success of the company is attributable to its built-in integrative techniques. The company makes networking a core value and central activity. Taking a close look at how the firm achieves level-two integration gives you a menu of choices to consider when you plan how you'll integrate your organization.

Capital Partners is differentiated, of course; all organizations are divided in one way or another. The firm's arranged in three main groups: office, retail, and industrial real estate development (horizontal differentiation). It has separate offices located throughout its market catchment area (spatial differentiation). And it has various levels—senior partners, partners, leasing agents, and support staff (vertical differentiation). Even though the firm is differentiated, there's a key difference between Capital Partners and most companies: The firm doesn't let differentiation become the strong force. Instead, Capital Partners is organized and run in such a way that integration is the strong force. Let's see how.

Capital Partners CEO Michael Mach bases his company on the blueprint of the network organization. In fact, he often refers to his firm as a "lattice" organization, a term he learned from W. L. Gore and Associates. (Lattice is just one of several synonyms for network.) The concept of a network (or lattice) organization departs fundamentally from the traditional organizational blueprint, the hierarchy. Consider, for example, how Capital Partners' network design differs from a classic hierarchy:

- *Horizontal Relationships.* Capital Partners strongly emphasizes *horizontal* relationships—the ties that unite and integrate. In a hierarchy, *vertical* relationships are given primacy, such as those drawn on the organization chart. The vertical implication of an organization chart is so antithetical to Capital Partners that the firm doesn't even have one!

- *Project-Based Teams.* Capital Partners is built around project-based teams, not specialized functions. Teams are multidisciplinary, multilevel, flexible, free-forming, self-managed, self-directing. By nature, such teams are integrative. Other real estate firms are organized as hierarchies, collections of specialized functions. The patterns of movement are strikingly different. In a network organization, *people move to projects.* Different people join a team focused on taking a total project from start to finish. In a hierarchy, *projects move to people.* People pass a project from department to department after each one completes a specialized task.

- *Informal Influence.* In a network organization, the power to influence others is based on expertise, experience, ideas, ability to marshal resources, and quality of relationships. A leasing agent who is intimately familiar with local market conditions has much more influence over leasing decisions than a senior partner who doesn't have day-to-day contact with the market. In a hierarchy, power is based on formal position and rank. Hierarchies have "bosses" who command, control, and intimidate; network-based firms like Capital Partners have leaders who inspire, coach, and empower.

■ *Direct Person-to-Person Communication.* Capital Partners emphasizes direct, personal, face-to-face interaction. A hierarchy, in contrast, stresses written, impersonal modes of communication—memos, reports, and so on. Direct person-to-person communication at Capital Partners is encouraged by deliberate avoidance of written communication, an open-office design, project-based teams, mentoring relationships, and an antibureaucratic value system. The goal is to make sure everyone knows everyone else. This isn't practical in a large organization, of course, so the idea is to have dense networks within market groups, and to have market groups linked by a network of teams.

■ *Network of Teams.* Sophisticated network organizations integrate multiple teams by establishing a network of teams. At Capital Partners, the partners themselves formed an integrating network that united the various market groups. In a hierarchy, the integration of functions or departments occurs only by moving up until a common manager is found. In a large hierarchy, this method is so impractical that integration just doesn't happen; groups are left to operate in a decentralized, autonomous fashion.

Rationale and Benefits

Why does Capital Partners attempt level-two integration? Why do they pursue the lattice ideal? They want it for some very good bottom-line reasons: Level-two integration yields great competitive advantages.

Better Service. By nature, real estate is project-based, project-driven. Each real estate project is unique and requires a customized mix of people. A good project team is assembled with people drawn from different disciplines and parts of the company. Developing a multiuse facility, for example, may require an expert from the retail group and another from the office group. Without the typical unscalable walls between departments, flexible cross-cutting ties help team leaders put together the right teams and deliver high-quality customized service.

Lower Costs. The emphasis on teams and networks of teams means professionals are better trained and cross-trained. They get real-world experience in all types and all phases of real estate development. As a result, project teams can be small and efficient, and that means lower labor costs. Cross-trained professionals—generalists—easily shift from phase to phase as a project progresses. Unlike their counterparts in traditional real estate firms, they learn everything from soup to nuts, from initiating new projects to leasing and managing the final product. As markets wax and wane, professionals transfer from development activities in weak markets (like office real estate) to strong markets (like retail real estate). Overhead is reduced because cross-trained professionals don't need the expertise of internal staff consultants or expensive outside consultants.

Improved Marketing.   The lattice design means lots of information sharing and excellent personal intelligence systems (Chapter 3). Professionals from different parts of the firm talk with each other a lot. They know on a real-time basis what's happening in each market. They learn what customers are thinking and anticipate their needs. When a customer wants a proposal, they learn of it before their competitors do. Bridges help to "cross-sell" customers. When the industrial group develops warehouses for a client, for example, it might learn of the client's needs for office space as well. Because the industrial and office groups are bridged, this lead will be relayed quickly to a trusted colleague in the office group.

Common Values and a Strong Unified Culture.   When groups aren't integrated, they go their own ways. They develop their own values and subcultures, their own ways of thinking and working. In a well-integrated company, however, people share information, build consensus, work for the common good. They develop a common set of values and a shared world view. This commonality is more than a humanitarian nicety. It saves money. With common values and a strong unified culture, you don't need expensive formal systems to monitor and "control" everyone. Given the Capital Partners' environment, people exercise *self-control*. Common values and shared information also enable Capital Partners to present "one front" to brokers, agents, municipalities, zoning boards, and other outside groups, avoiding the mixed messages that always arise when one group doesn't know what the other's doing.

Building Bridges at Capital Partners

How does Capital Partners implement its organizational strategy? What do they do, exactly? It's one thing to have the lattice blueprint in mind, quite another to put it into practice. Here are some of the specific ways they build and reinforce bridges.

Take Great Care to Hire the Right People. The senior partners are very picky about whom they hire. They look for more than just technical knowledge and skills. The right people are those who combine solid technical abilities with good *network assets* (the portable contacts a new hire brings to the job) and good *networking abilities* (the motivation and ability to make contacts and build relationships). In other words, they look for those who can network smart, people with good interpersonal skills who will thrive in the lattice culture. To make sure they get the right people, senior partners use a lengthy and intensive recruitment process, including repeated interviews and mandatory participation at social events and recreational activities. The whole process can take months.

Train Professionals to Be Generalists. The last type of person wanted at Capital Partners is a reclusive, narrow specialist. Generalists are preferred, but not just because they're more efficient than specialists—generalists are natural bridge builders. As a senior partner described, "I deal in all aspects of the business. We're not specialists in finance or zoning. I'm well-versed in all aspects of the business; therefore, I come in contact with more people in the organization—accounting, property management, and so on."[22]

Once they hire the right kind of person, they provide the right kind of environment—they manage conditions to enable people to become generalists. New hires learn by example. Each leasing agent is assigned a mentor, a partner who already is a real estate generalist. Leasing agents are qualified to become partners only when they know the whole real estate business inside and out.

Avoid Written Communications. Memos, letters, and other written documents inhibit quick communication, face-to-face interaction, and relationship building. Such written communications are avoided whenever possible. Doing so forces everyone to meet and talk frequently. People have to interact to get information, set priorities, build consensus, define their jobs, and so on. Avoiding impersonal forms of communication forces people to build bridges.

Use a Facility Design That Encourages Interaction. Capital Partners uses an "open office" layout—no private offices, not even dividers between desks. Even the CEO's desk is out in the open. This physical design promotes easy interaction, chance encounters, conversation. The open-office design symbolizes and reinforces the open corporate culture.

Underspecify Roles, Responsibilities, and Reporting Relationships. This sounds strange, I know. Management theory extols the virtues of clearly defined roles, responsibilities, and reporting relationships. In practice, however, precise job descriptions actually *reduce* communication because they define what one is supposed to do and *not* do, whom one is supposed to report to and *not* to. It's important to communicate a clear mission and broad guidelines, but after that being vague about roles, responsibilities, and reporting lines forces everyone to assume broader responsibilities and to interact with a wider and more diverse range of people.

Encourage Interaction between Professionals and Support Staff. In the typical real estate firm, professionals and support staff—accountants, project engineers, maintenance people—are estranged and distant groups. Bridging this gulf can yield great benefits. Better relationships between partners and accountants ensure quick and accurate transmission of vital information. "We want accountability in a personal way," a senior partner told me, "not just pushing the numbers, but pushing the numbers for *someone.*" To build bridges between professionals and support staff, both groups are located in the same offices. Support staff are included on teams. Accountants visit real estate projects under development to get a feel for the property.

Build Redundant Ties. No one should be the sole bridge between two groups. Exclusivity of this kind makes an organization much too fragile and vulnerable. Redundancy, the existence of multiple bridges, strengthens the organization by providing parallel channels. When I analyzed the networks at Capital Partners, I discovered a startling fact: The CEO had built so many redundant ties that he was "expendable"! He was central in the firm's networks, but he wasn't a "critical node": If he were hit by a bus, the firm's networks wouldn't disintegrate. It takes courage to make oneself "expendable" in this way, but it's part of the lattice design. And it's testimony to the CEO's commitment as a networking manager.

Pay for Performance. Money is used as a motivator at Capital Partners. Of course, the firm motivates by powerful nonmonetary means as well. Conditions are managed so that people enjoy real opportunities for personal and professional growth, achievement, camaraderie, friendship, and so on. The company is a high-spirited, exciting, empowering place to work. But it's also a place where you can make a lot of money. One of my messages in this book is that people work for more than money, but that doesn't imply people work for nothing. Effective managers provide a healthy mix of monetary *and* nonmonetary motivators.

Cooperation is important at Capital Partners, so the company's compensation scheme reinforces cooperative behavior. Partner pay, for example, depends on both *group* and *individual* performance. Partners receive a base salary of $25,000, with most of their compensation based on equity ownership in real estate properties. The equity partnerships are constructed so that a partner's compensation is linked to the performance of his or her *market group* and to the performance of the *firm as a whole*. Leasing agents also receive a base salary of $25,000, with most of their money earned via leasing commissions; they receive equity ownership once they become partners. Support staff are paid via salary and merit bonus, and senior staff also participate in an employee-owned partnership.

Manage Growth. Rapid growth and large size make it difficult to build and maintain relationships. It's simple arithmetic. Add 1 person to a group of 50. Group size has increased by just 1, but the number of potential new relationships has increased by 50! (The 51st person could establish ties with each of the original 50.) If you add 2 people to a group of 50, the number of potential ties jumps by 101! This simple arithmetic fact means that growth and large size overwhelm people—after some point, there are simply too many possible relationships to contend with. You can't know everyone well; you may not be able to ever know some. As a result, growth and bigness inhibit communication, create bottlenecks, and make it tougher and tougher to build bridges.

The leaders of Capital Partners recognized the negative unintended consequences of growth and large size. That's why they manage growth. They're not *anti*growth. They just understand that size exacerbates the bottleneck problem and makes it hard to build bridges. Other leading firms realize it, too. Upstart computer maker CompuAdd, for example, splits off any division that gets too big, making it its own company.[23] Goliath IBM is breaking itself up into a loose federation of Baby Blues.[24] And Sam Walton was contemplating breaking giant Wal-Mart into smaller, more cohesive companies![25]

Practice What You Preach. The senior partners at Capital Partners are excellent role models. They practice what they preach, the principles of networking smart. The partners don't delegate hiring, for example; they invest enormous amounts of time and energy in the recruiting process. They invest even more time and energy in close mentoring relationships. Their desks are out in the open. They dispense with the usual flurry of memos and communiques, communicating and "managing by wandering around" instead (MBWA).[26] They also wander around in the company's environment, cultivating ties with all sorts of outside people and organizations.

The partners drop by, socialize, invite people to lunch, play sports. They live in the same neighborhoods. They have built redundancy in the firm's networks to make themselves "expendable." And they put their money where their mouths are: They pay for performance. Finally, they avoid the fatal temptation of most real estate development firms: They control growth.

And they strive to better understand their company and their people. For example, they invited me to investigate and evaluate how well the firm was integrated. I administered a companywide survey of informal networks and quantitatively measured the extent of actual integration against the standard of perfect integration.[27] Capital Partners is, I confirmed, a well-integrated, network-style organization. They weren't perfect, but they had achieved level-two integration in practice.

What You Can Do *Now*

Bottlenecks are commonplace. Most companies still exhibit the debilitating symptoms associated with silos, turf, stovepipes, and empires. Most still suffer from the same level-one integration problems as Post Chemical Company. The signs are usually obvious. At Post Chemical, for example, bottleneck problems manifested themselves as personnel resignations, infighting, politics, long delays, missed deadlines, and—most important—customer reports of deep dissatisfaction and frustration. What you can do *now* is diagnose your bottleneck problems and understand their symptoms and causes.

To help, I've put together the following "A Spotter's Guide to Bottlenecks." I borrowed the idea of a spotter's guide from the World War II practice of training observers to scan the skies and spot enemy warplanes. As a guide, they were issued a booklet of warplane silhouettes, their *Spotter's Guide.* Your Spotter's Guide can help you identify the symptoms and causes of bottlenecks in your organization.

To use the Guide, target two or three groups that have a history of strained and troubled relationships. If your company is divided into traditional functions, it's a safe bet that production, marketing, and R&D don't get along. But you can target any set of groups—project teams, geographic units, divisions, and so on—and repeat as necessary for various sets of target groups.

A Spotter's Guide to Bottlenecks

Instructions: Consider each question as it applies to relationships between your target groups. Circle the number of each question to which you answer yes.

1. Do these groups have different objectives and goals?

2. Do members of these groups have different orientations to time?

3. Do members of these groups have different orientations to interpersonal relationships?

4. Does one group operate with informal structures and the other with formal structure?

5. Do people have straight vertical career ladders within the same function or group (as opposed to career paths that zigzag across functional lines)?

6. Are everyone's roles, responsibilities, and reporting relationships clearly and precisely defined?

7. Are groups separated by time and/or space—different offices, buildings, floors, work shifts, time zones, etc.?

8. Is there a lack of people designated as official bridges, liaisons, and integrators?

9. Is one person the sole bridge between groups?

10. Are memos, letters, and other forms of written communications the preferred form of interaction between groups?

11. Do you lack the new electronic communication technologies, especially peer-to-peer networking?

12. Are managers explicitly or implicitly discouraged from crossing group boundaries? Do they have to go "upstairs" to get permission to do so?

13. Is frequent informal interaction discouraged between groups? Between staff and line? Between professionals and support staff?

14. Are narrow specialists hired instead of generalists?

15. Are people hired primarily for *technical* skills?

16. Once people are hired, do they work only within their narrow specialties?

(Continued)

17. Are monetary rewards based on individual performance only? Do you lack pooled rewards linked to joint performance?

18. Are you experiencing explosive growth? (Rapid growth adds new people who must be integrated into the network of relationships.)

19. Are you experiencing high turnover or rapid downsizing? (Turnover and downsizing disrupt existing connections and impede the formation of new ones.)

20. Are you globalizing? (Globalization creates the need to integrate across time zones, places, national boundaries, and cultural differences.)

21. Have you decentralized into autonomous units (teams) without coordinating across units (e.g., networks of teams)?

Count the number of yes answers. If you answered yes to 5 or fewer questions, relationships between your target groups are in good shape. (Repeat this exercise for a different set of target groups. If you still don't identify bottleneck problems, skip to "What You Can Do in the *Long Run*" at the end of this chapter.) If you answered yes to more than 5 but fewer than 10, you have bottleneck problems to attend to. And if you answered yes to more than 10, you have severe bottleneck problems.

In addition to the Spotter's Guide, you may want systematic and hard scientific data about bottlenecks. If so, you can conduct a formal network analysis. That's what I did when I analyzed the integration of Capital Partners. Formal network analysis includes four steps: (1) defining the target groups or population, (2) designing a customized questionnaire to collect network data, (3) analyzing these data (often with computer programs designed to map and model networks), and (4) interpreting and communicating results. The findings reveal relationship disorders, like bottlenecks, and help you figure out where to intervene and take corrective action. Sometimes a follow-up network survey is used to evaluate how well the corrections worked.

If you want to do this sort of formal network analysis, I recommend that you contact independent network analysts/consultants or management consulting firms specializing in formal network analysis. Many university researchers work as independent network analysts. Before you contract with a management consulting firm, ask some pointed questions. I've talked with several national brand-name firms (I shouldn't name them here) who *claim* to do network analysis, but there's no substance behind their smoke and mirrors. One notable exception is Netmap International, now part of KPMG Peat Marwick. This group specializes in organizational network analysis, using its ORGMAP™ system to help clients map information flows and identify communication bottlenecks.

What You Can Do **Soon**

Now that you've diagnosed bottleneck problems, what you can do *soon* is take corrective action. Note, however, that it's not as simple as making mechanical adjustments; an organization is not a machine. People from different groups naturally develop divergent goals and ways of thinking, working, and feeling. These differences take root and resist change. I've found, for example, that insecure managers *like* bottlenecks: Bottlenecks protect their turf, their power and resource base. To overcome such natural resistance, you must help threatened managers see *different* sources of power: the power of integration, the power of multifunctional teams. But it's hard to change old, ingrained ways of thinking and working. Support structural changes by helping everyone improve their interpersonal skills. Provide education and training in the so-called soft skills—observation, active listening, giving and getting feedback, group dynamics, and team building.

Your pattern of yes and no answers to the Spotter's Guide offers hints and clues about what you can do soon. If you answered yes to questions 1 to 7, for example, then your groups suffer from classic level-one integration problems, just like Post Chemical. At a minimum, increase awareness and sensitivity by providing soft-skills training and education.

If groups are separated by time and/or space (question 7), unite them in a common space or link them via peer-to-peer electronic networking (question 11). Relocation may be easier than you think. One of my business associates was able to "relocate" his separated groups simply by moving dividers and trading space with another manager who wanted to do the same with his divided group.

If you answered yes to questions 8 and 9, appoint additional people as official bridges and liaisons between groups. Affirmative answers to questions 10 to 13 indicate a culture in which top managers discourage networking. The antinetworking culture is reinforced if people are hired for technical reasons, stay in their narrow specialties on the job, and are rewarded on an individual basis only (questions 14 to 17). These problems are tough to fix. Begin with soft-skills training and education. Once people become more aware of the problems, appoint a *planning team* to explore the concept of multidisciplinary teams.

A planning team is a group drawn from various functions, departments, and levels that investigates and applies the concept of multidisciplinary teams. In essence, this is what Jerome Simpson used as he began to revitalize Navigation Devices. Simpson created a 20-person planning team of workers, managers, and union representatives and charged them with "developing and implementing a plan to mobilize all employees to accomplish Navigation Devices' business goals."[28] The planning team's conclusion? "[B]arriers to cross-functional coordination needed to be overcome." This put Navigation Devices on the road to establishing a wide range of multifunctional teams. If you try this idea, give your planning team a loose mission and let them work out the details on their own.

Yes answers to questions 18 to 20 indicate massive changes in size and structure. Expansion and contraction move the company in opposite directions, but they create similar networking problems: lack of relationships, lack of integration. New hires lack relationships with current employees; turnover or layoffs sever existing relationships. In all cases, be sure to consider *network assets* and *networking abilities* before you hire, fire, or transfer. Charge your planning team with the task of exploring sensible ways to take network assets and networking abilities into account.

An affirmative answer to question 21 indicates a problem of level-two integration: uncoordinated teams. If you have this problem, you're more fortunate than most—you're ahead of many companies that haven't yet experimented with the networking concept. If your teams are uncoordinated, ask your planning team to investigate the problem and propose ways to establish a *network of teams* (see next section).

What You Can Do in the *Long Run*

What you can do in the long run is consider deep changes in organizational design that will permanently break bottlenecks and build bridges. This means transforming your organization into a *network of project-based teams*, the primary vehicle for competing successfully in the business world of the 1990s and beyond.

The transformation takes the two great principles of organization, differentiation and integration, and switches their traditional order of importance. Integration now becomes the strong force. That's the underlying structural change you want to make. Note, however, that some differentiation is still required, even when integration dominates. Even the best network organizations, like Capital Partners, are differentiated into vertical levels of authority, horizontal groups (such as market-focused teams), and multiple geographic locations. There are good reasons for doing so. Multiple office locations, for example, enable Capital Partners to stay in close contact with clients. But the network design ensures that differentiation doesn't become the strong force. Those who network smart make sure the centrifugal force of differentiation is offset by the centripetal force of integration.

With your planning team, explore changes at two levels: making teams the organization's primary building blocks and coordinating multiple teams via a network of teams. To accomplish the first change, look for opportunities to create multidisciplinary project-based teams. The PIM commercialization project at Post Chemical, for example, presented a golden opportunity. The company's approach—figuring out a way to shift the PIM project *from* R&D *to* Business Development—was the *traditional* solution to an integration problem. A better alternative would be to establish a commercialization team composed of members from Business Development, R&D, production, and marketing. Key customers and suppliers could also be included. Though Post Chemical didn't recognize it, the company had a perfect opportunity to inaugurate the organization's transition from level-one integration to level-two. A successful team approach could have served as a role model for the rest of the organization.

As you find (or create) opportunities to establish teams, be sure to follow a few simple guidelines:

1. Make sure the team is multidisciplinary and the right disciplines are represented. Consider including key customers and suppliers on the team.

2. Make sure the team gets the resources it needs—people, money, materials, a common work space, moral support, senior sponsorship, and so on. Have team members take soft-skills training together.

3. Give each team a loose mission. You have to set parameters, but after that let them go about their work without undue interference.

4. Link compensation, such as bonuses, to the performance of the team as a whole. Be sure to include symbolic rewards as well—celebrations, awards, announcements, etc.

5. Disband the team after its mission is complete. Disbanding is hard to do. It's painful for all involved. Manage expectations from the beginning by announcing the "disbanding rule" at the start. Provide for a "postmortem" debriefing of team dynamics.

6. Make teams commonplace: provide exciting new projects as soon as possible.

As teams become commonplace, a new coordination problem will arise: the need to integrate multiple teams. Managers often fail to recognize the need for integration at a higher level. But forewarned is forearmed. Your planning team should anticipate the problem and explore different ways to develop a coordinating network of teams. There are plenty of examples in this chapter to consider. Encourage your planning team to use the concept of "best practices"—see who does it well and borrow the ideas. GE's Corporate Executive Council, for example, is a model that could be imitated on many levels and in many different types of companies.

Royal Dutch/Shell reveals other possibilities. As Fred Guterl describes in *Business Month,* the company stumbled on a workable solution to a severe problem of integration caused by excessive decentralization. "[T]he Anglo-Dutch oil company," says Guterl, "is probably the ultimate decentralized organization—actually a collection of several hundred separate operating companies around the globe."[29] This mode of organization doesn't make Royal Dutch/Shell much different from most large companies; decentralization has been a fashionable practice for many years. But large companies like Royal Dutch/Shell are discovering that decentralization works well only in good times. Tough times demand efficiencies that can be achieved only by greater integration of disparate operations. That's where the oil company's global electronic networks became an accidental solution. Originally planned as a conventional database system, managers started to use the electronic system in unintended, unplanned, almost surreptitious ways. They turned it into a worldwide communications network, using it to swap information, negotiate, make decisions, even settle disputes. In effect, the network became an *electronic meeting place,* a virtual reality where managers from around the globe could interact, learn, and participate as if they were located in the same place. This positive unintended result enabled the oil company to integrate its diverse companies.

6
Managing Serendipity

Chance favors the prepared mind.
LOUIS PASTEUR

"Returning to his laboratory late one night," writes historian Theodore Remer, "Dr. Alexander Fleming noted a pile of petri dishes which had been contaminated during use. By accident, Dr. Fleming observed a remarkably clean area ringing the contamination in one of the dishes. His curiosity aroused, he observed under a microscope that as microbes approached the contamination (mold) they appeared to be dissolved, thereby enlarging the clean area. Later the work of other scientists brought to fruition this chance discovery."[1]

What did Dr. Fleming discover by accident? Penicillin.

Luck? Maybe. But this kind of luck strikes all the time—some of the most famous advances in science and technology were triggered by accidental discoveries: insulin, dynamite, teflon, polyethylene (plastics), Lexan (GE's unbreakable glazing material), 3M's post-it notes, floating soap, and countless others were discovered by luck and happenstance.[2] Serendipity struck again on a sunny day in July 1992 when Lori Vermeulen, a chemistry graduate student at Princeton University, walked across campus carrying a white powdery substance she used to study electrochemical reactions.[3] The substance turned an unexpected blue. With Professor Mark E. Thompson, Vermeulen discovered why it changed color: It stored solar energy. Experts believe this chance discovery could lead to a revolution in solar power.

Accidental discovery is so common and plays such an important role in the creative process that our language has a word for it: *serendipity*. Serendipity, coined by Horace Walpole in 1754, comes from the title of the fairy-tale *The Three Princes of Serendip* (a former name of Sri Lanka), the heroes of which "were always making discoveries, by accident and sagacity, of things they were not in quest of."[4]

The importance of accidental discovery—serendipity—is conspicuous in science and technology, but it's important whenever and wherever something new and original must be created. Serendipity is an essential ingredient in developing new products, brainstorming, conceiving an advertising campaign, doing creative financing, troubleshooting production problems, and so on. Even writing benefits from serendipity.[5] In this chapter, I describe how you can boost your own creativity and the creativity of others by managing conditions that improve the odds of serendipity. I conclude with concrete advice on what you can do now, what you can do soon, what you can do in the long run.

Creating the Right Conditions

Unfortunately, the importance of "accidents" reinforces the belief that creativity is a great mystery—an ineffable process impervious to attempts to understand it, never mind *manage* it. How could you ever hope to "manage" accident and luck? Well, you can't manage serendipity *directly*—it's a prime example of the dilemma of indirect management. But, as Max Gunther says in *The Luck Factor*, it's possible "to improve the odds in favor of good luck and diminish the odds of bad luck."[6] There *are* things you can do.

Harvard University's Howard Gardner gives us a clue. He observed that creative people first *master* the knowledge in their fields before they make original contributions.[7] With mastery, they are prepared to recognize accidents for what they really are. They can perceive the value in them. Dr. Fleming, for example, didn't discard the contaminated petri dishes or close the door and leave the lab in disgust; he saw something curious and investigated. This illustrates the true nature of serendipity—accident *and* sagacity. Whether sagacity is called intelligence, inspiration, openness, intuition, leap of imagination, or flash of genius, those who make accidental discoveries expect the unexpected.

There's an essential network ingredient as well. So-called lucky people, says Max Gunther, build a "spiderweb structure" that catches lots of different bits of information in its web.[8] Creativity depends critically on getting information, on keeping up with developments, on staying in the know. The romantic myth of the lone inventor is pure bunk. Even early inventors—Franklin, Watt, Edison, Bell—were active participants in learned societies and communications.[9] Intense interaction with colleagues is indispensable in the process of formulating and solving problems. Werner Heisenberg and Niels Bohr, two founders of quantum physics, held endless conversations as they wrestled with the revolution of modern physics.[10] Creative types, as I describe in this chapter, develop extensive and far-ranging intelligence networks.

What you can do to boost your own creativity or improve the creativity of others is to *manage conditions that improve the odds of accidental discovery*.[11] British humorist John Cleese (of Monty Python fame) has it right with the serious advice he gave in a speech to the British-American Chamber of Commerce: "...there are certain conditions I could describe that might help you become more creative, [but] they can only really be provided by your bosses."[12] Managers who recognize this fact can manage conditions that will improve serendipity anywhere—in the lab, in the marketing department, on the shop floor, even in the executive suite.

Tennant Company: A Role Model

Minneapolis-based Tennant Company creates conditions that enhance serendipity.[13] Tennant is the world's leading manufacturer of industrial floor maintenance equipment (floor and street sweepers, scrubbers, floor coatings, etc.). In the 1970s and early 1980s, however, the company struggled with productivity and cost competitiveness. Tennant was known for making high-quality equipment, but some customers—particularly its Japanese customers—complained about hydraulic leaks. This was a puzzle, as Tennant president and CEO Roger Hale recalled: "Why were the hydraulic leaks happening only in the machines we sent to Japan and not in those we were selling in the United States, where, in fact, we were selling many *more* of the same models? As it turned out, the leaks weren't just happening in Japan. The machines we sold here at home were leaking too. The difference was that U.S. customers accepted the leaks....In Japan, the leak was cause for complaint."[14]

Tennant discovered the leaky hydraulics problem by accident. Until Japanese customers complained, the company's managers didn't even know about it. In a sense, the "problem" didn't exist, like the proverbial tree falling unheard in the forest. Tennant's first *real* problem was to discover problems. Management began to suspect that quality problems existed, but they didn't know *what* specific problems existed or *where* they were. But those closest to the work—workers on the shop floor—knew all about the problems. So the first management task was to create a way to find out what workers already knew. Early on, for example, Tennant instituted the Error Cause Identification (ECI) program to do just that. Over 1200 ECI forms were received in the first six months! At its peak in 1981, 3400 ECI forms were generated. The company buckled under the weight of such a massive response, but eventually it was able to solve 90 percent of all ECIs within 30 days. Interestingly, the formal ECI system is becoming obsolete. As CEO Hale and colleagues write in *Quest for Quality*, "The number of ECIs has dropped...to about 149 in 1988. This doesn't mean we only have 149 problems in the company. It does mean we're learning how to work together to solve the problems we have without filling out forms. We hope to eliminate the ECI system within the next few years as people develop trust in the informal system."[15] In other words, Tennant is developing internal intelligence networks to aid problem identification.

Once quality problems are discovered, the next problem is solving them. Yet management suffers from a peculiar predicament—managers can't solve the problems themselves. They don't have the technical know-how, direct experience, or time. But they can create conditions that help. For Tennant, the *small group* is the formula for solving problems.[16] At this point, most workers have participated in these small groups. The origin of the company's small-group solution was the Japanese model of quality circles, but Tennant modified it to suit its needs and situation. Tennant evolved the following working principles:

- *Groups are small*—only 8 to 10 people.

- *Group composition is loosely regulated.* Each group is "vertically integrated." Each includes workers with firsthand experience and one or more managers who help secure resources, get information, eliminate barriers, and implement plans.

- *Groups are self-forming.* Any worker, manager, or department can form a group to solve a particular problem. Management, however, must approve the group's goal.

- *A group is disbanded when its problem is solved.* This prevents a group from taking on a life of its own.

- *Groups get the resources they need.* This includes giving group members technical and interpersonal tools and training. Training includes everything from statistical control methods and communication skills to group dynamics.

- *Membership is rotated.* Rotation imports fresh insights. Participation in multiple groups builds a broad view of the company and criss-crossing networks of contacts.

- *Group progress and success are recognized.* This includes everything from informal celebrations, announcements in the company newsletter, positive reinforcement, formal awards, and monetary benefits (e.g., share of cost savings).

Is Tennant's quality program a success? Here are just a few of the quantitative results: Manufacturing rework (for machines incorrectly or incompletely assembled) fell from 34,000 hours in 1980 to just 4600 hours in 1988. The number of rework mechanics was reduced by half, with actual wages paid for rework activities cut by 68 percent! (Displaced rework mechanics were transferred to other comparable jobs.) If the trend in rework had continued without quality improvements, actual wages would have *doubled* by 1988. Problems at installation have dropped from a 19 percent defect rate in 1980 to 6.6 percent in 1988. And Tennant's supplier partnership program pushed reject rates for supplied parts to just 25 percent of the rate eight years earlier.[17] All told, Tennant's quest for quality reduced costs by $8 million. Yes, Tennant's program is a smashing success. (Tennant documents its supplier partnership program in the company's second book, *Made in the U.S.A.* I discuss supplier partnerships and Tennant's supplier program in Chapter 12.)

Three Factors That Influence Serendipity

Serendipity can be managed, but only indirectly. Like Tennant Company, you must *create conditions* that boost communication and interaction and improve the odds of accidental discovery. You have three factors at your disposal: proximity and facility design, information gatekeepers and liaisons, and group composition. Each factor is a powerful action lever. By deliberately managing each one, you can stimulate serendipity.

Proximity and Facility Design

Britain's brand new Institute of Cancer and Developmental Biology in Cambridge features a unique research environment, as Alun Anderson describes in *Science:*[18] "In its physical design—laid out by scientists for scientists—the institute is unique. Corridors circle around, vanishing abruptly in open-plan laboratories. The idea is not simply to save space but to *maximize chance encounters* by forcing researchers to pass through other laboratories to get to their own. The point: The researchers behind this lab believe that critical conversation and *chance encounters are the lifeblood of scientific creativity.*"

Anderson continues: "There is no library; journals, after all, can be passed along and provide yet other opportunities for interaction. But there is a central facility that all the researchers agree is extremely important—a sunny and spacious tea room. There everyone, regardless of interests, is expected to mingle. 'The plan is to make people bump into one another,' says [senior scientist] Gordon. 'After all, interesting scientific ideas come in an unplanned way.'"

The physical layout of Britain's new institute highlights how serendipity can be managed—indirectly—by manipulating the physical environment. Serendipity requires communication; communication depends on proximity. The greater the distance between researchers, the less likely it is that they will talk. Distance doesn't have to be great to become an obstacle. Thomas Allen, who studies the effect of physical configuration on communication in research and engineering settings, found that people more than 10 meters apart have only a 9 percent probability of communicating at least once a week![19] The unique design of Britain's lab improves these odds. It compels scientists to mix and mingle; it encourages chance encounters.

Proximity is important wherever serendipity depends on communication and interaction. In my field, business research, collaboration is common; not only does it increase productivity, it stimulates new ideas and new ways of thinking. When I joined the University of Chicago faculty, other new hires and I were given offices on the fifth floor of Walker Museum, one of several business school buildings. Disciplines were deliberately mixed on the fifth floor—marketing, business policy, sociology, psychology, economics, statistics. Out of this multidisciplinary stew came numerous chance encounters that led to cross-disciplinary research. For example, I met Ananth Iyer, a professor in the operations and production area, simply because we were habitues of the fifth floor. In most other business schools, we would be housed in offices far apart and never meet. Through a series of chance encounters and free-ranging conversations, we discovered common interests and complementary knowledge. Our conversations generated new ideas—new problems to work on—that required the mixing of what I know and what Ananth knows. The result was greater than the sum of its parts. We have since published collaborative, cross-disciplinary work.[20] And our work is only one example of what has become known at the business school as the "fifth-floor effect."

Capital Partners (Chapter 4) knows the importance of proximity; that's why professionals and support staff are located together in an open-office layout. Chrysler, too, has discovered the importance of proximity. The auto maker's L/H design team is isolated and grouped together in a small office building 20 miles from engineering headquarters.[21] Eventually, the team occupied its own floor in Chrysler's new Technology Center. Why? By grouping together diverse disciplines in one location, managers stimulate serendipity and reduce outside interference. The results are quite positive: The new "cab forward" design has received great accolades from *Car & Driver* and other car-testing organizations, and it is selling very well.

IBM is learning the same lesson. When Big Blue spun off Lexmark, a first-rate maker of printers, typewriters, and keyboards, turning the unit into an independent private company, orphanhood was a blessing in disguise.[22] The typical IBM project is subdivided and dispersed to multiple sites, with all the inefficiencies and coordination problems you can imagine. The new Lexmark, however, created a superb new laser printer in record time by having people from marketing, manufacturing, and R&D work side by side in a single location. One reason for this success, I'm sure, was encouragement of the random encounters that produce serendipity. Excellent companies everywhere, as Peters and Waterman found, create campuses—Kodak's Kodak Park, P&G's Cincinnati center, 3M's St. Paul campus—where researchers from important disciplines are brought together under one roof.[23]

Gatekeepers and Liaisons

Information is essential to the creative process. This is where your personal intelligence network comes into play (see Chapter 3). To create its quality improvement program, for example, Tennant execs had to learn what other companies were doing to improve quality. So they tapped their personal intelligence networks: "During the late 1970s," recalls vice president Douglas Hoelscher, "Americans heard and read a great deal about Japanese quality, management styles, and quality circles. Some of what I read made sense to me, some didn't. To find out more, [quality consultant] Phil Crosby and I traveled to Japan in 1980. We planned to visit a number of Japanese companies and find out more about their management and quality practices. Thanks to the Tennant Company/Fuji Heavy Industries joint venture and Phil Crosby's reputation, we had access to top-level executives and managers in several companies."[24] (See Chapter 14, for more on strategic alliances.)

Tennant's experience illustrates the importance of what are called "boundary spanners" in the flow of information.[25] Douglas Hoelscher and Phil Crosby, for example, spanned the boundary between two companies to collect vital information. They were able to supply first-hand knowledge and insights about Japanese practices to their colleagues back home. Columbia's innovation expert Michael Tushman argues that a creative group's success depends on its ability to gather information from and transmit information to other groups.[26] And we know from TQM that communication across group boundaries is essential. In the initial phase of idea generation, such as Tennant's investigation of Japanese practices, information about new methods, products, or perspectives is found outside the group. In later phases, such as testing and implementation, information is exchanged frequently among various internal groups.

Boundary spanners come in many forms and guises. Tushman distinguishes three types—*gatekeepers, organizational liaisons,* and *laboratory liaisons.*[27] Each plays a vital role in the flow of information:

- *Gatekeepers link the unit with the organization's larger environment.* Gatekeepers are a key source of advice and information for others inside the unit.[28] R&D gatekeepers, for example, link their units with universities, professional societies, and the scientific literature. Gatekeepers in technical service areas link their units with customers, vendors, and suppliers.

- *Organizational liaisons link the unit with external groups inside the larger organization.* Every unit is incomplete and depends on other groups for resources—money, time, talent, and management attention. The success of a company's R&D effort, for example, depends on positive ties with sales, production, corporate staff, product-development teams, and so on.

- *Laboratory liaisons link the unit internally, communicating across the unit's internal groups.* Laboratory should be construed broadly—it could mean R&D scientists making new discoveries, brand managers coming up with new promotions, or bankers doing creative financings.

The role of boundary spanners in the creative process is part of a larger concept known as the "diffusion of innovations." Diffusion of innovations, as authority Everett Rogers summarizes, involves any idea, practice, or object perceived as "new" that is communicated over time among members of a social system.[29] Organizational liaisons between marketing and R&D, for example, bring critical information about customer needs to the attention of R&D scientists and engineers. Gatekeepers attend trade shows, conferences, professional associations, and so on to learn about new products and ideas, which they introduce to their home organizations when they return.

From the manager's point of view, the challenge is to assist interchanges of information about innovations. But there's a key dilemma, based on the similarity principle (Chapter 2). Effective communication occurs easily between people who are *similar.* When people share beliefs, use similar technical language, and have similar levels of education and social status, communication is likely to lead to real gains in knowledge and real changes in attitudes and behaviors. The diffusion of innovations, however, also depends on communication between people who are *different.* Similar people know the same things; people who are different—those with diverse backgrounds, who travel in disparate social circles, or hold different positions in the organization—know different things. And it's the interaction of different people that brings new information into the system and stimulates serendipity. To accelerate the diffusion of innovations, a manager must help people overcome the natural tendency to associate with others like themselves. The techniques I describe in the how-to sections below will help.

Diverse Group Composition

Tennant Company uses diverse small groups to solve problems. "One major factor in their success," write CEO Roger Hale and colleagues, "is that many are vertically integrated. This means that they are composed not only of people who have firsthand knowledge of the problems, but also of people who can remove the obstacles to a solution."[30] Vertical integration helps, they conclude, because it enables the group to cross departmental lines, secure resources, get budgets approved, and "clear the way" with top management. In other words, vertically integrated, diverse groups break the bottleneck problems I described in Chapter 5. But I believe there's another important reason: Diversity sparks serendipity. A mix of people and backgrounds is essential in a problem-solving group. Diversity aids serendipity because it draws together and links different ideas, experiences, and ways of thinking. This is what psychologist Donald Campbell calls his "fish-scale theory" of creativity: True innovation is most likely to arise where two disciplines overlap, like the scales on a fish.[31] Indeed, research shows that heterogeneous teams usually outperform homogeneous teams:

- The multifunctional team is the most successful way to spur product innovation, reports Arthur D. Little in its 1991 worldwide survey of the product innovation process.[32]

- Diversity aids innovation in hospitals. The greater the number of medical specialties in a hospital, the more administrative innovations and medical innovations are adopted.[33]

- Innovative banks—adopters of technical innovations like new products or computer systems, and such administrative innovations as new compensation plans or training programs—are governed by a well-educated top team with diverse functional areas of expertise.[34]

- The "fifth-floor phenomenon" at the University of Chicago Graduate School of Business (which I described above) works because people from diverse disciplines meet and interact.

- General manager Jerome Simpson tapped the power of diverse teams to revitalize Fairweather Corporation's Navigation Devices (described in Chapter 5).[35]

Diversity is essential, but the manager of serendipity must realize that it violates the similarity principle. Status, for example, can stand in the way. In their study of R&D labs, Allen and Thomas observed that scientists with Ph.D. degrees (the "high status" types) are, well, snooty.[36] These scientists talk frequently among themselves but routinely snub those whom they regard as "low status," scientists without the Ph.D. They certainly don't go to non-Ph.D.s for advice or assistance.

Difference in education is only one of many barriers. Gender, race, ethnicity, religion, age, rank—all are barriers to communication and optimal group performance. Working in diverse groups can cause psychological discomfort, even outright conflict. To tap the power of diversity, therefore, you must help people work in diverse groups by overcoming their natural preference for similarity. The best solutions I've seen tackle the problem head on. Leaders of diverse groups provide education and training that address the natural difficulty and great potential of diversity (see Chapter 7). They help new teams get off to a running start by providing team-building counseling and exercises and offer ongoing assistance as needed. After a team has completed its tasks, the best leaders arrange for "postmortem" debriefings.

What You Can Do *Now*

What you can do now is *evaluate* the current conditions of creativity in your organization. To start, pick a particular group with an important ongoing project. Almost any problem-solving group will do. It could be a new-product development team, a quality circle, a personnel team developing new compensation systems, or a marketing group brainstorming new product ideas. Once you pick a group, ask three fundamental questions[37]:

1. What information does the group need?
2. What are the group's current capacities and means for obtaining and processing information?
3. Is there a match between information requirements and information capacities (for example, the group's intelligence-gathering system)?

Information needs depend on three factors. First, the nature of the group's task is important: Custom tasks require more information than routine tasks. In pure science, for example, the "problem" is not even known and must be invented or created.[38] (Scientists call this "coming up with a researchable problem.") Second, information needs escalate when other groups are involved. If a group must coordinate and interact with many other groups, perhaps as part of a network of teams, it needs much more information. Third, information needs depend on the state of the larger environment. When the environment is fast-paced, turbulent, and quick-changing—as it is now throughout the business world—even more information must be obtained and processed.

Once you assess the creative group's information needs, you can evaluate the group's current information capabilities. Creative groups in R&D settings function well when information needs match capabilities, observes Michael Tushman.[39] This principle is true for all types of creative groups, not just those in R&D. Any group with high information needs, for example, must be able to collect and process vast amounts of information. To do so, the group should include diverse specialties and multiple functions working in close proximity. The group needs a sophisticated and well-developed intelligence network (see Chapter 3). Numerous liaisons, for example, should link the group internally and with other groups, while gatekeepers build bridges with the outside world. Without these features, the creative group would fail to collect vital information on a timely basis. (For example, the worst excuse an investment banker can give for not getting a particular deal from a client—called "deals done away"—is that he or she didn't know about it until a competitor had already won it.) A group with low information needs, however, would collapse from information overload with the same features.

The cardinal rule is that information needs must *match* information processing capacity.[40] When a high-need group lacks capacity, it misses the boat. It gets stale news, misses opportunities, fails to obtain vital information; it simply doesn't get enough of the chance encounters essential to serendipity. When a low-need group has too much capacity, it wastes time, money, and energy. To be successful, investment banks, for example, must have a keen ability to do creative financing. Therefore, they match their heavy information needs with heavy-duty information capabilities. Consider just a handful of the ways investment banks use group composition, proximity, and gatekeepers and liaisons to turn the organization into a vast information-processing machine[41]:

- A *client team,* composed of a diverse mix of product specialists and relationship managers, is assigned to each customer account.

- Product specialists and relationship managers *work on different teams simultaneously.* Multiple membership builds information bridges between teams.

- Traders and brokers work shoulder-to-shoulder in *open trading rooms* that permit quick information exchange.

- Two managers *share responsibility for the same unit,* such as coheads of the same department. This gives the unit two information gatekeepers.

- *Dual reporting lines* are used to build bridges. A new product development team, for example, may report to different departments.

- *Rotational training programs* and *cross-departmental career paths* build cross-cutting ties.

The grand result is an organization with dense, flexible, well-integrated information networks. These impressive networks match the bankers' needs for vast amounts of information to get their jobs done.

What You Can Do Soon

It may surprise you to learn that organizational factors are typically the greatest obstacles to creativity.[42] This is good news for managers because it means you can *do* something. What you can do soon is use what you learned from your analysis to change conditions and spur the chance encounters that feed serendipity.

Let's say you uncover the typical problem: deficient information capabilities. Aside from the vague feeling that your group just doesn't seem as creative as it should be, any number of symptoms may appear:

- Everyone seems to be the same; the group lacks diversity. Critical specialties or functions are missing.

- The group is dispersed and spread out among various offices or facilities.

- Members of the group tend to work alone.

- Written forms of communication (letters, memos) are used instead of face-to-face interaction.

- The group exhibits a pronounced us-versus-them attitude and has a record of conflict with other groups.

- The group routinely fails to deliver the goods on time. It's always behind schedule and/or over budget.

- The group lacks positive relationships with the other groups it must interact and coordinate with.

- The group stays by itself; members don't mingle or mix with others at formal or informal gatherings.

- No one in the group acts as a liaison with other groups or with the outside world; members of the group "stay at home" and don't attend conferences, trade shows, other labs, etc.

If your group has these symptoms, you can take a number of steps. Each factor—proximity and facility design, gatekeepers and liaisons, and group composition—is a managerial action lever. By making changes in one or more factor, you can improve the conditions of serendipity. Because you can't manage serendipity directly, your objective is to make changes that improve the odds of chance encounters and increase information flow. A few words of caution—don't change everything at once. Use a light touch. Consider all the suggestions I list in the accompanying box, but start with the smallest change that yields the biggest impact in your particular situation. And remember: creativity is an uncertain game; results won't appear overnight.

Managing Serendipity

Proximity and Facility Design

- Consolidate a divided group into one physical location.
- Rent a temporary facility to house the entire group.
- Encourage integration of multiple locations via job rotation and temporary reassignments.
- Create project teams that bring together people from each location. Rotate membership.
- Adopt an open office design. Get rid of private offices, dividers, and barriers. This includes managers, not just subordinates.
- Convene the entire group offsite on a regular basis.
- Build a new facility with close proximity in mind.

Gatekeepers and Liaisons

- Appoint and reward liaisons who act as bridges within the group.
- Recognize informal gatekeepers and liaisons.
- Establish formal liaisons between groups.
- Set up communication channels between groups (such as Tennant's Error Cause Identification (ECI) system).
- Establish regular meetings of groups that must coordinate with each other.
- Assign dual reporting relationships so that the group must report to different departments.
- Fund trips to outside conferences, trade association meetings, professional societies, and other work-related gatherings.
- Develop internal forums for information exchange, such as weekly lunch meetings, occasional outside speakers. Sponsor conferences with invitees from other companies and industries.
- Recruit people from outside the group to act as the group's eyes and ears. Salespeople, customers, service personnel, suppliers, and others can be gatekeepers and liaisons.

Group Composition

- Make sure all critical specialties and disciplines are represented in the group.

- If a group doesn't include a manager, add one. The manager's job is to help secure resources, get information, and eliminate barriers, *not* to take charge and direct the group.

- Make sure the group has members with firsthand experience with the problem.

- Make sure the group includes people directly affected by the group's work.

- Add diversity by insisting group members get new technical or interpersonal skill training.

- Rotate membership among groups; have people work on multiple teams concurrently.

- Recruit and hire talent you need; get someone "on loan" or temporary assignment.

- Add a *wildcard*—someone completely different—who will stir things up.

What You Can Do in the *Long Run*

So far I have focused on existing creative groups. What you can do in the long run is design a creative group from scratch. Designing a creative group is an exciting prospect; it gives you a chance to put together the right ingredients, right from the start. Don't restrict your attention to traditional creative groups like R&D. Creativity is required in almost all endeavors. You can decide to design almost any type of creative group—a production quality circle, a marketing research team, a new product development team, a finance group, and so on. The point is to pick a significant problem to work on, design the group, and set it loose.

Picking a significant problem is easier said than done. In a way, this is an assignment in creativity itself—what psychologist Jacob Getzels calls "the problem of the problem."[43] Often, coming up with the right problem, asking the right question, is the critical task of creativity. "The formulation of the problem," said Albert Einstein, "is often more essential than its solution, which may be merely a matter of mathematical or experimental skill. To raise new questions, new possibilities, to regard old questions from a new angle, requires creative imagination and marks real advances in science."[44]

So, how do you pick a significant problem for a creative group to work on? Here's my suggestions, based on Donald G. Marquis' analysis of 567 technical innovations.[45] Three out of four successful innovations, says Marquis, began with the recognition of a *market demand* or *production need.* Tennant Company, which I used as a role model in this chapter, began its quality improvement drive by focusing on a market demand and production need, what company executives called their "most persistent and embarrassing problem."[46] What was that? Oil leaks from hydraulic joints.

So, this is where I suggest you start: Form your creative group around real market demands and production needs. What do customers want? What problems are customers complaining about? What kind of production problems do you have? What do your people on the front lines identify as the biggest problems they have? What is your closest analogy to Tennant's most persistent and embarrassing problem?

Once you identify your significant problem, organize a diverse team to investigate specific problems and solutions. Give them a loose mission. Remember: a solution to the dilemma of indirect management I described in the Introduction is to organize the right group with a vague mission and they'll figure out what really needs to be done—and become a part of the solution rather than a part of the problem. To stimulate planning, the Fronts and Phases worksheet on the following page outlines three universal fronts—group composition, facility design, and gatekeepers and liaisons—with typical phases for each. Some boxes are left blank to encourage you to fill them in. Expand and revise the worksheet as appropriate to suit your situation.

Worksheet for Fronts and Phases (Partial Example Only)

Designing a creative group	Phase 1	Phase 2	Phase 3	Phase 4
Front 1: Group composition	Identify required types and number of disciplines, functions, expertise	Identify candidates inside and outside your group	Recruit qualified candidates	(fill in)
Front 2: Facility design	Identify appropriate facility design	Investigate access to current or new facilities	Secure use of appropriate facility	(fill in)
Front 3: Gatekeepers and liaisons	Identify need for information from internal and external groups	Identify formal and informal mechanisms	Create mechanisms and conditions; provide resources and rewards	(fill in)
Front 4: Other fronts (money, budget, management approval, etc.)	(fill in)	(fill in)	(fill in)	(fill in)

7

Tapping the Power of Diversity

In our diversity is our greatest strength.
CAROL MOSELEY-BRAUN
1992 Democratic National Convention

Xerox hired its first large group of black professionals in the 1970s. Members of the group soon suffered the same plight as their peers in many other companies: exclusion from the informal networks.[1] From the networking point of view, exclusion consigned them to the worst fate possible. Even a gifted person will fail without access to the informal network of information, support, advice, and mentoring.

So what did they do? They taught themselves how to network smart. They broke out of their involuntary confinement by actively building relationships and networks. They began by forming caucus groups. The first was San Francisco-based BABE (Bay Area Black Employees) which helped to establish a kindred group in Los Angeles. Similar groups arose spontaneously in Washington, D.C., New York City, Dallas, Chicago, and Xerox's hometown of Rochester, New York. The black caucus groups fought to revise hiring and promotion policies and gain equitable treatment of blacks. They worked to recruit and hire new black employees. They provided support, encouragement, and advice. The groups became places to swap information, build intelligence networks, nurture mentoring relationships, and secure informal training.

Xerox top managers were not pleased at first. I'm sure some felt threatened by such curious developments, as anyone might be who didn't appreciate the positive power of relationships. A few, for example, feared the national conference was the start of a budding union. Some black leaders reportedly received veiled threats that their activities wouldn't be good for their careers.[2]

But the caucuses were such a resounding success that attitudes swung from suspicion to open encouragement. And, if imitation is the sincerest form of flattery, then the early black professionals were supremely honored: By the end of the 1980s, Xerox was using the black caucuses as role models for similar groups for women, Asians, and Hispanics. And Xerox's black caucus groups are used now by GE as an example of "best practices" in human resource management!

The Xerox story is a fitting introduction to this chapter because it illustrates both the problem and power of managing diversity. As I discuss in this chapter, the problem of diversity is the same everywhere: a minority group—women, blacks, Hispanics, the young, the old, even white men in some cases—is denied access to the informal network of relationships. This is a grave problem, we know, because everyone *must* have relationships to get his or her job done. The plight of ostracized groups is much worse than Bill Hansen's problem (Introduction). Bill did it to himself; he caused his own misfortune by excluding himself from the informal network. It's a much different situation when a group is excluded against its will.

You may have been surprised that I included white men in the preceding paragraph. I included this category because it's important to recognize the broad focus of the challenge of managing diversity. We usually think of minority groups as women, blacks, Hispanics, Asians, individuals with disabilities, and other groups not numbered among white men. But exclusion from networks and stereotyping can happen to anyone who's in a numerical minority.[3] As the American Psychological Association summarized in its *amicus curiae* brief for the U.S. Supreme Court, "When there are very few employees who are members of a particular group, those employees are considerably more likely to be stereotyped than if the group of which they are a part is represented in large numbers"[4] It can happen to anyone who is "different" than the majority—the only political liberal in a group of conservatives, an engineer in a sales group, the sole lawyer in a company. Therefore, the proper focus of managing diversity is wide and broad. It includes all people, without regard to such personal attributes as race, national origin, gender, religion, birth region, or age. Networking smart means creating a situation in which such attributes become unimportant and inconsequential. In this chapter, I'll tell you how you can get started.

Now let me ask a devil's-advocate question: Why should you manage diversity? Why should you, apart from the noble American values of equality, liberty, and fairness? You should because managing diversity well is a powerful competitive force. I did say that the Xerox story illustrates the *power* of diversity, not just the problem. Let's see why.

The disenfranchised black professionals revealed themselves as extraordinary people. They *had* to be in order to respond so constructively to such a difficult situation. And their positive response taught Xerox an important lesson about organizational learning and development. The black caucuses helped the company grow and mature; they introduced an important innovation in human resource management that was copied with great success throughout the company (and by other companies as well). That's the power of diversity. By bringing fresh viewpoints, different experiences, and new knowledge, diversity has the potential to enliven, invigorate, and recreate. Diversity can help an organization flourish.

Like the case of black caucus groups at Xerox, diversity can yield all sorts of benefits. Diversity is the cornerstone of a sophisticated intelligence network. A diverse workforce links you and the organization to a sweeping array of social circles; diversity offers eyes and ears into the varied nooks and crannies of the world. Diversity keeps the organization in close touch with demographic and social trends. Without it, says Hudson Institute researcher William B. Johnson, companies become isolated from and unfamiliar with such issues as dual careers, child care, and sexual harassment.[5] Diversity is the well-spring of serendipity; managing diversity well enhances serendipity in all its forms. And cultivating a diverse workforce puts you in the right position to tap the best and the brightest—whoever and wherever they may be.

Without diversity, an organization ossifies like bone into rigid practices, customs, and attitudes. Like the dinosaurs, a company is doomed when it can't adapt to changing conditions and circumstances. That, in my opinion, is a chief cause of the problems of beleaguered corporate giants such as Sears and General Motors. For decades these dinosaurs had a policy of promoting from within, reproducing generation after generation of like-thinking, like-acting, inward-looking managers.[6] When Sears, Roebuck hired McKinsey consultant Phil Purcell in 1978 as vice president of corporate planning, he was the *first* senior level manager to be hired from the outside since Roebuck himself hired General Wood in 1920![7] Inbreeding can be as bad for organizations as it is for families. It weakens the organization.

What companies like Sears and GM really need is a megadose of diversity of all kinds.

Japan is another example of problems caused by too little diversity. Japan is cited as a role model for just about every good business practice under the sun. But not for managing diversity. Despite its considerable strengths, Japanese culture has a great built-in shortcoming: lack of diversity. The society at large has gender diversity (of course), but Japanese society suffers from deep-rooted sexist attitudes. These extreme attitudes permeate the Japanese workplace.

When Japanese managers come to the United States, their inexperience with diversity and ignorance of U.S. equal opportunity laws combine to get them in lots of trouble. American executives testified at recent U.S. Congressional hearings that Japanese owners treat them as "trophy managers," used just to attract new business; women complained of sexual harassment; both women and minorities cited gross insensitivity and job discrimination.[8] Japanese managers are coming to the realization that they have to do something, according to a recent poll of 400 Japanese executives working in the United States.[9] Fully 82 percent reported that they want to import U.S. human resource practices concerning minorities and women.

Diversity is a U.S. national treasure. We still have a long way to go, but we do much better than many. And the promise of diversity is unlimited.

The Glass Ceiling as a Relationship Problem

The glass ceiling is the well-known invisible barrier that traps women and minorities in low-level jobs. Some people think of the glass ceiling as a barrier to *top* jobs, but I think of it more broadly. To me, the glass ceiling is any limit to upward mobility based on race, national origin, gender, religion, birth region, age, or any other personal attribute that has nothing to do with ability and performance.

There's been some success in breaking the glass ceiling, but it's still a prominent feature of corporate America. Consider, for example, the trends for women and minorities in the white-collar workforce, 1981 to 1991 (Table 7-1). The proportion of women in all white-collar jobs remained relatively stable over the 10-year period, with women making up over half of all white-collar jobs. The trend for women in executive, administrative, and managerial positions has moved in the right direction, getting much closer to proportional representation by 1991. The proportion of women in professional and technical jobs is even

Table 7-1. Percentage Composition of Women and Minorities in the Workforce, Selected White-Collar Occupations, 1981–1991

Occupation	1981	1991	10-year change
Women in the Workforce			
Total white-collar jobs	53.6	56.2	+2.6
Executive, administrative, and managerial	28.0	40.6	+12.6
Professional/technical specialties	44.7	51.6	+6.9
Blacks and Hispanics in the Workforce			
Total white-collar jobs	8.6	13.4	+4.8
Executive, administrative, and managerial	5.4	9.7	+4.3
Professional/technical specialties	9.2	10.1	+0.9

SOURCE: Compiled from U.S. Bureau of Labor Statistics, *Employment and Earnings* (Washington, D.C.: Government Printing Office).

closer. These are real improvements, of course, but the numbers don't indicate big differences in the upper-level ranks. According to a recent *Business Week* cover story, women remain grossly underrepresented in the senior executive ranks (those who report directly to the CEO).[10] Only 3 percent of senior executives in 1991 are women, up from just 1 percent a decade earlier. And there's only one female CEO among the *Business Week* 1000 largest companies.

A similar story can be told for blacks and Hispanics. These minority groups were underrepresented in total white-collar jobs in 1981, but the situation improved by 1991 (Table 7-1). The proportion of blacks and Hispanics in executive, administrative, and managerial positions almost doubled in the 10-year period, but the figure still remains well below proportional representation. And there's been virtually no improvement for blacks and Hispanics in professional and technical specialties.

There's still a long way to go for women and minorities.

The glass ceiling is built from resilient materials. Good old-fashioned discrimination is one. People may discriminate because of deep-seated sexist and racist beliefs or simply because of threats of intensified competition and fear of loss of power and rewards. But I think the glass ceiling is more complicated than just that and more subtle. No one can succeed or be promoted without building good relationships. No one. A glass ceiling exists for *anyone* who lacks relationships, minority or not. Because women and minorities are excluded from the networks (like Xerox's black managers), they're placed at a serious relationship disadvantage: They're barred from developing the ties that anyone would need to be successful. The glass ceiling would start to dematerialize if men, women, and minorities were enabled to build relationships.

That's what happened at Xerox. Black managers overcame relationship obstacles by networking—building the ties, contacts, and connections they needed for success. And that's the powerful logic behind success strategies advocated by female executives. Networking is the single most popular strategy reported in a 1992 *Business Week* survey of 400 women executives at large companies.[11] Eighty-three percent of women executives agreed that "women should build networks with other women to help each other." I would go one step further and say that women should build relationships with women *and* men. Focusing on building only women's networks may be counterproductive. Research by Harvard Business School Professor Herminia Ibarra on men's and women's networks suggests a balanced strategy: Women must build ties to *both* men and women if they want to obtain access to the same resources men are able to get from other men.[12]

Because exclusion from the networks is a chief culprit, it's important to understand *why* exclusion occurs; it may be raw prejudice, but it doesn't have to be. The similarity principle I introduced in Chapter 2 is one of the most common and stubborn tendencies in human society: People prefer to associate with people like themselves. The glass ceiling occurs, at least in part, because diversity violates the similarity principle. It's simply easier to operate at a high level of understanding (see Chapter 2) when both parties share the same culture, customs, background, and language. Even a good manager may drop to a low level of understanding when confronted with people from widely dissimilar backgrounds.

People have trouble forming relationships with those who are different for reasons that may have little to do with prejudice. Similar people share the same language and ways of looking at the world, so communication and problem solving are fast and efficient. Diversity, however, disrupts the smooth operation of groups, at least at first. "Tokens," says Harvard's Rosabeth Moss Kanter, "cannot be assumed to share the same unspoken understandings that the rest of the members share because of their common membership in a social category...."[13] Diversity makes mutual understanding more difficult.

To understand the depth of the problem of mutual understanding, let's consider an impressive 15-year study of relations among black and white managers at a large corporation, conducted by Clayton Alderfer and associates.[14] It's one of the best long-term studies of corporate race relations. The Alderfer team began the study back in the late 1970s, diagnosing the then-current state of race relations among black and white managers at "XYZ Corporation," a company of about 11,000 employees, including 2000 managers of whom 150 were black. Based on their results, the company embarked on an ongoing program to rectify the problems identified and improve race relations. (I'll discuss this program in a moment.) The team evaluated both the short-term and long-term impacts of these interventions.

For now, consider the state of affairs when race relations were first diagnosed. Back in the late 1970s, XYZ already was a progressive company in promoting good race relations. "The corporation had taken the lead in its community to recruit and promote competent black managers," note Alderfer and associates, "before any explicit government pressure was exerted to do so."[15] The company was also working hard to accelerate its affirmative action commitments.

Nonetheless, black and white managers perceived the quality of race relations quite differently. White managers saw a much rosier picture than their black counterparts (see Table 7-2). Most white managers thought race relations were good, for example, but most black managers thought just the opposite. White managers weren't troubled by the quality of relationships between black and white managers, but most black managers were. The gap between white and black managers widens into a vast chasm as we look at perceptions of specific behaviors and practices—hiring, training, expectations, evaluation, and promotion (questions 4–9). Most black managers felt they weren't given the same level of training as whites, they're expected to fail, they're rarely evaluated fairly by white managers, and that most whites think black managers get promoted even if they're doing a mediocre job.

Such enormous differences in perceptions are formidable obstacles to managing diversity.[16] Without deliberate intervention, black-white relationships would deteriorate. White managers, believing everything's okay now, won't see the need to change. Black managers, already feeling unfairness, would interpret such behavior on the part of white managers as disinterest, insensitivity, or outright prejudice. Voicing their frustration would only get them looks of puzzlement, even anger. You can imagine how this lack of mutual understanding could spin downward into cycles of repeated misunderstandings and negative reactions.

Fortunately, the enlightened executives at XYZ used the diagnosis of race relations to make real changes.[17] Back in the late 1970s, black managers felt senior executives did little to advance their cause (question 10). That changed in the following years. XYZ put into place an action program to address the problems of race relations. The program had high visibility and senior-level commitment right from the start.

Table 7-2. Quality and Characteristics of Race Relations among XYZ Managers

	Percent agreeing with statements			
	White males	White females	Black males	Black females
1. Race relations within XYZ are good.	89	86	45	55
2. Good one-to-one black-white relationships are common at XYZ.	74	76	40	59
3. I am troubled by the quality of relationships between black and white managers at XYZ.	25	23	69	61
4. Black managers are hired on the basis of competence.	64	62	90	76
5. Whites receive better training than blacks for assignments.	6	1	65	62
6. Black managers are often given assignments with the expectation that they will fail.	5	8	70	62
7. Blacks are almost never evaluated fairly by white supervisors.	12	6	60	59
8. Blacks get promoted even if they are doing a mediocre job.	57	55	5	4
9. White managers share vital growth and career-related information with black managers.	89	90	42	41
10. XYZ officers do little to advance the cause of black managers.	8	7	74	81

SOURCE: Adapted with permission from NTL Institute, "Diagnosing Race Relations in Management" by Clayton P. Alderfer, Charleen J. Alderfer, Leota Tucker, and Robert Tucker, pp. 135–166, *Journal of Applied Behavioral Science*, vol. 16, no. 2, copyright 1980.

For example, the Race Relations Advisory Group, a temporary committee formed to assist the change effort, was converted into a permanent body.

The company tackled head-on the problem of misunderstanding by providing education and training on diversity. A workshop on race relations, for example, is offered on a regular basis. To break the glass ceiling, the company changed its promotion policies and procedures. A special task force, for instance, was created to evaluate *all* candidates for upward mobility. This task force includes balanced numbers of men, women, and minorities. More women and minorities were placed on the company's standing personnel committees so that all groups could participate directly in promotion decisions for managers.

The results? Did XYZ's race relations program change anything? Consider some facts from the Alderfer team follow-up studies.[18] Black managers in lower management positions, for example, grew from 4 percent of the total in 1976 to 6.7 percent in 1986. The proportion of black managers in middle and upper management jobs rose tenfold to 7 percent during the same period. And the proportion of black managers on standing personnel committees increased by a factor of seven, up to 14.4 percent in 1987. XYZ's program didn't shatter the glass ceiling, but it did inflict serious damage to it.

What about mutual understanding? Do black and white managers now see race relations in the same way? There are considerable areas of agreement. Most blacks and most whites feel that more black representation on personnel committees helps race relations and helps the company. Most blacks and most whites feel the diversity workshop improves race relations and helps the company. But blacks and whites differ in attitudes toward promotion policies. The majority of blacks feel the managerial promotion program helps race relations and helps XYZ company, but a much smaller percentage of whites agrees. The vast majority of blacks feel XYZ's promotion program should be strengthened, but three of four whites feel the program should be kept as is or weakened.

Real improvements, yes, but the results also show that differences in opinion and understanding remain quite pronounced. There are many reasons, but an important one is the effect of numbers and proportions on social relations. The proportions of XYZ black managers on committees and management positions are still small enough that they impede the formation of black-white relationships. In the next section, we'll see why by exploring the special role of numbers and proportions in managing diversity.

Numbers, Proportions, and Critical Mass

Numbers influence social interaction, a great truth captured in maxim and adage. With lovers, for example, two's company but three's a crowd or, no one wants to be the fifth wheel. Such folk wisdom has a firm basis in scientific fact: Numbers impact the quality of relationships, quite apart from the influence of prejudice, sentiment, or bias. From the networking perspective, this is good news. It means you can manage diversity by managing numbers.

Georg Simmel, one of the founding fathers of sociology, was the first to analyze the profound impact of numbers on social interaction.[19] Many others have since documented how numbers play out in a variety of social contexts.[20] Though there's always a *tendency* to associate with similar people—the similarity principle—the extent of associations between *different* kinds of people is influenced by the heterogeneity of a particular context. People tend to choose marriage partners and friends with similar backgrounds, but their decisions are constrained and shaped by opportunities for contact and available choices. Research shows that increasing diversity increases intergroup relationships. Increase the ethnic diversity of a community, for example, and the rate of ethnic intermarriage goes up.[21] Increase the racial integration of a classroom, and more interracial friendships are formed.[22]

So too in organizations. Change the demographic makeup of the workforce and you change the number and quality of relationships between members of various groups. Rosabeth Moss Kanter was among the first to analyze the effects of gender mix on the behavior of men and women in corporate life.[23] What she said about women is true for any group in the numerical minority: "The life of women in the corporation was influenced by the proportions in which they found themselves."[24]

Reconsider, for example, the situation of black managers at XYZ Corporation. Blacks made up less than 10 percent of lower-level managers and less than 10 percent of upper-level managers. Kanter calls this a *skewed group*. Skewed groups occur when one category makes up less than 15 percent of the total. When this occurs, as it does at XYZ, behavior takes on the familiar ring of *tokenism*. "Tokens," says Kanter, "...are often treated as representatives of their category, as symbols rather than individuals."[25] The women executives polled by *Business Week* report that tokenism is alive and well today. Seventy-seven percent said their companies have a "tendency to put women in token positions without any real power or operating authority." And they recognize the dominance of the male majority: 70 percent report that "a male-dominated corporate culture" is an obstacle to success at their companies.[26]

Almost anyone who has been numbered among the few knows what it's like to be treated as a token. When I was in graduate school at Northwestern University in the 1970s, for example, only 10 percent of my entering class were men. This was quite a reversal from undergraduate days where I was among the numerical majority. I experienced an inkling, however brief, of what it's like to be a token, treated more as a stereotypical representative of the category "all men" rather than as an individual. Edward Jones described the feeling of tokenism in his *Harvard Business Review* article on being a black manager in the 1970s: "I entered the first formal training phase, in which I was the only black trainee in a department of over 8,000 employees....I developed the feeling that I was considered a black first and an individual second by many of the people I came into contact with....Everyone knew my name, and I constantly had the feeling of being on stage."[27] Jones's feeling is echoed today by anyone numbered among the few in an organization.

The next situation is what Kanter calls the *tilted group.* Tilted groups still suffer an unequal ratio of one category to another (about 65:35) but it's better than the skewed group extreme. In this situation, the few grow in number and begin to approach *critical mass:* a size and weight that tips the scales in favor of a more equitable balance of power. "Minority members have potential allies among each other, can form coalitions, and can affect the culture of the group," says Kantor. "They begin to become individuals differentiated from each other as well as a type differentiated from each other."[28]

Finally, a *balanced* group occurs when the ratio of one category to another exceeds 60:40, up to 50:50. The weight of equal numbers forces members of each group to deal with each other on equal footing. The salient attribute—gender, race, national origin, or what have you— fades in importance. The system starts to become an impartial meritocracy in which success depends more and more on the right factors: personal ability, experience, track record, networking skills, and so forth. By 1991 the ratio of men to women in executive, managerial, and administrative positions *just* achieved a balanced group ratio (59 percent versus 41 percent). Even so, female middle managers are still paid less than their male counterparts, even when both groups are similarly educated and work in similar functions.[29] It will take a while for the balanced numbers to exert their force.

Current social trends are changing numbers and proportions in the workplace in ways that aid the management of diversity. Changes in demographics lead the push toward diversity, says columnist Carol Kleiman, who writes regularly in *The Chicago Tribune* on jobs and employment.[30] Consider, for example, the massive shift in workplace demographics evident in U.S. Labor Department projections.[31] By the year 2000, more and more women and minorities will move into the white-collar workforce and compete for management jobs. White men will become the numerical minority—only 45 percent of the total workforce. The main source of growth in the workforce—as much as 80 percent of the increase—will come from women, minorities, and immigrants. The business leaders of the year 2000 must know how to tap the power of this new multicultural workforce.

These projections represent sweeping demographic trends; the numbers don't reflect changes in the top jobs. Despite the trends, the composition of top executive ranks in the year 2000 will be very close to what it was in 1991. Demographic trends lead the push toward diversity and can help you balance your workforce, but you still need to manage diversity deliberately to make real changes.

Breaking the Glass Ceiling

Breaking the glass ceiling means eliminating artificial barriers to upward mobility for everyone. From the networking perspective, this means eliminating obstacles to the free formation of relationships. By doing so, you empower everyone, and in the process, serve the interests of the organization as well. Blocked opportunity, warns Kanter, is bad for everyone, not just those in positions of powerlessness. "Aside from the cost to such individuals—often women, but also men—organizations are wasting a large measure of their human talent."[32]

In one way or another, good strategies incorporate the networking principles I introduced in Chapter 2. Good strategies tap and direct the raw human energy contained in the fundamental human need for relationships (principle 1). These strategies recognize that expectations can be self-fulfilling (principle 2), so they create expectations of fair play and equitable treatment. The similarity principle (principle 3) is the root of the problem of diversity, but the operation of the principle can be turned back on itself by overriding *personal* similarity (race, gender) with *group identity* (teams, peer groups, committees) as a basis of similarity and affiliation. Good strategies enforce repeated interaction between diverse groups because it encourages cooperation (principle 4).

Here are six basic strategies companies use to manage diversity and tap its power:

Senior-Level Commitment

Commitment at senior levels may sound obvious, but I can't emphasize it enough. Without official support from the top, most attempts to manage diversity and tap its power are doomed. Top-level support is one of the most important success ingredients for groups like Xerox's black caucuses, as diversity experts Ray Friedman and Donna Carter discovered in their extensive study of these movements.[33] Xerox executives, for example, eventually saw the immense value of the grass-roots black caucus groups and became active supporters. And, XYZ executives stand behind and firmly promote the company's race relations program.

Education and Training

Because discrimination has its roots in attitudes and beliefs, education and training make up one of the first steps companies take. The initial objective is to increase awareness of and sensitivity to the problem of diversity. Training and orientation programs are used by such leading companies as McDonnell Douglas, Hewlett-Packard, Ortho Pharmaceuticals, Corning, Digital Equipment, Xerox, and Procter & Gamble.[34] "Two types of training are most popular: awareness and skill building," says University of Michigan business school professor Taylor Cox. "The former introduces the topic of managing diversity and generally includes information on workforce demographics, the meaning of diversity, and exercises to get participants thinking about relevant issues and raising their own self-awareness."[35] For effective awareness training, I've found it's important to include hard data about relationships, such as XYZ's survey findings about race relations. Hard data speak loudly; they document the state of affairs for all to see.

Progressive companies go further by educating about the *power* of diversity as well. Even basic training about diversity is helpful, researchers report, for people to see and appreciate its advantages.[36] Most blacks and most whites at XYZ Corporation, for example, reported that diversity training improved race relations and should be continued.[37] Corning learned that gender training (coupled with career planning and mentoring programs) cut the dropout rate by half for women managers and executives.[38]

"The skill-building training," continues Cox, "provides more specific information on cultural norms of different groups and how they may affect work behavior."[39] Here, again, I've found that it's difficult to beat hard data. Cultural differences can be measured and documented. By doing so, you can circumvent a lot of factless discussion and move to the real differences. It's also important to include training in "generic" interpersonal skills: group dynamics, giving and getting feedback, observation, and so on. These skills are useful in any social setting and are particularly important for managing diversity.

It's absolutely essential that all levels be involved in education and training efforts. That includes—especially—top managers and executives. It may be a bitter pill to swallow, but most people at the top don't see problems of diversity. Let me tell you a story that illustrates this natural phenomenon.

A few years ago I was traveling the Outer Banks of North Carolina, a long, thin barrier island stretching the entire length of the coast. The Outer Banks is rich in myth and mystery. It's known, for example, as the Graveyard of the Atlantic, a name earned from countless shipwrecks on its treacherous shoals.

I started my trek up north, near Kitty Hawk, and traveled south, stopping for a few days on Ocracoke Island, near the southern tip of the Outer Banks. Ocracoke is an isolated, tiny community populated hundreds of years ago by shipwreck survivors. While I was exploring the island, I had a curious experience talking with the native islanders. One was a middle-aged son of the island who had returned to Ocracoke after living on the mainland for several years. "The best thing I like about Ocracoke," he said, "is that it's a classless society. Everyone's equal." Later that day, I met a native son with a different point of view. "The thing I hate most about Ocracoke," he said bitterly, "is that it's such a rigid class-based society."

Why the different views? It would be too easy to dismiss the divergence of opinion as personality differences. I learned the real reason after asking more questions. Two classes of people sailed on ships— the passengers and senior officers, mostly of upper-class origins, and the crew, mostly of lower-class origins. When a shipwreck occurred, the survivors recreated their class differences on the island. The upper class claimed the high ground on the island, the point; they became known as "pointers." The lower-class survivors took the low ground, the creeks, and became known as "creekers." The first person I talked with came from a pointer family; his great-great-grandfather had been a ship captain. As a pointer, he just didn't see class differences. But the second person, born into a creeker family, was all too aware of the island's class structure.

The Ocracoke principle holds true in organizations. Those at the top don't see the problems of diversity; those at the bottom are all too aware of them. That's why it's essential that senior levels are included in education and training about diversity.

Jobs and Career Paths

Another early strategy is to ensure equal access to job openings and favorable career paths. Public job posting, for example, is used to advertise openings and make them available to all qualified candidates.[40] Job posting should be a companywide practice. Note, however, that official job posting won't solve the problem of *unofficial* exclusion from jobs. In many cases, openings are posted as a formality, and people with the "inside track" get the jobs. Public posting is necessary but not sufficient. You have to do more.

Good managers of diversity identify upward mobility job chains, the job-to-job ladders that lead to top positions. Xerox, for example, discovered that its executives had all followed the same career path (such as line sales manager to branch manager to a regional-level job). "Pivotal" jobs are those that are links in an upward chain. To increase the odds of upward movement, Xerox placed women and minorities in pivotal jobs. Similarly, Anheuser-Busch Companies of St. Louis has instituted a formal management development program that moves women and minorities from jobs in inventory to higher-level management positions.[41]

It's possible to go too far. For years, Xerox worked hard to hire women and minorities. But it may have overdone it, discouraging white men from applying or being hired. To solve the reverse problem, Xerox established what some have called the first affirmative action program for white males.[42] Its purpose: hiring white men as entry-level engineers.

Formal and Informal Minority Groups

Formal minority committees and groups send strong signals from high places. Official and high-visibility committees like Xerox's Employee Resource Advisory Committee and XYZ's Race Relations Advisory Group are signals of top-level recognition of and commitment to affirmative action. These signals help to set up the right expectations (networking principle 2) about managing diversity. Of course, along with the right message you might have to make minority promotion a part of a supervisor's performance evaluation.

Official committees work best when most (or many) members are representatives of minority groups, and when they're given an open-ended mission: Investigate any and all minority-related issues. These committees can unearth all sorts of practices in need of reform. Remember, however, that such committee work puts extra time burdens on minority managers. This can be a disadvantage for minority managers unless participation is factored in as part of a manager's overall performance evaluation.

Informal groups are vitally important. Good managers of diversity endorse and support grass-roots minority groups like the black caucus groups at Xerox and help them become role models for the whole organization. Some managers may fear that such groups are the start of a labor union movement, but the opposite is true. Grass-roots caucus groups indicate a willingness to work *within* the system, not out-side it; if anything, the odds of a labor union go *down* when these groups arise. Remember: everyone needs a "home base"—a place to belong and build close ties (networking principle 1). That's part of the power of The Company of the Table. For the majority, the organization itself contains lots of home bases. That's not true for a minority, at least until the organization achieves a balanced ratio.

Favorable Numbers and Proportions

Tokenism, in large part, is a number problem. Because it's caused by unfavorable proportions, one solution is to balance numbers.[43] Balanced numbers invoke the operation of the fourth networking prin-ciple: Repeated interaction encourages cooperation. Just like a critical mass of fissionable material sustains a nuclear chain reaction, when women and minorities appear in greater-than-token numbers, they can obtain a critical mass that sustains organizational change. Critical mass changes attitudes, breaks stereotypes, promotes intergroup rela-tionships, lowers resistance to diversity, and enhances appreciation of its benefits.[44]

Trying to balance numbers, however, faces a built-in predicament—the fact that some groups are numerical minorities in the population at large. Women are just over 50 percent of the U.S. population, but blacks, Asians, Hispanics, and other groups each comprise a much smaller fraction. You can *improve* proportions in your organization by balancing numbers, but equal representation (versus proportional rep-resentation) is impossible, especially if other organizations are com-peting with you to recruit the same people.

Kanter recommends that women (or any minority) be hired in *batches* rather than one by one and then *clustered* in various locations instead of spread around the company.[45] These tactics may help, but they can also create new artificial barriers and reinforce stereotypes. Such tac-tics won't work if women and/or minorities are placed in *weak* groups. I would rather see women and minorities dispersed around a com-pany in powerful positions and powerful departments than clustered together in peripheral, low-power groups.

If women and/or minorities are dispersed, use compensatory mech-anisms. Job rotation, committee assignments, task forces, and multi-functional project teams can help the few members of a scattered minority group get together for task-related purposes.[46] To make this work, however, you have to do more than encourage such assign-ments; you have to sponsor women and minorities and recommend them for membership in groups, teams, and committees.

Kanter recommends developing a women's network to provide moral support, information, and feedback not available from immediate coworkers. Carol Kleiman gives the same advice in *Women's Networks*.[47] Such networks can help, but remember that focusing on developing *only* a women's network can be counterproductive. Women need to network with women *and* with men.[48] (The same is true, of course, for minorities.)

Networking should be internal and external. In particular, encourage and support participation in *outside* networking clubs. Outside clubs can provide the same moral support and encouragement as internal networking groups but have the added benefits of helping women and minorities build their external intelligence networks, as well as augment the organization's intelligence network. (Networking groups abound. See Chapter 13 for suggestions, as well as Carol Kleiman's useful book.[49])

Organizational Redesign

Some authorities advocate redesigning organizations to empower women and minorities.[50] Redesigning would help, of course, but it's hard to imagine hard-pressed businesses making radical changes for the sake of managing diversity alone. Diversity is a very real and very serious issue, but it competes for attention with many other serious issues. Fortunately, some of the fundamental changes taking place in the business world are redesigning organizations in ways that can help you manage diversity.

The increasing use of multifunctional teams, for example, can be a boon to managing diversity. By design, a multifunctional team includes representatives from diverse disciplines, functions, and departments. Multifunctional teams are learning laboratories. Participating in a team increases awareness of the value of diversity, and it provides participants with direct experience working with people from different backgrounds. To reap the full benefits of multifunctional teams, however, women and minorities must be included on them.

Globalization increases diversity. Business is no longer confined to the domestic economy; business must now span diverse places, time zones, cultures, and nations. In a way, this added diversity is a blessing: The need to compete globally forces managers to deal head-on with the issue of diversity and makes managing diversity well an absolute necessity. Globalization also provides new opportunities for learning. Making "foreign" assignments part of a manager's career development creates the right conditions for learning how to appreciate and manage diversity.

The rise of network organizations—probably the most radical organizational redesign of all—creates new opportunities for managing diversity. As companies replace hierarchies with networks, they tear down the walls between departments, functions, and divisions; companies remove external walls and build partnerships with customers, suppliers, and competitors. These changes turn an organization upside down, disrupt the traditional power structure, and create unprecedented opportunities for networking. These opportunities are available for anyone who recognizes and seizes them.

Not all the fundamental changes taking place make it easier to manage diversity. Downsizing, for example, can make it harder. Because downsizing imposes wider spans of management and heavier work loads, managers have less time to worry about managing diversity. Worse, companies downsize without paying attention to diversity. Consider, for example, the plight of Alberta's oil industry. In response to falling oil prices, oil companies are laying off veteran workers and refusing to hire new people, according to an industry study, reported by Gordon Jaremko, in the *Calgary Herald*. "The result of cost-cutting with blunt instruments," says Jaremko, "is found to be a homogeneous workforce of demoralized white males in their late 30s who lack both veteran mentors and infusions of fresh talent needed for healthy performance."[51] A more thoughtful approach to downsizing would take into account the effects on the diversity of the workforce. That's tough to do, however, given the bedlam and hysteria often created by rapid downsizing.

What You Can Do *Now*

Diversity is managed at all levels. It's not just the concern of top executives; all those who network smart try to tap the power of diversity. Managing diversity well boosts the performance of your group as a whole. What you can do *now* is identify the current status of diversity in your group and target areas of improvement. In your evaluation, focus on the relationship aspects of diversity. The glass ceiling is primarily a networking problem. You can crack it by helping everyone become avid and skillful relationship builders.

How do your people *feel* about diversity? What do they know about it? Do they recognize the power of diversity, such as its role in organizational intelligence systems or in serendipity? Do women and minorities in your group feel left out or disenfranchised? One good way to find out is to bring the topic up at your regular informal get-togethers. Ask your people directly. Tell them about what you've learned in this chapter on diversity. Get their input, thoughts, concerns, ideas.

In the accompanying box is a checklist you can use to assess the state of diversity in your group. You can put these questions on the table during one of your informal sessions. You may also find it helpful to conduct a survey of attitudes, feelings, and knowledge about diversity. If so, you can use the checklist as a guide to constructing a questionnaire.

Checklist for Assessing Diversity

1. How may women and/or minorities are in your group?
2. Are women and/or minorities represented at all levels?
3. What are their numbers and proportions?
4. Is tokenism a problem? Are members of any particular category in the numerical minority?
5. If you discover unfavorable proportions, how far away are you from balanced proportions?
6. Once hired, do you cluster women and/or minorities, or do you spread them around various locations or offices?
7. Are women and/or minorities located in low-power, peripheral positions or groups?
8. Does your company provide education and skill-training programs on diversity?
9. Do your people attend these programs? Have *you* attended?
10. Does your company provide objective information and hard data about diversity, stereotyping, and the glass ceiling?
11. Are women and/or minorities stuck in dead-end jobs in your group? Do they have restricted access to favorable career paths—the tracks that lead upward to better and better positions?
12. Do you use public job posting when a position becomes available? Do you also use the informal grapevine?
13. Are there *formal* minority committees and groups? Do you include participation as part of a member's performance review and appraisal?
14. Are there *informal* committees and groups, such as Xerox's black caucuses? Do you support and encourage them?
15. Is there a formal or informal mentoring program?
16. Are women and/or minorities represented in balanced numbers on personnel committees?
17. Do you use 360-degree performance evaluations (Chapter 4) to reduce bias and ensure more accurate performance appraisals?

18. Do you encourage everyone to get involved in outside networking groups? Do you give them time off? Do you pay for membership dues, fees, travel, and other expenses?
19. When considering changes in organizational design, do you take into account their impact on networking and relationship building, especially for women and minorities?
20. Do you provide hard incentives for managing diversity well? Do you include requirements for managing diversity in performance reviews and appraisals?

What You Can Do *Soon*

Once you've used the checklist to assess the status of diversity in your group, what you can do soon is use it to target changes. Before you make changes in policies and procedures, however, you can begin simply by working on your personal relationships with women and minority coworkers. Pay particular attention to subordinate relationships. As the boss, you're in a special position to help subordinates integrate themselves in the organization.

As I described in Chapter 4, it can be difficult to understand those you work with if they're different from you. If your people come from diverse backgrounds, then differences in language, custom, and styles of interaction make achieving mutual understanding difficult. Even managers who operate at high levels of understanding when working with people like themselves can drop to a low level when working with people from different backgrounds. Part of the solution is to recognize that such difficulty is *natural*. Diversity can impede mutual understanding. By becoming aware of it, you're less likely to blame others for lack of mutual understanding and more likely to seek the real cause of a problem. You're less likely to confuse differences in *style* with differences in *substance*. Men and women, for example, may express frustration differently yet be frustrated by the same thing.

As a leader, you shoulder the responsibility of developing and empowering your people. As part of your job, do you initiate and develop mentoring relationships with women and minority subordinates? At Capital Partners, the commercial real estate firm I featured in Chapter 5, partners are assigned routinely as mentors to new leasing agents. You can assign yourself, formally or informally, as a mentor. You don't have to make official announcements; you can simply recognize and act on your mentoring responsibilities.

Use the secret formula for managing relationships I described in Chapter 4. Include women and minorities in your personal intelligence networks. Encourage them to "wander around" in the company and its wider environment. Support participation in informal caucus groups. Encourage everyone to join outside networking clubs (see Chapter 13); give people time off to attend outside networking events, and pay for travel expenses, membership dues, conference fees. Sponsor and promote women and minorities as members of multi-functional teams, task forces, special projects, and other work-related group assignments that integrate them in the organization. And remember: the more successful your people are, the more successful you are. By empowering others, you empower yourself.

A good mentor is supportive and constructively critical. A good mentor activates the Pygmalion principle by setting appropriately high expectations. "A unique characteristic of superior managers," says J. Sterling Livingston, who wrote about the Pygmalion effect in management, "is the ability to create high performance expectations that subordinates fulfill."[52] Unfortunately, stereotypes set *wrong* expectations. Managers who stereotype women and minorities may communicate expectations of failure, subtly or not, and trigger a vicious cycle of declining performance and falling expectations. To fight this problem, you may have to help fellow managers overcome negative stereotypes and develop positive expectations. Hard incentives may be necessary to signal seriousness and to motivate stubborn managers.

Objective information, education, and training about diversity can help. If your people haven't had such education and training, then I recommend that you begin by arranging for diversity awareness and skill-building programs. In-house programs are generally better (they're geared to your company's specific situation), but consider outside courses and programs as well.

A few words of advice before you take additional steps. Some changes are much easier to make than others. Consider high payoff strategies—those where a small change makes a big difference. Use "flock" strategies—those that kill several birds with one stone. If you need to build bridges between groups, for example, think of ways you can do so that will improve the management of diversity as well. By sending a minority member of one group as an emissary to another group, you build bridges *and* help minorities develop their personal networks. Look for natural synergies. Due to the similarity principle, natural cross-group alliances are possible when each group includes members of the same minority. Finally, you must consider government regulations, requirements, and guidelines before you make changes in hiring, retention, and promotion; be sure to check with your human resources and legal departments.

What You Can Do in the *Long Run*

Managing diversity is a continuous process. What you can do in the long run is set up systems that continuously integrate men, women, and minorities in your organization. Due to the dilemma of indirect management, however, you can't force anyone to manage diversity well. What you can do instead is establish the right conditions, the right environment, the right climate for managing diversity well. By managing conditions, you can manage diversity.

The first action you should take for the long run is to propose and sponsor the establishment of *formal* committees for minorities and women. Be sure to staff them with minorities and/or women (and recognize the added work load by including such assignments in performance reviews and appraisals). Charge the committees with a general mission: to explore and investigate any and all issues related to the problems and promise of diversity. Such committees serve multiple functions. They broadcast a high-powered signal about the importance of diversity. They serve as a seedbed for networking. And they provide new insights into policies and practices in need of reform.

Consider targets for desired workforce composition. This involves *benchmarking* the company against some standard. A rough-and-ready standard is the demographic composition of surrounding communities, though this is just a starting point. Xerox, for example, develops "availability estimates" for jobs in which women and minorities were underutilized.[53] These estimates take into account such factors as population, unemployment, total workforce, requisite skills, internal availability, and training. Developing such availability estimates is tricky, and government regulations and guidelines must be taken into account. You can participate in the effort, perhaps as its impetus, but it should be a companywide effort approved and sponsored by top executives.

Investigate and improve career management practices. Identify upward-mobility job chains, the pivotal jobs and job-to-job sequences that lead to top positions in your company. To increase the odds of upward movement, place qualified women and minorities in pivotal jobs. Institute a formal management development program that moves qualified women and minorities into successful job chains.

Anticipate *new* strategies for managing successful careers. The deep changes in the business world will alter (or even eliminate) *current* upward-mobility job chains, making today's advice about tomorrow's successful careers more and more irrelevant. What will be the *new* job patterns that lead to success in the emerging business order?

- Frequent participation on multifunctional teams is becoming mandatory for a successful career. Advertise this fact, establish procedures so that women and minorities are included on teams, and provide incentives for doing so.

- Globalization means that stints abroad must become part of everyone's career development. Advertise this fact, establish procedures, provide incentives.

- External alliances with customers, suppliers, and competitors provide good opportunities for networking. A successful career includes participation in external partnerships. Be sure women and minorities are given the opportunity to become involved in these partnerships.

- This rise of network organizations casts aside the standard "good advice" on managing careers. We do know, however, that successful career paths will look less like "ladders" (the appropriate image for a hierarchy) and more like zig-zagging, meandering paths. In network organizations, a successful career will include more *lateral moves* than ever before.

Coordinate all major changes in organizational design with efforts to manage diversity. Always ask, "How will this change impact the diversity of our organization? How will it impact networking?" If you're downsizing, for example, are you doing so in ways that recreate the personnel problems plaguing the Alberta oil industry? Are you creating a homogeneous workforce by laying off women, minorities, the young and the old? Are you cutting mentoring relationships by forcing out veteran managers? Are you destroying internal bridges or external alliances as well?

A few final words. Managing diversity isn't easy. "Learning to manage diversity is a change process," writes R. Roosevelt Thomas, Jr., in the *Harvard Business Review*, "and the managers involved are change agents."[54] If you're at the cutting edge of managing diversity, he says, you're a "pioneer"—and a pioneer explores unknown territory.

Diversity is our greatest strength. You don't want to eradicate differences; rejoice in diversity and learn how to tap its great power. "The correct question today," says Thomas, "is not 'How are we doing on race relations?' or 'Are we promoting enough minority people and women?' but rather 'Given the diverse work force I've got, am I getting the productivity, does it work as smoothly, is morale as high, as if every person in the company was the same sex and race and nationality?'"[55]

8

Networking through the Organizational Life Cycle

Everything flows and nothing stays.
HERACLITUS

Do you remember Head skis? I know they're still around, but I mean the *original* Heads: the black metal skis that were the hottest items on the slopes in the 1960s.[1] Head enjoyed the triple-crown distinction of high quality, great performance, and cachet—a status symbol that actually improved your skiing. I learned to ski when I was in high school in the late 1960s, right at the peak of Head's fame and success, and I coveted a pair of Head skis (alas, my tastes exceeded my financial grasp).

Howard Head's career is the typical story of ardent inventor turned reluctant business manager. Like many inventors, in the beginning he was much more interested in solving an engineering puzzle than in building a business. His real goal was to build a better ski, not to run a business. But his solution to the engineering puzzle became a spectacular business success. Head came out with the first successful metal ski five years before the competition and rode the crest of the swelling recreational ski market throughout the 1960s. By 1967 Head was the biggest U.S. ski maker, outselling its nearest competitor, Hart, by a ratio of almost 3 to 1.

Crisis was right around the corner. Like many inventors whose success propels them into business management, Howard found himself increasingly encumbered with the day-to-day details of running a business. The company's needs soon eclipsed Howard's management abilities, and the business became more and more disorganized. Head Ski was falling victim to its own success. Howard had a problem on his hands.

To his credit, Howard did something that many founders find impossible to do: He stepped aside and hired a professional manager. Harold J. Seigle, former head of the consumer products division of Arvin Industries, joined Head Ski as president in 1965. Seigle's goal was to turn Head Ski into a professionally run company. He did a lot of the right things, such as introducing standard business practices and procedures. But he also took the company on a wild acquisition spree. The spree was intended to break the company's dependence on a single seasonal product; it broke the company instead. Financial strain and heavy losses in newly acquired subsidiaries forced Seigle to sell the company to AMF in May 1971. (About 20 years later, AMF spun off Head Ski, and it once again stands as an independent company.)

The Head Ski story illustrates a basic fact of organizational life: An organization, like a person, moves through a natural life cycle, a sequence of predictable stages and crises.[2] Head Ski was teetering at the critical transition between organizational childhood and adolescence, the time when a company has outgrown the business skills of the founder. This classic crisis is only the first of several a company faces as it grows and develops. Had Head Ski survived this transition, its victory would have lasted only until it faced the next crisis in its life cycle.

Life-cycle crises are inescapable parts of organizational life. Those who network smart aren't taken by surprise when crisis hits. They learn to *anticipate* crisis and manage in ways that help them and their organizations withstand the strains of crisis and successfully negotiate the transition into the next stage. In this chapter, I describe the six predictable stages in the organizational life cycle and the typical crises associated with them. I describe the networking challenges, both personal and organizational, that arise in each stage. I tell you how to build networks that can help you and your organization survive and, as Tom Peters puts it, thrive on crisis.[3] With the right networks, you can turn crisis into a powerful energizing force.

The Organizational Life Cycle

Many leaders know that organizations move through stages of development, but only a few use this knowledge to anticipate crisis. I've been guilty of this myself. When I worked as a senior manager in a Washington, D.C.–based management consulting firm, I participated in a painful transition similar to Head Ski's. Back then, however, I didn't recognize it as a natural and predictable problem. It seemed unique and uniquely distressing to me. The founders of the firm were growing restless with increasing management burdens, and they wanted to move on to create a new venture. But it was hard for them to let go. Only after considerable squabbling and anguish were we able to devise a satisfactory solution to the same transition Head Ski tried to make. If we had recognized that our transition was not unique, we would have predicted the leadership crisis and prepared for it in advance. We could have short-circuited some of the hard feelings and turmoil.

Many crises, like the one I went through, are growing pains caused by an organization's progress through the life cycle. Crises are predictable because a new one follows each stage. Larry Greiner, in one of my favorite *Harvard Business Review* articles, "Evolution and Revolution as Organizations Grow," describes natural stages of organizational development.[4] To be useful to us, however, his model of the life cycle must be modified and extended. Greiner came up with it long before organizations faced the now-widespread restructuring and downsizing trend, as well as the rise of network organizations. So, I've updated his model for our use. Greiner's model includes five stages of organizational growth.[5] I retain his first four stages (creativity, direction, delegation, coordination), but I replace his fifth growth stage (collaboration) with *downsizing*, the first stage of organizational contraction. And, I add an entirely new stage of organizational development, *networking* (stage six).

The six stages in the organizational life cycle and their crises are illustrated in Figure 8-1. The diagonal line represents the growth path of an organization as a function of its size (vertical dimension) and its age (horizontal dimension). Of course, the slope of the line can be steeper or flatter. A fast-growing (or fast-shrinking) company, for example, would follow a much steeper path, moving through each stage and confronting each crisis sooner than a slow-moving company.

It's possible, of course, to *skip* a stage. Company leaders might foresee the pitfalls of an upcoming stage of development and jump over it.

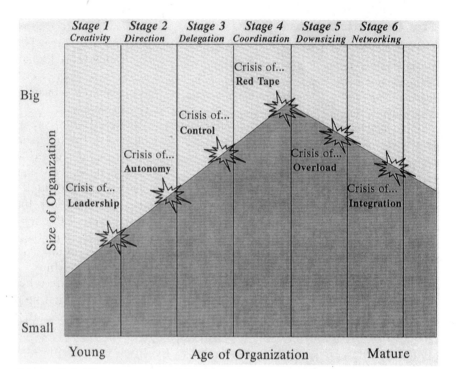

Figure 8-1. The organizational life cycle. (Source: *Modified and reprinted by permission of* Harvard Business Review. *An exhibit from Larry E. Greiner, "Evolution and Revolution as Organizations Grow," July–August 1972. Copyright © 1972 by the President and Fellows of Harvard College; all rights reserved.)*

After watching what's been happening to corporate behemoths like Sears, General Motors, and IBM, for example, insightful leaders wouldn't let their companies turn into bloated bureaucracies, and so they can skip the painful "downsizing" stage. And some leaders might recognize the virtues of the network form of organization and go right to it from the start. Capital Partners, the "network-style" organization I described in Chapter 5, is one such company.

Six Predictable Stages and Crises

Stage 1: Creativity and the Crisis of Leadership[6]

Stage 1 is the organization's birth and initial growth spurt. Head Ski was in this stage and was just on the verge of growing out of it. The original inspiration of the founder—like Howard Head's perfection of the metal ski—is the organization's momentum and driving force. The company's small size allows it to be run informally, much more like an informal social group than a formal organization. Networks are flexible, adaptable. Coordination and control are accomplished via face-to-face interaction, casual meetings, and spontaneous networking.

The very success of the company in stage 1 creates its first major crisis. As with Howard Head, the organization outgrows the business skills of its founders. Several of the networking problems I discussed in previous chapters crop up at the end of stage 1. For example, sheer size impedes informal communication, making it necessary to build intelligence networks (Chapter 3). New people are hired who may lack the dedication (and ownership stake) of the original few, creating the need to actively manage up, down, and sideways (Chapter 4) and to manage diversity (Chapter 7). Networking becomes less and less spontaneous, so managers must now actively help their people build relationships.

Like Head Ski, the organization at the end of stage 1 hits what Greiner calls a *leadership crisis.*[7] To meet it, the founders must step aside and bring in a professional business manager. For Head Ski, that was Harold Seigle.

Stage 2: Direction and the Autonomy Crisis[8]

The new professional manager provides *direction* to the firm by instituting standard business practices and rationalizing everyday business life. Depending on the situation, the new manager may redesign the organization (often establishing a functional structure), formalize budgets and accounting procedures, formalize communication, and so on. This is what Seigle should have emphasized at Head Ski instead of his wild acquisition spree. Had he attended only to the details appropriate for stage 2—getting the house in order—Head Ski would have survived and thrived. Instead, he tried to jump stages, like an adolescent who tries to act like an adult, and put the company in jeopardy.

For a time, business rationalization propels the company into a period of renewed growth. From the networking perspective, however, something's been lost. The good old days of spontaneous networking are gone. Tight control at the top becomes an impediment to the flexible networking required for continued success. The functional form of organization creates bottlenecks that managers are not free to bridge (Chapter 5). Indeed, lower-level managers, says Greiner, are "treated more as functional specialists than as autonomous decision-making managers."[9]

This stage is a particularly dangerous time in an organization's life. Research conducted by organizational experts David Krackhardt and Robert Stern, and Reed Nelson, reveals an important fact about networks and crisis management: Organizations with lots of *bridges* between groups are better able to handle crisis than organizations without them.[10] The functional structure created in stage 2, however, lacks cross-unit bridges, thus making the organization unable to handle crises well. Excessive departmentalization splits the organization into a number of warring factions. When crisis hits, these departments won't cooperate. Instead, each one perceives crisis as a threat to its power base, resources, and autonomy; each department withdraws, turns inward, defends itself. Any preexisting conflicts between groups are aggravated.[11] Each unit becomes a well-defended fortress, just the opposite of what you want in a crisis. Departments cooperate *less* during crisis, but adaptation to crisis requires *more* cooperation between units, not less.[12]

Stage 2 ushers in its own revolution: what Greiner calls the *autonomy crisis*.[13] Managers who are close to products and markets clamor to be free from the constraints of overcentralization and bureaucracy. Their instincts are right. Those on the firing line in a large organization know more about customers and products than top managers do. And to better handle crisis, the organization needs bridges across its various departments and functions. To solve the crisis, top managers must *delegate*.

Stage 3: Delegation and the Control Crisis[14]

Delegation means converting the organization from a centralized structure to a decentralized structure. Top managers get their hands out of day-to-day operations, focusing instead on long-run strategy and resource acquisition and allocation. The functional form of organization gives way to autonomous profit centers, each run by a general manager with multifunctional responsibilities.

Delegation fuels the next growth burst. Companies that were first in their industries to adopt the use of autonomous profit centers—DuPont, General Motors, General Electric—leapfrogged their competitors.[15] Profit centers are a more efficient solution than the functional form to problems created by large size and complexity. Placing multiple functions under a single manager helps to build crisis-handling bridges across functions.

After a while, however, delegation precipitates a new crisis, the *crisis of control*.[16] Top managers, who backed away from operations, now feel they're losing control, getting out of touch. And they're right. The autonomous units become independent operations; the company appears to be little more than a conglomerate, a holding company. It's an understatement to say that coordinating links or bridges across units don't exist.

If you know GE's history, you know when the company hit its crisis of control.[17] In the years after World War II, Ralph Cordiner turned GE into an extremely decentralized organization. He reorganized the company into 120 separate business units, each headed by a department manager with total profit and loss responsibility. His excessive delegation allowed the company to degrade into a collection of uncoordinated, autonomous units. True to the doctrine of decentralization, Cordiner ran the show strictly by the numbers. (Indeed, his insistence on making the numbers is often cited as a cause of GE's involvement in the infamous price-fixing conspiracies of the 1950s, which Rob Faulkner and I analyze in detail.[18]) The situation got worse in the 1960s under Cordiner's successor, Fred Borch, as GE grew to 170 different units. This excessive decentralization resulted in lackluster performance and precipitated the crisis of control.

To solve the stage 3 crisis of control, top managers must find a way to regain control without resorting to centralization (appropriate only for stage 1 crisis). They must find a way to build the bridges the organization desperately needs to boost its crisis-handling ability. The solution is what Greiner calls *coordination*.[19]

Stage 4: Coordination and the Red Tape Crisis

Coordination, says Greiner, "is characterized by the use of formal systems for achieving greater coordination and by top executives taking responsibility for the initiation and administration of these new systems."[20] Changes include merging decentralized units into product groups, increasing headquarters staff, establishing formal planning and review procedures, close monitoring and coordination of capital expenditures, and so on. These actions spur growth by achieving a more efficient use of the company's scarce resources. At GE, for example, greater coordination and more efficient use of resources were achieved, in part, by the implementation in the 1970s of GE's vaunted strategic planning and management system.

In this stage, top managers formally build bridges between groups.[21] These bridges solve the bottleneck problems between groups (Chapter 3) and prepare the organization to respond better to crisis. Bridges help an organization handle crisis for three reasons[22]:

- *Interaction leads to positive sentiment and feelings.*[23] This is a direct application of the fourth networking principle: repeated interaction encourages cooperation (Chapter 2). When people from different groups interact, they tend to form positive and trusting relationships—not always, but it's a strong tendency.

- *Bridges counteract the similarity principle.* Crisis aggravates the natural tendency for people to associate with others like themselves. Frequent contact counteracts this tendency. Bridges are information conduits and the basis of external loyalties. Bridges help to break down stereotypes and overcome narrow self-interest.

- *Bridges are channels for dispute resolution.* When bridges don't exist, unresolved grievances build up; problems aren't solved in the normal course of business before they blow up. Established bridges ensure the familiarity and trust so necessary to settling differences and finding mutually beneficial solutions.

But the next crisis is right around the corner. Companies often go too far in stage 4, and end up solving the crisis of control by *over*coordinating. They become control freaks, disciples of the philosophy of bureaucratic control (see Introduction). Those who do the work (the line) and those who audit and monitor the work (the staff) become estranged. Animosity erupts between line and staff. The organization becomes big and bloated, too many people, too many staff types, too many layers—a fat "corpocracy."

Overcoordination stifles networking. Far too many relationships are *prescribed*; free, flexible networking is almost entirely absent. The heavy use of formal systems and procedures creates what Greiner calls a *crisis of red tape.*[24] The solution, which Greiner didn't foresee, is *downsizing.*

Stage 5: Downsizing and the Overload Crisis

The large, overgrown corporations of the 1970s and 1980s exhibited the crisis symptoms associated with overcoordination. Many solved the problem by downsizing—making massive layoffs, selling divisions unrelated to core competencies, paring corporate staff, cutting layers, widening spans of control, and so on. GE, for example, made these tough changes under Jack Welch's leadership in the 1980s (see Chapter 15 for details). Some companies went too far, we know, spurred on by followers of the cult of the deal; along with the fat, they cut bone and muscle. For those that didn't go too far, however, downsizing was an appropriate (if quite painful) cure for the excesses of coordination.

Downsizing helps the company focus on building and exploiting its core strength. But it eventually creates its own revolution, what I call the *overload crisis.* I've seen it in many companies that have downsized. Here are some symptoms: Forced retirement of large numbers of veterans means the loss of organizational memory and the loss of key relationships with customers and suppliers. Many jobs and layers have been cut, but the amount of work remains the same; those who are left must shoulder a bigger and bigger burden. Wider spans of control overwhelm managers, who now must manage large numbers of relationships. The old authoritarian techniques associated with the philosophy of control don't work any more. Many people are searching for better approaches, but they haven't found them yet. They express their struggle, vaguely, as the need to "reconceive their jobs" and "empower people," but they don't know how.

The solution to the overload crisis is *networking.*

Stage 6: Networking and the Integration Crisis

Networking lifts organizations out of the chaos of downsizing. It helps to rebuild organizations, making them more efficient, effective, and empowering for the people in them. Stage 6 includes all the networking practices I advocate in this book: the emphasis on building relationships and networks, multifunctional teams, external alliances and partnerships, and so on. Teams, in particular, are a critical feature of networking. In a sense, teams recreate the informality of organizations in stage 1. Each team becomes a stage 1 organization in miniature, creating the conditions that empower people, help them network, and allow them to flourish.

Networking done on a grand scale helps to turn the organization into the fast and flexible *network organization.* As I've mentioned, these new organizational forms go by many names—GE's boundaryless organization, Capital Partners' lattice organization, the virtual enterprise. But no matter which name's used, in practice the organization's the same: a seamless network of internal and external relationships. (See Chapter 15 for a description of GE.)

We know that every solution contains the seeds of the next crisis. So what crisis will arise from the network organization? In the drive to create multifunctional project-driven teams, many leaders fail to recognize the need for *cross-team integration.* To get closer to customers, for example, some companies decentralize and create multiple customer-focused teams but then forget to reintegrate by building a *network of teams.* StorageAmerica is just one of many companies with this problem (as I described in Chapter 5). Without a network of teams, a company suffers all sorts of problems: wasteful duplication of effort (such as redundant systems or procedures), absence of cross-team learning, lack of a unifying set of values, uncoordinated relationships with customers, suppliers, investors, and other external groups.

In stage 6, the crisis appears to be the challenge of integrating multiple teams, what I call the *crisis of integration*. As a company becomes a true network organization, it must learn how to develop a *network of teams*. This is the challenge of level-two integration I described in Chapter 5.

What You Can Do *Now*

You can't get where you want to go if you don't know where you are. What you should do first is assess *where* your group or organization is on the growth path. Which stage are you in? Review the six stages and see which one most closely matches your situation. How far along are you in whatever stage you're in? Have you just resolved a crisis and advanced into a relatively calm period, or is a new crisis right around the corner? If you're near a critical transition, you'll have to do something fast to prepare your group or organization.

If crisis is imminent—or you're already in one—here's what I recommend: immediately establish a *crisis task force* composed of members of different key groups. Forming it immediately alerts everyone to the crisis and serves as a rallying point. The task force's multifunctional composition induces bridge building and gets you at least some of the benefits of cross-group ties. And a multifunctional task force will likely devise a solution to the crisis that'll be supported by different constituencies.

If crisis isn't imminent, you should continue your analysis of where your organization is on the growth path. Networking problems and their solutions vary by stage of development. In stage 1, small size and informality induce natural networking. You may have to prod it along, but in most cases sufficient integrating ties already exist and you don't have to do much. (And you're preoccupied already with just getting the firm off the ground.)

Once you've entered stage 2, direction, real networking problems crop up. In this stage, the organization is recast into a functional structure. The organizational mishmash of stage 1 is departmentalized into production, sales, finance, R&D, and so on. This new design boosts growth for a while, but we know from Chapter 5 that a departmentalized structure eventually creates extreme bottlenecks. An organization in the thick of stage 2 is very vulnerable. Tall walls between departments weaken crisis-handling capability. If you're in stage 2, you have to act soon (more on what to do in a moment).

Stage 3, delegation, presents severe networking problems. In this stage, the autonomy crisis has been solved by organizing the company into autonomous profit centers. This may solve the networking problem *within* each unit because each one contains multiple functions under the unified command of a general manager. But the networking problem doesn't go away; it's pushed up to the next level: No networking takes place *between* profit centers. That's the nature of the control crisis wrought by stage 3 success. The stage 3 organization is very vulnerable because it lacks crisis-handling bridges between profit centers. You have to act soon. Bridges must be established *before* crisis occurs. Once it hits, it's too late.

At first, stage 4, coordination, doesn't suffer from the same networking limitations as stages 2 and 3. The control crisis from stage 3 is solved in stage 4 by reorganizing and creating *formal* bridges between divisions. This works, but I prefer *informal* solutions. Informal solutions are adaptable, flexible, and don't take on a life of their own. Formal solutions become rigid and long outlive their original purpose. Indeed, the red tape crisis arising in stage 4 is produced by a rigid network-stifling bureaucracy. Coordination increases crisis-handling ability with formal bridges, and you still have to encourage informal bridges.

Stage 5, downsizing, is a special situation. In a sense, downsizing is a crisis itself, quite apart from the crisis of red tape it resolves. Downsizing severs relationships. Too often, key bridgers are let go or forced into retirement. Even when bridges haven't been destroyed through downsizing, those who are left are so overwhelmed that bridging activities are given short shrift. Even though you're preoccupied with many other problems, it's essential that you take the time to reconstitute the bridges between groups.

In stage 6, networking, the overload crisis created by downsizing is solved by adopting the new philosophy, the networking concepts in this book. What you can do in this stage is aid the process. Arrange for training and skill-building workshops centered around networking and relationship management. Help create a climate and context that empowers you and your people to build and maintain the relationships all of you need to get your jobs done.

What You Can Do *Soon*

Once you've figured out which stage your organization is in, you're ready to take action. Bridges are so important to an organization's ability to handle crisis that you should emphasize bridge building. If you're in stage 2 (direction), for example, you need bridges to span the boundaries created by a departmentalized structure. If you're in stage 3 (delegation), you need bridges to unite autonomous units in concerted effort. If you're in stage 5 (downsizing), you need bridges to link the broken pieces left by restructuring. And, if you're in stage 6 (networking), you need bridge building as part of your network of teams.

What you can do *soon* is encourage the organization to build crisis-handling bridges. But remember that *forced* cooperation doesn't work well. You can't mandate cooperation. To get the crisis-handling benefits of bridges, you have to find a way to *indirectly* encourage their formation long before you actually need them. Fortunately, the bridges that solve the bottleneck problem I talked about in Chapter 5 can serve double duty. Bridges that bust bottlenecks enable the organization to handle crisis as well.

I recommend that you create a multifunctional crisis task force, no matter what stage you're in. Because a crisis is always just around the corner, you can justify creating a task force even when crisis isn't imminent. Charge the task force with the job of mapping stages of development and their crises and formulating a plan to handle them. Make sure the task force reviews and considers the many bridge-building techniques I presented in Chapter 5, as well as the networking approach to managing diversity (Chapter 7).

Don't keep the task force a secret or allow its existence to be interpreted as a cause for alarm. Tell your people about it and why it exists. Educate them on the concept of the organizational life cycle and predictable crises. Make education one of the task force's chief responsibilities.

You may find festering conflicts between groups that already exist and obstruct change efforts. If so, you may have to address this conflict before you can go on. Organizational consultant Rosemarie Barbeau told me about a great exercise for helping warring groups work out their differences.[25] I've since used it to help groups understand and overcome their differences. It's called *mirroring.* Each group, privately, writes flip charts answering four questions: (1) How do we see ourselves? (2) How do we think the other group sees us? (3) How do we see the other group? (4) What would we like the relationship to be? The two groups are brought together, and the charts are put up on the walls. "How we see ourselves" is placed next to "how they see us," for example. The comparisons are eye-opening. No one can deny the problems when the data are available for everyone to see. After large-group discussions, small groups formed from members of each conflicting group meet and work out solutions to improve their relationships in the future.

What You Can Do
in the *Long Run*

What you can do in the long run is to consider changes in organizational design that will encourage network building. To do so, I recommend that you "piggyback" on changes made for other reasons. The practice of multifunctional project-based teams, for example, should be adopted for multiple reasons, only one of which is improved crisis handling. Multifunctional teams boost innovation, cut time to market, increase responsiveness to customers, *and* induce widespread bridge building. By design, a multifunctional team includes people from diverse disciplines, functions, and departments; getting these people together on the same team builds bridges.

Find ways to reward cooperation and bridge building. Some competition between groups may be healthy, but too much impedes the formation of cooperative links. Compensation is an important action lever. If you want two groups to cooperate, tie rewards to their combined performance. Even investment bankers—avid promoters of the cult of the deal—recognize the benefits of group-level bonus systems.[26]

Numbers and proportions play roles in managing intergroup relationships, just as they do in managing diversity (Chapter 7). If you're smart about it, you can improve bridge building *and* manage diversity at the same time. As a general rule, groups of equal size have more cross-group interaction than groups of unequal size. The larger a group is, the less likely its members will interact with outsiders. When the opportunity arises to change group size, create favorable numbers and proportions by balancing groups.

Demographics—age, seniority, ethnicity, gender, and so forth—also play roles in the likelihood of interaction between groups. If members of two groups are similar, it's more likely that they'll interact (the similarity principle). Over the long run, you can create a more conducive context for bridges by balancing the demographics of various groups.

We know that physical layout influences interaction (see Chapters 5 and 6). Bridge building is hampered by separation and distance. Often, correcting problems caused by physical layout is a long-term proposition. The law firm I featured in Chapter 4, for example, grew so rapidly that it occupied several floors in its original office building. The firm's leaders clearly recognized the obstacles created by physical separation, but they had to wait until better office space could be found and remodeled. Eventually, the firm moved to a new location and designed an open-office layout.

Here's my most radical suggestion: Engineer a jump to stage 6, networking. Human beings can't skip stages of development, but organizations can. Doing so can save you the pain, strife, and turmoil caused by following the traditional path of organizational development. GE got to stage 6 by moving through all six stages of organizational development, including the agony of downsizing (see Chapter 15). But other companies, like Capital Partners, adopted the network form of organization right from the start (see Chapter 5). They, like others, skipped the crises of autonomy, control, and red tape, jumping right to the networking mode of organization. Many companies are trying to do the same right now. Is it possible for your company?

Finally, keep in mind that crises are predictable outcomes of organizational change and development. Crises are inevitable. Forewarned is forearmed: Knowing that a new crisis will come—even if you don't know what shape it will take—prepares you to better respond to it.

PART 3

Managing Relationships and Networks outside the Organization

9

Finding
Good People
(or Changing Jobs)

Cultivate networks, maintain visibility.
PAUL HIRSCH
*Pack Your Own Parachute: How to
Survive Mergers, Takeovers, and Other
Corporate Disasters*[1]

The concept of networking got its start in the context of job seeking and head hunting. To some, that's all networking means. By now, however, you know that networking is something far, far more. I'm not implying, however, that the traditional use of networking is obsolete. Far from it. With the new career realities we all face today—the end of job security as a clause in the new implicit employer-employee contract—knowing how to network to find jobs is a required survival skill.[2] But networking today in the context of jobs does mean something more than the traditional (mis)conceptions. Networking *smart* to find good jobs means using your personal networks responsibly and ethically. And it means using the same resourcefulness when you're on the "other side" of the fence, using your networking skills to find good people for jobs in your company. With the increased rate of job hopping in the new business order, everyone must become more and more adept at using networks to find good people.

My personal education about the role of networks in matching people and jobs began when I was a job seeker, tapping my personal contacts to find a good job. Given the new career realities, this is a good place to start. It was 1980 and I stood before the great abyss all Ph.D.

185

candidates must confront sooner or later: impending graduation and the need to find gainful employment. In fact, as the first member of my Ph.D. cohort at Northwestern University to seriously consider a job as a reasonable alternative to perpetual education, I was confronting the abyss sooner than most. I applied the final touches to my dissertation about networks in the world of finance[3] and set out on a job search that ended a few months later with a fine position in a management consulting firm in Washington, D.C.

To tell you how I got from Northwestern to my consulting job, however, I have to tell you about a piano. My landlord at the time, Allan Farmer, who was also a faculty member on my doctoral dissertation committee, bought a used upright. And, of course, he needed help moving it. Though I reluctantly offered my assistance, I would have jumped at the opportunity had I known then that this piano-moving affair would supply the chance encounter that would lead me to Washington, D.C., and a steady paycheck. For along with a few captive graduate students, Al had enlisted the aid of an old friend, Joe Schwartz, who had been a fellow graduate student years ago at the University of Chicago. As we wrestled with the piano, Joe listened to my story. When he heard I would consider relocating, he offered to send my résumé to Dave Murray, a friend from college days at the University of California, now the head of a management consulting firm in Washington, D.C. "Dave's probably not hiring," Joe said, "but he knows everyone who's anyone in Washington. He'll know whom to put you in touch with." It seemed like a long shot, but I had nothing to lose, so I gave my résumé to Joe.

This seemingly insignificant encounter triggered a quick series of events. Joe sent my résumé to Dave. Dave looked it over and passed it to his partner Alice Caprelli. One of Alice's senior project managers had just given notice, and she needed a replacement right away. My credentials fit. She called and arranged a preliminary interview. We hit it off immediately. Before I went back for the second round of interviews, however, Dave checked me out. Now the chain worked in reverse. Dave called Joe. Joe called Al. Al supplied Dave with a personal reference on my behalf. (Dave didn't know it, but I was also using the information chain to get the inside scoop on him and his firm.) After I completed the second round, Alice hired me on the spot. Months before I graduated, I landed a good-paying job, working for a great boss in a young, exciting company. I stayed at the firm for several years, eventually rising to become a partner with Dave and Alice.

My story is not unusual, particulars aside. Most people find jobs and most employers find good people via personal contacts. Outplacement firm Drake Beam Morin reports that almost 70 percent of its candidates in the 1980s found jobs through personal contacts.[4] My story illustrates all the elements common to the experiences of those who use personal contacts to find good people or good jobs:

- You never know who will give you the key lead.

- The person who gives you the key lead is not someone you know well or even talk with often.

- You get the job only if you deserve it. The old adage "It's not what you know but whom you know" is only half correct. It's what you know *and* whom you know.

- You're more likely to be satisfied and paid well in a job you find through your personal contacts.

You *can* find good people (or a good job) by using the traditional methods—classified advertisements, direct mail campaigns, job fairs, headhunters, professional search firms—but study after study shows that you're much more likely to find good people (or get a good job) by tapping personal contacts.[5]

Just about everyone uses personal contacts to find jobs. According to the National Longitudinal Survey of Youth (which tracks people throughout their lives), blue-collar workers are more likely to use personal connections than white-collar workers. In his classic study of how managers, professionals, and technical workers find jobs, sociologist Mark Granovetter discovered that personal contacts is the preferred method of job finding regardless of religion, ethnic background, or level of education.[6] Age, however, does make a difference. Two-thirds of those over 34 use personal contacts, compared with just less than half of those under 34.[7] As you mature and move up the career ladder, personal contacts and networking skills become more and more essential for personal and professional success.

Why Use Networks?

People don't just find jobs through personal contacts—they find *better* jobs. Those who use personal contacts are more likely to be very satisfied with the jobs they get.[8] Job seekers who get jobs tailor-made for them are much more likely to have used personal ties. And, the higher a job seeker's income, the more likely it is that he or she used personal contacts.[9]

Smart employers know that they benefit from job networking as well as their employees. At Xerox, the black employee caucus groups I described in Chapter 7 used their informal ties to recruit new employees.[10] It was good for the minority employees; it was good for Xerox. There are plenty of good reasons to recruit through personal contacts. Job "stayers" (those who haven't considered looking for new jobs) are more likely to have found their jobs through personal contacts than did job "movers."[11] Personal contacts not only help employers get the right person for the job but they help find a person who is more likely to stay in the job. Good managers make referral networks an integral part of their personal intelligence networks (Chapter 3).

Why are personal contacts so helpful? Networks solve an age-old problem. Labor markets are notoriously inefficient: Buyers and sellers have a hard time getting together. Good employers and good job candidates often reside in different business and social circles, making it difficult to find each other. Using personal contacts is an efficient means for both sides to bridge these circles. Classified advertisements waste everyone's time by producing lots of inappropriate leads. At my consulting firm, for example, we always found the best candidates and made the best hires by using our personal networks. On the rare occasions when we suffered from mental lapses, we experimented with the classifieds. The classifieds always generated a deluge of applicants— well into the hundreds—and not one was the right person for the job.

Personal networks work because they provide better information about job seekers and jobs. Both sides get more and higher-quality information from personal contacts. "...[a] friend," says Granovetter, "gives more than a simple job-description—he [or she] may also indicate if prospective workmates are congenial, if the boss is neurotic, and if the company is moving forward or is stagnant."[12] Similarly, an employer who uses personal contacts gets insights and information that never appear on the candidate's résumé. Recall that Dave and I both used our personal contacts to get the inside story on each other!

What Types of Connections Are Important?

It may surprise you to learn that the most useful personal contacts are *weak* connections. Successful job seekers often use old contacts that have lain forgotten and dormant for years. Weak ties—an old school acquaintance, a former neighbor from the old neighborhood, or an acquaintance at a previous employer—are usually better sources of information about job openings than your strong ties—close friends, immediate coworkers, family. Why? You already know what your strong ties know; they don't have *new* information. Your *weak ties* have the new information you need. Strong ties *can* supply good job leads, but because you travel in the same social and business circles, you probably already know about them. Weak ties, however, are bridges between worlds; weak ties are privy to information about job openings you don't already know about. Indeed, weak ties are so effective as information conduits that Granovetter called this phenomenon "the *strength* of weak ties."[13]

Work-related contacts—the new employer, an acquaintance in the hiring company, an acquaintance in another company—are used twice as often as family and friends to find out about job openings. Employees already working for the hiring firm—inside contacts—are prime sources of information about job openings in the firm. As shown in Table 9-1, at least one out of four successful job seekers used an *inside* contact. Finding a contact inside the hiring firm is a very good strategy.

Referral networks operate differently for men and women. Men use inside contacts more frequently than women do (Table 9-1). There is also a same-sex referral bias: 87 percent of male job seekers used men as contacts, and 70 percent of women were referred by women. This bias is especially striking for managerial and professional positions. Eighty-two percent of men who find managerial or professional jobs used contacts with other men, while only 54 percent of women who secured similar jobs used contacts with women. This difference reflects, at least in part, the fact that men hold managerial and professional jobs in disproportionate numbers and are part of the infamous old-boys' network. Women who seek positions as managers and professionals, therefore, have a tougher time tapping into the personal contact network. If you're looking for good people who are women or minorities, you have to make special efforts.

Table 9-1. Men and Women Referred by Employees of the Hiring Firm

	Men	Women	All Workers
Managerial and professional	31%	20%	25%
Technical	25%	15%	20%
Sales	36%	28%	31%
Administrative support/clerical	42%	31%	33%
Service	39%	26%	32%

SOURCE: National Longitudinal Survey of Youth, reported in James D. Montgomery, "Social Networks and Persistent Inequality in the Labor Market," manuscript, Northwestern University, Department of Economics, 1992. Table reprinted with permission of the author.

It's important at this time to discuss the difference between referrals and references. A referral puts you and a job candidate together; it isn't a recommendation or testimony to the candidate's qualifications and character. A reference, in contrast, is a personal endorsement: The reference gives a personal evaluation of the candidate, attesting to credentials and suitability for the position. Although a referral can also be a reference, don't confuse the two.

Weak ties—those bridges to other circles—are sources of *referrals*. They are your eyes and ears. They let you know about job candidates and they let job seekers know about openings, but they don't testify to qualifications or requirements. One reason weak ties are likely to give information to a job seeker is that one doesn't ask for much—a job seeker doesn't ask for a job or a personal reference, only factual information.

References, unlike referrals, are put under pressure: You ask people to take a stand and put their reputations on the line. If it works out, it reflects well on them; if it doesn't, it may tarnish their reputations or jeopardize relationships. You won't get the job if you don't deserve it. Getting in the door is half the battle, but you must have a good product—you—to sell once you get in.

The Dark Side: A Cautionary Tale

Most of the time, getting jobs through personal contacts is good for everyone: job seekers land better jobs, employers fill positions with the right people, the number of mismatches is reduced, and organizations function more smoothly. If networking is done on a grand scale, it helps the labor market work efficiently and society benefits. But networking has a dark side as well, of which all employers must be aware.

Consider a medium-size manufacturing firm studied by network expert Ronald Burt.[14] Its main manufacturing plant is racked by internal conflict and hostility. Workers resist management initiatives. In fact, workers hate management, so much so that the CEO and his family have received bomb threats. The entire plant seems to be governed by forces outside management's control. It is. And the reason is rooted in the ways personal contacts were used to find and hire new workers.

When the plant first opened, workers were recruited from the surrounding communities via local community leaders. Job applicants secured employment by using their connections with doctors, ministers, priests, teachers, local businesspeople, and political leaders. The result was a work force firmly rooted in the local community and strongly influenced by outside opinion, expectations, and social norms. Things changed. Over time, new hires came from the families of people already working for the company. Current employees became the primary source of referrals and personal references for new hires. Community leaders were rarely used anymore for referrals or references. As a result, the work force became a little society of its own, inbred and detached from outside influences and public opinion. Informal leaders inside the firm replaced community leaders. Hostile factions arose, composed of family and friends with close personal allegiances and sympathies. Each faction has its own agenda—which didn't include the best interests of the company at large.

It's a well-known fact that people tend to refer others like themselves. This is yet another instance of the similarity principle I described in Chapter 2. In the case of this firm, the similarity principle created a hostile workforce that undermined management. But it was management's ignorance of basic networking principles that allowed it to happen. By abrogating its responsibility to *manage* the referral and recruitment process, management allowed the excessive use of family contacts and the withering of community leader contacts. A managed balance of the two sources of referrals and references—inside contacts and outside contacts—would have averted the firm's current catastrophe.

What You Can Do *Now*

Your current personal contacts are the raw material for a job-search network. What you can do now is to *organize* this raw material by starting a database of personal contacts. Format doesn't matter. A rolodex, index cards, paper files, or a computerized database will do, as long as the result is an easy-to-use, easy-to-update inventory of personal contacts. Even if you love your job and have no intention of job-hopping, start your database now. The same is true for finding good people. The perfect time to organize a network database is when you *don't* need it. Remember that it's not a question of "if" you'll need it, it's a question of "when." This is the era of job *in*security. The increased rate of job jumping in the new business order means it's mandatory to know how to network smart to find jobs and to find good people.

Right now you have more contacts than you may realize. The typical professional knows an estimated 3500 people! Skeptical? I was when I first heard this estimate. The reason is that we can't think in the abstract of but a small fraction of our personal contacts. Memories

Table 9-2. Your Primary Contact List

Friends and acquaintances
Relatives and in-laws
Former employers
Fellow workers from previous jobs
Colleagues
Bankers and brokers
Accountants
Lawyers and paralegals
Entrepreneurs and venture capitalists
High school friends, alumni, and teachers
College friends, alumni, and teachers
Graduate school friends, alumni, and teachers
Community and civic leaders
Church, parish, synagogue members
Sales personnel and marketing representatives
Journalists and reporters
Doctors, dentists, nurses
Consultants
Insurance agents and brokers
Real estate agents and brokers
Officers and administrators of professional associations
Health club members
Social club members
Secretaries and receptionists

---

must be prompted by a specific question, event, or unexpected encounter with a long-forgotten acquaintance. Just to prompt you for a moment, consider the list in Table 9-2, which Ellie Workman, director of Alumni Career Management at the University of Chicago's Graduate School of Business, gives to job seekers. (I've added several of my own recommendations.)

As you skim the list, you realize that you *do* know lots of people. And this is just a list of your *primary* contacts, those in your *first-order zone* of contacts. (As I described in Chapter 2, your first-order zone contains the people you know personally.) We know from the fifth networking principle—it's a small world—that you also have a much, much larger number of contacts in your *second-order zone* (the primary contacts of *your* primary contacts). Considering together your primary and secondary contacts, you can begin to comprehend the vastness of the network of contacts you're connected to. This enormous network is an excellent conduit for job information.

Successful matches of good jobs and good people often involve long chains of primary and secondary contacts. Consider, for example, the chain leading to my management consulting job in Washington, D.C. It began with a direct contact with Allan Farmer, and then ran through three indirect links: Me to Allan to Joe to Dave to Alice. Often, secondary contacts are your ultimate destinations: They have the job information or jobs you want. Even though you can't build an inventory of secondary contacts (you don't know them yet), it's important to remember that you do indeed have a large number of secondary contacts, and you can find and activate them via networking.

The beginning of your networking database is on your desk: your rolodex (or an electronic version of it). Who's in it? Is it up to date? Have you lost contact with anyone? Have you committed the cardinal sin of networking—removing and throwing away a rolodex card? If you edit your rolodex so it contains only active contacts, place the inactive entries in a secondary rolodex (or electronic file). One day you'll need it. Never throw out an old rolodex, or delete an entry, especially when you change employers—past workmates are a prime source of job leads and job candidates.

What other lists do you have or can you get? School yearbooks, conference proceedings, company phone directories, employee rosters, committee or team assignments, membership directories of trade and professional associations—collect and keep every list you come across. Every list of names is raw material for your networking database. Scan each list and make a special note of the people you know.

As you build and update a database, it's helpful to record at least the following information:

- Person's full name (and nickname)
- Title, position, name of company
- Phone and fax numbers (office and home)
- Address (office and home)
- How you do know this person? (referred by another person, coworker, fellow member of an association, met at conference, etc.)

If you get in touch with the person as part of a job or candidate search, add:

- Date of contact
- Results of contact—information about job openings and referrals to third parties (secondary contacts)
- Dates and action for follow-up, thank you notes

What You Can Do *Soon*

Your personal network of contacts grows naturally over time. What you can do soon is speed up the process by consciously making new contacts. By this I don't mean becoming a glad-handing nuisance flitting from person to person; I mean becoming more *aware* of the networking potential in every situation. Those who network smart use decorum and discretion. Many times, business contacts are best formed while you're doing something else, a by-product of the day-to-day rounds of business and social life. What you can do soon, therefore, is adopt the positive mental outlook of the networking leader: the person who understands the world as a vast network of relationships.

Here's a helpful technique. For the next two weeks, jot down on your calendar or day timer (or electronic equivalent) all the people you meet or talk with during the course of each day. Indicate the "networking potential" of each contact: Is he or she an inside contact or outside contact? (An inside contact is someone you know inside your company.) If the person's an inside contact, is she or he well-connected? People in sales, marketing, purchasing, and customer service are excellent contacts for jobs and candidates outside the company; in their daily routines, they make contact with a wide and diverse range of outside people. In contrast, those who never get out of the office are poor sources of outside contacts. At the end of the two weeks, draw up a ledger of your contacts and their networking potential. On the left side, list all your outside contacts and your inside contacts with extensive external networks. On the right side, list those with limited or narrow ranges of outside contacts. If the left column is considerably shorter than the right, you have a network deficit and need to adopt a deliberate strategy for building contacts.

Mobility is the key to network building. Mobility keeps you in the swim of things; it provides you with new venues, new places and people, new opportunities to make contacts. Volunteer to take a temporary assignment to another group, division, or subsidiary. Join new committees and teams, especially those with representatives from other functions or departments. Attend and participate in company-sponsored business and social events. Avoid a back-office assignment that's devoid of networking potential. The worst thing you can do is toil in the company's underground and limit your own contact-making opportunities. Richard Thain, late dean of External Affairs at the University of Chicago, said it well in his paraphrase of an elegy written by British poet Thomas Gray: "Do not remain a flower that blooms unseen and wastes its fragrance on the desert air."[15]

Select an outside meeting or conference that you can attend in the next few months. Management seminars, professional conferences, trade association meetings, trade shows, and other business-related gatherings are natural candidates, but consider trying something different. Remember: the point is to meet *different* people from *diverse* backgrounds; these are the *weak ties* that bridge different business and social circles. Try a town or village meeting, charitable event, fashion show, school-board meeting, art lecture, networking club, or any organized event where you can naturally meet and mix. Contact making should remain a by-product of the event, so pick an event where your principal reason for participating is interest, education, duty, or simple curiosity.

What You Can Do in the *Long Run*

Most of us set sights on a long-term career objective. Its outlines might be hazy, but we have a sense of trajectory, direction, purpose. It might be owning your own business, running a division, working for the ideal company, gaining political office, switching careers, working in another country, or making a major career change. My long-term objective, for example, was to secure a faculty position at a top university. To get there, however, I first had to go someplace else. I needed a halfway house. For me, that turned out to be Harvard Business School. (No insult intended by applying the term halfway house!) I traded my consulting job for a two-year position as a research fellow (a position I found, of course, through a weak tie). My halfway house enabled me to gain the experience and contacts I needed to reenter the world of academia in a way that was positive for me.

Halfway houses and intermediate steps bridge the gap between where you are and where you want to be. The critical network concept is *targeted networking*. Targeted networking is the gradual, long-term development of a sequence of personal contacts that moves you toward your long-run work objective. Targeted networking puts you on potential employers' "radar screens" and identifies you as a promising job candidate for the future.

Many people leave long-term networking to chance. Chance, as we know from Chapter 6, plays an important role, but you don't have to leave it all to luck and happenstance. What you can do in the *long run* is make targeted networking a deliberate long-term career strategy.

The first step in targeted networking is to identify holes in your personal network. Holes are gaps between your current job and targeted jobs. How wide is the gap? How far away is your ideal job? Do you have contacts already in the company or industry, or do you need to find a point of entry? Will you need a halfway house?

Major career changes require building a network of contacts to a new occupational world. Even if you're well-connected in your current line of work, connections to job opportunities in the new one may be sparse. What types of information will you need to find out about job opportunities? Who is likely to have the information? To start building a network of contacts to aid a future move, consider:

- Regular attendance and participation in industry or career-related meetings, conferences, and seminars in your field of choice

- Intermediate job changes that move you closer to your ultimate job

- Participation in business, social, or health clubs frequented by people in your targeted field

- Relocations or reassignments, temporary or permanent, that put you in the vicinity of the people you want to meet

No matter how you build contacts, it's important to keep a record of the contacts you make. Often the key lead is supplied by a chance encounter with a long-forgotten acquaintance. Memory fades, so improve the odds by maintaining an inventory of contacts. And chance is fickle, so stay in circulation and increase the odds that you'll encounter the right people at the right time.

10

Building Relationships with Customers and Clients

The people at Mark Twain Bancshares of St. Louis, Missouri, know how to build relationships with customers.[2] They do so in a very innovative way. Mark Twain is a $2.2 billion regional bank with 28 locations in Missouri, Illinois, and Kansas. If Mark Twain were operated like most banks, all its locations would be mere bank branches. Instead, Mark Twain is organized into 14 distinct banking units, each with its own president and advisory board of directors. Add to these 14 local boards Mark Twain's holding company board, Commercial and Industrial Board, Medical Industries Board, Trust and Financial Services board, and Monday Board (made up of long-time advisors who meet the first Monday of each month), and you get a grand total of over 300 directors!

This may seem like a cumbersome and unwieldy number of directors, but the arrangement works extremely well. Mark Twain is organized this way because the founders know how to network smart and
build strong customer ties. Each bank draws its directors from the
local community. Most are owners of successful small and medium-
size businesses; all directors *must be* customers of the bank. "Other
banks won't take a director if he does business with the bank," Mark
Twain founder and emeritus board chair Adam Aronson told me.
"Mark Twain won't take a director *unless* he does business with the
bank."[3] In fact, lending to directors is *encouraged,* not frowned upon.
Having major customers as directors is good for business. Board membership solidifies the relationship between Mark Twain and its clients,
and that boosts volume: Directors are prolific and reliable sources of
business. And the directors become avid promoters of Mark Twain,
encouraging friends, neighbors, and associates to do business with the
bank.

Having local business people as directors is also good business
because the 300+ directors make an impressive intelligence network.
They link Mark Twain with local communities, keeping the bankers
abreast of local trends and developments. Director input improves
loan qualification. With 300+ directors spread throughout the market,
it's almost certain they know any loan applicant. "The chance that they
won't know the guy you want to lend to is remote," Aronson said.[4]
Local directors can attest to an applicant's creditworthiness, business
reputation, and personal character. It's a great way to get the information you need that doesn't show up on an application form. And, since
directors invest as shareholders in Mark Twain, they're unlikely to let
friendship or personal sympathies with an applicant override a sound
business decision.

Skeptical? Mark Twain's networking philosophy sounds great, but
does it influence performance? Well, the numbers speak volumes. "In
terms of the growth rate of the bank," says executive vice president
Peter F. Benoist in a *Bank Marketing* interview, "there is no question in
our mind that the advisory boards have been one of the primary reasons for our success, if not the primary reason for our success."[5] Mark
Twain has used its unique director arrangement since its founding 28
years ago, and assets have grown from $4 million in 1964 to $2.23 billion in 1992. Earnings have grown over the last five years at a com-
pound growth rate of 19.0 percent, and year-to-date return on equity
for the second quarter 1992 is 16.85 percent. Loan quality is superb.
Nonperforming assets were only 2.0 percent of loans in 1991, and
that's dropped to 1.79 percent by the second quarter of 1992. This out-

standing record puts Mark Twain at the same level as the best per-
forming banks in the country. Mark Twain's networking strategy pays
off handsomely.

The Mark Twain story is a fitting introduction to the main theme of
this chapter: *relationship marketing*. Mark Twain bankers are masters at
building strong ties with customers. In this chapter, I describe the
growing trend toward relationship marketing and describe how many
companies build strong relationships. I conclude the chapter with
advice on how to diagnose your customer relationships and build
strong ties; as always, I tell you what you can do now, what you can
do soon, and what you can do in the long run.

The Rise of Relationship Marketing

The growing importance of relationship marketing is a profound
transformation in ways of thinking about customers: It represents the
shift from a product (or deal) orientation to a strong relationship orientation. Relationship marketing—building strong customer partnerships—is the marketing trend of the 1990s. You can see evidence
everywhere that this is true. Companies with the best-rated sales
forces, for example, such as Hewlett-Packard, Scott Paper, and Hyatt
Hotels, all make building customer relationships a top priority.[6]

Marketing authorities Philip Kotler of Northwestern and Theodore
Levitt of Harvard both predict that relationship marketing will
become ever more important in the future.[7] But relationship marketing
is still experimental. Many marketers still stick stubbornly to the mis-
guided teachings of the cult of the deal. Keep your distance from customers, they say, be wary. It's a zero-sum game out there; the customer's gain is your loss. Those who network smart know better:
"Build good relationships," advises Kotler, "and profitable transactions will follow."[8]

The celebrated partnership between marketing legends Procter &
Gamble and Wal-Mart is a great example of a successful conversion in
ways of doing business.[9] "Before 1985," says former P&G vice president of sales Lou Pritchett in a *Supermarket Business* interview, "no
executive above field sales manager had ever called on the Wal-Mart
Co."[10] Now P&G has a 37-person multifunctional team living at Wal-
Mart hometown Bentonville, Arkansas. And Wal-Mart has its own special team dedicated to working with its P&G counterpart. The joint
teams work at various levels—organizational, operations, and sys-

tems—to strengthen the company-to-company bond and achieve mutual benefits. This is a splendid example of what marketing experts Jan Heide and George John call "joint action" in customer-supplier relationships. "Organizational boundaries become interpenetrated," they say, "by the integration of activities as the supplier becomes involved in activities that traditionally are considered the buyer's responsibility and vice versa."[11] In other words, a true partnership.

Why are relationships like the P&G/Wal-Mart alliance profitable? There are many good reasons, but I think they boil down to two bedrock truths:

1. *Old customers are better than new customers.* New customers are hard and expensive to get. It costs 3 to 5 times as much to get a new customer as it does to keep an old one.[12] And steady customers provide a stream of revenues. "Loyal customers—the ones not lost because of bad service—"say William Davidow and Bro Uttal in *Total Customer Service,* "are worth thousands of dollars in sales over the life of their relationship with a company."[13] Abide by the ancient wisdom: "Forsake not an old friend; for the new is not comparable to him."[14]

2. *Strong ties are solid competitive barriers.* Strong customer ties blunt a competitor's efforts to steal your customers. They slam shut the marketing window, as Donald Potter puts it in his award-winning article, "Success under Fire."[15] And these strong ties make it difficult for competitors to use the same relationship strategy. Excellent service, say Davidow and Uttal, gives you a *self-perpetuating advantage* and puts your competitors in a situation of *self-perpetuating disadvantage.*[16]

It's usually unwise to make a blanket recommendation, and I'm not making one here. Relationship marketing isn't for everyone or for all situations. Building relationships is premature and wasted effort if your product or service isn't great to begin with, if you haven't made investments in a relationship culture, or if you've targeted the wrong market segment (one that just doesn't want such strong ties).[17] For some customers, for example, it's possible to provide *too much* service, levels they don't want and would rather not pay for. The proliferation of self-service (gasoline, food, routine banking, etc.) over the second half of this century is a case in point. In an ironic twist of fate, Japanese consumers now complain about excessive attention to personal service (such as painstakingly overwrapped purchases).[18] Despite these important exceptions, however, in many situations building strong relationships is still the right marketing prescription.

Social and Business Ties: The Embeddedness Phenomena

At the heart of relationship marketing is a great sociological truth: Business and personal ties become intermixed in a long-term relationship. This phenomenon is what sociologist Mark Granovetter calls *embeddedness:* Business decisions are enmeshed and entwined in networks of social relationships.[19] Embeddedness is exactly what cultists of the deal abhor; they despise the mix of personal, social, and business ties. For them, business deals should take place in an "interpersonal vacuum."[20] But all good businesspeople know that embeddedness is a natural part of the real business world. Networking smart means making embeddedness a marketing objective.

Direct selling—the primary distribution channel for such organizations as Tupperware, Amway, A. L. Williams (insurance), and Mary Kay—is a great example of the embeddedness phenomenon. The direct selling industry is huge. It sold $14.1 *billion* of goods and services in 1992, according to the Direct Selling Association. These sales were generated through an estimated 5.5 million people.[21] A. L. Williams, an insurance company, was selling more term life insurance by 1986 than Prudential![22]

Sociologist Nicole Woolsey Biggart captured the essence of direct selling in her book *Charismatic Capitalism.* "Whereas bureaucratic firms seek to exclude nonwork social relations in order to control workers," she says, "the direct selling industry pursues profit in the opposite way, *by making social networks serve business ends.*"[23] Consider, for example, how a typical "home party" works.[24] A company sales representative or demonstrator works with the party hostess to organize a home party. The hostess identifies and invites guests to her (sometimes his) home for the party. (Many of these guests are past hostesses who gave parties attended by the current hostess.) The representative exhibits products, answers questions, and emphasizes that the hostess will receive bigger and better gifts when guests buy more and/or book a future party themselves. Guests know that purchases benefit the hostess through gifts and sales commissions.

How, exactly, do direct selling companies make social networks serve business ends? Harry Davis and Jonathan Frenzen, two of my colleagues at the University of Chicago, analyzed in depth how purchasing decisions are influenced by social ties at home parties.[25] Here's what they found out:

- Guests with stronger social ties with the hostess are more likely to make a purchase. (The strength of a social tie reflects the degree of intimacy, closeness, help, and assistance between guest and hostess.)

- Guests with stronger social ties with the demonstrator are more likely to make a purchase.

- Guests who have a "social obligation" to the hostess are more likely to make a purchase. A guest "owes" the hostess if the current hostess has attended more parties given by the guest, compared with the number of parties the guest has attended that were given by the current hostess.

The overlap of social and business ties in home-party purchasing is but an instance of the common embeddedness phenomenon. MCI's Friends and Family long-distance discount program, for example, is an interesting twist on the embeddedness idea. I use the program, so I can tell you how it works from a customer's point of view. When I signed up, I gave MCI a list of my frequently called numbers. I get a 20 percent discount on calls to anyone on the list who is also an MCI customer. With my permission, MCI contacts those on the list who aren't current MCI customers and invites them to join MCI as their long-distance service. In principle, MCI's program works just like home parties: nonbusiness social networks are tapped to increase sales. The results are impressive: Over 10 million customers signed up with the Friends and Family program in just 22 months.[26] (By the way, I've never had the complaint, as AT&T implies in its advertising, that letting MCI call people on my list is some sort of violation of relationships. If my friends don't want to sign up when MCI calls, they just say so.)

Sociologist James Coleman coined the term *social capital* to describe how business ties, in general, are embedded in and supported by social networks.[27] Credit unions are great examples. These cooperative savings and loan associations are founded on "common bonds"—shared neighborhood, employer, or ethnic ties. Indeed, common bonds (or social capital) must be demonstrated before a new credit union can be legally chartered. The New York diamond market is one of Coleman's favorite examples of a business institution built on rich social capital. Expensive diamonds are exchanged with nothing more than a handshake because ethnicity, religion, and ties of blood and marriage (rich social capital) create a high level of trust and confidence.

When I talk about using embeddedness to manage customer relationships, my advice is often met with skepticism or suspicion. One common objection I hear is that social ties *confound* business relationships; social ties muddy up hard-nosed, rational decision making. But this objection is based on the erroneous assumption that business decisions are made in an interpersonal vacuum. Quite the opposite is the truth: *All economic decisions are supported by social relationships.*[28] Social ties are not obstacles to rational decisions; they permit business decisions to be made. A rational decision maker would *want* to get the assurance of high levels of social capital—it's better than a written guarantee of conscientious performance. The economic benefits of social relationships are always there. Mark Twain Bancshares, we know, obtains the hard business benefits of superior loan origination and qualification by mixing social and business ties.

A second common objection I hear is that social ties with customers create *conflicts of interest*. Simply put, a marketing manager or product engineer might become an advocate of the customer, putting the customer's interests ahead of the company's. *But customer advocacy is exactly what you want.* You want to place the customer's interests *first* in order to drive a strong customer orientation into the company's forebrain. Instead of compromising the company's interests, customer advocacy furthers your interests by putting customer needs in their rightful place.

The Spectrum of Relationships

Building relationships with customers, like all areas of networking, involves a *spectrum* of relationships. This spectrum, as I described in Chapter 2, varies from *weak ties* on one end to *strong ties* on the other.[29] A weak tie is the embodiment of the cult of the deal; in particular, it lacks the embeddedness phenomenon I talked about above. A strong tie is the opposite. It's a long-term commitment in which business ties are firmly embedded in layers of social relationships. Between the weak and strong extremes lie varying degrees of relationships.

STAR Industries, a national electrical equipment manufacturer, is a great example of incorporating the spectrum of relationships in a well-tailored marketing policy.[30] In June 1990 STAR rolled out its STAR Distributor Marketing Program. This was a grand departure from the strategy they had used throughout the company's history. "Prior to 1990," says STAR director of marketing Harry Michaelson, "we had a one-size-fits-all policy for our distribution. As the market grew and matured, we realized we couldn't continue to be all things to all people." The problem was one size *didn't* fit all; some distributors paid for services they didn't want, others wanted services they would pay for but couldn't get. STAR's solution: tailor-made relationships. STAR unbundled services and created four relationship categories, each reflecting different levels of needs, commitments, and service:

1. *One STAR.*   For a small distributor serving a small market, this option gives access to the full STAR product line and requires a small inventory commitment. Minimum services are provided. Salespeople don't call; the distributor places orders by phone or mail. Merchandising support and other services are available at additional cost.

2. *Two STAR.*   This option is for the distributor who needs access to a narrow product line. The distributor selects which products to stock, and access to additional products depends on commitment to invest in inventory. Services include field sales support (e.g., market planning, end user calls, training), sales support material (e.g., end user advertising, literature), merchandising and displays, quick shipments, and quantity discounts.

3. *Three STAR.*   This option gives full access to all STAR products. The distributor commits to support and inventory STAR's five core products plus at least 50 additional products, and to merchandise, display, and promote STAR. Like the Two STAR option, services include field sales support, sales support materials, merchandising and displays, but add merchandising distribution specialist service (personal service at the store level), 48-hour shipments, and more favorable pricing options.

4. *Four STAR.*   For the large, high-volume distributor who makes STAR its *exclusive* stocking supplier. The distributor must have purchased $50,000 or more of STAR products in the prior year (or year to date). The distributor agrees to merchandise, display, and promote STAR and to develop and implement an annual business marketing plan. Services include all *Three-STAR* services, no freight charges, no minimum billings, branch order packing service at no cost, more favorable pricing and return policies, cooperative advertising, and sales rebates.

Now distributors can work with STAR in ways that best suit their specific needs. If they want a weaker tie, they can choose the One-STAR or Two-STAR option; if they want a strong tie—a *partnership*—they can choose the Four-STAR option. Using the spectrum of options boosts STAR's sales. The market response is overwhelmingly positive. STAR overshot projections of distributors who took the Four-STAR option: quadruple the number of locations, triple the sales volume. Networking smart, like STAR, means using the *spectrum* of relationships to manage relationships with customers.

Diagnosing Relationships

Now for a touch of theory, but just a light touch. A little theory goes a long way. A little is helpful for diagnosing your customer relationships. Once diagnosed, you can better plan how to build relationships.

The relationship grid I introduced in Chapter 2 is a useful tool for understanding customer relationships.[31] I've reproduced it here in Figure 10-1, with some important additional features. As shown, the Grid compares your orientation along the spectrum of relationships against your customers'. Of course, you may use multiple marketing strategies or you may serve customer segments who have different purchasing strategies. The objective is to array *each* customer (or homogeneous customer segment) against the strategy you explicitly or implicitly use. You should do this for current *and* potential customers.

Type 1. Spot Market:
Deal-Deal Match

If you and your customer are located in the upper-left quadrant, both of you value deals above all. Because orientations match, this is a stable situation; both parties can achieve mutual satisfaction. Indeed, the

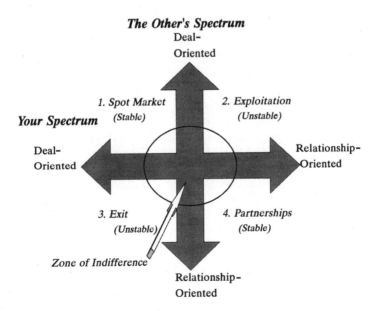

Figure 10-1. The relationship grid.

spot market deal mentality can be appropriate in some situations. Marketing expert Barbara Bund Jackson advises marketers to use "transaction marketing" when customers have a short time horizon and low switching costs (few investments in people, policies, and procedures). Relationship marketing, she argues, is costly and ineffective with such customers.[32] There's truth in her argument, and some marketers live happily in a deal-dominated world. If the deal mentality fits, use it. But consider the possibility that greater benefits may be obtained by becoming more relationship oriented.

Type 2. Exploitation:
Relationship-Deal Mismatch

Unhappiness reigns in the upper-right quadrant: You want relationships but your customers don't. This is the situation in which many marketers find themselves, and they often find themselves exploited by it. Relationship-oriented marketers make concessions and provide incentives as investments in long-run relationships. A marketer hopes customers will respond to these inducements, make similar investments in return, and develop a loyal, close relationship. If customers are deal-oriented, however, they'll grab the concessions and incentives but rebuff the marketer's advances. A loss-leader strategy, for example, just leads to losses, not repeat purchases.

You may feel powerless when faced with stubborn deal-oriented customers. In some cases, you may have to protect yourself by withdrawing from the exchange and finding new customers with more appropriate orientations. But don't give up too quickly on the possibility of building relationships with deal-oriented customers. It's rare when there isn't *some* opportunity to create value, find mutual benefits, and build stronger relationships. And, given the widespread trend toward external partnerships and alliances, more customers (and marketers) are beginning to see the light.

You can build relationships even for what may seem to be fleeting, one-shot encounters if you search for ways to *create real value* by linking transactions over time.[33] The objective is to make repeated purchases with you more attractive than shopping around every time. With extreme deal-oriented customers, your objective must be realistically modest, just some increase in the probability of repeated transactions. Here are some examples:

- Commercial bankers include an automatic rollover feature in certificates of deposit (CD) to make it easier for customers to renew CDs. Without the automatic feature, customers are more likely to shop around at renewal time.

- With its POWERSHIP program, Federal Express installs free computer equipment in customers' offices, hooking them directly with the courier's tracking system. Customers themselves can now track the delivery of packages they send. This technology link increases the odds that customers will use Federal Express more frequently— maybe exclusively.[34]

- Airline carriers use frequent flyer programs to convert deal-fixated customers into repeat purchasers. These programs don't guarantee that a passenger will fly with the same airline, but they improve the odds.

- American Hospital Supply's ASAP system converts deal-oriented hospitals into relationship customers.[35] With ASAP's computerized ordering and inventory management system, American Hospital Supply develops sole-source relationships with hospitals for a variety of commodity-type products.

- Jeffrey Lant, author of *Money Talks: The Complete Guide to Creating a Profitable Workshop or Seminar in Any Field*, cultivates relationships with participants in his workshops and seminars around the country.[36] He lets them know when he's returning to their area by sending a course brochure or enclosing a letter in the sponsoring organization's brochure. Past program participants may get a special discount for the next seminar. He's available for consulting when he's there, or arranges for a limited access follow-up course for alumni only.

Type 3. Exit:
Deal-Relationship Mismatch

In the third quadrant, you desire deals, but your customers value relationships. This mismatch may seem like an improbable situation. Don't all marketers now claim to want relationships? Yes, they do, but talk is cheap. Many companies, I've found, "talk" relationships but treat customers in a deal-oriented manner. I hear such talk on Wall Street all the time; investment bankers love to talk about building customer relationships, but they often act quite differently. After all, they're prime purveyors of the cult of the deal (as I described in Chapter 1).

Look past your marketing rhetoric. Actions speak louder than words. How do you actually *treat* your customers? What does your *behavior* tell you? Most important, find out how customers *feel* they're treated. You're lucky if your customers want relationships, but your luck will run out and your customers will *exit* unless you invest in a relationship culture and infrastructure. (I tell you about investing in infrastructure in the next main section.)

Type 4. Partnerships:
Relationship-Relationship Match

The fourth quadrant represents loyal, long-term, mutually beneficial relationships: partnerships between buyers and sellers. Often, this is the state in which people and organizations achieve their highest performance. Customer partnerships yield all sorts of benefits. Relationships save money because it costs less to keep an old customer than it does to get a new one.[37] Loyal customers provide a steady stream of revenues.[38] And strong relationships are solid competitive barriers.[39]

If you're in quadrant 4, applaud your good fortune and work diligently to build and maintain strong relationships. Keep in mind, however, that you can build different kinds of relationships, some stronger, others weaker. In our recent *California Management Review* article, Rob Faulkner and I present a framework for analyzing customer-supplier relationships. A relationship is made up of two components, *products* and *transactions*.[40] A *product* could be a hard good or a service. A *transaction* is the actual purchase of a good or execution of a service.

The key marketing question is whether *value* can be created by linking products and/or linking transactions. An airline frequent flyer program, for example, creates customer value (free tickets, upgrades) by linking transactions over time. I call this a *narrow* relationship because it connects deals over time but is limited to a single product. The customer would obtain other products, such as a rental car or hotel, from other providers. The customer would have *multiple* narrow relationships, illustrated in Figure 10-2 as separate horizontal bars. But, add a rental car discount or a hotel discount each time a passenger flies with the same carrier and you create customer value—lower total cost and greater convenience—by linking products (air transportation + ground transportation + hotel). I call this a *wide* relationship because it links products *and* it links transactions over time. As shown in Figure 10-2, a wide relationship covers multiple products and transactions. STAR Industries' Four-STAR option is a good example of a wide relationship.

The Zone of Indifference

The zone of indifference, illustrated by the circle in Figure 10-1, is an area of both risk and opportunity. It's risky to be in the circle because customers are not committed to relationships or to deals. They're indifferent, and they could easily be swayed one way or the other. A competitor could step in and steal waffling customers by building relationships and moving them out of the zone. Once out, customers are no longer indifferent; they're committed to one strategy. But the circle contains opportunity because *you* can shift indifferent customers outside the circle. By resolving your indifference, you can adopt a more aggressive relationship-building strategy and make customers loyal to you. That's what STAR did. Its new customer program moved distributors out of their zone of indifference.

Investing in a Relationship-Building Infrastructure

Building relationships is an investment, typically big. Keeping relationship-oriented customers in the "Partnerships" quadrant (type 4) requires continuous attention, devotion, and investment. And moving customers out of the zone of indifference or the spot market quadrant (type 1) demands even more. Here's a way to think about it. Davidow and Uttal say in *Total Customer Service* that the backbone of great service is *infrastructure:* "networks of people, physical facilities, and information."[41] In a similar way, if you want to forge and sustain strong ties with customers, you have to establish a *relationship-building infrastructure.* A relationship-building infrastructure is the backbone of healthy partnerships with customers and clients.

Many different sorts of investments are required to establish a relationship-building infrastructure. You have to put into place a complex of practices, customs, policies, procedures, and people that are all oriented in one direction: building solid customer relationships. You may have to uproot old attitudes. Marketers schooled in the cult of the deal, for example, want to hold customers at bay; they'll resist your investments in relationship infrastructure. Training and education may be necessary to help such people develop a different attitude about external alliances.

Know Thy Market

Customer-oriented companies know who their customers are and precisely target them. "Know thy market" is the first rule extolled by Capital Partners CEO Michael Mach for his commercial real estate firm: "We operate the business in the markets we know and are located in."[42] Know thy market is good general advice. But I mean more than the usual marketing prescriptions. From the networking perspective, knowing your customers well means knowing their locations on the spectrum of relationships. If you're going to make the investment in a relationship infrastructure, *it's absolutely critical that your customers*

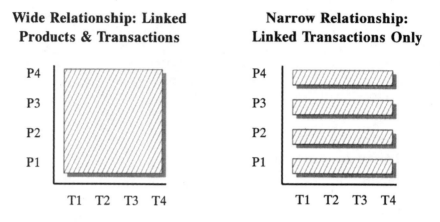

Figure 10-2. Wide and narrow relationships. (*Source: Modified from Figure 1 in Wayne E. Baker and Robert R. Faulkner, "Strategies for Managing Suppliers of Professional Services." Copyright 1991 by the Regents of the University of California. Reprinted from the* California Management Review, *vol. 33, no. 4, by permission of the Regents.*)

be relationship-oriented. This can't be a wish; it has to be reality. You have to be located in the "Partnerships" quadrant of the relationship grid (Figure 10-1), or be absolutely sure that you can bring your customers there.

This caution may seem obvious, but I know many marketers who *believe* their customers desire relationships when in fact they don't. Sears, Roebuck is the classic example. For years, executives at Sears have spoken of the giant retailer's "covenant" with the U.S. consumer, long after consumers made it clear that it had become a case of unrequited love. Lack of mutual understanding is a common problem in marketing relationships, just as much as it is in personal relationships (Chapter 4). Marketers who network smart make critical investments in the right kind of marketing research—the kind that investigates and reveals customers' *true* relationship preferences.

Set High Performance Expectations

Setting high expectations works at multiple levels. At one level, effective marketers carefully manage customer expectations. Davidow and Uttal recommend setting customer expectations at levels that distinguish you from competitors, but at a level somewhat below what you can actually deliver—as a way to ensure superior performance.[43] Their recommendation makes a lot of sense. I am especially pleased with Federal Express, for example, because my packages are often delivered *before* the 10 a.m. deadline.

But it's important to set performance expectations at another level: the goals that drive your people to produce stellar performance. We know from the second networking principle—the Pygmalion principle—that setting and communicating high performance expectations motivates people to excel. And we know from total quality management (TQM) that "stretch objectives" often push people to break frames of conventional thinking and achieve unprecedented levels of productivity. If your defect rate is 10 percent, for example, setting a target of 5 percent is too reasonable: People aren't pushed to change the way they work. Setting a *zero* defect rate forces people to think and behave differently. To achieve the "unreasonable" goal of zero defects, people have to reconceive their jobs; they must evaluate anew the kind of work that's done and the way it's done. When people do so—when they think in completely new ways about what they do—they can achieve outstanding performance.

So, setting high performance expectations is a balancing act. To build strong relationships, you have to deliver the goods. You don't want to promise too much and disappoint customers, but you also don't want to pull back on performance expectations and be "too reasonable" about just how good your goods or services can be. Help your people achieve new heights, and help your customers understand and appreciate what you can deliver.

Set High Relationship Expectations

We usually think of expectations as they relate to individual achievement and performance. But the Pygmalion principle also applies to the *continuity of a relationship* itself. When a marketer and customer *expect* their relationship to continue, it does. Research has documented that expectations of continuity in buyer-seller relationships are self-fulfilling prophesies.[44]

Because expectations of continuity are self-fulfilling, it's paramount that marketers set high *relationship* expectations. To activate the Pygmalion principle, you must communicate relentlessly the expectation that relationships with customers will continue. But you have to do it carefully so your message won't be misconstrued. Expectations of continuity should not invite complacency or nonchalance. Expectations should bolster everyone's commitment to making long-term investments in the customer relationship, the kinds of investments that sustain it and make expectations of continuity self-fulfilling.

Make Sure Top Levels Stay
Informed about Relationships

When building relationships is so important, it's critical that those at the top stay current about customer satisfaction. Fast feedback channels must be incorporated in top-level intelligence networks (Chapter 3). At Zap Computers, for example, top managers use frequent operational meetings to relay, share, and discuss market and customer information.[45] All reports of service problems must reach Network Equipment Technologies (NET) CEO Bruce D. Smith within four hours.[46] A division of forest-products company Trus Joist sends its customers a customer service card and rolodex insert, both of which include the home phone numbers of 10 customer service, plant, and production managers.[47] And, GE uses its Quick Market Intelligence (GMI) to take the pulse of the market every week (Chapter 3). Those who network smart keep themselves in touch with their customers.

Have Executives and Senior
Managers Adopt Customers

One way to keep in touch with the market and ensure the highest levels of performance is to have executives and senior managers *adopt* big customers. Adoption means they're responsible for the care and welfare of their charges. Mark Twain's local directors develop such intimate ties with various businesses and community organizations. NET officers adopt groups of customers and visit them several times a year.[48]

Adopting customers implies more than occasional phone calls and visits. It includes enough direct personal contact to invoke the fourth networking principle (repeated interaction encourages cooperation). Adoption means getting to know your customers and their people personally; it means embedding business, personal, and social relationships.

Hire Great People, Train Them
Well, Reward Them Well

Great people are talented individuals with superior *technical skills* and abilities, coupled with excellent *networking capabilities*. Both qualifications are essential. Technical skills alone aren't enough because solid customer relationships are built on strong *personal* relationships. You need competent people operating at high levels of interpersonal understanding to build strong customer relationships.

Customer-oriented companies recognize the importance of great people, and you see the practice of hiring the best anywhere you see strong customer ties. Mark Twain hires the highest caliber people; even though it's a regional bank, it rewards them on par with the biggest financial institutions.[49] To find and hire the best new college graduates, Dow Chemical builds strong relationships with the colleges it recruits from. "We make sure our relationship with each school is like our relationship with a supplier," says Dow human resources vice president Robert M. Baughman in *Sales & Marketing Management*.[50]

Put Managers and Service People in the Field and Keep Them There

Make the fourth networking principle work for you by managing conditions that boost repeated interaction with customers. Put managers and service people out there, nose to nose with customers, talking, listening, observing. Hyatt Hotels, for example, with its renewed customer emphasis, recently moved 10 middle managers out of its Chicago home office and made them divisional directors of sales and marketing, each with an office in one of the hotels in his or her region.[51] Tennant Company, the world's leading manufacturer of floor maintenance equipment I featured in Chapter 6, uses its sales force as "quality eyes and ears" in the company's total quality improvement program.[52] Cray Research maintains several regional service operations and often locates engineers at customer sites.

It's important to keep your people in the field long enough to build strong relationships. As a rule, U.S. companies rotate people too quickly. Some rotation is helpful, of course, because it provides varied experiences and opportunities to make new contacts. But excessive rotation disrupts relationships. Companies in the United States often rotate account managers too quickly in Asia, a context where it takes a long time to cultivate strong relationships. An Asia marketing manager for a big U.S. company impressed upon me how much Asian customers don't like the U.S. practice of churning account managers.[53] A minimum commitment of *five years* is needed, he said, to build a solid foundation of trust and mutual understanding.

The five-year hurdle is interesting. I bet Japanese authorities know five is the magic number. Did you know that the tax status of a foreign executive working in Japan changes unfavorably at the five-year mark? Before then, a U.S. executive working in Japan pays taxes only for income earned and paid in Japan. After five years, the exec becomes a "permanent resident" and must pay Japanese income tax for *worldwide* income, money earned and paid anywhere.[54] Many U.S. execs avoid the penalty by leaving before their five-year anniversary.

Thus, Japanese income tax law is an effective nontariff trade barrier— it disrupts the long-term cultivation of relationships so necessary for doing business in Japan.

What You Can Do *Now*

"If you don't know where you're going," said Casey Stengel, "you might end up somewhere else."[55] And to figure out where you're going, you first have to know where you are. You need hard data, real information. What you can do *now* is figure out where you are by diagnosing three categories of customer relationships—*lost* customers, *current* customers, and *potential* customers.

Use the relationship grid in your diagnosis. Start with current customers. A bird in hand is worth two in the bush. Lost and potential customers are bush birds; you might be able to patch up broken relationships or win new customers, but right now your fate is determined by the customers you have. And it's cheaper to keep a customer than it is to get a new one. After you analyze current customers, you can return and analyze why you lost customers (and what it'll take to retrieve them), as well as target new customers with relationship orientations compatible with yours.

Array each customer (or homogeneous customer segment) against your actual marketing strategy. I recommend that you conduct this exercise in a group. Try it out first in one of your informal Donuts with Ditch sessions. After a trial run there, create a *customer relationship task force*. Give the task force this mission: Diagnose customer relationships and the company's relationship-marketing strategy. The task force should be staffed with people from sales, marketing, and service, from both field and corporate offices. Include people who *know* customers personally as well as those who are closely involved in providing customer service.

A warning: This exercise is more difficult than you think. You have to get beyond your company's marketing rhetoric. I've observed many marketers who talk relationships but treat customers transactionally. Customers, too, can talk relationships but switch suppliers for the flimsiest of reasons. Look past the rhetoric. Actions speak louder than words. How do you actually *treat* your customers? What does your *behavior* tell you? And how do your customers *behave*? How do they *treat* their suppliers—companies like yours?

If you can get hard, quantitative data on customer purchase histories, use them. If you can get hard data on purchases made from you *and* from your competitors (investment bankers call these "deals done away"), even better. Hard data cut through rhetoric and misconception. I once conducted a detailed quantitative analysis of the five-year purchasing histories of 1530 companies to determine the strategies they used to acquire investment banking services.[56] Conventional wisdom had it that relationships were dead, but I discovered that 3 out of 10 customers still had *exclusive* relationships with their investment banks. By analyzing purchasing histories, you may learn that your customer base follows the famous 80/20 rule: 80 percent of sales are made by 20 percent of your customers.[57] The 20 percent core (it may be more or less) is the main source of repeat business. Make it a primary focus of relationship-strengthening activities.

For any major relationship in which you contemplate additional investments, I recommend that you conduct a formal *relationship audit* before you do. A relationship audit is the systematic and periodic evaluation of performance, strengths and weakness, and areas of improvement. Typically, relationship audits are initiated by *buyers* who use audits to evaluate the performance of their *suppliers*. I propose you take the initiative and turn tables: Apply the practice of audits to *customers*. I know this may sound like a strange idea, but it's a helpful way to understand customers and their orientations toward you. After all, if you make big investments in a relationship, you want to be confident that the customer wants relationships and will reciprocate.

A relationship audit can be a time-consuming undertaking, so it's important to devise the right evaluation criteria. Obvious criteria include sales volume, profitability, purchase history, payment and credit history, and so forth. These criteria are important, of course, and should be included. But you also want to include *relationship* factors, those that indicate the customer's receptivity to relationship marketing:

- *Demonstrated relationship orientation.* Where is the customer on the relationship grid? Does the customer already have successful partnerships with other suppliers?

- *Quality-oriented leadership.* Is the customer at the forefront of the quality revolution? Does the customer have a demonstrated commitment to total quality service for its own customers?

- *Team commitment.* Has the customer dedicated a group or team to your relationship? Or are you dependent on one or two people?

- *Quality and level of personnel.* Do you get the customer's best and brightest? Are top executives and managers involved in the relationship?

- *Communication.* Does the customer communicate frequently with you? Do they initiate conversations? Do they keep you informed?

Do they visit you regularly? Do their people "live" at your facilities?

- *Embeddedness.*   Have your people and your customer's developed strong *personalized* relationships?

- *Relationship investments.*   Has the supplier made investments in your relationship? Investments include people, new technologies, policies, and procedures that support the relationship.

- *Expectations of continuity.*   Does the customer expect the relationship to continue? Expectations of continuity are self-fulfilling prophesies (the Pygmalion principle), because those who expect to stay in a relationship make the investments that sustain it.[58]

- *Continuous relationship improvement.*   Is the customer committed to continuously improving and strengthening the relationship with you?

What You Can Do *Soon*

You're blessed if the relationship grid reveals a close match between your marketing strategy and your customers'. If you're like most, however, you've discovered significant mismatches, at least for a few customer segments or a few important customers. If so, you have four generic options:

1. *Adopt a marketing strategy that matches your customer's purchasing style.*   If customers want relationships but you haven't accommodated, abandon your deal orientation and adopt a relationship style. Note, however, that you have to invest in infrastructure before you lose dissatisfied customers. This option is impractical if customers love deals but you've invested in a relationship infrastructure. You would have to abandon it and adopt a foreign low-cost culture (where your edge comes from manufacturing and distribution efficiencies).

2. *Convert your customers to your marketing style.*   If you're deal oriented but your customers are not, you could elevate their affection for deals, but I don't recommend it (take option 1 instead). If the situation is reversed, you must find ways to convert deal-oriented customers and build relationships (more on how in a moment).

3. *Exit and find new customers whose purchasing style matches yours.*   If you prefer a deal style (or can't make relationship investments), you may be delighted to divorce relationship customers and play the field. If the situation is reversed, and you've exhausted efforts

to convert deal-oriented customers, redirect resources to a more receptive customer segment.

4. *Exit the business altogether.* Drop a particular line of business—for good. A last resort, yes, but it's appropriate at times. If you drop products where you can't achieve a proper match between you and your customers, you free resources that can be rededicated to a more compatible customer group.

If you decide to strengthen existing ties or convert deal-oriented customers, the following are several relationship-building techniques:

Use the Spectrum of Relationships. Some marketers err by treating all customers alike. If your analysis reveals distinct customer segments with different relationship orientations, revise your marketing program accordingly. Like STAR Industries, you can unbundle services and offer them in customized packages designed to meet the needs of targeted segments.

Get Involved Earlier in the Process. Help customers *define* their needs, not just meet those presented to you. Japanese suppliers locate in close proximity to their big customers so they can work together easily and participate in joint product design and development.[59]

Increase Frequency of Interaction. Just increasing the frequency of interaction can invoke the fourth networking principle. It can begin as simply as making sure salespeople drop in and check up on customers. It doesn't have to be a formal sales call. Stopping by signals commitment, and provides a mechanism for quick feedback about problems *as they occur.* Customers might be vexed over a problem when it occurs but forget to tell you later. Specific memories fade, but the accumulation of ill will doesn't.

Provide incentives that increase the frequency of interaction. For the next six months, institute a formal calling and relationship-building program. Mark Twain, for example, was one of the first banks to use a systematic calling program for its salespeople.

Involve More Internal Groups and Functions. Customer satisfaction isn't just the responsibility of sales and marketing. Customer problems are best solved through the joint action of manufacturing, R&D, sales, finance, and so on. To achieve this, however, you have to have solved the bottleneck problem (see Chapter 5).

Involve Higher Management Levels. Before P&G and Wal-Mart formed their partnership, no one above field sales manager called on

Wal-Mart; now high-level executives from both sides get in the act. Few actions signal commitment more than having company execs meet with customers. It's a fast channel for communication and problem resolution and a good way to keep top levels informed about service performance. Have executives go even further and *adopt* important customers.

Create "Client Champions."   A client champion adopts an important client or customer, becoming the client's advocate, point person, and sponsor. Each client champion develops strong personal ties with the client, makes sure the client's interests are served, and does whatever it takes to marshal resources to do so.

Involve the Customer.   Make customers promoters and partners in the discovery of new market opportunities. Textile manufacturer Milliken put together over 1000 customer action teams (CATs), as Tom Peters reports.[60] To form a CAT, both Milliken and the customer put together a joint team with people from various departments and functions. The customer-supplier team works to find or create new areas of mutual benefit.

Participate in Customer Intelligence Networks.   Customers, like you, build their own intelligence networks (see Chapter 3). Become a critical node in their networks by offering them facts, data, tidbits, and gossip relevant to their business.

Create Value via Linkage.   Find ways to increase the probability of repeat purchases by making it in the customer's interest to do so. Frequent buyer programs create value by offering discounts or additional services. STAR Industries offers more services and lower prices to distributors who make long-term commitments. Irvine Company, a big real estate developer in southern California, assigns all unlawful detainer business to one law firm in return for discounted legal fees.[61]

Multiple purchases invoke the fourth networking principle: Repeated interaction encourages cooperation. Customers might respond at first simply to the economic value you've created, but over time continuing association stimulates information sharing, mutual understanding, and cooperation. Business relationships become embedded in social ties, and mutual benefit is generated via the joint pursuit and creation of value.

Make Creative Use of the New Electronic Technologies.   The new information and communication technologies are great opportunities for building value and strengthening customer relationships. For a great example, consider the sophisticated use of technology in the Federal

Express POWERSHIP automated shipping system.[62] Federal Express installs free computer equipment and/or software that links the POWERSHIP customer directly with Federal Express. The system gives the customer unprecedented control over shipping activities. The customer can track and monitor the status of any package at any time. The system generates reports that enable the customer to better understand and manage shipping activity. (The system also does all sorts of useful routine tasks. It's self-invoicing; it prints shipping labels, which eliminate airbills; it lets you order supplies and schedule courier pick-up.) The more advanced POWERSHIP options can even prepare paperwork for customs and international invoicing, or link together the customer's mainframe with Federal Express's mainframe.

Federal Express's POWERSHIP technology-based link is good for the company, good for the customer. Federal Express gets more business; the customer gets more control and better service. "The benefits to Federal Express are accrued via a stronger relationship, through technology, with each POWERSHIP customer," says Federal Express marketing manager Kathryn Milano.[63] "Better technology means better service, and better service builds business."

Embed Business Ties in Social Relationships.   If you implement my recommendations, the embeddedness phenomena will occur naturally. Relationships are a fundamental human need (principle 1), and people from both sides will naturally form personal ties. You should also boost this natural process by actively seeking opportunities to forge social ties. Mark Twain, for example, encourages its local bank presidents to get involved in the social life of their communities. Direct-selling companies piggyback purchases on the social networks of their home-party hostesses.

If you follow my advice by using all these techniques, you'll have ample opportunity to embed ties. Give the process time; it'll take a while. Give customer relationships the room they need to germinate and mature. Don't rotate your people so quickly that you sever budding relationships. (Remember, for example, the five-year relationship hurdle in Asia.)

What You Can Do in the *Long Run*

What you've done so far is get your marketing house in order. But you've yet to make *fundamental* and *sweeping* changes in the company's marketing philosophy. What you can do in the *long run* is set up a mechanism for overhauling your marketing program and designing a comprehensive new relationship strategy.

To begin the process, establish a client partnership task force. Its goal: Investigate and recommend specific investments in infrastructure that will create a long-term, sustained, self-perpetuating advantage for the company. I use the term *partnership* here in two senses. The first is obvious—the objective of long-term, win-win relationships with customers. The second is less obvious. By partnership I also mean involving *customers and clients* as full participating members of the task force. You can't design a solid relationship strategy in a vacuum. You have to do it *with* customers. Pick a small number of customers—ones who rely on you as much as you rely on them—and approach them with the idea. (If they've read Chapter 12, "Building Supplier Partnerships," they'll meet you more than halfway.)

Here's an early assignment for the task force: Explore the idea of establishing a companywide *customer complaint management system.*[64] This system is a comprehensive program for listening and responding to customers; when used well, it can turn complaints and problems into a wealth of information that can help you and the task force improve and reshape the marketing program. Let me introduce the idea by asking you a question: What's the worst kind of customer complaint? Answer: the one you never hear. One of the worst marketing problems is plummeting sales caused by dissatisfied customers who simply exit and never voice their complaints to you. (Of course, as I describe in the next chapter, they'll spoil additional sales by badmouthing you and your products to potential customers.) A customer complaint management system can avert this all-too-common problem.

The core of the system is what marketing experts Roland T. Rust, Bala Subramanian, and Mark Wells call the "problem impact tree," or PIT, illustrated in Figure 10-3.[65] The PIT is a very useful management tool for understanding customers and improving service. By using the PIT as a diagnostic tool, say Rust, Subramanian, and Wells, you can learn to avoid problems from the start, increase the proportion of customers who report problems, and resolve a higher proportion of reported problems.[66]

The PIT divides and redivides customers according to their experiences and behaviors. To begin, at the top of the tree are "all customers" for a particular product or service. This category is divided at the first branch into customers who have "no problems" and customers who "have problems." The overall objective here, of course, is to maximize the number of customers who take the "left" branch of no problems; these satisfied customers make the best repeat purchasers and informal emissaries of goodwill for the company. The percentage of customers without problems is a yardstick to measure quality improvement or customer satisfaction programs.

Of those customers who experience problems, some "report problems" and some "don't report problems." The big challenge is to get those who don't report problems to do so. A postpurchase survey can help (and may be your only option). If possible, however, it's much better to learn of problems as they occur. Hotels, the example used by Rust, Subramanian, and Wells, put out tent cards and lobby signs to encourage reporting.[67] Tennant Company uses a formal reporting system in which a salesperson fills out an installation report each time a machine is delivered; defects are reported immediately to the company's warranty and quality departments.[68]

At the final branch, customers who report problems are divided into "problem resolved" and "problem not resolved." The objective, of course, is to increase the percentage of resolved problems. If a cus-

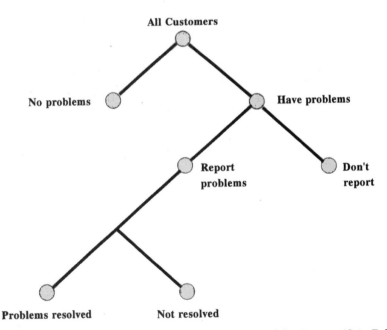

Figure 10-3. The problem impact tree. (*Source: Exhibit I on p. 42 in Roland T. Rust, Bala Subramanian, and Mark Wells, "Making Complaints a Management Tool,"* Marketing Management, *vol. 1, 1992, pp. 41–45. Copyright 1992 by The American Marketing Association. Reprinted (with minor adaptations) by permission.)*

tomer's problem is resolved on the spot and the customer is satisfied, there's a very good chance the customer will buy again and make positive word-of-mouth recommendations (see next chapter).

With a customer complaint management system, you can focus strategic efforts to improve service and build customer relationships. You can improve product performance and service to increase the percentage of customers who never experience problems (and become company loyalists and advocates). You increase the percentage of people who report problems, and minimize the worst problem of all—those who experience problems and just walk away, never to be seen again. Sometimes, learning where and why you fail can be the most important information you ever get. And it can help you learn how to focus efforts to resolve problems once reported. Remember: It costs a lot more to get a new customer than it does to keep an old one. Learn what your customers think and feel, and make the necessary investments to build strong customer relationships.

11

Word-of-Mouth Marketing

Forget about market surveys and analyst reports. Word of mouth is probably the most powerful form of communication in the business world.

REGIS MCKENNA
The Regis Touch[1]

What do business books, luxury automobiles, and men's underwear have in common? All three are marketed through word of mouth. *In Search of Excellence*, the best-selling business book of all time, was marketed aggressively by word of mouth during the two years prior to actual publication. As Tom Peters describes in *Thriving on Chaos* (also a best-seller), he and coauthor Bob Waterman bound a 125-page presentation of the book's main findings and circulated copies of it among business managers and executives. Eventually, they printed and distributed 15,000 copies to meet the "underground demand." They also courted media opinion leaders who would write favorable reviews. "Thus, within days of the book's launching," recalls Peters, "supportive reviews appeared, and the network of 15,000 (plus at least an equal number of photocopied knockoffs) hurried to buy the real thing, often in bulk for their subordinates."[2] That's word-of-mouth marketing.

What about luxury automobiles? These, too, are marketed through word-of-mouth networks. In fall 1992, BMW began promoting its new 740i sedan by asking executives in the southern United States to test-drive it free for a week. BMW sweetens the deal by putting Chicago composer-musician Keith Hooper's *Implosion* album in the car's stereo system. Executives get to keep *Implosion* as a gift—a take-away reminder of pleasant associations with the new 740i.[3] BMW's test-drive program isn't new; it's just an updated version the same word-of-mouth marketing technique Ford used when it introduced the Thunderbird in the 1950s. Of the 15,000 executives who took the Thunderbird for a day of free test-driving, 84 percent said they would recommend it to friends.[4]

And now underwear. The men's undergarment industry has often used athletic celebrities like Michael Jordan or Jim Palmer to endorse its products. Recently, Chicago-based Fruit of the Loom, Inc., took a brave step for the common man by using bus and taxi drivers to test and endorse underwear.[5] To launch its newly designed men's and boys' briefs, Fruit of the Loom, Inc., invited drivers in cities across the United States to take the Comfort Challenge—"test ride" the briefs for a week and report back via a comfort survey. This unique word-of-mouth marketing campaign is a smashing success. The Comfort Challenge attracts both local and national media interest. The Challenge and its results have been featured on local TV news and in local newspapers (including front-page stories in some cities), as well as coverage by national newspapers, magazines, and news programs.

And this is just the beginning of Fruit of the Loom's word-of-mouth efforts. "Word-of-mouth communication is a powerful form of influence," says CEO William Farley, "and Fruit of the Loom, Inc., is trying to develop this approach in a systematic way. This is one of our first steps of many in our word-of-mouth marketing strategy." The latest to take the Comfort Challenge? A triple-A baseball farm team. Word of mouth works.

Word of mouth—information passed through personal networks—is one of the most powerful forms of communication in the market. Think about it: All but the most trivial purchases are influenced by the knowledge and opinions of others. Despite its power, word of mouth is one of the most neglected of all marketing techniques. "You never see a 'word-of-mouth communications' section in marketing plans," says expert Regis McKenna.[6] But networking smart means becoming much more systematic about marketing via word of mouth. In this chapter, I describe some of the key facts about word-of-mouth marketing. I then tell you how you can boost sales by incorporating word-of-mouth networking techniques in your marketing programs.

Why Word of Mouth Is Powerful

Word of mouth is an extremely effective marketing communications device. It differs in important ways, however, from conventional communication methods. These differences are why word of mouth exerts such a powerful influence in the decision-making process. Regis McKenna, an authority who advocates proactive word-of-mouth marketing campaigns, notes that word of mouth is a powerful influence because it is a live, direct, experienced, person-to-person process.[7] Unlike an impersonal advertisement, word of mouth takes place in an interpersonal context. The person-to-person "channel" is a wide band: It transmits meaning in multiple ways—words, emotions, inflection, body language. The channel is interactive; it allows two-way feedback, queries, and replies.

Even so, the interpersonal nature of word-of-mouth communication isn't enough, by itself, to make word of mouth so powerful. There's one more essential element: *source credibility*. Word of mouth influences decision making because it typically comes from credible, believable sources—friends, colleagues, associates, or known experts. In contrast, when a salesperson talks and makes a pitch, we discount the message because we know he or she wants to make a sale. There's conflict of interest. But when a friend or colleague makes a recommendation, we're much more likely to believe it because we trust the person. We know a friend or colleague isn't getting a finder's fee or earning a sales commission. We also know that the person has put his or her "reputation" on the line (so we might come back and complain if the product doesn't meet expectations). And, if we know the recommender well enough, we also know whether his or her tastes and preferences match our own.

Source credibility in word-of-mouth communication is based on our old friend, the similarity principle. People are more likely to believe those who are similar to themselves. Evidence of the role of similarity in word-of-mouth communication comes from a broad field of research called the "diffusion of innovations."[8] One of the field's best-documented facts is that "interpersonal diffusion" is more likely to occur between people who are similar—similar backgrounds, education, age, occupation, and so forth.[9] Similarity is a sound basis for credibility, but not always. The trust we naturally place in similar others can be the basis of trickery and fraud.

Finally, word of mouth is powerful because it capitalizes on the fifth networking principle: It's a small world. According to this principle, we know that every time you increase your network of direct contacts by a single person, you also tap into a vast network of indirect contacts. Think of opinion leaders as your direct contacts, and their followers—the customers you want—as your indirect contacts. Every time you convince an opinion leader of the merits of your new product or service, you also indirectly convince a large number of customers to buy it.

The small-world principle helps you *broadcast* information about new products and services. Be forewarned, however, that the word-of-mouth network can carry positive *and* negative information. Word of mouth will backfire if customers are unhappy with your products or services. McKenna offers this rule of thumb: "If a customer has a good experience, he'll tell three other people. If he has a bad experience, he'll tell ten other people."[10]

Now that I've mentioned the possibility of bad-mouthing, it's a good time to bring up some of your ethical responsibilities in word-of-mouth marketing. Ralph Waldo Emerson, the U.S. poet and philosopher, can help us. "If a man make a better mouse-trap than his neighbor," he said, "though he build his house in the woods, the world will make a beaten path to his door." Ralph didn't know much about marketing. You need marketing to tell the world about your superior mousetrap and where to get a good map to your door. But Ralph did get this part right: You had better have a better mousetrap. If you have a superior product that meets real customer needs, then customers want to know about it. If you don't, you may trick them once or twice, but you won't get away with it for long. "If there is little or no trust," says Stephen R. Covey, author of the business best-sellers *The Seven Habits of Highly Effective People* and *Principle-Centered Leadership*, "there is no foundation for permanent success."[11]

Word-of-Mouth Networks

Personal networks play a powerful, vital role in word of mouth. "Adoption of a new idea," says diffusion expert Everett Rogers, "is the result of human interaction through interpersonal networks."[12] Rogers is widely acknowledged as the foremost authority on the diffusion of innovations; his comprehensive *Diffusion of Innovations* is considered the definitive source on the subject.[13] In this work, he synthesizes over 3100 publications on diffusion, documenting conclusively that new ideas, new practices, new products and services, and new opportunities (such as job openings) "diffuse" or spread through networks of personal contacts. Consider the role of such word-of-mouth networks in just a few different situations:

- As stockbrokers get older (and wiser), they build networks of personal contacts and rely more and more on word of mouth to sell stock. Senior managers at pension funds, insurance companies, and other institutional investors are prized mostly for their personal networks. Networking makes sense because individual and institutional investors alike get information leading to the purchase of stock from word of mouth.[14]

- Doctors learn about new pharmaceutical drugs from drug companies, but they're persuaded to adopt them in practice only when they hear about successful use from fellow physicians. Well-connected doctors adopt earlier than isolated doctors.[15]

- When hybrid corn was invented by Iowa State University and first came available, farmers didn't use it right away. They relied on word of mouth to evaluate it. Farmers heard about the innovation from company salespeople, but personal references by neighboring farmers persuaded them to switch.[16] Farmers still rely on word of mouth, today more than ever. Corn is genetically rich; thousands of hybrid varieties exist, with many of the so-called supersweets hybridized just in the last five years. Word of mouth is the only efficient way to sort through the bewildering number of choices.

- The oil-drilling industry is a tight network. Because oil-field services are sold on a per-hole basis, those who get the new business learn via personal contacts and word of mouth about when and where holes will be drilled.[17]

- Most people find out about job openings through their personal contacts. Job finding via personal networks is the norm for both white-collar and blue-collar occupations (see Chapter 9).

For those who market by networking smart, the prime objective is to find and tap into influential diffusion networks. You have to figure out the best way to enter a network and spread the good word about your products and services. To do that, however, you have to understand the cast of characters involved in word-of-mouth networking.

The Cast: Adopters, Opinion Leaders, Change Agents

If you want to play a part in the drama of word-of-mouth networking, three roles are available: adopters, opinion leaders, and change agents.[18] An *adopter* is any person who decides to use a new idea or purchase a new product or service. A customer is an adopter. When you purchased your first personal computer, for example, you were an adopter. If you were among the first to buy one, you were an "early" adopter; if you just bought one, you're numbered among the "late majority." (More on adopter types in a moment.)

An *opinion leader* is someone whom adopters go to for advice and recommendations about a product or service. If you consulted your office's resident computer guru about which PC to buy, for example, then you were influenced by an opinion leader. Of course, opinion leaders can be adopters, too. Opinion leaders are often *early* adopters who influence the decisions of *later* adopters. But opinion leaders don't have to actually adopt; they can recommend a product without ever having bought it. Only 14 percent of the executives who test-drove the Thunderbird said they would *buy* it, for example, but 84 percent said they would recommend it to friends.[19]

Opinion leaders play a special role in word-of-mouth networks because they influence large numbers of adopters. Their special role is good news for word-of-mouth marketers: It means you don't have to get the message out to *all* potential customers (adopters). You just have to target the small number of opinion leaders. Get the message to them, convince them of the merits of your product or service, and they'll send a positive "buy" recommendation to countless others.

And now the third dramatic role, the *change agent*. "A change agent," says Rogers, "is an individual who influences clients' innovation decisions in a direction deemed desirable by a change agency."[20] Translation: If you're a marketer, then you're the change agent. Your company's the change agency. As a marketer, you try to get customers (adopters) to buy (adopt) your products or services. For word-of-mouth marketing, your objective is clear: Speed up the "rate of adoption" of your product or service. You want to get *more people* to *adopt faster* than they would otherwise. You want your new product or service to move quickly and completely through the entire network of potential customers.

Five Types of Adopters

Not all adopters are alike. Some buy a new product right after it's launched; others hesitate and buy only after the product has been out for a time; still others delay and lag far behind the crowd. If you want to market via word of mouth, it's important to understand various types of adopters and their key differences. You'll save a lot of time, money, and aggravation.

Over 30 years ago, Everett Rogers proposed a method of adopter classification that has since become the universal standard in diffusion studies.[21] As such, I use it here.[22] Rogers' method arrays categories of adopters along two dimensions: time sequence and size of category. Time sequence is the order in which different categories first bought a product, used a service, or accepted an idea. Size of category is the proportion of all potential adopters a particular category represents. Using this method, Rogers distinguishes five types of adopters:

Innovators. Innovators are wild adventurers, the brash and daring explorers of the unknown. They seek whatever's new and risky; they love to experiment with new products. The first users of microcomputers—back in the 1970s—were the innovators in this fledgling industry. Few of us are true innovators; typically, less than 3 percent of all people who adopt an innovation are in this vanguard group. Yet innovators play an important role as *information gatekeepers.* They build extensive external intelligence networks to learn about innovations, and they're the first to import a new idea from the outside. The problem is that they're so wildly different from everyone else that they're not really respected. The similarity principle—networking principle 3—works against innovators. Because most adopters don't look to innovators for advice, as a change agent, you shouldn't focus your efforts on them.

Early Adopters. Early adopters buy or learn about new products and services early in the diffusion process but not as soon as innovators. Members of this category bought PCs in the early 1980s. Early adopters aren't a large segment of the market, less than 15 percent of all adopters, but they're very influential opinion leaders for later adopters. As a rule, early adopters are much more respectable (in the eyes of most potential adopters) than innovators. They serve as good role models. "Potential adopters look to early adopters for advice and information about the innovation," says Rogers. "The early adopter is considered by many as 'the individual to check with' before using a new idea."[23]

Of course, any of the five types of adopters could be opinion leaders. By definition, any adopter who influences another person's decision to adopt is an opinion leader. The real question is, who are *most likely* to be opinion leaders for the bulk of the market? To get the biggest bang for your marketing buck, you have to play the odds. And the odds say early adopters are your best bet. Early adopters are critical links with the large numbers of customers who adopt later on. If you're a word-of-mouth marketer, the early adopter is your prime target.

Early Majority. Members of the early majority buy new products or services just *before* the average person does. This category is important because it's the first big group of customers, about one-third of all adopters. Members of the early majority are not important opinion leaders. Once you break into this category, however, you're well on your way. Adoption of a new idea starts slowly, but research shows that it really takes off once you break the "sound barrier" of 25 percent adoption. You break the 25 percent barrier as you penetrate the early majority. After you do, the momentum is so great that it's almost impossible to stop the spread of an innovation. As a word-of-mouth marketer, 25 percent adoption is the critical point you must shoot for.

Late Majority. The late majority buys new products just *after* the average person does. Members of this large group (about one-third of all adopters) seem to adopt reluctantly. They're cautious. Typical members of the late majority have fewer resources than earlier adopters, so they can't afford to take too much risk. They prefer to wait and make sure an innovation will work before they adopt it. The late majority may adopt out of economic necessity, but usually they need *peer pressure* before they buy anything new. When it comes to PCs, for example, the late majority hears (and heeds) comments like "I can't believe you still write everything in longhand!" or "You're still making your secretary take dictation?"

Laggards. Laggards are the very last to adopt an innovation. They tend to be traditional, skeptical, and suspicious of new ideas. Laggards insulate themselves from outside influences; they're social isolates and prefer only the company of others with similar traditional values. And they distrust change agents, like you. The good news for word-of-mouth marketers is that laggards make up only a small fraction of total adopters, about 15 percent or so.

Laggards do adopt, eventually, but they're hard to get to and hard to influence. That doesn't mean you should neglect them entirely, at least not until you learn *why* they lag behind. The label "laggard" just means "late to adopt" (it doesn't imply any sort of disrespect). Lagging behind is often rational. The typical member of this category lacks resources, so he or she can't afford to take risks. A laggard might be working for a company that discourages risk taking and severely punishes those who make mistakes. I know several large organizations, for example, that languish still in the information dark ages. To this day, PCs are nonexistent; workers rely entirely on clunky mainframes. On that fateful day they're dragged kicking and screaming into the PC age, you can be sure they won't buy low-cost clones or the latest hot box. For them, their guide will be the motto, "No one was ever fired for buying IBM."

What Are Opinion Leaders Like?

Getting to opinion leaders is your goal; they influence large numbers to buy (or reject) your products and services. Because opinion leaders play such a key role, it's essential to know what they're like.

A lot of research has been conducted on opinion leaders and those who follow their advice.[24] Opinion leaders and their followers are somewhat different, which Rogers captures in several well-documented generalizations.[25] Opinion leaders are more active seekers of information about new ideas, products, and services. They keep abreast of news as it breaks by building sophisticated intelligence networks (Chapter 3). Opinion leaders are more open to the mass media—newspapers, magazines, journals, radio, TV, and so on. They're the ones in your company who seem to have chronic cases of wanderlust; they frequent trade shows, seminars, conferences, networking clubs (Chapter 13), and so on. And opinion leaders are superb network builders. They seek, promote, and maintain personal networks with both change agents (to get the news) and with followers (to relay the news).

Opinion leaders often have somewhat higher social status than their followers do. People of higher status are influential when higher status is associated with greater credibility. This fact may seem to contradict the similarity principle, but it really doesn't. Opinion leaders can't be *too* different from those they influence. Leaders, like followers, must conform to the same social norms and conventions. Opinion leaders are a little more innovative than their followers, but these leaders don't deviate too much from the average person. Opinion leaders aren't innovative when they work in traditional organizations, for example, but they're very innovative when they work in innovative places.

So what's the bottom line? For word-of-mouth marketers, the most encouraging conclusion is this: *Opinion leaders know how to network smart.* They're proactive network builders. They work hard to build networks that maximize their exposure to information about new products and services. They *want* contact with change agents. You'll find opinion leaders to be a receptive audience, once you find them. That's your task: finding and contacting those who lead opinions for your product or service. These people want to hear your message. If they like it, they'll become your best salespeople.

Developing Word-of-Mouth Marketing Campaigns

It won't be easy, at first, to incorporate systematic word of mouth in your marketing programs. You'll run into plenty of skeptics, especially those schooled in the standard marketing approaches. Word of mouth doesn't yet have the "stamp of approval" from the marketing discipline. Indeed, the phenomenon is something of a puzzle to them.[26] Don't let their puzzlement lead you astray. Like the drunk who searches for car keys under the street lamp because the light's better, many market researchers spend too much time studying things they can easily observe, such as media buys, formal advertising campaigns, and sales promotions. Traditional marketing underemphasizes the importance of personal networks and word of mouth.

Practitioners and consultants everywhere know better. They fully recognize the vast importance of word of mouth. Tom Peters, for example, devotes an entire section in *Thriving on Chaos* to it; he advises marketers to "use *systematic* word-of-mouth campaigns as the keystone for launching all new products and services."[27] The trick is to learn how to activate and use word-of-mouth networks.

Start with the Right Product or Service

You can pick almost any product or service to start with. It could be a sparkling new product, or an existing product that you relaunch via word of mouth. In either case, I recommend that you start with one of your clearly superior products, something that's a big improvement over competing products. I don't recommend a commodity product, a minor product-line extension, or something that's only a small incremental improvement. Starting with a clearly superior product makes it easier to drum up enthusiasm and support among your corps of change agents (salespeople) and the opinion leaders you want to influence. And it gets a better product into customers' hands.

Word-of-mouth marketing should be used alongside traditional marketing and advertising programs. Word of mouth is not a *substitute*; it's a *supplement*. Systematic word-of-mouth programs can become, of course, your most important channel of communication for some products, but it still should be used in conjunction with other programs. Mass media advertising, for example, helps build *awareness* of your new product, whereas word-of-mouth recommendations persuade customers to make purchases.

Identify Qualified Opinion Leaders

Word-of-mouth marketers don't target all potential customers. Instead, they identify and go after the much smaller set of opinion leaders for a new product or service. Consider Mark Twain Bancshares, the very successful commercial bank I introduced in Chapter 10. This company makes a science out of word-of-mouth marketing. Mark Twain bankers don't try to reach directly each and every potential customer; rather, they "sign up" local opinion leaders in the communities they serve. And just who are those local opinion leaders? Their directors. Each of their 300+ board directors is a prominent business or civic leader—an *opinion* leader—in his or her local community. These opinion leaders are the potent sales force behind Mark Twain.

It's important to *qualify* opinion leaders, just like you qualify sales leads. Word-of-mouth marketers make two common mistakes when they go about identifying opinion leaders, both of which are caused by failure to qualify. The first mistake is the case of mistaken identity: Innovators are confused with opinion leaders.[28] It's an easy mistake. Opinion leaders, like innovators, *seek* contact with change agents. They're open to new ideas. But innovators are so outside the norm that they can't persuade people to adopt. A good opinion leader is someone who is open to your ideas *and* who is similar enough to the average adopter. Mark Twain's directors are qualified opinion leaders. Each director is a successful business leader in his or her local community. Adopters of Mark Twain's financial products listen to and take the advice of these directors; in contrast, they wouldn't listen to endorsements made by big shots on Wall Street.

The second common mistake is to identify opinion leaders who adopt too late. All adopters, no matter when they adopt, can influence others to do the same. As a rule, however, the earlier, the better. *Earlier* adopters (except innovators) are more qualified as opinion leaders than later adopters. Later adopters typically don't have much of a following—people don't go to them for recommendations. And, if they're too late in the diffusion process, like the late majority or laggards, then few potential adopters are left to make recommendations to.

When you hunt for qualified opinion leaders, be sure to cover all their possible locations and habitats. You and other experts in your company have a good sense of "who's who" among possible opinion leaders, but they'll differ for each of your products or services. And you'll be surprised where they'll turn up, so it pays to cast a wide net. As a prompt, consider the following generic opinion-leader categories (some are McKenna's, some mine) and how they apply specifically to your selected product or service[29]:

- The financial community (brokers, commercial bankers, investment bankers, analysts, venture capitalists, informal investors)

- Industry observers (consultants, advisory services, watchdog and consumer advocacy groups)

- Current and old customers [If you've built strong ties with your customers (Chapter 10), now's the time to tap them.]

- Suppliers of goods, parts, capital, training, professional services, etc. (see Chapter 12)

- Competitors with whom you have cooperative alliances (see Chapter 14)

- Professional and trade associations

- Scientific societies and user groups

- Organized networking clubs (see Chapter 13)

- The press/journalists/writers (local and national, business press, trade press, general and popular press, newsletters, electronic billboards)

- The community (anyone who interacts in any way with your company or its products and services)

Opinion leaders may be links in a long chain between final customers and you, the change agent. If so, then you have to trace the chain for your selected product or service and identify qualified opinion leaders all along the way. Consider, for example, the typical chain of opinion leaders between customers (end users) and manufacturers in the personal computer industry, as described by McKenna: *End users* learn about an exciting new PC from the *business and trade press*, who are informed by *financial analysts* and such industry "luminaries" as *consultants* or *key users*, who are influenced by *third-party software developers* and *independent software vendors*, who are developing software products to be used with this great new PC.[30]

Building Lines of Communication

Building lines of communication with opinion leaders follows the "secret formula" I described in Chapter 4: mutual understanding plus mutual exchange. Mutual understanding begins with the recognition that both sides—opinion leader and change agent—need each other. Opinion leaders want to learn about new products and services; for them, change agents like you provide welcome links to timely information and intelligence. As a word-of-mouth marketer, you need opinion leaders to broadcast buy recommendations for your products and services. These complementary needs may sound like the basis of a natural, mutually beneficial exchange. Unfortunately, mutual understanding often ends right there.

Change agents frequently fail to understand opinion leaders well enough to make exchanges work in the long run. Opinion leaders need change agents who are credible; to provide real service to opinion leaders, word-of-mouth marketers must be technically competent and knowledgeable. Too often, however, just the opposite is true. Lack of credibility is one of the biggest causes of change agent failure. I'm sure you've been frustrated by salespeople who lack credibility because they're ill-trained and poorly informed.[31] They're just pushing the product of the week, and they don't really understand the product or its capabilities. They end up wasting your time and squandering their company's goodwill. If you want to build solid lines of communication with opinion leaders, you have to avoid this common problem. As a responsible word-of-mouth marketer, one of your duties is to make sure those who contact opinion leaders are trained, knowledgeable, and competent.

To work with opinion leaders, you also have to understand the constraints they live with. Effective change agents "lead" opinion leaders, providing them with informal education and training in new technologies, ideas, products, and services. But you can't go overboard. Overenthusiastic word-of-mouth marketers push opinion leaders too far ahead of the pack, too far outside the norm, and convert opinion leaders into innovators without followers. Or, marketers just get too chummy and cozy with opinion leaders and alienate them from their followers.[32] If you go too far, you'll know the signs: The opinion leader will be said to have "sold out" or "gone native" (as anthropologists are fond of saying, and sometimes doing). The ethics of word-of-mouth marketing include sensitivity to the needs and norms of opinion leaders and the worlds in which they live.

Get Your Message Out

Once lines of communication are built with qualified opinion leaders, the next task is to get the message out. There are many ways to do so, including:

- *Provide prototypes, early releases, or "test" versions of a product* (this works for services as well). BMW promotes its new 740i sedan by asking corporate executives to test-drive it free for a week. And Fruit of the Loom, Inc., reaches its blue-collar customers by using cab drivers to test and endorse underwear.

- *Brief opinion leaders on your products or services.* Intel briefed technology guru and noted opinion leader Gordon Bell when they introduced their first 32-bit microprocessor.[33] Opinion leaders often write articles and commentaries in trade or industry publications, so you can find them by combing published sources.

- *Provide sample versions to high-influence customers.* Perfume companies place tear-and-sniff samples of new fragrances in leading fashion magazines. Software companies place discs with short versions of new software programs in top computer magazines.

- *Court future opinion leaders.* PC makers donate (or provide on very favorable terms) new equipment to high schools, colleges, and universities so students will become users and advocates.

- *Talk up your products and services at any credible forum.* Make presentations at trade association meetings, trade shows, professional societies, community activities and events.

- *Secure testimonials from satisfied customers.* Bring opinion leaders and potential customers together at events with satisfied customers.[34]

Follow Up

I'm always surprised at how seldom people follow up. A survey of sales executives by the National Research Bureau, Inc., for example, found that "80 percent of all sales are made after the fifth call." But 9 out of 10 salespeople quit before they get that far. Persistence pays off, but few persist.

Polite persistence is required to build and maintain lines of communication with opinion leaders and to get your message out. You have to keep in touch with opinion leaders to build mutual understanding. Repeated interaction encourages cooperation (networking principle 4). And you need to check back with opinion leaders to learn about their reactions to your message. If you provided prototypes, for example, how well are they working? Have opinion leaders run into snags or glitches? What's their *opinion* of your new product or service? Do they think it can be improved? How?

What You Can Do *Now*

You could try to embark right now on a systematic word-of-mouth marketing program, but I recommend that you first learn more about how word of mouth is used for your products and services. This knowledge will help you pick the right product or service for a systematic word-of-mouth program, as well as help to identify qualified opinion leaders. What you can do *now* is pick one of your best products or services and evaluate how customers find out about it.

Checklist for Word-of-Mouth Survey

Which of the following did you use to find out about our product or service (check all that apply)?	Customer name	Customer name	Customer name	Customer name
Company sales representative				
Company advertisement				
Another customer/user				
A supplier				
A competitor				
Friend, relative, nonbusiness contact				
Other third party (specify)				
Trade shows, conventions				
Trade or industry publication				
Other publication (specify)				
Other, not above (specify)				

Conduct an informal poll of your customers. In the future you can conduct a *formal* customer survey, but for now I recommend an informal one. You'll need the assistance of sales and marketing personnel, preferably those who have been around for a while and have direct customer contact. Over the next month, have your informal pollsters ask their key customers how they first learned about your selected product or service. Provide pollsters with the following questionnaire. (This is a suggested format. Expand and enlarge as appropriate.)

Be sure your informal pollsters record several pieces of critical information:

- How did the customer first *learn* about the product or service? Which *sources* of information were important?
- Approximately *when* did the customer first learn about it?
- How was the customer *persuaded* to use the product or service? Was it a third-party endorsement, recommendation from a friend or business associate, or what? Record identifying details about the medium of persuasion—trade journal name, recommender's name, and so on.
- Approximately *when* did the customer first *purchase or use* the product or service? That is, when did he or she first *adopt* the innovation?

At the end of the month, collect checklists from your pollsters and compile the results in a simple summary report. Convene a meeting of the group and discuss the results. During that meeting, assess the status of word of mouth in your company's marketing strategy. It's probably absent. This shortcoming can be a great opportunity for you because your competitors probably don't use systematic word of mouth either. Armed with your new data on word of mouth, you can become a marketing opinion leader: Persuade others in your company to establish a formal word-of-mouth marketing campaign.

What You Can Do **Soon**

Now that you know more about how customers use word of mouth, you're in a position to establish a *pilot program* for word-of-mouth marketing. What you can do soon is *plan and implement* a pilot program, following the five steps I described above and review here:

1. Pick one of your *clearly superior products*. It could be a new product or service or one that you wish to relaunch. Just make sure that it's a great product so the pilot program will be a fair test. You don't want the pilot program to fail because the product's mediocre.

Be sure that you can *support* word of mouth for your selected product or service. Do you have enough resources—people, time, and money—to dedicate to a thorough word-of-mouth program? And do you have the productive capacity to meet the surge in demand once you break the 25 percent sound barrier? It would be a shame to approach 25 percent adoption and then falter because you can't meet the demand for your product or service.

2. Who are the likely opinion leaders for your selected product? Start with the leads you obtained from your earlier analysis of word-of-mouth networks. Tap your intelligence networks, both internal and external. Who inside your organization might know—or know of—outside opinion leaders? Who outside the organization might know? Run through the list of opinion leader sources I listed above. If there's a chain of opinion leaders between you and the final customer, you'll have to identify opinion leaders all along it.

Be sure opinion leaders are *qualified*. They can't be too early (innovators) or too late in the adoption process. The biggest companies aren't necessarily the best opinion leaders. Signing up a giant household-name company sounds great, but it's tough to do because big companies tend to be late adopters. This is the rule, but there are more and more exceptions. Past research shows that big firms are conservative, holding back to let other firms assume the risk of trying new ideas.[35] This is true *if* the big firms are *traditional* and *bureaucratic* organizations. Large companies reorganizing around the principles of networking, like GE, are becoming much more receptive to innovative ideas, products, and services from the outside (for GE, see Chapter 15). As this trend continues, you'll have more opportunities to sign up big endorsers. For now, however, you have to evaluate which kind of big company you're dealing with.

3. Make contact with qualified opinion leaders. Make sure those who contact opinion leaders are technically qualified and knowledgeable. They also must have good interpersonal skills and understand the formula for building relationships (Chapter 4).

4. Get your message out by providing prototypes, early releases, samples, or test (beta) versions. Conduct briefings with opinion leaders. Have your best people make presentations at trade shows, conventions, scientific meetings, users groups, community events, and so on. Talk up your products and services at any credible forum.

5. Follow up, follow up, follow up. You can establish a systematic call program for contacting and recontacting opinion leaders, just as you do for making sales calls. Provide incentives so your corps of change agents will be compensated for their efforts. Despite the advice to follow up, be careful not to burn out or wear out your opinion leaders. Don't place too many demands on any particular one. To avoid this common problem, cast a wide net in step 3 and make sure your list of potential opinion leaders is long enough to avoid making excessive demands.

6. Sweeten the whole pilot program by rewarding word-of-mouth successes. When one of your people "lands" a big opinion leader,

reward him or her with cash and symbolic awards. Be sure to accompany roll-out with plenty of fanfare. And publicize the success of the pilot program. The practice of word-of-mouth marketing is an innovation that should diffuse throughout the entire organization.

What You Can Do in the *Long Run*

Now that you have a success under your belt, what you can do in the long run is expand the pilot program and make word of mouth an explicit part of every marketing program.

There are two approaches, the first more centralized than the second. Establish a formal *word-of-mouth marketing committee,* staffed with key marketing, advertising, and product people. The committee's role is to become the in-house champion of word of mouth. It would review marketing plans to make sure word of mouth is an explicit component of each one. The committee would act as central source of information and experience about how to do systematic word-of-mouth marketing.

You can also promote word-of-mouth marketing in a more decentralized fashion. Place a member of the successful pilot program in each marketing unit or group. Each of these members is a "seed" for growing word of mouth from within. Each would be a local champion for promoting and implementing word-of-mouth programs in his or her unit.

12
Building Supplier Partnerships

In the fall of 1991, I went in search of a critical supplier. I needed this
supplier to help me solve a networking problem. I had written the
proposal for this book, I wanted to find a good publisher. But I didn't
have relationships with the right publishing houses. I had contacts with
academic publishers, those who publish small-volume technical books
for specialized audiences, but I lacked access to the professional book
publishers required for *Networking Smart*. I needed an intermediary, a
go-between, someone who could supply me with those relationships.
What I needed was a literary agent, one of the professional go-
betweens in the world of publishing.

This solution presented me with yet another networking problem.
How should I find a reputable literary agent? I could consult directo-

ries such as *Literary Market Place* or lists provided by The Independent Literary Agents Association, but those aren't the best ways to find a good agent. Directories and lists tell you nothing about what *really* matters—reputation, personality, track record, access to and clout with the right publishers. Instead, I used my personal networks to find a good agent. I knew three authors who had recently published books aimed at the audience I was writing for. Two were colleagues at the University of Chicago's Graduate School of Business; one didn't use an agent, the other graciously offered to put me in touch with his.

The third author, Allan Cox, I had known from my graduate school days when I helped design the questionnaire he used to research *The Cox Report on the American Corporation*. Allan is a Chicago consultant who helps corporations develop their missions and improve their teams. He's also an accomplished author with numerous articles and six books to his credit, including *Confessions of a Corporate Headhunter* and his recent *Straight Talk for Monday Morning*. Allan knows the power of networking, and he kindly put me in touch with his agent for *Straight Talk*, Ken Shelton, who heads Executive Excellence Literary Agency. Allan gave Ken and his agency a resounding endorsement. They have a stellar track record, I learned, representing best-selling books like Stephen R. Covey's *The Seven Habits of Highly Effective People* and *Principle-Centered Leadership*. Now *this* was the agency for me.

Well, one thing led to another; I won't bore you with all the details except to say that the world of book publishing runs on networks,[2] like most businesses do, and applying the principles of networking leads to superior results. I'm very satisfied with my agent's performance and pleased to have *Networking Smart* published by McGraw-Hill.

The larger significance of my personal anecdote is the illustration of two key points about managing suppliers: (1) careful selection of suppliers is critical, and (2) nothing beats word of mouth and personal endorsement by a trusted associate for finding good suppliers. Your personal and organizational success depends mightily on building relationships with the right suppliers. No company is an island. About half of the cost of a typical manufacturer's product, for example, comes from components made and supplied by other companies.

Ultimately, I wanted to be *your* supplier; I wanted this book to be in your hands. But I couldn't get my product to you directly. I depended completely on the faithful performance of a chain of suppliers:

- I needed to find the right supplier of publisher relationships—a reputable literary agency. I used my personal contacts to find one.

- In turn, literary agents are suppliers to publishers. My agency tapped its contacts to place *Networking Smart* with the right publisher, McGraw-Hill. Agents help publishers solve their networking problem. Publishers are deluged with a torrential supply of unsolicited book proposals that come in "over the transom." Literary agents screen the flow, sifting and sorting to find a few promising ideas that they target to the right publishers.

- Once a book is published, publishers become suppliers and use their relationships, selling the book to wholesalers, distributors, national chains, and other book buyers.

- At chain's end, distributors, retailers, and book clubs are *your* suppliers. They close the final gap between you and me.

Managing suppliers, the subject of this chapter, is the flip side of the previous chapter; it looks at the buyer-seller relationship from the buyer's side. I've found that many smart managers dutifully build strong ties with customers, but oddly neglect to do the same with suppliers, even though suppliers make up one of the basic competitive forces in an industry.[3] Networking smart means managing *all* external relationships, including customers (Chapters 10 and 11), suppliers (this chapter), and competitors (Chapter 14). In this chapter, I describe how to use word-of-mouth networks to find new suppliers. I tell you why those who network smart are developing strong partnerships with suppliers of goods and services, but are using different strategies for suppliers of professional services—law firms, investment banks, advertising agencies, management consulting firms. I conclude the chapter with concrete advice on how you can put into practice what you know about building supplier partnerships.

Using Word of Mouth to Find Suppliers

Imagine that you run a thriving business in sore need of an infusion of new capital. Let's say you've exhausted your credit lines and can't finance from retained earnings or internal cash flow, so you must look to external sources of supply. What should you do? You could seek financing from traditional money suppliers—professional venture capitalists or the public capital markets. But if you don't (or don't want to) meet the stringent requirements for using these sources, you could do what many other business people do: tap the informal capital market. This market is a vast, unofficial network of business associates, friends, friends of friends, and others. These personal contacts make up the *finance grapevine* through which many a happy marriage of investors and capital seekers has been made.

How big do you think the informal capital market is? Huge. A study conducted for the U.S. Small Business Administration investigated the size and scope of the informal capital market in the United States.[4] Each year, an estimated 700,000 informal investors supply equity investments of over $30 billion, as well as more than $20 billion of loans and loan guarantees. That's a whopping total of more than $50 billion annually! The informal capital market is the single largest source of external funds for start-ups and small businesses. And there's even more good news for someone who's looking for financing: over half of the informal investors want to invest *more* money but can't find acceptable opportunities. Beyond actual investments, there's an enormous pool of available but untapped investment capital—to the tune of $20 billion or more per year!

How do people tap the informal capital market? How do investors find out about promising investment opportunities? By word of mouth. The study shows that business associates and friends are the most frequently used sources of information. Traditional go-betweens—investment bankers and investment brokers—are seldom used. And business associates and friends are rated as more *reliable* sources of information about investment opportunities than traditional sources.

The finance grapevine isn't limited to the informal capital market. The grapevine is also part of the highly organized, official capital market as well (like the stock market). Both institutional investors and individual investors get information via the finance grapevine. That's what two economists, Yale's Robert Shiller and Harvard's John Pound, found out. They fielded a survey of both types of investors and asked them directly how they got information that led to stock purchases.[5] The majority of their respondents, institutional and individual investors alike, said it was word of mouth: via colleagues, friends, business associates, and investment professionals.

Word of mouth plays a key role in getting suppliers and customers together (see also Chapter 11). Customers want to find good suppliers; suppliers want to find good customers. It's seldom talked about, but word of mouth is used everywhere. Add the examples from this chapter to those from Chapter 11 and you glimpse the enormous diversity of situations in which word of mouth plays a key role: authors in quest of literary agents, literary agents seeking publishers, companies searching for informal investors, doctors looking for new pharmaceutical drugs, farmers learning about hybrid corn, oil drillers in need of oil field services. When you seek suppliers, word of mouth is one of your very best sources of information.

The Trend toward Supplier Partnerships

Detroit auto makers were devoted disciples of the cult of the deal. Up until the early 1980s, they used *thousands* of parts suppliers. General Motors itself had a staggering 3500 suppliers, not counting material suppliers![6] GM and its peers awarded short-term contracts, changed suppliers for tiny price differences, and pitted supplier against supplier in an annual bidding contest with victory determined by price, not quality.

Times are changing. Today, U.S. auto makers are developing long-term relationships with suppliers. Auto makers use fewer suppliers than ever before. They do more subcontracting, enter into longer-term contracts, and involve their suppliers in design, planning, and quality improvement procedures.[7] This deals-to-relationships trend is widespread in U.S. industry. Frito-Lay once maintained a base of over 30 suppliers of flexible packaging; today they have only four.[8] Xerox and Boeing drastically cut their pool of suppliers, training the chosen few in quality control and including them in the design and development process.[9] And Digital Equipment's partnerships with its suppliers include joint planning and action at the strategic, technical, and professional levels.[10]

Why the trend toward partnerships? In a word: *quality*. Strong relationships are the road to high quality. The auto makers' deal-oriented attitude created all sorts of quality problems. Working with a large number of suppliers in such a detached way made it impossible for an auto company's engineers to know personally their supplier counterparts. Personal ties would have permitted them to resolve problems quickly and to tap the expertise of their suppliers. Without personal ties, they were forced to manage clumsily via impersonal specifications, blueprints, and contracts. Japanese auto makers, in contrast, have long achieved high quality by working closely with a few key suppliers. These close ties encourage regular communication, frequent interaction, personalized relationships, mutual understanding, and the evolution of trust—all necessary ingredients for quality.

Tennant Company, the world's leading manufacturer of floor maintenance equipment, is a U.S. firm that's learned the Japanese lesson well. It develops strong ties with most of its suppliers. In January 1988, for example, Tennant and Ford Motor Company made a sole-source commitment. Ford would be Tennant's only supplier of new 1.1 and 1.3 liter engines. Their reason? Quality. Before the partnership was established, says Tennant CEO Roger L. Hale and associates, "we were using four or five engine suppliers and had to adjust or repair more than half the engines we bought. That extra work was costing us money, and we knew the problems were preventable. Today our engines work right out of the box."[11] Most manufacturers like Tennant, who build supplier partnerships, report improved quality—zero defects, on-time delivery, quick problem resolution, well-designed parts, and innovative ideas.

The relationship trend is the result of a long battle between two competing philosophies—the cult of the deal versus the relationship paradigm. Deal cultists advise you to use lots of suppliers and to make them compete; with only a few suppliers, they warn, you become so dependent that avaricious suppliers extort all sorts of concessions from you. Not so, say the relationship advocates. The pathway to quality is the cultivation of strong—often exclusive—partnerships with suppliers. Long-term commitments enable both sides to make long-term relationship investments and work toward mutual understanding and mutual benefit. And strong supplier ties yield lower costs as well.[12]

Strong external ties, what Rosabeth Moss Kanter calls "stakeholder alliances," enable companies to "do more with less."[13] Digital Equipment Corporation (DEC) recognized the need. "In the future," says a DEC manager in Kanter's *When Giants Learn to Dance*, "we are not going to be able to build everything that we will be selling. We just don't have the resources to do that. We had better rely on other than Digital employees to help us deliver goods and services ourselves."[14] DEC has saved money and improved quality by cutting its supplier base and building supplier partnerships.

Partnerships are good for suppliers, too. Mutual benefit is the prime objective in managing supplier relationships, just as it is in managing personal relationships (Chapter 4). "We don't start every week wondering if we have the business," says National Purity president Jack Spillane, Tennant Company's sole-source supplier of certain chemicals. "We don't worry from day to day about losing business. We're tied right into Tennant's growth as long as we do what they need."[15] With mutual commitment, suppliers can redirect money and effort from marketing to the partnership itself. And marketing new business actually gets easier. Having a satisfied, long-term customer is the best credential a supplier could ask for.

Mutual benefit is critical. You can't build strong supplier ties without it. Too many large U.S. companies bully and exploit their suppliers in the name of "relationships" and "partnerships." Some GM suppliers, for example, accuse the ailing auto maker of roughshod treatment.[16] I've heard many stories about big companies who force their suppliers into just-in-time (JIT) delivery but don't make corresponding changes in their own systems and ways of doing business. Reducing inventory—on both sides—is a primary goal of JIT; the delivery system can yield *mutual* benefits. But the bullies just dump their inventory problems on suppliers, who are now forced to hold large inventories to accommodate their buyer's JIT demands.

Sadly, Wal-Mart, too, may be giving in to a similar temptation, despite its celebrated alliance with P&G. Wal-Mart and other so-called power retailers—Kmart, Toys 'R' Us, Target, Home Depot, Circuit City, Costco, and others—stand accused of wielding their vast market power to force concessions from suppliers, as reported in a recent *Business Week* cover story.[17]

On the face of it, the giant retailers' behavior doesn't sound too bad. It could be argued, for example, that they know the customer better than manufacturers do. And, by using their muscle on manufacturers, they save consumers money. But some retailers seem to be going too far, taking actions outside the spirit of true partnerships, demanding big discounts, lots of free samples, and big penalties and fines for errors and mistakes.[18] We consumers benefit now from the power struggle between retailers and suppliers, but the long-run outcome is unclear. Smaller suppliers are being squeezed out, unable to compete for the power retail business. Consolidation may create an industry populated by a few giant retailers and a few giant suppliers—and result in less innovation and higher prices.[19]

Transplanting Japanese Supplier Practices: How Far?

U.S. manufacturers are learning that the Japanese model works better. Still, many companies have a way to go to catch up with Japan's sophisticated use of suppliers. American companies still use more suppliers than their Japanese counterparts. They have fewer sole-source relationships (contrary to conventional wisdom, however, Japanese firms don't rely *predominately* on sole sources).[20] And they still subcontract less. GM, for example, produces 70 percent of the value of its cars, whereas Toyota itself produces only 20 percent.[21] Toyota, says economist John McMillan, even subcontracts *"the entire responsibility for some models' design and manufacture."*[22] And Japanese manufacturer-supplier relationships are deeply embedded in all sorts of social and business ties: interlocking directorates, joint ownership, equity investments, personal and informal allegiances. Japanese business is a dense, interwoven tapestry of business and social ties.

Skeptics say U.S. companies can't go as far. Japanese practices work in Japan because, well, they're so *Japanese:* Their culture and national mind set support close-knit supplier relationships. Americans, they say, are just too ornery and cantankerous; our individualistic culture is hostile to Japanese practices. They're wrong. Japanese practices are quite hardy and will thrive in foreign soil. Richard Florida and Martin Kenney took a close look at so-called *transplants*—Japanese auto makers like Honda, Nissan, and Toyota with manufacturing plants operating in the United States—and showed that Japanese practices *can* be successfully transplanted here.[23]

Here are some of the similarities between supplier relationships in Japan and those used by transplants in the United States[24]:

- *Close geographic proximity* of supplier and manufacturer. Forty percent are within a two-hour shipping radius; 90 percent within an eight-hour radius.

- *Continuous interaction and communication.* Almost all transplant suppliers are contacted immediately when they deliver a defective product, and almost all manufacturers make regular on-site visits to their suppliers.

- *Joint product design and development.* Transplants and their suppliers work closely together, exchanging engineers and shop-floor workers, to develop new products, processes, and techniques.

- *Supplier pyramids.* Transplants in the United States, like companies in Japan, use interlinked tiers of suppliers (each lower-level tier supplies the next-higher level). Often, they are linked by closely coordinated just-in-time delivery systems.[25]

Of course, transplanting a Japanese auto assembler here is different than overhauling a U.S. company well-entrenched in American-style management practices. The important point is this: Our culture is not *hostile* to Japanese supplier practices.[26]

What's the real impediment to Japanese practices? Not U.S. workers; they've adapted readily to the Japanese system. Indeed, those working in Japanese-style organizations fear a return to U.S. management methods. (Read *Rivethead* by ex-GM riveter Ben Hamper if you want a close-up view of how terrible traditional factory life has been at GM.) The real impediment, I'm sorry to say, is the attitude of middle managers. "During site visits and interviews," say Florida and Kenney, "we were told repeatedly that American middle managers, especially those recruited from U.S. automobile corporations, have experienced great difficulty adapting to Japanese production organization and management."[27]

Attitudes mean a lot. It's the Pygmalion principle: People tend to do what's expected of them (Chapter 2). Traditional U.S. manufacturers expect laziness, lack of initiative, and sloppy work; they employ the management teachings of the whips-and-chains philosophy. Because expectations are self-fulfilling, they end up getting just what they expect. But poor productivity and carelessness are not intrinsic or natural; they're caused by low expectations and destructive management practices. Japanese companies and their transplants hold loftier expectations of their workers and suppliers. They expect—*and set up the right conditions to encourage*—high performance, personal commitment, emotional involvement, and routine behavior above and beyond the call of duty.

How far can we go with Japanese supplier practices? As far as our attitudes and expectations will let us.

Tennant Company: Role Model, Again

Back in Chapter 6, I used Tennant Company as a role model of how to manage serendipity. The firm is back, this time as an exemplar of building strong supplier partnerships. Tennant's *Quest for Quality* (title of their first book) extends outward to embrace their supplier community as well.

Minneapolis-based Tennant Company, as you recall, is a manufacturer of world-class quality industrial and commercial surface equipment, supplies, and floor treating materials. Tennant's new book about quality, *Made in the USA: Strategic Supplier Quality Management,* written by CEO Roger L. Hale, Director of Manufacturing Ronald E. Kowal, Corporate Procurement Manager Donald D. Carlton, and Purchasing Engineering Manager Tim K. Sehnert, describes just how important good suppliers are to producing world-class quality products.[28] Tennant makes supplier excellence a cornerstone of its quality policy (see accompanying box).

Based on their experience, Tennant has developed a seven-point critical success factor program for building relationships with suppliers. Of everything I've learned about managing suppliers, their program impresses me the most; it's clear, simple, complete—and it works.[29]

1. *Top-down emphasis on quality.* Top managers from both sides must be committed to quality-generating relationships. Tennant executives meet with their top-level supplier counterparts right from the start. Having top levels involved sends the right signal and sets the right high expectations. People tend to do what is expected of them (the Pygmalion principle).

Tennant Quality Policy

Commitment to Excellence

TENNANT is committed to continuous improvement in identifying and satisfying worldwide customer needs at each and every point of contact.

We believe that to achieve this continuous improvement we must strive for employee excellence, group excellence, and supplier excellence.

- Achieving individual excellence for each employee

  Training and skill building
  Recognition and respect for each employee
  Universal involvement and empowerment

- Achieving group excellence

  Communication
  Effective, efficient, reliable processes for serving customers
  Achieve comprehensive understanding of how each of our roles combines to meet customer needs

- Achieving supplier excellence

  Partnership—mutually beneficial
  Top management commitment—long-term relationship
  Mutual trust—open and candid communication

SOURCE: Roger L. Hale, Ronald E. Kowal, Donald D. Carlton, and Tim K. Sehnert, *Made in the USA: Strategic Supplier Quality Management* (Tennant Company, Minneapolis, Minnesota, 1991), p. 11. Copyright 1991 by Tennant Company. Reproduced with permission.

---

2. *Sense of employee ownership: a corporate team approach.* This critical success factor applies the first networking principle: Relationships are a fundamental human need. This factor taps the basic need to belong, to contribute, to be a member of The Company of the Table. But it doesn't always come easily. The corporate team approach requires diverse functions—production, marketing, purchasing, R&D, etc.—to pull together. Tennant first had to overcome the bottleneck problem (Chapter 5).

3. *Customer/supplier partnership.* In a real partnership, the corrosive attitude of the cult of the deal is replaced with a positive attitude of cooperation, trust, and mutuality. A healthy customer-supplier partnership resembles a healthy personal relationship. Both partners strive for mutual understanding and mutual benefit. Both try to operate at the highest levels of understanding of interpersonal problems; when a problem does crop up, both work cooperatively to resolve it. A partnership is a win-win situation, not zero-sum.

Humility helps. Sometimes the customer causes the so-called supplier problem. Cessna Fluid Power Company was one of the first suppliers Tennant worked with to build a strong relationship. A "binding" spool valve was one of Tennant's main complaints with Cessna's parts. During a joint tour of Tennant's production plant, however, Cessna engineers saw the real source of the problem. "It was at that time," says Purchasing Engineering Manager Tim K. Sehnert, "Cessna pointed out how Tennant was incorrectly using a vise to hold the valves in place for the sub-assembly operation. Our mistake caused the castings to be distorted which made the spools bind."[30] It takes a lot of self-confidence and integrity to own one's problems (and tell us in their book!) and not blame the other party.

4. *Preventing problems from reaching the customer.* The customer shouldn't be the testing ground for products. At Tennant, preventing problems from reaching the customer means suppliers and Tennant work closely, starting in the design stage and continuing through production. Joint design not only ensures problem-free products for the customer but also improves the quality of product design from the beginning. Joint design is a common practice in Japanese manufacturer-supplier partnerships; some manufacturers, like Toyota, go even further, subcontracting responsibility for design and R&D of critical components to trusted suppliers.[31]

5. *Measuring and reporting quality.* You're flying blind without data. If you don't have hard data on quality, you can't judge suppliers, monitor improvements, or prevent unpleasant surprises. In a real partnership, both parties develop what Tennant calls *data consciousness.*[32] Data-conscious people look for opportunities to collect, report, and share data about quality, reliability, and delivery.

A word of caution: Don't add to the information problem I talked about in Chapter 3. Just adding data exacerbates the information problem because you have to sort and sift data to get useful information.[33] And just adding more data can contribute to a worse decision by giving you the illusion of control and confidence.[34] Develop judicious data consciousness. And along with your quantitative measures of performance and quality, build a network of supporting intelligence relationships (Chapter 3).

6. *Qualifying suppliers.* This success factor is all about setting high expectations and finding suppliers who can meet them. Tennant Company has developed rigorous qualification criteria to evaluate supplier performance. "Suppliers should meet qualification criteria within a specified time," says CEO Hale and associates, "and maintain it during the entire relationship. They should meet expectations."[35] Top-ranked suppliers enjoy long-term purchasing commitments and the opportunity to bid first on new business. Tennant publicizes stellar performance with awards and celebrations.

7. *Annual business management sessions.* Mutual understanding is the heart of supplier partnerships. Tennant uses annual business management meetings to review, discuss, and plan with suppliers. All levels of management can be involved. Of course, these important annual meetings are just part of the continuous dialogue between Tennant and its suppliers. As in the best personal relationships, Tennant and its suppliers strive to achieve a high level of mutual understanding.

The Big Exception: Professional Service Suppliers[36]

What do Burger King and IBM have in common? In the late 1980s, each advertiser dropped its traditional advertising firm and split accounts among multiple agencies. Burger King cut its strong tie with N W Ayer, replacing it with what the fast-food executives called a "dual agency structure." Brand identity or chain-image advertising went to D'Arcy Masius Benton and Bowles; short-term and product-specific advertising went to Saatchi and Saatchi Advertising. Big Blue made similar changes. IBM dropped its traditional relationship with the Lord Geller agency, splitting its $100+ million advertising account between two agencies, Lintas and Wells, Rich, Greene.

Burger King and IBM are but two examples of a big exception to the trend toward supplier partnerships. While relationships with suppliers of parts, components, and goods are moving from weak to strong ties, the opposite trend is taking place in relations with advertising agencies, investment banks, law firms, and professional service firms. Once, companies *did* have strong, often exclusive, ties with their professional service providers, but that's no longer true. My research with Robert Faulkner shows that most companies have abandoned traditional professional-services partnerships and instead opt for more detached, multiple-source strategies. Such strategies are founded, of course, on the cult of the deal (Chapter 1).

Even some Japanese companies consider professional services to be a big exception to the rule of strong partnerships. Our research revealed that the U.S. subsidiaries of Japanese auto makers, for example, show *less* loyalty to their advertising agencies than their U.S. counterparts. Honda and Nissan switch U.S. agencies and split accounts more often than do GM or Ford.[37] One of my Japanese MBA students reports a similar story about one of the largest construction and engineering firms in Japan.[38] The company's Engineering Design Group (EDG) works with small and medium-size engineering consultant companies who are hired on a project-by-project basis. EDG prefers to pay a fixed fee per drawing or design and will contract only for the first stages of a project. EDG managers even try to obtain early work on a free trial basis. If quality isn't acceptable, suppliers are simply dropped. No attempt is made to work with suppliers and improve their skills.

Why the big exception? There are several reasons, which Rob Faulkner and I analyze in our *California Management Review* article on managing suppliers of professional services,[39] but I think it comes down to this: Too many U.S. professional service firms became too opportunistic in the 1980s. They became champions of the cult of the deal, often to the shock and detriment of their long-term customers. For example, 15 years ago banks rarely financed hostile takeovers, but doing so became standard operating procedure in the 1980s—even when it trod upon traditional relationships. The corporate community abounds with tales of investment banks double-crossing clients.[40] Corporate customers had to become more deal oriented to protect themselves from the cult of the deal. In relationships between firms, just as between people, behavior sinks to the lowest common denominator.

To be fair, however, I have to point out that some corporate clients exacerbate the decline of supplier partnerships. Professional service relationships can't help but suffer when corporate finance managers become obsessed with minimizing fees on financings, or corporate advertisers continually put accounts up for review, or corporate lawyers force law firms into frenetic bidding contests. When this happens, corporate customers and their professional service suppliers succumb to a mutually defeating game of tit-for-tat.

It's also important to recognize the exceptions to my big exception. There are some cases where professional service suppliers and their clients develop strong, mutually beneficial partnerships. Capital Partners, for example, the highly successful commercial real estate developer I described in Chapter 5, builds strong exclusive ties with architects and contractors. I'm working right now with two law firms that are exceptions. Both are seriously exploring the application of total quality management (TQM) principles to legal services. Building strong, mutually beneficial customer-supplier partnerships is a big part of their TQM efforts.

Chicago-based advertising agency Leo Burnett Co. is another shining exception.[41] Burnett is renowned for its long-standing tradition of high-quality, personalized customer service. Most ad agencies are losing accounts left and right, but Burnett enjoys uncommon client loyalty. Of the agency's 33 U.S. clients, 15 have been with Burnett for more than 20 years; two-thirds of their total clientele for more than 10 years.

Burnett's clients are uncommonly loyal because the agency knows how to build genuine, mutually beneficial partnerships. Burnett has created a true relationship-building infrastructure (see Chapter 10). They know their market: a small, select list of blue-chip clients. A small roster means the agency can dedicate time, resources, and staff to each client. Burnett isn't trying to become the world's largest agency (a strategy that undid Saatchi and Saatchi). That doesn't mean Burnett is a small business. In 1992, the agency generated billings of $4.3 billion worldwide.

Burnett sets high performance expectations. The agency's mission is clear and focused: create the best advertising. The corporate logo—a hand reaching for the stars—says it all. Burnett sets high relationship expectations. The entire organization is oriented to providing unparalleled service and building long-term client partnerships. The partnership tradition permeates the culture. The agency builds strong employee relationships. Burnett enjoys a very high retention rate. Burnett hires the best and rewards them well. The typical Burnetter makes his or her entire career at the agency. (Burnett was cited recently as one of the 100 best U.S. companies to work for, the only ad agency on the list.) And the partnership tradition extends even to stockholders, all of whom are active, long-term employees. (Burnett is privately held, which allows the agency to take a long-run, partnership-building perspective.)

All levels are informed and intimately involved with clients. The agency stresses getting to know each client and its business. High employee retention permits the agency to embed and reinforce its business relationships with close personal ties. Burnetters travel frequently, visiting clients regularly no matter where they are. If necessary, the agency will even "loan" its people to fill open positions in client organizations. A Burnetter might, for example, fill in for a person on maternity leave or for a position vacated by staff changes.

Leo Burnett Co. is a true exception. Burnett is a role model for any professional service firm that wants to buck the trend and build genuine customer-supplier partnerships.

Unless you're lucky enough to find a progressive firm like Leo Burnett or Capital Partners, however, most attempts to build partnerships with professional service suppliers lead to problems. If you try to build relationships with deal-oriented suppliers, you're in the unhappy region of the relationship grid I call *exploitation* (see Figure 10-1 in Chapter 10). And it's *you* who gets taken advantage of. If you find yourself stuck in this unhappy situation, consider using four guidelines Rob Faulkner and I derived from our research on managing suppliers of professional services.[42]

1. *Use multiple-source strategies.* I wish I could advise you to build partnerships with professional service suppliers. Some companies do so, with great success. As a rule, however, a multiple-source strategy is usually necessary to get professional service suppliers to behave properly. But keep in mind that a little goes a long way: just moving from one to two suppliers may be all you need. I particularly like Motorola's "two-lawyer rule." To ensure quality, every piece of work done by one lawyer is reviewed by another lawyer.

2. *Develop credible internal alternatives.* Developing internal alternatives is a good way to avoid dependence on opportunistic suppliers and to get the experience you need to deal more effectively with them. Examples: Companies can meet more of their legal needs internally or avoid litigation altogether by arbitrating or mediating instead. Advertisers can use in-house media managers. And corporate finance officers can seek financing directly from institutional investors, circumventing their bankers.[43]

3. *Link pay and performance.* Some people think linking pay and performance is impossible to do for professional services, but that's not true. Corporate finance managers, for example, can insist on a "firm commitment" instead of "best efforts" from underwriters of new issues of stocks or bonds. Establish incentives for superior service and/or quantity discounts. The traditional 15 percent advertising commission is only used now by a minority of companies. Negotiate fees and replace straight commissions with nontraditional arrangements (fee for service, commission plus fee, sliding-scale fees, or contingency fees). If establishing a fee structure is difficult, renegotiate compensation for each phase or step individually.

4. *Increase accountability by monitoring and auditing.* You know what the typical bill for professional services looks like:

> For professional services rendered.
>
> TOTAL NOW DUE: $ (big number)

The typical bill is too aggregated, vague, and uninformative to be of much use. To be more effective, insist on detailed and itemized bills. You can even hire outside auditors, evaluators, and monitors to assist you.

What You Can Do *Now*

How good are your suppliers? Who are your best? Your worst? The average? You may not know. Even Tennant didn't know when they embarked on their supplier excellence program.[44] Not only that, but Tennant discovered they didn't even have the right data to figure it out. What you can do *now* is figure it out for your critical purchased products and services: How good are your suppliers?

To answer, you need to develop supplier evaluation criteria, tailored to your circumstances. The checklist for supplier evaluation criteria shown in the box will get you started, but customize it to apply to your suppliers. Consider technical performance, but don't forget the personal, relationship, and fuzzy cultural criteria, even those that seem intangible and subjective. Everything can't be quantified. Along with hard data, you need to get a feel for the supplier. What's the supplier's philosophy? What's the culture of the organization like? Do you like the people? Is the "chemistry" right?

Above all, remember that you're building an implicit *relationship contract* with every supplier, consciously or not. Just as in a relationship between two people (see Chapter 4), a customer and supplier develop tacit understandings about roles, responsibilities, and performance. As you apply the checklist for supplier evaluation, keep in mind the concept of the relationship contract. What kind of implicit agreement are you developing? What are its terms and conditions? Are the terms and conditions mutually beneficial?

If your company's like most, you don't have all the data you need at your fingertips. To collect data, you have to tap a variety of sources. Your direct experience with a supplier is an important one. Like Tennant, you may have to set up formalized systems to collect and track data. Information is also available directly from suppliers: make on-site visits; look the place over; get a feel for it. Check secondary data sources (financial statements, credit ratings, security analysts reports, articles in the business press). Don't forget the most important critical source of all: word-of-mouth networks. Activate your personal intelligence network to collect all the positive and negative information you can get.

Supplier Evaluation Criteria

General Performance Criteria

- *Financial strength.* How financially viable is the supplier? What are its long-term prospects? Examine the supplier's balance sheet, income statement, credit history, reputation in the financial community, etc.

- *Corporate strategy.* What is the supplier's overall strategy? What markets does it serve and how is that changing? Has the supplier targeted your market as a critical growth area, or is it pulling out and investing in other areas?

- *Life-cycle stage of development.* Look back at Chapter 8. What *stage* of the organizational life cycle is the supplier in? Is the supplier on the verge of a major transition—such as the leadership crisis—that could disrupt supplier relationships?

- *Innovativeness.* Is the supplier a leader or a follower? How much does it invest in R&D? Is the supplier innovative on the *organizational front*—a stiff bureaucracy with a bottleneck problem (Chapter 5) or a flexible and dynamic network organization (Chapter 15)?

- *Quality leadership.* Is the supplier on the forefront of the total quality improvement revolution? Does it have a demonstrated commitment to total customer service? Can it deliver the quality you need, both now and in the future?

- *Top-management strength.* What capabilities do managers have? Is it a one-person show? How deep and strong is the bench? Is top management succession worked out?

Technical Performance Criteria

- *Product/service reliability.* Does the product or service perform to your specifications and expectations? Does it meet (or exceed) expected life? Are *your* customers happy with it? Is it a source of complaints from them?

- *Defects.* Does the supplier meet (or exceed) your established defect targets? Defect rates vary with product complexity. Tennant, for

(Continued)

example, has a defect goal of 1 per 1000 for hydraulic hoses and fittings, but 10 per 1000 for engines and electric motors.[45] Are there established procedures for quick-handling defective components or services?

- *Delivery.* Do you get what you want when you need it? If you use just-in-time (JIT), does the supplier meet your JIT goals?

- *Ordering procedures.* Does the supplier use old-fashioned purchase-order-and-invoice methods, or advanced real-time technology, such as electronic data interchange or similar methods?

- *After-purchase support.* Does the supplier provide satisfactory technical support after purchase and delivery?

- *Continuous technical improvement.* Is the supplier making continuous progress for improving technical performance?

Relationship Performance Criteria

- *Relationship orientation.* Where is the supplier on the spectrum of relationships? Is the supplier primarily *deal-oriented* or *relationship-oriented?* Does it already have successful partnerships with other customers?

- *Communication and interaction.* Does the supplier communicate frequently with you? Do they initiate conversations? Do they keep you informed? Do they tell you about problems *first?* Do you interact regularly with multiple people from multiple functions? Do they visit you regularly? Do their people *live* at your facilities?

- *New electronic technologies.* Has the supplier invested in the new information and communication technologies? Has the supplier explored electronic link-ups with you? Over 2600 of Kmart's 3000 suppliers, for example, have electronic linkages with the power retailer.[46]

- *Quality of personnel.* Do you get the supplier's best and brightest? Do you have access to different departments and functions when you need it?

- *Top-management involvement.* Are top executives and managers involved in the relationship? Do they sit in on meetings? Do they visit you? Do you have access to them as the need arises?

- *Problem resolution.* How quickly can you resolve problems and conflicts? Are there established channels and procedures? Is there a sense of urgency?

- *Embeddedness.* Have your people and your suppliers developed strong *personalized* relationships? Do they know each other well? Have you seen them together at more than business events? Do they get along?

- *Relationship investments.* Has the supplier made investments in your relationship? Have they dedicated teams of people? Do they provide specialized training? Do they invest in equipment and establish procedures designed to serve you better? Has the supplier relocated near you?

- *Expectations of continuity.* Does the supplier expect the relationship to continue in the long run? Expectations of continuity are self-fulfilling prophesies (the Pygmalion principle), because those who expect to stay in a relationship make the investments that sustain it.[47]

- *Continuous relationship improvement.* Is the supplier committed to continuously improving and strengthening the relationship with you?

What You Can Do *Soon*

If you are able now to answer the question "How good are your suppliers?" then what you can do *soon* is consider improvements in your supplier relationships. Based on your previous analysis, prioritize your supplier relationships into three categories:

- *Invest* is your strategy for supplier relationships that are critical and have great potential for true partnerships.

- *Hold* is your strategy for supplier relationships that are fine and don't need additional investment at this time. (This doesn't mean they're unimportant or that you should neglect them. Maintenance-level investments are still required.)

- *Divest* is your strategy for suppliers who are unsatisfactory and hold little potential for improvement. A supplier who's withdrawing from your market, or who's adamantly deal oriented, is a prime candidate for divestment.

Building strong ties with suppliers is accomplished in many ways. The most important step is to *involve your suppliers* in discussion and dialogue. Joint action is essential for *mutual understanding* and *mutual benefit*. Only together can you find ways to create value in the relationship and tap the power of The Company of the Table.

- *Meet with your suppliers.* Explain your intentions. Invite their input, help, and assistance. (If they've read Chapter 10, "Building Relationships with Customers and Clients," they'll welcome your advances.)

- *Establish regular communication channels.* Open dialogue and keep it open. Visit suppliers; have them visit you. Become a critical node in supplier intelligence networks.

- *Increase frequency of interaction.* More interaction invokes the fourth networking principle—repeated interaction encourages cooperation. Give your people time, resources, and incentives to interact more.

- *Get suppliers involved earlier.* Solicit supplier input in the brainstorming and design stages. Make use of supplier expertise.

- *Involve higher levels.* Have top-level managers meet with suppliers, and keep top levels engaged in the process of developing partnerships.

- *Involve more internal groups and functions.* Purchasing may take the lead, but other internal functions influence the quality of the relationship. Get others involved—manufacturing, quality assurance, R&D, sales, finance, and so on. (But you have to have solved your bottleneck problem—see Chapter 5.)

- *Use "vendor champions."*[48] A vendor champion adopts an important supplier and becomes the supplier's advocate, point person, sponsor. Each vendor champion develops strong personalized ties with the supplier, makes sure the supplier's interests are served, and does whatever it takes to marshal resources to do so.

- *Create supplier action teams.* These are the counterparts of your customer action teams (Chapter 10). A supplier action team is a *joint* effort, including people from both sides. Remember that diversity aids serendipity (Chapter 6): Make sure participants come from multiple functions, disciplines, and departments.

- *Embed business ties in social relationships.* If you implement my recommendations, the embeddedness phenomena will occur naturally. Relationships are a fundamental human need (principle 1), and people from both sides will naturally build personal ties. Boost this natural process by actively seeking opportunities to forge social links with key suppliers.

Building strong relationships is a positive experience, and you'll be tempted to spend all your time with your favorite ones. But you must also face the difficult task of cutting ties. If your company's like most, you're using too many suppliers. You have to *divest*. Sometimes suppliers make it easy. You're not important to them, and they let you know it. They won't meet with you, delay returning phone calls, or just send low-level managers. Some suppliers simply aren't interested in partnerships. Divesting these suppliers isn't difficult. But even if suppliers don't make it easy, you still have to shrink your supplier pool to a manageable size. Working with a few select suppliers makes it possible for you and your people to build personalized relationships with them. Just as you can't be intimate friends with dozens and dozens of people, you can't develop close ties with an excessive number of suppliers.

Reducing the number of suppliers frees time and energy to rededicate to favored suppliers. It also enables you to allocate more business to them. One of the best ways to invest in partnerships is by rewarding treasured suppliers with *more* business. Allocating more business naturally invokes two powerful networking principles. Repeated interaction encourages cooperation (principle 4), and expectations are self-fulfilling (principle 2). By rewarding superior performance, you build expectations of continuity. With such expectations, favored suppliers can make relationship-strengthening investments with confidence.

What You Can Do in the *Long Run*

Building solid supplier partnerships is a long-term proposition. Even now, more than a decade after Tennant started building supplier partnerships, CEO Roger Hale and his associates feel the journey has just begun.[49] The substantial but incremental successes of the 1980s must be surpassed by quantum improvements in delivery, product development, and response to customers. What you can do in the long run is establish a mechanism to explore ways to make quantum improvements in your supplier relationships.

To begin, establish a *supplier partnership task force,* the organizational companion of the client partnership task force I recommend in Chapter

10. The task force's goal is to devise a comprehensive supplier selection, management, and improvement program. It's critical that you involve key suppliers as full participating members of the task force. You can't design a solid relationship strategy in a vacuum; it has to be a joint endeavor. Pick a small number of trusted suppliers and discuss the idea with them. If they're networking smart, like you, they're already forming a client partnership task force to make quantum improvements in customer relationships—and that means you.

13
Networking
Clubs

When you have an idea or thought or need,
you have a huge network of people to pull
from. Members are very goal directed toward
making your business successful.
MARGARET BELECKIS, VICE PRESIDENT, OPPEN-
HEIMER & CO., COMMENTING ON HER EXPERIENCE
IN TWO WOMEN'S NETWORKING GROUPS[1]

A good networking club can mean the difference between success and
failure. That's been Mac McDowell's experience, president of Exectech
Microsystems, a quick-response computer maintenance service in
Schaumburg, Illinois.[2] "If any one company in our group can say that
this was a survival vehicle, it's us," says Mac. "I never was one to
believe in networking—until now."

Mac is an active member of *NSACI Networkers*, a networking club
organized by the Northwest Suburban (Chicago) Association of
Commerce and Industry.* The recession and the sudden defection of
his key sales partner (with major customers) had put Exectech
Microsystems on the brink and left Mac struggling to make sales. A
chance encounter with a NSACI Networker introduced him to the
group. "I attended two sessions," says Mac, "and was enthralled with

---

*Addresses and phone numbers for networking clubs named in this chapter are listed at
the end of the chapter.

the process." Within six months after joining, the group was generating a steady stream of sales for him. And it saved Mac's company. "It has been truly a godsend for me and my company," declares Mac. "It meant survival for me through the recession—it was the business coming in from this group. After the recession, it put us over the top." Exectech Microsystems just enjoyed its best quarter yet, with 80 percent of new sales coming through NSACI Networkers.

A good networking club provides more than just sales leads. A good club's a great opportunity to learn and develop professional relationships. "It's a peer group," says Mac. "The vast majority of members are entrepreneurs and principals in the organizations they're representing. Several people are sounding boards for me. There's also the intangible reward of associating with similar professionals. And there's the learning—every week there are two business presentations. Learning about these businesses broadens your knowledge." Oppenheimer & Co. vice president Margaret Beleckis agrees. A good group, she says, "helps you grow and develop in your own business." But you have to have the right frame of mind. "If you go there with the attitude that you just want to get business," she warns, "you won't get much from the organization."

Like Mac, when I first heard of organized networking clubs, I was a little skeptical. I firmly believe in the power of networking, of course, but I was unsure of the value of a formally organized club with the avowed purpose of networking. Sometimes networking works best when we aren't so, well, *obvious* about it, when it's a by-product of other events and activities. I was wrong. After talking with people like Mac McDowell, I've become a true believer. Networking works when we *are* obvious about it, and networking *smart* means seriously considering the proven value of organized networking clubs. And that goes for small *and* big companies. Networking clubs can help anyone boost sales, collect intelligence, and find peer support.

I've become such a believer that I've devoted an entire chapter to the topic of organized networking clubs. This chapter can be used in conjunction with most of the other chapters. For example, networking clubs help you build your own intelligence networks (Chapter 3), find good people or change jobs yourself (Chapter 9), market via word of mouth (Chapter 11), and find and qualify new suppliers (Chapter 12). In this chapter, I first discuss the small-world principle, the logic on which networking clubs are based. I then describe the various types of clubs and what makes a good club to join. I conclude the chapter with advice on how you can incorporate networking clubs into your networking activities.

It's a Small World, Inc.

Networking clubs institutionalize the small-world networking principle (Chapter 2). This principle is based on simple yet powerful arithmetic. Each of us has two zones of contacts. Your first-order zone contains all of your *direct* contacts. (The typical professional has about 3500.) Your second-order zone contains all of your *indirect* contacts, everyone linked to your first-order contacts but not directly to you. Every time you add one direct contact, you gain access (potentially) to a huge number of new indirect, second-order contacts. The problem, of course, is that you can't always get access to your new-found second-order contacts. You don't know who they are (they're indirectly linked to you), and it's considered impolite and pushy to probe and try to find out. (I'm sure you've had the unpleasant experience of an associate who becomes a direct-sales fanatic and tries to sell through you to all of your friends and associates.) Usually, you have to wait until a direct contact *volunteers* to make a referral on your behalf.

Organized networking clubs solve the problem. Making contacts and referrals is the raison-d'être of a networking club. That's what everyone's there for, that's what everyone's agreed to do. At Mac McDowell's networking club, NSACI Networkers, every member is *required* to make an average of two referrals a week. Referrals are recorded and reported monthly, so none can duck the requirement.

When you join a networking club, you immediately get a new set of *direct* contacts, all committed to the concept of networking. Your new direct contacts are good sources of business themselves. Member-to-member transactions, as they're called, yield new sales directly. But it's the *indirect* contacts that really make a difference. Your new direct contacts willingly give you access to their contacts. They're bridges to your newly expanded second-order zone. And you're not pushy when you ask for access to your new indirect contacts—asking for and giving referrals are requirements.

Free access to the second-order zone is the real power of organized networking clubs. "We're not just selling to our first-level referrals," says Mac. "We are down to our *fourth* level and just hit our *fifth*-level referrals." A first-level referral is a friend of a friend. For Mac, it's a direct referral from one of his fellow NSACI Networkers, like this: Mac to A to B. A fifth-level referral is a much longer chain that really illustrates networking power. It looks like this: Mac to A to B to C to D to E to F. All the intermediaries between Mac and F are satisfied customers or those who are so impressed with Mac's reputation that they made the referral.

Utilizing the power of the small-world principle depends on two rules of conduct. The first is reciprocity. Networking clubs work if and only if everyone gives and receives referrals. The second is trust. Clubs require members to make referrals, but the recipient has to make good. A referral becomes a reference: a testimonial to quality performance. A networker who makes a referral entrusts the recipient with a valued personal contact. The recipient must handle the contact responsibly and live up to expectations.

When you perform well, the news of your superior performance spreads throughout the word-of-mouth network. Mac has received many referrals from unsolicited testimonials about his excellent performance. But remember that word-of-mouth networks carry positive *and* negative news—and negative news spreads faster.[3] If you fail to perform, or abuse a referral, everyone quickly finds out and you won't get any more referrals.

An Infinite Variety

For many people, the idea of a networking club conjures up a specific mental image. Depending on your experience or what you've heard, you might think of a networking club as a small group of close associates, or as a huge disorganized social event, or something between these extremes. And you'd be right. There's an infinite variety of networking clubs, and you can find one that fits any description.

Organized networking clubs differ in four key ways: focus of interest, size, membership composition, and rules and procedures. It's important to keep these characteristics in mind when you go looking for a club. Networking clubs differ so much that you can't pick one at random. You have to find one that can meet your needs.

Focus of Interest

Networking clubs vary enormously in focus of interest. Some have very general missions, and others are dedicated to specific activities, such as sales or job finding. Some concentrate their efforts in particular geographic areas, while others are national or international in scope.

NSACI Networkers, for example, serves a local business community. This club's devoted to increasing members' sales of products and services in Schaumburg and Hoffman Estates, two large and dynamic suburbs northwest of Chicago. (Hoffman Estates is where Sears moved when it abandoned Sears Tower in Chicago.) Similarly, Greater O'Hare Networking Executives and The Women's Professional Sales

Network of Wilmette, Illinois, are local forums for making sales, building contacts, and getting peer support.

Increasing sales isn't always the main reason for networking groups. Some groups serve a much broader mission. A few of these groups are quite exclusive and acquire new members by invitation only. As such, they are not useful to most people. Others, however, serve the broad needs of large constituencies. For example, The National Association of Women Business Owners with 50 local chapters and the National Association for Female Executives (NAFE) with over 300 local networks serve the career development and networking needs of women executives (some affiliates admit men). The National Association of Negro Business and Professional Women's Clubs, Inc., has over 350 local affiliates that serve similar networking needs.

The Young Presidents Organization (YPO) is another group with a very broad mission. The YPO is devoted to the continuing education and professional development of young CEOs. To qualify, you have to be a CEO of a sizable company before you reach age 40. (And at 50, you have to leave.) Through its local chapters, national meetings, and international conferences, the YPO is an ideal forum for learning about business and developing leadership skills. Gordon Segal, CEO of Crate & Barrel, found the YPO to be an important part of his personal and professional growth. As Howard Haas describes in *The Leader Within,* "it wasn't until [Segal] joined the Young President's Organization that he realized the true value of networking. He had emerged from a management cocoon he himself had built as the Crate's founder, entrepreneur, and CEO. It wasn't until he met other young chief executives that he realized they too had problems similar to his own, problems he thought were unique. He no longer felt isolated."[4]

Some networking clubs are very specialized. The Business Network (Ohio) and the Boston-area 128 Venture Group (named for the famous high-technology region around Boston)[5] are "match makers" that bring together informal investors and high-tech innovators in need of financing. For example, the 128 Venture Group's charter describes its mission as follows: "Provide a forum where the technical innovators seeking to start or build a firm can meet informally with the venture community representatives and individual investors who provide seed capital and venture funding as well as potential candidates for their management team."[6] Networking clubs such as these formalize the finance grapevine I described in Chapter 11. And they work quite well. The 128 Venture Group, for example, has thrived for over 10 years.

The majority of organized networking clubs are devoted to career development and job hunting. These groups formalize the networking lessons from Chapter 9. For example, the Forty Plus Clubs (with locations nationwide) focus on job hunting and related services (career counseling, résumé preparation, etc.). Many colleges and universities develop formal networking services to assist students and alums. For example, my alma mater Northwestern University has AlumNet—a career service for students and alumni that includes job counseling, access to kiNexus, Inc. (the nation's largest on-line candidate search service), and an electronic billboard linking colleges and companies.

Size of Membership

Some networking clubs are small and strictly limit their membership. NSACI Networkers restricts its membership to a maximum of 45 individuals, based on the philosophy that members should get to know each other well. At the other end of the spectrum, an average of 250 members attend the Business After Hours networking events sponsored by the Chicagoland Association of Commerce and Industry, with some events breaking the 500 attendance mark. Large and small clubs offer opportunities for different types of networking.

Membership Composition

With the infinite variety of networking clubs, it's no surprise that the composition of membership varies widely. Business people from all walks of life join networking clubs. Some clubs are restricted to business owners or corporate executives, others are wide open. Some attract small businesses, others draw representatives from large companies. Some career development groups serve the networking needs of those early in their careers, whereas others are intended to serve the professional development needs of people who are older and well along in their careers. Given the infinite variety, it's important to find a networking group that's suitable for you.

Rules and Procedures

Networking clubs are organized quite differently. Some are very informal and loosely organized. They meet sporadically, change locations, and impose few rules and regulations. To me, such groups seem more like excuses for having a good time, the kind of "shmooz-fests" that give networking a bad name. To really benefit from organized networking, I recommend clubs that are serious, well-organized, and well-run. Mac's club, NSACI Networkers, is one such group. They were founded by the local chamber of commerce with an explicit goal:

"to generate new and additional business through members aggressively promoting each other."[7] The club has established sound rules and regulations. Membership is held to a maximum of 45 to make sure everyone gets to know each other well. Competing businesses are not allowed, and any new applicant is rejected if only one member objects.

NSACI Networkers meet every Thursday from 7:30 to 9 a.m. Breakfast is provided (covered by mandatory dues). Each meeting follows a set format, which includes two 15-minute presentations by different Networkers who describe their companies, products and services, and kind of referrals they need. The club demands active participation. "Everyone is expected to do their fair share," says NSACI vice president of programs Carol Pape.[8] Networkers are expected to attend a majority of the weekly meetings (Mac has missed only two in two years) and give an average of one referral a week. Attendance is recorded, and members report details of referrals given and received. Statistics are compiled and reported each month.

What You Can Do *Now*

What you can do *now* is consider joining a formal networking club. Before you jump in, however, take a moment to figure out *why* you want to join a networking club. Ask yourself three questions:

1. *What's my reason for joining?* You may be looking for sales leads in a particular area, or you could be more interested in moral support, rubbing elbows with peers, and so on. Be sure of your motivation before you join up.

2. *Am I prepared to make the commitment?* Above all, a good networking club takes time. You must be prepared to commit to regular attendance over the long run. There may also be some monetary commitment (like dues or meal expenses).

3. *Am I expecting immediate results?* Organized networking clubs speed up the natural networking process, but you still need patience and reasonable expectations. Mac's investment, for example, really didn't begin to pay off for six months. It takes time to build up trust among your fellow networkers.

Talk with others who are members of networking clubs. Ask them what their experience is. What were their motivations and expectations? What do they get out of participating? What would they do differently?

What You Can Do *Soon*

If you think a networking club's for you, what you can do *soon* is find and join a good one. Use the checklist in the accompanying box to pick one that's right for you. Above all, be sure there's a good fit between the networking club and your needs. And, when you evaluate a group, remember that a good networking club offers more than just sales leads; it can be a productive forum for learning and professional development.

How do you *find* a networking club? For starters, at the end of this chapter, I've provided you with a list of the networking clubs I've mentioned in this chapter. Some of these are national organizations with hundreds of local affiliates and chapters; be sure to check with the national headquarters to find one close to you. One of the best ways to find a good networking club is through word of mouth: someone (or someone who knows someone) who's an active and satisfied member of a networking club. It's a small world; ask around.

What You Can Do
in the *Long Run*

What you can do in the long run is establish your own networking club. You might be thinking that you won't need to do this. But it's not so unlikely. Perhaps you can't find a satisfactory networking club, or you're excluded from good clubs due to a noncompetition rule. Or it could be that you're an active member of a good club and you wish to expand the networking club concept into new areas and markets.

If you've found a good networking club but can't join, or you want to expand the club into new areas, propose a joint venture. A joint venture with an existing club is better than trying to start a new club from scratch. An existing club lends credibility, and its format can serve as a model for the new one. You may be permitted to review the club's current waiting list to find prospective members.

If you have to start from scratch (or need to supplement a waiting list), use word-of-mouth marketing to find good prospective members (Chapter 11). Don't advertise in the newspaper; be more selective than that. You probably know several people who would be good candidates. Approach them with the idea, have them suggest more good candidates, who themselves will suggest more, and so on. Think of your customers, suppliers, former employers—anyone who might be appropriate. To spur ideas, review the primary contact list in Chapter 9.

Strive for diversity. We know from Chapter 6 that diversity stimulates serendipity, and you want to raise the odds of the chance encounters that bring new leads into the group. If everyone is similar, you'll

How to Pick a Good Networking Club

1. What's the specific purpose of the club? Does it serve your specific needs?

2. Does it *primarily* serve the market or geographic region you're interested in?

3. Do your products or services or needs fit the club's mission?

4. Is the composition of the membership suitable for meeting your needs? Can the members help you learn and grow professionally?

5. If the club is oriented toward sales, are club members themselves potential customers?

6. How often does the club meet? (Weekly or biweekly is best.)

7. When does the club meet? (Early morning sessions are usually more productive than after hours.)

8. Can you arrive early and stay late for informal networking, follow up, etc.?

9. Does the club have formal rules and regulations? (Clubs with established policies and procedures work best.)

10. Is membership limited to a reasonable number so members get to know each other well?

11. Do members have regular opportunities to make presentations to the group?

12. Are referrals required, recorded, and reported?

13. What's the club's track record? (It's a good sign if the club keeps records of performance, such as number of referrals given, dollars invoiced, etc.)

14. Are competing businesses allowed in the group? (Avoid clubs that allow competitors to join.)

15. Do current members have a say in who's allowed to join?

16. Will the club let you sit in for a few sessions before joining?

17. Are there dues or other monetary requirements?

18. Can you join right away? Is there a waiting list?

get along marvelously (due to the similarity principle), but your personal networks will overlap too much. The group will lack reach into diverse business and social circles.

You should also strive for diversity to eliminate harmful competition within the networking club. I think the NSACI Networkers' rule of noncompeting business is productive; it reduces conflict and encourages trust and loyalty. Bob Burg, a founder of local networking clubs, offers similar advice.[9]

Make sure your new networking club is serious and well-organized. It should have rules and regulations. I recommend that you use NSACI Networkers as a role model, adapted to fit your needs and circumstances. Use the criteria I've provided in "How to Pick a Good Networking Club" as guidelines to designing a productive, well-run group. Make sure your new networking club is one that those who network smart would like to join.

Appendix: Directory of Networking Clubs

This directory lists the networking clubs I mentioned in this chapter. Several are national organizations with hundreds of local affiliates and chapters; contact them for information on those close to you. Check with your local chamber of commerce to see if it sponsors a networking club. Do the same with any college or university that you've attended. And check listings in local newspapers and business magazines.

National Organizations

Forty Plus Club of New York, Inc.
15 Park Row
New York, NY 10038
(212) 233-6086

National Association of Women
  Business Owners
1377 K Street, N. W., Suite 637
Washington, DC 20009
(301) 608-2590

National Association for Female
  Executives (NAFE)
127 W. 24th Street, 4th Floor
New York, NY 10011
(212) 645-1112

National Association of Negro
  Business and Professional
  Women's Clubs, Inc.
1806 New Hampshire Avenue, N.W.
Washington, DC 20009
(202) 483-4206

Local Clubs

NSACI Networkers
  Northwest Suburban Association
  of Commerce and Industry
1450 E. American Lane, Suite 140
Schaumburg, IL 60173
(708) 517-7110

The Chicagoland Chamber of
  Commerce
200 N. LaSalle
Chicago, IL 60601
(312) 580-6900

Women's Professional Sales
  Network
825 Green Bay Road, Suite 270
Wilmette, IL 60091
(708) 256-0264

Greater O'Hare Networking
  Executives
c/o Greater O'Hare Association of
  Industry and Commerce
1050 Busse Road, Suite 100
Bensonville, IL 60106
(708) 350-2944

The Business Network/Network of
  Small Businesses
5420 Mayfield Road
Suite 205
Lyndhurst, OH 44124
(216) 442-5600

14
Cooperating with Competitors

*Today the strategic challenge of doing more
with less leads corporations to look outward as
well as inward for solutions to the competitiveness dilemma....They can* pool *resources
with others,* ally *to exploit an opportunity, or*
link *systems in a partnership.*

ROSABETH MOSS KANTER
When Giants Learn to Dance[1]

The summer of 1991 was a time of great mystery and romance, corpo-
rate-wise: IBM and Apple Computer made it official and announced
their matrimonial intent.[2] Rumors of the unlikely romance circulated
soon after the pair began their courtship in secret a year earlier, but
the actual engagement still rocked the computer world. Skeptics
scoffed at the idea that this odd couple could make it last, but most
observers (and all competitors!) were awestruck by the fantastic potential of the new team-up.

In the time since their historic announcement, the budding romance
has blossomed. Apple will be using IBM's superfast RISC chips in its
popular Macintosh computers. Joint venture Taligent (*tal* for talent,
igent for intelligent) is developing next-generation operating systems
for personal computers. A sister joint venture, Kaleida, is working on
data-graphics-sound-video multimedia technology that IBM President
Jack Kuehler says will bring a "human-like quality" to computers.[3]
The PowerOpen project is developing a new version of Unix, an up-
scale operating system for workstations and larger computers.

The Apple-IBM alliance could solve vexing problems for each computer maker. Both Apple and IBM are experiencing falling market

274

share and earnings, their positions nibbled away by low-cost copycat competitors. Apple, maker of classy high-priced machines, has had to slash prices to spur sales. Its self-imposed inability to communicate directly with IBM machines locked itself out of the lucrative corporate market. And now it lacks the big bucks needed to create the next wave of revolutionary computer products.

Giant IBM has its own woes. Largely a hardware house, Big Blue lacks Apple's innovativeness and talent in software technology. It became too dependent on Bill Gates's Microsoft. For IBM, the alliance is a wedge to loosen Gates's iron grip on developing operating systems. (Jilted Microsoft has since formed a new alliance with Digital Equipment Corporation.)[4] The Apple alliance is also needed to break IBM's dependence on chip maker Intel. In a three-way pact, IBM's new RISC (reduced instruction set computing) chips will be made for Apple by Motorola.

The IBM-Apple alliance is sensational news; it makes great headlines. What doesn't make the headlines is an even more startling fact: IBM is already involved in over 400 strategic alliances worldwide![5] The IBM-Apple alliance is but one example of the widespread trend of cooperating with competitors. Indeed, competing companies everywhere—in industries as diverse as biotechnology, communications, automobiles, electronics, steel, pharmaceuticals, robotics, and others— are burying traditional rivalries and learning to compete more effectively by joining forces.

In this chapter, I tell you why more and more competitors are cooperating. I describe what kinds of alliances they make and why some work and some don't. I provide concrete advice on how you can assess your need for alliances and find the right alliance partners. You may think that the making of alliances is a task reserved for those at the top. It's not. No matter where you are in the organization, seeking alliances is part of your networking job. Did you think IBM's interest in Apple originated at the top? No, it began as a suggestion by IBM's research team for advanced microprocessors.[6]

The Spectrum of Alliances

When it comes to dealing with competitors, traditional managers are accustomed to thinking in binary terms: compete or acquire. Competitors are either bitter adversaries to be bested (and eliminated) in battle or hapless victims to be taken over and gobbled up. The compete-acquire binary mentality is the oversimplified view of the world taught by disciples of the cult of the deal.[7] In reality, however, there's a wide *spectrum of relationships* between the compete-acquire poles. Networking smart means using the entire spectrum to find new ways to cooperate with competitors.

Consider, for example, some of the ways competitors link up and cooperate:

- *Joint venture.* A joint venture is an independent organization set up and jointly owned by two (or more) companies. It's typically dedicated to a specific goal. So far, IBM and Apple have created two joint ventures, *Taligent* (new operating systems) and *Kaleida* (multimedia technology). Parents of the joint venture may contribute money, time, people, and other resources to their joint-venture offspring.

- *Technology sharing.* This occurs when one company allows another, often through licensing arrangements, to use a proprietary design, plan, or process. For example, Apple plans to use IBM's RISC chips, codeveloped and manufactured by Motorola.

- *Marketing and distribution.* Here, one company piggybacks on the marketing and distribution capabilities of a competitor. New biotech firms, for example, have lots of innovations but no way to market them. So, they tap the existing networks of the large integrated pharmaceutical companies.[8]

- *Manufacturing and assembly.* In this arrangement, one company lets a competitor make and produce its product. In the biotech industry, for example, manufacturing *and* marketing agreements may go hand in hand.[9]

- *Equity investment.* An equity investment occurs when one competitor owns some of the stock in another. In the 1980s, for example, Ford made equity investments in Aston Martin, ACCAR, Mazda, and Kia; General Motors had similar equity ties to Isuzu, Suzuki, and Daewoo.[10]

It's important to recognize that different types of alliances are not mutually exclusive. A single alliance can be a many-splendored thing, a strong tie that grows layer by layer as the two firms build trust and mutual understanding. The Ford-Mazda alliance, one of the most successful and celebrated affiliations in the auto industry, is a strong tie made of many strands. It began in 1979 with Ford's 25 percent equity stake in Mazda and grew to include all the alliance types described above: The two auto makers share manufacturing, product, and process technology; they're 50-50 owners of joint venture AutoAlliance International, which operates the Flat Rock, Michigan, automobile plant built by Mazda (Probes are made at Flat Rock); each company owns part of Autorama, which distributes Mazda-made Fords and Ford-made Fords throughout Japan.[11]

Why Cooperate?

The new biotechnology is one of the hottest (and most controversial) growth industries in the United States. In its short life of only 20 years, the industry has already produced sensational discoveries—human insulin, growth hormones, and genetically engineered vaccines, just to name a few. In the twenty-first century, it will make fact out of the wildest science fiction.

It couldn't happen without alliances. Along with all the scientific breakthroughs, the new biotech has spawned a prodigious number of alliances between competitors, which several sociologists have studied in detail.[12] Here's why we see so much cooperation among competitors in this new industry.

The new biotech created a huge imbalance with all the makings of a good old-fashioned horse trade. On one side, dozens of new biotech companies are founded each year to explore and exploit the new technology. These start-ups are rich in R&D expertise but poor in everything else, desperate for funds and such basic business capabilities as production, marketing, and distribution. On the other side, the large established pharmaceutical companies are threatened with obsolescence and extinction. Their knowledge is based on an older biotechnology (organic chemistry), whereas the new biotech is based on recent Nobel-prizewinning breakthroughs in immunology and molecular biology, like techniques to cut-and-paste DNA (a.k.a. genetic engineering). "[The] established firms were unable to create internally the kind of research environment that fostered innovation and discovery," say sociologists Woody Powell and Peter Brantley, but they "...were flush with cash and controlled established worldwide marketing channels."[13] Hence the horse trade: New biotech firms and established companies struck dozens upon dozens of alliances.

The biotech story illustrates several good reasons for cooperating with competitors. The new biotech firms need alliances to obtain capital, secure basic business expertise, and gain access to worldwide markets. They also need to bask in the glow of big-firm corporate halos; it gives them instant legitimacy in the eyes of the business and investment communities. The big established companies need alliances for one big reason: access to new technology. Without links to the new biotech firms, they'd be cut off from the stream of innovations.

Alliances in biotech are based on the principle of *complementarity*. Each side has what the other lacks. Complementarity drives alliances in many industries. It's the logic behind Ford's alliances with Jaguar, Kia, Lio Ho, Mazda, and Nissan.[14] Ford and Jaguar make a natural match-up, for example, because the British car maker needs access to deep pockets, and Ford wants a prestige product in the high-end luxury sports car market. Complementarity is the logic behind the recent joint venture between Motorola and Northern Telecom. U.S.-based Motorola is a leading maker of cellular telephones and equipment; Canada-based Northern Telecom is a leading maker of network switching equipment. And the new alliance between Time-Warner and U.S. West—formed to create an "information superhighway"—is yet another example of complementarity.

Alliances are also based on the principle of *pooling*. Instead of matches based on different and complementary assets, competitors with *similar resources* combine them to strengthen their collective position and do things together they can't do apart. Pooling alliances are common in the auto industry. The three-way Fiat-PSA-Renault alliance, for example, enables these small (relatively speaking) auto makers to enjoy *scale economies* they couldn't otherwise get. By putting their resources in one pot, they have the wherewithal to conduct joint research and to manufacture common components[15] (just like the way Chevrolet, Pontiac, and Buick use common GM parts). But the pooling logic doesn't work so well in biotech. Few alliances occur between new biotech firms,[16] for example, because there's nothing to be gained—they're already innovative and would still lack capital and downstream business capabilities.

What Rosabeth Moss Kanter calls "service alliances" are based on a pooling logic. Industry research consortia are good examples.[17] Consortia enable member firms to conduct research or other activities that would be too expensive or too difficult to do alone. PAFT, the Programme for Alternative Fluorocarbon Toxicity Testing, is the chemical industry's worldwide alliance to test and promote ozone-friendly substitutes for chlorine-containing compounds. Other examples include International Partners in Glass Research, the Center for Advanced Television Studies (includes network giants ABC, NBC, PBS, among others), and Bellcore, formed by the Baby Bells after the breakup of giant AT&T.

The University Hospital Consortium (UHC), a nonprofit alliance of 62 major academic medical centers, illustrates the creative use of pooling logic. The UHC's Technology Advancement Center (TAC), for example, fosters the placement and performance of industry-sponsored preclinical and clinical trials in its member hospitals.[18] TAC acts as a coordinator and go-between, bringing together industry sponsors and medical researchers. TAC worked with industry and its member hospitals to develop standardized approval documents, cut bureaucratic red tape, and streamline the entire process. For example, TAC has "cut the time to identify investigators interested in clinical trials from several months to two weeks," according to TAC Director Dr. David Burnett.[19]

The pooling idea extends beyond the business sphere into the political as well. It's not common to think of it this way, but companies pool *political* resources when they join forces to influence politics and regulations.[20] They do so, for example, when they jointly support a trade association that monitors the regulatory process and lobbies on their behalf. Firms also pool resources when they build an unofficial network of companies that informally coordinates lobbying activities or makes contributions to PACs (political action committees).[21]

All alliances are vehicles for learning. Indeed, Powell and Brantley call the webwork of alliances in biotech *networks of learning* because they enable firms to keep up with rapid scientific and marketing developments.[22] But learning isn't limited to the specific technology or process at hand. There's also what I call *fortuitous learning*—gaining access to information and expertise well beyond the manifest purpose and scope of the alliance itself. When Tennant Company was putting together its total quality improvement program (see Chapters 6 and 12), they needed to learn more about Japanese quality practices. Instead of relying on hearsay and secondary sources, they tapped one of their Japanese joint ventures, their alliance with Fuji Heavy Industries. This bridge gave Tennant access to executives and managers in several Japanese companies and got them the information they sought, right from the original sources.[23] Chrysler, too, wanted to learn more about Japanese practices. The U.S. car maker reached out to alliance partner Mitsubishi to learn Japanese organizational principles for developing new products. And they learned the lessons well. Using Japanese-style teams, Chrysler created its spectacular, award-winning L/H line of cars—and it did so much faster and for much less money than it would have with its traditional new product development methods. Networking smart means incorporating alliances into your external intelligence network (Chapter 3).

What Makes an Alliance Work?

Building strong alliances has a lot in common with building strong personal relationships (Chapter 4). Both person-to-person and company-to-company relationships depend on the same "secret formula": mutual understanding + mutual benefit. When there's true mutual understanding, each party understands why the other acts in a particular way and accepts the behavior as legitimate and authentic, despite the tension or inconvenience it might cause. Each party understands the other's motives and feelings and can take the role of the other with great empathy. When there's true mutual benefit, both parties get what they need from the relationship. Each helps the other find benefits. The partners develop a win-win relationship contract.

Both ingredients—mutual understanding and mutual benefit—may seem obvious to you, but they're not so obvious in many alliances we see. Too many companies enter into alliances with a short-term outlook, expecting quick results, and they don't make the heavy investments in time, energy, and personal contact that are absolutely necessary. Without these investments, however, mutual understanding is impossible, and the alliance is destined to fall apart. Other companies enter into alliances with good intentions but fail to find mutual benefits. It may be that real synergies just don't exist and never will, or that the hard work of building the relationship and finding mutual benefits was never done. Without mutual understanding *and* mutual benefit, an alliance is doomed.

Mutual understanding is a lot harder than we think. Remember from Chapter 4 the study of "spousal predictions"—how well husbands and wives really know each other's preferences?[24] Spouses were very confident of their predictions, and they were very wrong: The typical spouse was correct only 2 times out of 10! The same problem plagues alliances, but it's magnified many times over because the marriage of two companies means the marriage of many people from each side. The starting point for cooperating with competitors, therefore, is to admit that mutual understanding is going to be a lot of hard work. If you can't (or don't want to) commit the resources it'll take, then alliances aren't for you.

Some experts advocate looking for partners with similar cultures, but I'm not so sure that's a good idea. At one level their advice does make sense: By virtue of the similarity principle, it's easier for managers from related cultures to understand each other. But would Apple be as attractive if it were just a smaller IBM? I doubt it. Apple's attractive because it's so *different*. Its open and spirited culture—the opposite of IBM's stiff buttoned-down style—promotes Apple's creativity, and that's what makes Apple so appealing. Different cultures *do* make mutual understanding more difficult, but opposites attract when you're looking for mutual benefits.

My research on alliances, along with that of others, points to six factors that promote mutual understanding and mutual benefits.[25] Keep these factors in mind as you negotiate and renegotiate the "relationship contract" with your alliance partner.

1. *Long-term commitment.* It's critical that both parties make a lasting commitment to the alliance. We know that expectations are self-fulfilling prophesies; that's the Pygmalion principle in operation (Chapter 2). It works here, too. If you and your partner both expect the alliance to continue indefinitely, each of you is more likely to make the investments that encourage mutual understanding and sustain the relationship.[26] If even one party isn't ready to commit, the alliance can't make it.

Commitment must come from all levels. "At the operating level," says alliance expert Jordan D. Lewis, "alliances don't go far without enthusiasm."[27] An alliance works better when there's a *champion* on each side who can cut through organizational static and nonsense and marshal resources to support the alliance. And commitment from the top is absolutely essential.[28] Apple recently upped its commitment at the top by making John Sculley in charge of finding and building strategic alliances.

2. *Strong-tie expectations.* Good alliances start small and think big. You may initiate an alliance to solve a specific and immediate problem (a need for capital or access to markets), but the relationship should have the potential to grow into a strong tie of many strands. The Mazda-Ford alliance, for example, began as an equity investment but grew to embrace multiple relationships. The best alliance partners are always on the lookout for new ways to create mutual benefits and invest in the relationship. Because expectations are so critical for longevity and success, it's essential that both partners *expect* the alliance to grow, develop, and blossom.

3. *Interaction and communication.* How do you know what your partner's intentions are? How do you know if your partner's ready for commitment—or that the commitment is changing? How do you know about frustrations, problems, or grievances? The only way to know is by constant meeting, talking, and interacting. The Japanese, for example, have always appreciated the necessity of nurturing partnerships. They invest willingly in the gradual process of building trust, mutual expectations, and strong personal contacts. Veteran alliance makers know it, too. They make alliances integral parts of their intelligence networks (Chapter 3) and their personal relationships.

The process of building an alliance invokes the operation of the fourth networking principle: Repeated interaction encourages cooperation (Chapter 2). It's part of the good sense behind lots of interaction and communication. Good alliances begin with frank and open discussion, plenty of it. Continual dialogue, mutual visits, informal socializing—at all levels—are essential to build the groundwork for mutual understanding and to find mutual benefits. "An alliance will have enormous problems," says the chief financial officer (CFO) of a large joint venture, "if after the signing the senior players of the two partners do not continue to work (kind of like a marriage) to make the alliance a success. An alliance, especially in the early days, needs a great deal of nurturing."[29] And even when the alliance is well established, intensive interaction isn't over; it's just begun—like any relationship, an ongoing alliance needs continuous tending to stay healthy.

4. *Embeddedness.* Good alliances are *embedded* relationships, just like partnerships with suppliers and customers (Chapters 10 and 12). Business, social, and personal ties are blended together, uniting and supporting the alliance. Corning, which has so many successful joint ventures that it thinks of itself as a network of alliances, encourages embeddedness by moving people in and out of its alliances.[30] This practice builds layer after layer of dense, cross-cutting ties that bind the alliance network together.

Embeddedness helps an alliance in several ways. The network of ties that criss-cross organizational boundaries creates fast feedback channels. Personal relationships encourage quick problem identification, communication, and resolution. Personal ties are essential for managing the inevitable conflict that arises in even the healthiest relationships. And when a company's network of alliances becomes embedded in personal, social, and professional ties, the network itself can undergo a profound transformation: It develops a shared system of values and a common culture that unite the alliances in concerned effort and mutual benefit.

5. *Real mutual benefits.* A healthy alliance is based on the principle behind The Company of the Table: Powerful groups are built on relationships that grow out of the *natural interests* and *common bonds* of the parties involved. What's odd about alliances is that the enemy has been invited to the table. Traditionally, your "natural" interest was victory, not cooperation. To make alliances succeed, however, you and your partner must overcome narrow unilateral self-interest and work hard to find *real mutual benefits,* gains for both parties. This doesn't mean you abandon self-interest. It means that you maximize *self*-interest by maximizing *joint* interest. If you reframe the situation and think creatively, cooperation can gain you more than the spoils of one-sided "victory."

Benefits can take all sorts of forms. Alliance expert Kathryn Rudie Harrigan divides benefits (what she calls motivations) of joint ventures and other cooperative arrangements into three large categories.[31]

The first is *increasing internal strengths*. Alliances strengthen a company by sharing costs, spreading risks, and providing access to resources the company couldn't secure alone or grow itself—financing, new customers, new technologies, new manufacturing processes, intelligence, and innovative management practices and systems.

Improving competitiveness is the second main category. Alliances can help influence an industry's direction and rate of change. The new biotech is a perfect example. Alliances improve competitiveness by granting early access to prime resources, customers, or technologies. When a new entity is created, such as a joint venture, the child may not suffer the limitations of the parents. Like many parents, I'm sure Apple and IBM pray their offspring will be different enough to achieve what each parent couldn't do alone.

And *changing strategic direction* is the third category of benefits. Alliances can help a company diversify into different businesses, even create new businesses altogether. Alliances are ways to explore the unknown. Every company must change; the question is *where* it should change. To find out, you have to keep your hand in and get the news as it breaks. But the pace of change is so swift that it's impossible to keep your hand in everywhere without alliances. Remember my discussion of luck and serendipity in Chapter 6? Lucky people build wide, diverse networks—spiderwebs—that improve the odds of good fortune. Lucky companies do the same: They explore possible new strategic directions by spinning a spiderweb of alliances that lets them peer into the future.

No matter what benefits you seek in an alliance, the key is to make sure *both* parties obtain real benefits. Without mutuality, an alliance won't survive or thrive in the long run. That doesn't mean the "relationship books" have to balance at each and every moment. But it does mean the books have to balance in the long run, that each partner sees and reaps real benefits from the alliance. As in any true relationship, each alliance partner has a duty to help the other understand, articulate, and meet its needs.

6. *Flexibility and autonomy.* I've always found it curious that alliance-founding organizations are called "parents" and the entities they found are called "children." Linguistic usage always reveals beliefs and attitudes, and here the terms "parents" and "children" tell us a lot about prevailing attitudes toward alliances. All too often, alliances are treated (or mistreated) just like children. In some cases, the alliance isn't allowed to grow up. The venture remains forever a stunted child trapped by arrested development. In other cases, the alliance becomes a clone of one parent. This was the anticipated result of the Apple-IBM

link-up. (The joke circulating in Silicon Valley at the time went something like this. Question: What do you get with an alliance between Apple and IBM? Answer: IBM.) Alliances that don't grow up, or remain little versions of their parents, don't succeed.

It's paramount that an alliance be given sufficient room to grow, develop, and mature. Networking smart in alliances, like most business areas, means managing by *managing conditions*, not by micromanaging or making decisions unilaterally. Top executives need to keep in touch and stay informed, but the alliance's operating level should be given autonomy to work within broad policy outlines. Autonomy lets operating decisions be made at the right level—the firing line—and it permits the venture to adapt to changing circumstances.

Alliance culture is an important success factor. "A successful joint venture must develop its own culture," says the CFO of a large joint venture.[32] One reason Corning's alliances work so well, says a Management Committee member, is Corning's willingness to let its ventures run independently. Corning insists on results, but it doesn't foist its culture, structure, or practices on alliances.[33]

One of the surest ways to create a distinctive culture is the infusion of new blood into the alliance—new employees that don't come from either parent. "[T]he addition of new employees who come from the outside," says the joint-venture CFO, "...helps to diffuse the old cultures and leads to the development of a new, vibrant joint-venture culture."[34] We've seen this idea in action before: It's the power of diversity, tapped by managing numbers. We know from Chapter 7 that numbers and proportions significantly influence interaction. If too many alliance employees come from one parent, the odds are too high the alliance will become a clone of that parent. If the numbers from each parent are balanced, cloning isn't the concern, but you may suffer a contest of corporate wills. If you bring in enough new employees from the outside, however, you can create a productive mixture: some from one parent, some from the other, and a healthy number from neither. This gives you the best odds of creating a distinctive alliance culture.

The Biggest Obstacle

Do you know what the biggest obstacle to cooperation is? Antitrust hang-ups? Cultural differences? Size disparities? These factors matter a lot, of course, but the biggest obstacle is the enemy of networking smart everywhere: the cult of the deal. Just as the cult plagues anyone who manages relationships, it hampers the formation of cooperative ties between competitors. The traditional attitudes and shortsightedness of parent firms, argues Kathryn Harrigan, are major obstacles to alliances. "Their unwillingness to see that the nature of competition is changing," says Harrigan, "creates barriers to firms' effective uses of joint ventures or other cooperative strategies."[35] Traditional companies, trapped in cult-of-the-deal thinking, cooperate reluctantly, if at all. And when they do cooperate, their inability to open up, share information, and take risks leads to one inevitable outcome: failure. Then the traditionalists have the satisfaction of saying, "See? I told you so. Cooperation doesn't work." Their expectations of failure become self-fulfilling prophesies.

The deal mentality could undo the IBM-Apple alliance (I hope it doesn't). To be sure, their cultural differences are enormous: "It's like a surfer girl marrying a banker," quips *Computer Letter* publisher Richard Shaffer.[36] Spanning the cultural divide won't be easy. But it's the adversarial, deal-demented, go-it-alone mentality that's the real threat. To make the alliance work, both companies have to act in the true spirit of partnerships. IBM, however, is well known for its independent, domineering ways. (Remember the Silicon Valley joke!) It won't be easy for Big Blue to change its colors. But Apple's not much better. Along with its hang-loose culture is a fierce independence. Remember that Superbowl a few years ago when Steve Jobs began advertising Apple as the countercultural alternative to Orwellian "Big Brother" IBM?

You hear a lot of talk and hype about strategic alliances these days, but I think the dark truth is this: In their heart of hearts, traditional U.S. managers would rather fight than cooperate. If they could get away with it (and they no longer can), I suspect that IBM and Apple would rather not team up. "It is not in the tradition of rugged individualism for U.S. companies to cooperate," writes Robert McGough in *Finance World*. "But these days, that frontier mentality is no match for ferocious international competition."[37] Executives and managers today must confront what Tom Peters calls a master paradox: "More competition requires more cooperation."[38]

To make your alliances work, you have to combat the deeply ingrained deal mentality. Traditional managers enter alliances as if they were shotgun weddings—reluctantly—and with about the same prediction for long-term success. Networking smart means expecting cynicism and internal resistance from those schooled by the cult of the deal. And it means working hard to stamp it out, whenever and wherever you find it.

And now a dire warning: If you wait too long, if you don't adopt the networking philosophy soon enough, your company could end up without any alliances at all—all the good partners will be taken already. The history of alliances unfolds in three stages, and the chances of forming alliances and of making them work are different in each one.[39] Already, most industries are past the *early stage*—that initial period when cooperating with competitors was a rare and novel event, the time when alliances were unproven, almost illegitimate organizational innovations. It was hard to form alliances in the early period and hard to make them work. Those times are gone. Most industries are well into the *middle stage,* the spirited time when alliances are easier to form and sustain. Cooperation is "normal" and partners have learned how to make alliances work. Eventually, however, an industry passes into a *late stage,* the troubled period when it again becomes difficult to create alliances. Cooperation among competitors is still legitimate, but the pool of eligibles has become so small that new allies are hard to find. The industry becomes "crowded" and alliances compete with one another. If you wait until this late stage to get involved—to start forming alliances—your chances are slim and none.

Are Alliances Just Temporary Solutions?

And now the question at the heart of all alliances: Are they just temporary solutions to momentary problems? In the new biotech industry, for example, skeptics see the alliances of new firms and old money as nothing more than temporary marriages of convenience.[40] In time, they say, the huge imbalance will sort itself out and the industry will consolidate, driven by the inexorable forces of economic history. Those upstart start-ups and their pesky alliances will be eliminated or absorbed, leaving a stable industry dominated by a few corporate colossi.

Sociologists Powell and Brantley don't see it this way, and neither do I.[41] The world is changing. What Powell and Brantley call the "locus of innovation" has already shifted. It's moved the magic from industrial labs buried inside big companies out into the alliance network itself—the loose federation of start-ups, foreign firms, universities, large established companies, government laboratories, and nonprofit research outfits. Internal R&D isn't sufficient anymore. To be competitive today, firms need internal R&D *and* external collaborations. Internal R&D is needed to evaluate outside research; collaborative research is needed to gain fast access to and exploit knowledge generated in the outside network. The alliances aren't going away. By

1988, over 90 percent of all cooperative linkages ever formed in biotech were alive and well![42] Alliances aren't weakened as time goes by; they thrive in the new business environment.

A similar story can be told in industry after industry. The stable balance in the global automobile industry, for example, was altered forever by deep changes in basic economics—the oil shocks of the 1970s, changing customer preferences, and the ascendancy of Japanese auto makers.[43] Auto makers in the United States were left with obsolete capabilities when customers now demanded fuel-efficient, high-quality cars. Japanese firms, for all their strengths, were uncertain about their abilities to meet global demands. Neither side could go it alone anymore.

This is a time of great transition, the advent of a new business order in which alliances play an enduring part. In years past, value was created by *high-volume* enterprises, where profits came from scale and volume, says Harvard political economist Robert Reich (Clinton's Secretary of Labor) in *The Work of Nations*.[44] Now, the logic of high-volume is being replaced by *high-value*—where profits come from building a network that continuously discovers and links together solutions and needs. To succeed in the 1990s and beyond, companies must embrace and build what Reich calls *the global web*, the world-spanning network of alliances and partnerships.

In this web, there's no place for traditional companies that want to be the individualistic, disconnected, free-floating "atoms" their corporate ancestors were before. Organizational individualism is an increasingly obsolete idea, and the stand-alone corporation is an increasingly inaccurate image of business enterprise. "The new organizational webs of high-value enterprise," says Reich, "...are reaching across the globe. Thus there is coming to be no such organization as an 'American' (or British or French or Japanese or West German) corporation, nor any finished good called an 'American' (or British, French, Japanese, or West German) product."[45]

Those who network smart heartily embrace the image I proposed in the Preface to this book: *The world is a network*. Those who network smart see the business world changing and abandon the cult of the deal. They make the world change by finding new ways to create value by cooperating with competitors.

What You Can Do *Now*

No matter where you are in the organization, what you can do *now* is to start thinking about how alliances can help you. Everyone can come up with good alliance ideas. People on the firing line are in good positions to do so. The IBM researchers who proposed the Apple link-up, for example, knew better than anyone else what IBM's and their strengths and weaknesses are. People on the firing line have the close links with the outside world. They know trends; they spot emerging opportunities; they get the news as it breaks. If you're at the top, encourage everyone to be on the lookout for new alliance opportunities. And listen to what your people say. If you're on the firing line, speak up and let your voice be heard.

An alliance makes sense only if it gets you something you can't get another way. Your first step is a needs assessment. What needs do you have that could be met through alliances? What do you need *access* to that an alliance partner could provide you?

- *Access to funds.* Access to capital is a prime motivator behind many biotech alliances.

- *Access to downstream or upstream business capabilities.* Access to established business capabilities is another motivator for biotech alliances.

- *Access to new technologies.* Ford and Mazda swap expertise in manufacturing and process technologies; big pharmaceutical companies get access to the new biotechnology.

- *Access to new markets.* Instead of building links to new customers, you can piggyback on a competitor's networks by selling your new products through theirs. This generally gives you faster access, which is critical when new products suffer short life spans.

- *Access to foreign markets.* Access to some foreign markets requires joint ventures with local partners. Such link-ups may be mandated by law, or simply the quickest way to tap the market. Ford and Mazda, for example, jointly own Autorama to distribute cars in Japan.

- *Access to creativity.* IBM, for example, wants the Apple tie to get access to Apple's software-development talent.

- *Access to economies of scale.* Pooling alliances help smaller players realize the production or distribution efficiencies of a big player.

- *Access to political muscle.* Concerted lobbying works better than individual efforts. Pooling political resources is especially important in closely monitored industries or those that might be reregulated.

- *Access to intelligence networks.* An alliance offers great opportunities to augment your organization's intelligence network by linking up with others.

It's critical that your needs assessment doesn't stop with your needs only. Good alliances, like good relationships of all kinds, depend on finding *mutual* benefits. Your second step, therefore, is to take the role of the other: Look at the list above from the perspective of prospective partners. What do *they* need? What do *you* have to offer? What assets and resources do you have that could provide benefits to a new ally?

Your third step is to consider the *spectrum of alliances* and determine which could help you and a partner achieve mutual benefits. The menu of generic choices includes joint ventures, technology sharing, marketing and distribution arrangements, manufacturing, and equity investments.

What You Can Do *Soon*

Now that you've assessed your needs for alliances, what you can do *soon* is look for potential alliances. Jordan Lewis calls this *scanning for opportunities.*[46] Scanning methods, he notes, range from formal organized searches to the use of informal contacts. Formal methods work, but I prefer informal networking. You're looking for *new* opportunities, potential sources of synergy and value. By definition, these are ill-defined, incomplete, and hidden. They won't turn up in formal searches. You find them by networking. That's why you've built your own intelligence networks (Chapter 3). Tap your networks—and those of your people, suppliers, customers, and others—to discover new alliance opportunities.

Remember the ancient wisdom I cited in Chapter 10? "Forsake not an old friend; for the new is not comparable to him."[47] It applies to alliances as well. Your *current* alliance partners are the best sources of new opportunities. You already know them; you know you can work with them. Many opportunities aren't recognized as such until they're given shape and form through interaction, discussion, and brainstorming. And it's easier to do all of that with someone you already know. If you've picked the right partners, they already have strong-tie expectations. They want to find ways to add more cooperative value to the relationship. Organize wide-ranging, open discussions with current allies and partners to explore and define potential opportunities. Some enlightened companies do this in a very systematic way by holding annual "alliance fests" for all their partners and allies. In these organized get-togethers, everyone is encouraged to seek new link-ups with members of the network.

What should you look for in an alliance partner? Above all, there must be genuine sources of mutual benefit. That's rule one. Without real value—for both parties—an alliance doesn't make sense. The proposed match-up has to give you a real edge. It might get you to the market first; it might give you the capital you need; it might realign the industry in a way that gives you a big competitive advantage.

Does your prospective partner have prior commitments to any of your major competitors or allies? Past alliances and prior commitments may rule out potential partners due to conflicts of interest.[48] A few "relationship rules" can help sort it out. For building pooling coalitions, the rule "a friend's friend is my friend" (like the Fiat-PSA-Renault three-some) helps to define the eligible partners. For complementary alliances, the rule "my enemy's enemy is my friend" points out potential allies. IBM and Microsoft, for example, were once "friends." But Big Blue's alliance with Apple Computer alienated Microsoft's affections and drove it away. Microsoft then turned to an "enemy" of IBM—Digital Equipment—and "befriended" it in a new alliance.[49]

A third rule, "my enemy's friend is my enemy," helps sort out whom you should avoid. For example, Ford and GM (two enemies) never hold equity stakes in the same auto company. Ford's equity stake in its "friend" Mazda, for example, turns this Japanese auto com-pany into an "enemy" for GM, making Mazda ineligible as an equity investment. This rule doesn't seem to apply to joint ventures. Both Ford and GM have joint-venture partners in common (such as Volvo and Fiat). I think the difference occurs because an equity stake is a much stronger tie than a joint venture. An equity stake penetrates a company's governance structure, giving the equity holder decision-making authority, while a joint venture results in a third organization created outside the governance structure of each parent.

What makes a good ally? The secret formula for a good alliance (like any relationship) is *mutual understanding* and *mutual benefit*. Therefore, a good ally is a competitor who is capable of mutual understanding and with whom you can find mutual benefits. Remember that you're building an implicit *relationship contract* with every ally, consciously or not. Just as in a relationship between two people (see Chapter 4), members of an alliance develop tacit understandings about roles, responsibilities, and performance. As you apply the alliance evalua-tion criteria in the accompanying box, keep in mind the concept of the relationship contract. What kind of implicit agreement do you want? What are its terms and conditions? Are the terms and conditions mutually beneficial?

Picking the Right Alliance Partner

Technical Criteria

- *Type of Alliance.* What *type* of alliance are you looking for? One based on *pooling* or *complementarity?*

- *Resources and Capabilities.* Given the type of alliance you seek, does the potential ally have the right resources and capabilities for it? Do *you* have the resources and capabilities the potential ally seeks? Resources could be capital, creative personnel, top managers, manufacturing capabilities, marketing networks, new technologies, customers, suppliers, information, political muscle, and so on.

- *Corporate Strategy.* What is the ally's overall strategy? What markets does it serve and how is that changing? Does the potential alliance target a critical growth area for the partner, or is it investing in other areas?

- *Competitiveness.* Does the potential alliance improve your competitiveness? Does it give you early or preferred access to customers, markets, technologies, and so on? Does it help you shape your industry or influence its rate of change?

- *Strategic Reorientation.* Does the potential alliance place you in a position to learn? Does it improve your "luck" by being in the right place at the right time? Does it let you peer into the future? Does it help you keep in touch with new developments that could redirect your strategy?

Relationship Criteria

- *Relationship Orientation.* Where is the potential ally on the spectrum of relationships? Is the ally primarily *deal-oriented* or *relationship-oriented?*

- *Alliance Priority.* How important are alliances to your potential partner? Is a senior executive (like Apple's John Sculley or Corning's Jamie Houghton) dedicated to building alliances? Are alliances a vital part of overall strategy?

- *Quality of Personnel.* Will the ally's best and brightest be assigned to the alliance? Will top executives and managers be involved?

(Continued)

- *Prior Alliance Experience.* Does the potential ally already have a history of successful alliances and partnerships? Do any of the potential ally's current alliances preclude one with you? Are there conflicts of interest?

- *Long-Term Commitment.* Expectations of continuity are self-fulfilling. Is the potential ally willing to make a long-term commitment to the alliance? Are you?

- *Strong-Tie Expectations.* Does the potential ally expect the alliance to evolve into a strong tie of many strands? Or does the ally consider the alliance to be a narrow, short-term transaction? Is the proposed scope of the alliance wide enough for a strong tie to develop?

- *Life Cycle Stage of Development.* Look back at Chapter 8. What *stage* of the organizational life cycle is the ally in? Is the ally on the verge of a major transition—such as the leadership crisis—that could disrupt the alliance? Note, however, that a pending crisis could be the rationale for an alliance. Those about to enter the networking stage, for example, are hungry for alliances.

What You Can Do in the *Long Run*

The model company in the 1990s and beyond will be an active participant in a vast network of external alliances. Whether you're going to be that kind of company depends on what you're becoming *now*. What you can do in the *long run* is figure out how you're going to get there.

The networking prescription is this: Jump on the alliance bandwagon. I don't mean you should create alliances prematurely or go about it in a haphazard way. It's just that the network of companies you need to be a part of can't be assembled overnight. If you avoid cooperating with competitors, or you're planning to slow down or stop adding new alliances, you're putting yourself in grave danger of creating a self-perpetuating disadvantage.

You can't wait or slow down because the creation of new alliances is influenced by *previously formed* alliances. As more alliances are formed, the pool of eligible partners shrinks. You may not be able to ally with those who would be your best partners. Maybe they're already spoken for, or now they've become unattractive because they linked with an archrival. Those who network smart move first and fast, making sure they get the pick of the best.

You can't wait or slow down because your evolving network of companies is a vital part of *organizational learning.*[50] Consider what sociolo-

gist Ranjay Gulati discovered in his impressive study of alliance formation in three global industries—automobiles, new materials, and industrial automation.[51] He found that a company's prior experience with
alliances influences the likelihood of future alliance making. The more
alliances a company already has, the more likely it is to form new
alliances. And, a company with well-connected allies—those who
themselves have many alliances—is more likely to create new alliances,
compared with a firm whose alliance partners are isolated. Why?
Current alliances aid learning in two ways. Companies with lots of
alliance experience are more likely to form new alliances because
they've learned how to make alliances work. And, when a well-connected company seeks new allies, the network of alliances becomes a
vast information-processing machine for finding and learning about
good new partners.

Here's what I recommend: Create an *alliance exploration task force.*
Your mission: Investigate how the organization can *systematically* spot
new cooperative opportunities and explore alliance options. Don't
restrict your attention to the top. Top-level benedictions are necessary,
but good alliance proposals can come from anywhere in the organization. The task is to increase awareness of alliances as an additional
alternative to meet the organization's needs. When considering
options, everyone should now ask "Does an alliance make sense here?"
If yes (or even maybe), the next question should be "Who would be a
good alliance partner?" This change in perspective won't be so easy,
especially for those trapped in the cult of the deal. But it's absolutely
essential for preparing the organization to survive and thrive in the
intensified competitive environment of the new industrial order.

PART 4
Conclusion

15

The Boundaryless Organization: Role Model for the 1990s and Beyond

That's where we have to turn in the '90s—to the software of our companies—to the culture that drives them.

JOHN F. WELCH, JR., CHAIRMAN AND CHIEF EXECUTIVE OFFICER, GENERAL ELECTRIC COMPANY[1]

In General Electric's 1989 *Annual Report,* Jack Welch described his grand vision of GE in the coming decade:

> Our dream for the 1990s is a boundaryless Company, a Company where we knock down the walls that separate us from each other on the inside and from our key constituencies on the outside.
>
> The boundaryless Company we envision will remove the barriers among engineering, manufacturing, marketing, sales and customer service; it will recognize no distinction between "domestic" and "foreign" operations—we'll be as comfortable doing business in Budapest and Seoul as we are in Louisville and Schenectady. A boundaryless organization will ignore or erase group labels, such as "management," "salaried" or "hourly," which get in the way of people working together.
>
> A boundaryless Company will level its *external* walls as well, reaching out to key suppliers to make them part of a single process in which they and we join hands and intellects in a common purpose—satisfying customers.[2]

Jack Welch's grand vision of a boundaryless organization captures the networking message I've espoused in this book. This is an organization of *networks*—personal and organizational, internal and external. It's an organization of people who actively build and manage networks of productive relationships, networks they make and maintain in intelligent, resourceful, and ethical ways. It's the home of people who've learned how to network well and apply their knowledge responsibly. In short, it's a company that *networks smart.*

I believe Welch's vision of the boundaryless organization is a great role model for success in the 1990s and beyond. GE's still implementing the boundaryless idea, so the jury's still out, but since Welch started changing the "software" in the late 1980s, the results have been nothing short of spectacular. In addition to plenty of success stories, such as reduced cycle times, improved morale, and huge cost savings, the general performance indicators—sales, profits, and shareholder value—are just tremendous. Companies that want to thrive in the wild and turbulent times ahead need the same speed, flexibility, and dynamism as the new GE; they'll get there by learning how to network smart. And the people who thrive in these new organizations will be those who learn the same lessons.

In this concluding chapter, I offer the vision of the boundaryless organization as a unifying concept, a way to think about integrating the individual topics covered in the previous chapters. I describe GE's amazing transformation from a broadly diversified smokestack company to a focused global high-technology and services leader.[3] I highlight the four big management tools Welch employs to make GE's great cultural change—Work-Out, best practices, process managing, and education. As always, I conclude with practical advice on what you can do now, soon, and in the long run.

GE's Hardware Phase: The 1980s

When Jack Welch became chairman and CEO of General Electric in April 1981, he embarked on one of the biggest organizational transformations in U.S. corporate history. Getting the right mix of businesses—what Welch called fixing the *hardware*—was the first great problem he tackled. The company Welch inherited was a broadly diversified giant, a multinational conglomerate with over 350 different businesses. GE was financially sound, but Welch believed the company had to be streamlined and repositioned if it was going to dominate the "white-knuckle decade" of the 1990s.[4] He would have to convert the diversified smokestack company into a lean, focused, global high-technology and services leader.

Downsizing was the most painful part of GE's transformation. It earned Welch the nickname Neutron Jack (from the weapon that eliminates people but leaves buildings intact). By the end of the 1980s, GE had shed 100,000 jobs, reducing employment to under 300,000. (GE is now down to 230,000.) Fortunately, GE was in good financial shape, so it could provide a "soft landing" to many people who were let go.

Delayering went hand in hand with downsizing. To boost productivity, GE had to simplify, cut bureaucracy, remove layers. "Layers insulate," says Welch. "They slow things down. They garble. Leaders in highly layered organizations are like people who wear several sweaters outside on a freezing winter day. They remain warm and comfortable but are blissfully ignorant of the realities of their environments. They couldn't be further from what's going on."[5] Layers insulate managers from the outside environment; layers smother the creative energies and talents of those inside.

So, GE cut layer after layer, minimizing the number of management levels between workers and the CEO. (Some say Welch would be happiest with 230,000 direct reports!) The company eliminated its top management "superstructure"—sectors and groups. Eliminating sectors alone saved the company at least $40 million![6] The real impact, however, was *speed*—much faster decision making. And GE pared its vaunted corporate staff, eliminating what Welch calls "the questioners and the checkers, the nitpickers who bog down the process, people whose only role is to second-guess and kibitz, the people who clog communication inside the company." Cutting corporate staff is more than a change in numbers; it's a wholesale change in orientation: "[S]taff essentially reports to the field rather than the other way around."[7]

Fixing the hardware also meant changing and focusing the portfolio of businesses. Soon after he took over, Welch devised his now-famous three circles strategy. GE would concentrate its efforts in three major areas: core, services, and technology. The core includes traditional GE lines, such as major appliances, lighting, and power systems. Services include financial services (like GE Credit) and information services. Technology covers high-tech businesses like aircraft engines, medical systems, and industrial electronics. These three circles were Welch's best bets on where the global economy was heading and where GE could or could be positioned to win big.

All of GE's 350 existing businesses didn't fit the three circles. Welch placed each business in one of the circles or outside the circles entirely. Those inside the circles were the favored few; they would be nurtured and supported. Those outside were slated to be sold or closed, unless they could be fixed, quickly. His decision rule was simple: Every business had to be #1 or #2 in its market. If a business couldn't become a leader in its field, it was out. Welch divested $10 billion worth of businesses that couldn't be #1 or #2, and made $19 billion worth of acquisitions to help those that could. By the end of the 1980s, GE was pared to 13 key businesses that dominated their global markets.

The pieces were now in place.

GE's Software Phase: The 1990s

Fixing the hardware didn't really change anything fundamental to GE. Sweeping changes were made, of course, massive cuts and reallocations that affected thousands of lives, hundreds of communities. But hosts of companies were doing the same things in the 1980s (and companies such as IBM, GM, and Sears still are). In its heart and soul, GE was still the same old GE.

GE was captive to a century-old culture, the whips-and-chains philosophy of control. Indeed, for most of its history, GE was the *role model* of the whips-and-chains management style. GE wrote *The Book* on scientific management; its formal strategic planning process, for example, was widely admired and imitated. The old GE perfected the control techniques I described in the Introduction, ultra-control (specify everything in advance) and managing by the numbers (manage for short-term results). The hardware changes shook up the company, but GE was still a bureaucracy, a vertical command-and-control structure. Most GE managers still subscribed to the philosophy of control, managing through intimidation, fear, and punishment. Good workers, like good children, were seen and not heard. And GE managers still adhered to the not-invented-here policy, suspicious of any process, technique, or idea that wasn't grown in GE's own backyard.

Those old attitudes wouldn't cut it in the coming years. GE had to change more than its hardware. To win in the 1990s, Welch argues, companies have to change *culture*—values and beliefs, ways of thinking, feeling, working, interacting. It's the only way to achieve sustained growth in productivity. "We've spent the majority of our energy in the '80s working, appropriately, on the *hardware* of American business because that hardware had to be fixed," says Welch. "The Japanese, on the other hand, have the software, the culture which ties productivity to the human spirit—which has practically no limits. That's where we have to turn in the '90s—to the *software* of our companies—to the culture that drives them."[8]

To unleash the tremendous energy of its people, Welch turned to the "soft stuff"—the philosophy of empowerment. He calls it *soft values for a hard decade.*[9] What Welch wants is nothing short of total religious conversion: He wants to convert GE from the role model of control into the role model of empowerment. It's a very tough task, much tougher than fixing the hardware. It's much easier to buy, sell, and swap businesses than it is to change the way people think, feel, and act. Fixing GE's software is tough because it runs into a huge version of the *dilemma of indirect management:* How could Welch change the way 280,000 people work? His only hope was to figure out how to change behavior by *managing conditions.* And fixing the software is tough because Welch wasn't dealing with a small-scale enterprise. GE had been slimmed and restructured, but it was still a massive corporation, a globe-spanning giant with 280,000 people working in businesses ranging from light bulbs and banking to locomotives, medical systems, and robotics. In effect, Welch was attempting nothing less than the biggest cultural transformation in U.S. corporate history.

Empowerment has become the mantra of the 1990s. Many chant it, few have figured out how to do it. GE's figuring it out. One big reason I consider GE to be a good role model is that the company's making the deep changes required to oust the philosophy of control and truly empower people. Many companies talk empowerment, but they don't provide the tools, skills training, and education that help people learn how to work differently. GE is. Many managers tell their people "you're empowered," but they don't do anything to change basic processes of work. GE's doing something.

GE is using four big management tools to fix the software—Work-Out, best practices, process managing, and education. Each, in its own way, empowers by helping people help themselves. Each involves people in decision making; each provides ownership; each helps people figure out more productive ways to work and interact, think and feel. Together, the four tools move GE along the path to boundarylessness. They're turning GE into the ultimate network organization, a simplified, fast, and flexible company of self-confident networkers, an exhilarating company that sustains high productivity—fast decisions, high quality, quick response to customers, rapid innovation, short cycle times.

Work-Out

The seed of frustration that germinated Work-Out was planted in September 1988, when Jack Welch made one of his routine visits to

Crotonville, GE's Management Development Institute in New York.[10] In *The New GE*, Robert Slater tells what happened:

> The audience, comprising a mixture of upper and lower levels of GE management, bombarded him [Welch] with questions different from those in the past. Not about where he was taking the company or how GE would fare in the near future. But hard-hitting, specific queries about the businesses. A Power Generation employee started. Someone in Aerospace chimed in. As always, Welch was candid. If he knew the answer, he gave it. If he did not, he said simply, "I don't know. I hope you'll have the courage to ask that tough question of somebody who can do something about it when you go home."
>
> One member of the audience summed up the frustration that some other members had also experienced: "When I'm here at Crotonville, I understand what you're saying. I have a chance to talk about it. I get it. But back home it's not like that. It's not happening that way. We don't have this kind of dialogue with our managers."[11]

That was the problem. What happened at Crotonville—the dialogue, candor and openness, questioning of authority—wasn't happening on the job. It was still business as usual, still the same old GE.

With Crotonville head Jim Baughman, Welch came up with a solution that captured the spirit of what happened at Crotonville: Work-Out. Modeled after the New England town meeting, Work-Out would be a forum for people from all businesses, all levels, all functions to get together. The objective, summarized Baughman, was "to work on how we can get more speed, simplicity, and self-confidence into this operation."[12] The first Work-Out took place in 1989; soon after, the practice of Work-Out spread like wildfire throughout the company.

From the beginning, Work-Out had four major goals, as Noel Tichy and Stratford Sherman summarize in their book on the GE revolution: building trust, empowering employees, eliminating unncessary work, and implementing a new paradigm—the boundaryless organization.[13] The original Work-Outs began by focusing on the most concrete goal, eliminating unnecessary work, and in the process delivered on the other three more intangible goals.

Here's how a Work-Out session works. For three days, a group of 30 to 100 GE people assemble to discuss their business, openly and candidly. Each group is diverse, including hourly workers, salaried, managers—even labor union leaders. The bosses, however, are excluded until the third day, when they hear and make decisions on the proposals worked out by the group. Early Work-Out sessions were facilitated by outside consultants; as people gained experience and self-confidence, Work-Outs were conducted by the teams themselves, often without the knowledge of senior managers. Eventually, Work-Outs reached out to customers and suppliers, embracing them in the same extraordinary process.

The Work-Out group first tackled the problem of unnecessary work—all the inane procedures and counterproductive rules that had evolved over the long years under the old GE regime. "The sessions quickly became a shooting gallery," says Welch and associates in the 1990 *Annual Report,* "with the more egregious manifestations of bureaucracy as the targets—10 signatures on a minor requisition, non-sensical paperwork, wasteful work practices, artificial dress codes, pomposity. Most of these were abolished or reformed on the spot, not put 'in channels.'"[14] Part of the genius of Work-Out was the rule that bosses had to make decisions on the spot, right in the Work-Out session. They couldn't squirm out of making decisions. If a problem couldn't be solved immediately, the boss had to say when it would be. In practice, about 80 percent of all proposals were decided upon right in the Work-Out sessions.[15]

GE culture began to change. Slang and special terms are good indicators of a culture, and you can see a new one emerging when new terms begin to pop up.[16] One of the first new terms at GE was "low-hanging fruit"—the easy opportunities to spot and pick off.[17] "Rattlers" became problems that made noise and were easy to spot, easy to shoot. Another kind of snake—"pythons"—was different. Unlike rattlers, pythons were hard to spot and tough to kill: These were the hard problems that would take time and effort. But the objective of Work-Out was to kill both kinds of snakes, pythons and rattlers, and to grab all the low-hanging fruit.

How successful is Work-Out? Very. Work-Outs around GE picked bushels and bushels of low-hanging fruit, shot nest after nest of rattlers and pythons. There's no shortage of success stories. Consider two described in the 1991 *Annual Report*[18]:

> In 1987, at the Lynn [Massachusetts] plant, a combustor—a key part of a jet engine—took 30 weeks to make. Through Work-Out, that process was down to eight weeks in early '91; now it's four weeks, and the teams that run it are talking 10 *days.* Hardware product cycles are now down an average of 20% across the business, with 50% clearly in sight.
>
> And in our Schenectady turbine plant, another site with a century-old tradition of mistrust between labor and management, Work-Out has grown a team effort that is improving productivity beyond anything we ever envisioned. Just to name one area, in the critical steam turbine bucket machinery center, teams of hourly employees now run, without supervision, $20 million worth of new milling

machines that they specified, tested, and approved for purchase. The cycle time for the operation has dropped 80%. It is embarrassing to reflect that for probably 80 or 90 years, we've been dictating equipment needs and managing people who know how to do things much better and faster than we did.

Work-Outs are directly related to the jump in productivity at GE. For me, however, the most exciting aspects of Work-Out are what it does to empower, break barriers, and advance networking, both inside and outside of GE. Work-Outs represent the first times and places in which GE people from different ranks, functions, and specialties came together. The forums are overturning the traditional authoritarian relationship between superiors and subordinates, enabling workers and managers to forge new and more productive relationships. Work-Outs are helping to ease long-standing hostilities between labor and management. Once-skeptical union leaders—and once-skeptical GE managers—now embrace the process. Work-Outs are helping to break GE's age-old bottleneck problems—the silos and chimneys erected throughout the company; Work-Outs build bridges. Work-Outs are enabling people to tap the power of diversity and to boost serendipity. And Work-Outs are forging external alliances with suppliers and customers.

Work-Out is building the boundaryless organization.

Best Practices

Work-Out is the main vehicle used in GE's pursuit of boundarylessness, but one management tool wasn't enough. More were soon coming. Soon after Work-Out began, GE approached the best companies in the world to learn from them about improving productivity. The practice of learning from the best became known as "best practices," and it, too, spread quickly throughout the company.

Research on best practices started with a list of about 200 companies, which was culled to about two dozen companies with consistently better productivity than GE. Of these, half entered with GE into what I think of as *educational alliances:* a reciprocal arrangement to share with each other the secrets of success. Among those with whom GE struck such educational alliances are AMP, Wal-Mart, Chaparral Steel, Ford, Hewlett-Packard, Xerox, Sanyo, Toshiba, Honda, even the United Nations and Citicorp.[19]

Best practices is a complete about-face for GE. For decades, GE was the home of NIH, the not-invented-here syndrome. If GE didn't invent something, it wasn't worth much. Best practices, however, is based on a humbling premise: Some companies are much more productive than

GE, and GE has much to learn. That GE was humbled (and inspired!) by what they learned is evident in Welch's reflection on the company's educational alliance with Wal-Mart:

> We learned something everywhere, but nowhere did we learn as much as at Wal-Mart. [The late] Sam Walton and his strong team are something very special. Many of our management teams spent time there observing the speed, the bias for action, the utter customer fixation that drives Wal-Mart; and despite our progress, we came back feeling a bit plodding and ponderous, a little envious, but, ultimately, fiercely determined that we're going to do whatever it takes to get that fast.[20]

For example, GE recently borrowed a Wal-Mart practice and created QMI—Quick Market Intelligence.[21] As described in GE's 1992 *Annual Report*, "Quick Market Intelligence is our term for the magnificent boundary-busting technique pioneered by Wal-Mart that allows the entire Company to understand, to sense, to touch the changing desires of the customer and to act on them in almost real time."[22] QMI is a mechanism that incorporates GE salespeople and managers in an active intelligence-gathering network (see Chapter 3). Once a week, people in the field—those closest to the customer—report what they've learned, directly to key managers and the CEO of the business. With this timely information, responses are almost immediate. Some skeptics thought QMI would work well only for consumer products (like Wal-Mart's market), but GE has found that QMI works just as well for large industrial products, like steam turbines.

Best practices has taught GE a lot about improving productivity. Beyond learning specific operational techniques, however, best practices yields significant and lasting networking benefits. It quickens the development of a managerial mind-set better suited to the 1990s and beyond—the mind of the manager who networks smart.

Best practices broke the frame of conventional thinking—not just the NIH syndrome, but the way managers *conceive* of running a business. Consider what I think is the biggest lesson GE managers gleaned from best practices: The very best companies in the world all focus on managing *processes*.[23] Not people, not tasks, not functions, not the pieces, not the parts. The best companies manage the *network* of interrelationships. This emphasis on processes is the philosophical basis of the movement to reengineer the corporation.[24]

What GE learned through best practices is nothing less than the quantum view of organizations I introduced in the Preface. The quantum view prevails in modern physics, ecology, Eastern mysticism, and it is now replacing the outdated Newtonian parts-over-process model of organizations. What GE learned through best practices puts it at the leading edge of the revolution in organizational development. The company learned that it had to stop managing by the numbers (setting targets, measuring performance) and start changing the basic process-es and conditions of work. GE's mindset change was evident in a best practices workshop used to communicate the new orientation: "Process over Product."[25]

Best practices makes GE people look outward. It teaches them how to initiate, build, and maintain external alliances and partnerships. In fact, the theme of another best practices workshop was "Partnering with Suppliers."[26] The experience people gain from best practices enables them to have better relationships with any external organiza-tion—customer, supplier, or competitor. And the experience helps GE people build better *internal* relationships as they work to "diffuse" knowledge of best-practice innovations throughout the company. Best practices, like Work-Out, breaks boundaries.

Process Managing

Process managing is Welch's third great management technique. GE has made headlines with it, but many companies use it, such as Union Carbide, Ford, Boeing, GTE, Motorola, McDonnell Douglas, and AT&T.[27] And, though process managing is most commonly used in manufacturing, the technique is equally at home in services. For exam-ple, I've used the technique with a large law firm to map and improve legal work processes. This technique officially goes by the name process *mapping*, but I prefer the more inclusive term, *managing.* Mapping is the chief analytical tool used to diagnose work flow in a business operation process, but the results serve the larger purpose of improving the total management of an operation.

Process managing forces a team of workers and managers to dissect a business operation and understand it in detail. Once understood, they can figure out how to simplify and streamline the process, elimi-nating unnecessary work, needless steps, duplication, and other ineffi-ciencies. Applying the technique follows six basic steps[28]:

1. *Pick a critical process.* Workers or managers begin by selecting an important process that could stand improvement. Improvement could mean shorter cycle times, lower costs, less complexity, or higher quality.

2. *Define inputs and outputs.* Inputs include *everything* that goes into a process: people, parts, components, materials, money, information, and so on. Outputs include *everything* that comes out: product qual-

ity, delivery, profitability, etc., even psychic rewards like personal satisfaction, growth, achievement, and empowerment.

3. *Map the process.* Mapping the process means charting the flow of work from start to finish. It includes all activities, no matter how small, and all decisions and all people involved in the process. It maps *who* does *what* and *when.* The map shows the *sequence* of activities, as well as *elapsed times.*

4. *Analyze the process.* Once mapped, the process is analyzed to determine what specific improvements can be made. Improvements might be eliminating unnecessary steps or duplicative activities, rearranging people and equipment, installing new equipment, combining activities, removing obstacles, etc.

5. *Implement improvements.* Planned improvements are converted into concrete actions. Implementation includes *who* does *what, when,* and *how.*

6. *Monitor and repeat.* As improvements are implemented, it's important to monitor the process. Often, new problems pop up when old ones are solved. And the exercise can be repeated, in the true spirit of continuous improvements.

Process managing at GE yields extraordinary results: better quality, lower costs, compressed cycle times. GE has plenty of success stories; the best might be Quick Response, a program in GE's Major Appliance business.[29] It began as research in best practices. A manufacturing manager in Camco, a GE Canadian subsidiary, visited a New Zealand company with a reputation for slashing cycle times. He imported the company's methods and applied them at Camco. The results were smashing. As summarized in the 1992 *Annual Report,* Quick Response "has taken GE Appliances from an 18-week order-to-delivery cycle to a $3\frac{1}{2}$-week cycle at the present—on the way to *three days.* Quick Response has reduced average inventory in GE Appliances 50%, or almost $400 million, and will allow it to break through the 10-turn barrier in 1993—almost double the rate of 1989."[30] And, GE quickly spread this great innovation throughout other parts of the company.

Process managing yields fantastic improvements in productivity— higher quality, lower costs, faster response to customers. For me, however, the most exciting benefit is the contribution of process managing to GE's new culture of empowerment. To empower, as I argued in the Introduction, you must create the right conditions. The traditional hierarchy doesn't work because it creates the *wrong* conditions. By design, hierarchy is *disempowering;* it treats adults like children.[31] In contrast, process managing works because it creates the *right* conditions, those that empower workers and managers to be their best. The approach treats adults as adults. It assumes that people desire fulfilling and rewarding work. It assumes that those closest to the work know better than anyone else how to be productive, and it provides the means for them to release and focus their natural creativity and resourcefulness.

Process managing empowers in many ways. It empowers by fostering a genuine sense of ownership: Those who do the actual work learn how to diagnose what they do and improve what they do. It empowers by helping workers and managers learn how to work together in teams. And process managing empowers because it instills the networking perspective. It rejects the outdated Newtonian view of organizations as collections of disjointed parts—jobs, activities, roles, unconnected individuals. By nature, it compels everyone to focus on managing networks of relationships, not the parts or pieces. This is the *quantum* image of managing (see Preface). It's the world as a network, the world in which personal and organizational success come from networking smart.

Education

I've saved education for last, but not because it's the least important. I've saved it for last because in many ways the reeducation of GE is taking place through the practice of the other management techniques—Work-Out, best practices, process managing. All three contribute mightily to new ways of working, new ways of thinking, new ways of competing in the 1990s. And I've saved this management tool for last because I mean something far more than the usual connotations of "education." Education, at GE, is really *resocialization*—the inculcation of *new values*, not just the learning of new techniques. Through education—formal and informal—GE people are internalizing the philosophical principles of empowerment and networking.

Throughout Jack Welch's tenure as CEO and chairman, GE has defined its values—the social principles, goals, and standards of desired behavior. These values create a cultural center for a diverse, giant, global company. Without them, GE couldn't hold together. Values guide personal behavior by defining what's acceptable, what's not. The values provide standards for evaluating proposals and projects, for making decisions, for evaluating others. The values provide GE people with an image of what it means to be a leader in the new GE. Today, for example, GE defines four types of leaders.[32] The ideal type is the leader who shares the values and delivers on commitments. Such leaders empower and inspire great performance. The second type, a person who shares the values but doesn't deliver yet, is given new opportunities to become the first. The third and fourth types are the problems. Those who don't share the values yet make commitments to do so because they rule by the philosophy of control. In the long run, they won't succeed. And those who don't share the values and don't deliver, don't last long.

The values themselves have unfolded over time, defined and refined as the company evolves. In the 1980s, for example, values included honesty, candor, openness, and integrity. These standards helped people face reality and embrace the need for change. Today, GE builds on these basic values and emphasizes the behaviors demanded in the 1990s. For example: "create a clear, simple, reality-based customer-focused vision...have a passion for excellence...hate bureaucracy...have the self-confidence to empower others and behave in a boundaryless fashion...have, or have the capacity to develop, global brains and global sensitivity...stimulate and relish change...."[33]

Of course, listing values is one thing, getting people to believe and accept them is quite another. The best method is learning by doing. "The only learning which significantly influences behavior," says psychologist Carl Rogers, "is self-discovered, self-appropriated learning."[34] GE people learn, practice, and internalize GE values through Work-Out, best practices, and process managing. But there's another important vehicle for education, for communicating, and working out values: GE's vaunted management training center in Crotonville, New York.[35] The Crotonville experience begins right at the beginning. Every incoming class of new professional hires goes straight to Crotonville for the Corporate Entry Leadership Conference (CELC). Each year, over 10,000 GE people participate in Crotonville courses. These courses cover the waterfront, and change as GE needs and the environment change. Crotonville is so important for clarifying and communicating values—and for giving and getting feedback—that Jack Welch visits Crotonville almost once a week.

The Self-Renewing Enterprise

Do you know why bureaucracies are failing? They suffer from what's known as organizational inertia.[36] They can't change. Like the dinosaurs, they can't adapt to their rapidly changing environment. Bureaucratic inertia has put the titans of the U.S. corporate world—companies like General Motors, Sears, IBM—on the endangered species list.

General Electric is different. Unlike most of its corporate peers—the large, old U.S. companies—GE is taking the necessary actions to escape extinction. First it was the hardware, now it's the software, the most difficult task of all. If GE's great cultural revolution succeeds (and I predict it will), GE will escape the plight of organizational inertia. Network organizations—like Jack Welch's boundaryless GE, Michael Mach's lattice organization, high-tech Silicon Valley firms, or the virtual enterprise—evade organizational inertia by their very nature. They adapt, they adjust, they change. They're designed to accommodate tasks and environments that demand flexibility and innovation.[37]

The network organization is a *self-renewing enterprise*. A bureaucracy can't adapt. It's built to process routine problems; when new problems come along, bureaucrats can't cope. But the network organization easily molds itself to each problem. Network organizations recreate themselves anew each time a novel problem must be solved, a unique request must be satisfied. As I've written before, "The intrinsic ability of the network organization to repeatedly redesign itself to accommodate new tasks, unique problems, and changing environments enables such organizations to escape the plight of forms like bureaucracy that ossify and become incapable of change."[38]

And that is why my bet is on GE. While all the corporate dinosaurs are dying—Sears, GM, IBM—companies like GE will win because they're learning how to adapt, change, grow. They're creating self-renewing enterprises.

What You Can Do Now

Because I use GE as a role model in this concluding chapter, I bet you think my advice will be suitably grand. But what you can do right now is personal. GE is networking smart on a grand scale, but you can begin to do the same with the person in the mirror. My advice is this: Take each of Welch's management tools—Work-Out, best practices, process managing, and education—and use them in your own work group. It doesn't matter how small or large your group is. You may be running a big company or participating on a team of five people. It doesn't matter. These techniques work on any scale.

Plan a Work-Out for your group. (You could start with your informal Donuts with Ditch sessions.) If you feel you need help, bring in outside consultants to facilitate the sessions. Make sure all your people are included; give them this chapter to read. (Start with your own group members, but soon after you should be inviting people from other groups, internal and external customers, and suppliers.)

Just like GE Work-Outs, seek out all the unnecessary work—needless, senseless reports, meetings, measurements, and approvals. Which can be eliminated, improved? Pick low-hanging fruit. Hunt rattlers and pythons. Most important, *make decisions on the spot.* Don't squirm out of it; don't let anyone else off the hook either.

On to best practices. Where can you learn about increasing productivity? Which companies are role models in your industry? GE compiled its original list of candidates from public information, press reports, and reputations known by GE people. You can do the same. If you've built your own internal and external intelligence networks, use them now to find best practice candidates. Also consider contacting the American Productivity & Quality Center in Houston, Texas. This benchmarking institute provides training, networking, and information on benchmarking. Once you have your list, approach candidates in the same spirit as GE did: offer reciprocal learning arrangements. They share their secrets with you, you share your secrets with them. To break the ice, give them this chapter to read.

Then process managing. In some ways, this may be the hardest technique to implement, but it's critical because it really promotes the networking perspective. (Not to mention the real gains in productivity!) Bring up the idea of process managing in an early Work-Out session. Give people this chapter to read as background. Get them thinking about processes to work on.

If process managing is foreign to you and your group, you may have to go outside for training or mapping techniques. After training, give your people the time and resources they need to map selected processes. Use Work-Outs to decide which processes to begin with, as well as to discuss the results. And help them implement changes in processes. Champion the cause.

And education. What are your core values? Are your values explicit? Are values imposed from above or developed in partnership with those they affect? What mechanisms do you have for developing, clarifying, and communicating the principles of empowerment and networking? In the spirit of best practices, look to GE for guidance: What kind of training courses can you offer? Can you set up a management institute? Can you offer a tailored program at all levels, from entry-level courses for new hires to advanced courses for executives and senior managers?

What You Can Do Soon

Revolutions can start small. Your experience with Work-Outs, best practices, process managing, and education can become role models for organizational learning. Again, it doesn't matter where you are in the organization. Even if you're a new manager, you can do it. In the downsized, restructured, streamlined organizations we now live in, it's possible for you to have a bigger impact earlier in your career than ever before. Influence today is based much less on formal position and authority, much more on the quality of your ideas and the strength of your performance.

What you can do *soon* is explore ways to export your good experiences to other groups in the organization. One theme cuts through all of GE's experiences with its change efforts: Attitudes matter more than anything else. Your biggest obstacle will be traditional middle managers; they're the usual skeptics, the naysayers. You've got to find some way to reach the skeptics, or your efforts will fizzle out.

Here's an exercise you can use to get your message across. It's an exercise consultants Geary Rummler and Alan Brache use for process managing. Ask your skeptics to draw a picture of the organization. What they'll produce is something like the traditional organizational chart, a diagram with tiers of neat boxes and vertical lines.[39] Then you can discuss the limitations—and risks—of their traditional view of the organization. As Rummler and Brache say, "it doesn't show the products and services we provide. It leaves out the customers we serve. And it gives us no sense of the work flow through which we develop, produce and deliver our products. In short, the familiar organization chart doesn't show what we do, for whom we do it or how we do it."[40]

Now, *you* may be skeptical that this exercise can reveal much. Wouldn't any manager, traditional or not, draw a vertical diagram? Well, this is what happened when I gave a similar exercise to Michael Mach, CEO of Capital Partners, the real estate development firm I featured in Chapter 5. I asked him to draw an organization chart of his firm.[41] He did, but only under protest. "I don't see the firm this way," he grumbled. "We don't work this way. I'll try, but it's a completely misleading picture of the firm." The reason for his reluctance is obvious: Capital Partners is a *network organization*, a small-scale version of the boundaryless organization. The only accurate picture would be a *network*, criss-crossing lines going in all directions, not nice neat boxes and vertical lines. In fact, to be really precise, a still picture wouldn't do; you'd need a motion picture to capture the natural ebb and flow of a network organization.

What You Can Do in the *Long Run*

Creating world-class competitors out of today's organizations won't happen easily. And it won't happen by itself; real transformations of culture don't occur naturally. Change is always resisted. You have to make change happen.

Of all the weapons in your arsenal, one of the two mightiest is *education*. At GE's 1990 Annual Meeting of its share owners, Jack Welch stated that education and training make up one of the greatest challenges of the 1990s. "There is no more important investment this Company can make—because in the '90s, a decade that will roar with new technologies, geopolitical upheaval, cultural change, the difference between winning and losing will be how the men and women of our Company view change as it comes at them."[42] To make the change happen at GE, Welch is investing billions of dollars each year in education and training.

What you can do in the long run—for you, for your people, for your organization—is to become an active *student* and *teacher* of networking smart. As a student, you can teach yourself by studying and applying the lessons of this book. It won't be easy at first. As with learning any new skills, we're uncomfortable and a little awkward at first. It takes time and practice to become good at anything important. It's not enough to just read this book; you have to put into practice what you learn. To benefit from this book, you have to practice in daily life the lessons of networking smart. All the exercises, hands-on tools, and checklists I've provided throughout the book are there to help you. If you haven't experimented yet, go back, pick a chapter, and try out what you've learned.

As a teacher of networking smart, you can help others in many ways. Share this book—with your teammates, bosses, peers, suppliers, customers, and so on. Give selected chapters to them. For example, your immediate coworkers will benefit from Chapter 4, "Managing Up, Down, and Sideways." Groups or departments with a history of troubled relationships will benefit from the lessons in Chapter 5, "Bottlenecks and Bridges." Give Chapter 10, "Building Relationships with Customers and Clients," to your valued customers, and give Chapter 12, "Building Supplier Partnerships," to your key suppliers. And so on. The more people know about networking smart, the easier it is to build good relationships.

You teach best when you practice what you preach. Become a role model of networking smart. "Role models, relationships, and networks," says former Sealy CEO Howard Haas, "are the mechanisms by which important skills of leadership are transmitted."[43] Demonstrate by example how leaders build and manage networks of relationships in intelligent, resourceful, and ethical ways. Help those inside and outside your organization learn how to network well and apply their knowledge responsibly.

Finally, remember that we're at a turning point in the history of business leadership. The 1980s was the crest of the cult of the deal, with its greed, avarice, and utter disregard of relationships. Those who make it in the 1990s and beyond will take a more enlightened course. They will empower themselves and their people through networking smart, and they will turn their companies into exciting, fulfilling, vibrant network organizations.

Only connect!
Epigram from *Howards End*
E. M. FORSTER[44]

References

Preface

1. Margaret J. Wheatley, *Leadership and the New Science* (San Francisco, Calif.: Berrett-Kohler Publishers, 1992), p. 38. Quote is from a conversation Wheatley had with an unidentified friend.

2. For example, see Ed A. W. Boxman, Paul M. De Graaf, and Hendrick D. Flap, "The Impact of Social and Human Capital on the Income Attainment of Dutch Managers," *Social Networks*, vol. 13, 1991, pp. 51–73.

3. Ronald S. Burt, *Structural Holes* (Cambridge, Mass.: Harvard University Press, 1992).

4. See, for example, Mark. S. Granovetter, *Getting a Job: A Study of Contacts and Careers* (Cambridge, Mass.: Harvard University Press, 1974); National Longitudinal Survey of Youth, as, for example, reported in James D. Montgomery, "Social Networks and Persistent Inequality in the Labor Market," unpublished manuscript, Northwestern University, 1992.

5. See John J. Gabarro, *The Dynamics of Taking Charge* (Boston: Harvard Business School Press, 1987); see also John P. Kotter, *The General Managers* (New York: The Free Press, 1982), and Linda A. Hill, *Becoming a Manager* (Boston: Harvard Business School Press, 1992).

6. For example, see William H. Davidow and Bro Uttal, *Total Customer Service* (New York: Harper Collins Publishers, 1989), p. 30. See also, Thomas J. Peters and Robert H. Waterman, Jr., *In Search of Excellence* (New York: Harper and Row, 1982), p. 112.

7. For example, "[a] U.S. automobile executive estimates that about a quarter of the cost advantage of Japanese firms is due to the superior efficiency of their supplier networks." Quoted on p. 38 in John McMillan, "Managing Suppliers: Incentive Systems in Japanese and U.S. Industry," *California Management Review*, vol. 32, 1990, pp. 38–55. See also evidence presented in Chapter 12.

8. See, e.g., Fred Luthans, "Successful vs. Effective Real Managers," *Academy of Management Review*, vol. 2, 1988, pp. 127–132. Reams of supporting evidence are presented throughout my book.

9. A great deal of evidence supports these facts. See, for example, E. Diener, "Subjective Well-Being," *Psychological Bulletin*, vol. 95, 1984, pp. 542–575; J. A. House, *Work Stress and Social Support* (Reading, Mass.: Addison-Wesley, 1981); M. Jahoda, *Current Concepts of Positive Mental Health* (New York: Basic, 1958); S. S. Jouard and T. Landsman, *Healthy Personality: An*

Approach from the Viewpoint of Humanistic Psychology, 4th ed. (New York: Macmillan, 1980); Charles Kadushin, "Social Density and Mental Health," in Peter V. Marsden and Nan Lin (eds.), *Social Structure and Network Analysis,* pp. 147–158 (Beverly Hills, Calif.: Sage, 1982); S. R. Pinneau, "The Effects of Social Support on Psychological and Physiological Stress," unpublished doctoral dissertation, University of Michigan; C. Schaefer, J. C. Coyne, and R. S. Lazarus, "The Health-Related Functions of Social Support, *Journal of Behavioral Medicine,* vol. 4, 1981, pp. 381–406; S. E. Taylor and J. Brown, "Illusion and Well-Being: A Social Psychological Perspective on Mental Health," *Psychological Bulletin,* vol. 103, 1988, pp. 193–210; K. A. Wallston and B. S. Wallston, "Who Is Responsible for Your Health? The Construct of Health Locus of Control," in G. Saunders and J. Suls (eds.), *Social Psychology of Health and Illness,* pp. 65–95 (Hillsdale, N.J.: Erlbaum, 1982).

10. Lisa F. Berkman and S. Leonard Syme, "Social Networks, Host Resistance, and Mortality: A Nine-year Follow-up Study of Alameda County Residents," *American Journal of Epidemiology,* vol. 109, 1979, pp. 186–204.

11. See, for example, Mihaly Csikszentmihalyi, *Flow: The Psychology of Optimal Experience* (New York: Harper & Row, 1990), p. 164. He reports that the two most important factors are how we experience the work we do and the quality of our relationships with others.

12. See, for example, J. G. Parker and F. Asher, "Peer Relations and Later Adjustment," *Psychological Bulletin,* vol. 102, 1987, pp. 357–389.

13. Conclusion of a new study by Alice S. Baum and David W. Burnes, *A Nation in Denial: The Truth about Homelessness,* reported by William Raspberry, "Two Researchers Who Want Us to Face the Truth about Homelessness," *The Chicago Tribune,* January 4, 1993, sec. 1, p. 13. They reject the generally accepted argument that homelessness is caused by poverty and lack of affordable public housing. Poverty-stricken people don't become homeless if they have family, kin, church, or neighbors who can offer temporary shelter and other assistance.

14. These trends have been noted by many, but they are nicely summarized by Homa Bahrami in "The Emerging Flexible Organization: Perspectives from Silicon Valley," *California Management Review,* vol. 34, 1992, pp. 35–52. I elaborate these trends in the Introduction.

15. Robert B. Reich, *The Work of Nations: Preparing Ourselves for 21st-Century Capitalism* (New York: Vintage/Random House, 1992), p. 85. See especially Chapters 7 and 8 for his analysis.

16. Tom Peters, "Connectors Help: Don't Fear Them" from his "Peters on Excellence" column, *Union-News,* Springfield, Mass., September 8, 1992, pp. 1, 19.

17. From letter April 15, 1993. Used with permission.

18. Jeffrey Pfeffer, *Managing with Power* (Boston, Mass.: Harvard Business School Press, 1992), p. 17.

19. Charles Darwin, *The Origin of Species* (New York: Mentor, 1958[1859]), pp. 80–84.

20. This is the message in Fritjof Capra, *The Tao of Physics: An Exploration of the Parallels between Modern Physics and Eastern Mysticism*, 3d ed. (Boston: Shambhala, 1991). Capra's quote on p. 329.

21. Wheatley, *Leadership*, pp. 39, 71.

22. Peters, "Connectors Help," pp. 1, 19.

23. Michael Hammer and James Champy, *Reengineering the Corporation* (New York: HarperCollins, 1993).

Introduction

1. Philip B. Crosby, *The Eternally Successful Organization* (New York: Mentor, 1988), p. 61.

2. Noel M. Tichy, "Networks in Organizations," in Paul C. Nystrom and William H. Starbuck (eds.), *Handbook of Organizational Design*, vol. 2 (New York: Oxford University Press, 1981).

3. This story is based on interviews with industry participants. Company and individual names have been changed to ensure anonymity.

4. See, for example, John P. Kotter, *The General Managers* (New York: The Free Press, 1982).

5. See, for example, John J. Gabarro, *The Dynamics of Taking Charge* (Boston: Harvard Business School Press, 1987).

6. See, for example, Kotter, *The General Managers*, and Linda A. Hill, *Becoming a Manager: Mastery of a New Identity* (Boston: Harvard Business School Press, 1992). Studies cited throughout this book support the argument of the importance of relationships and networks.

7. See, for example, the impressive network evidence on this fact in Ronald S. Burt, *Structural Holes* (Cambridge, Mass.: Harvard University Press, 1992).

8. Estimate in "How to Track the Fast-Track Firms," *Chicago Tribune*, sec. 8, December 27, 1992, p. 1.

9. Estimates in Stephan Franklin, "For Workers and Their Employers, It Was a Wonderful Life," *Chicago Tribune*, December 22, 1992, sec. 3, pp. 1, 3. Sears made the changes official at the end of January 1993. See also Jolie Solomon, "The Fall of the Dinosaurs," *Newsweek*, February 8, 1993, pp. 42–44.

10. Quoted in Noel Tichy and Ram Charan, "Speed, Simplicity, Self-Confidence: An Interview with Jack Welch," *Harvard Business Review*, September–October 1989, p. 114,

11. In *Pack Your Own Parachute* (Reading, Mass.: Addison-Wesley, 1987), Paul Hirsch describes the changing employer-employee contract and the importance of building networks as a key survival strategy.

12. Many of these changes are documented in detail in Lee Sproull and Sara Kielser, *Connections: New Ways of Working in the Networked Organization* (Cambridge, Mass.: The MIT Press, 1992).

13. For discussion of control of information as a source of power, see Jeffrey Pfeffer, *Managing with Power* (Boston: Harvard Business School Press, 1992), Part II.

14. Bahrami, "Emerging Flexible Organization," p. 34.

15. See, for example, Joann S. Lublin, "Firms Ship Unit Headquarters Abroad," *The Wall Street Journal*, December 9, 1992, pp. B1, B8.

16. From a speech given by John F. Welch, Jr., "Managing for the Nineties," at the GE Annual Meeting of Share Owners, Waukesha, Wisconsin (April 27, 1988), used with permission; Tom Peters, *Liberation Management: Necessary Disorganization for the Nanosecond Nineties* (New York: Alfred A. Knopf, 1992).

17. Charles M. Savage, *Fifth Generation Management: Integrating Enterprises through Human Networking* (Digital Press, 1990), p. xiii.

18. See, for example, Bahrami, "Emerging Flexible Organization"; Wayne E. Baker, "The Network Organization in Theory and Practice," in Nitin Nohria and Robert G. Eccles (eds.), *Networks and Organizations* (Boston: Harvard Business School Press, 1992); Wayne E. Baker and Robert R. Faulkner, "Role as Resource in the Hollywood Film Industry," *American Journal of Sociology*, vol. 97, 1991, pp. 279–309; Robert G. Eccles and Dwight B. Crane, "Managing through Networks in Investment Banking," *California Management Review*, vol. 30, 1987, pp. 176–195.

19. Peters, *Liberation Management*.

20. Based on General Electric Annual Report, 1989. In the original text, "boundaryless" is hyphenated as "boundary-less." I have deleted the hyphen to make the term consistent with current usage at GE. See Chapter 15 for a fuller description of the boundaryless organization.

21. Jeffrey Pfeffer, *Managing with Power* (Boston: Harvard Business School Press, 1992), Part II.

22. See Allan Cohen and David Bradford, *Influence without Authority* (New York: Wiley, 1990).

23. Rosabeth Moss Kanter, *When Giants Learn to Dance* (New York: Simon & Schuster, 1989), p. 361.

24. Charles J. Fombrun, *Turning Points: Creating Strategic Change in Corporations* (New York: McGraw-Hill, 1992), quote from cover.

25. See, for example, Robert Slater, *The New GE*, (Homewood, Ill.: Business One Irwin, 1993), p. 210.

26. Robert Slater, *The New GE*, p. 210.

27. See Robert E. Lane, "Work as 'Disutility' and Money as 'Happiness': Cultural Origins of a Basic Market Error," *The Journal of Socio-Economics*, vol. 21, 1992, pp. 43–64.

28. Douglas McGregor, *The Human Side of Enterprise* (New York: McGraw-Hill, 1960); also Frederick Herzberg, *Work and the Nature of Man* (New York: New American Library, 1966, 1973). Parts of this paragraph are based on my "Pay, Motivation," *Chicago Tribune*, June 15, 1991.

29. Peter M. Senge, *The Fifth Discipline: The Art & Practice of the Learning Organization* (New York: Doubleday Currency, 1990), p. 140.

30. Robert Slater, *The New GE*, p. 210.

31. Donald M. Nerwick, A. Blanton Godfrey, and Jane Roessner, *Curing Health Care: New Strategies for Quality Improvement* (San Francisco, Calif.: Jossey-Bass, 1990), p. 35.

32. Ibid., p. 36.

33. Discovered, for example, by GE's exploration of "Best Practices" with companies such as Chaparral Steel, Ford, Hewlett-Packard, and others, reported by Noel M. Tichy and Stratford Sherman, *Control Your Destiny or Someone Else Will* (New York: Doubleday, 1993).

34. From a speech given by John F. Welch, Jr., "Managing for the Nineties," at the GE Annual Meeting of Share Owners, Waukesha, Wisconsin (April 27, 1988). Used with permission.

35. From John F. Welch, Jr., "Soft Values for a Hard Decade: A View on Winning in the '90s." An Executive Speech Reprint, General Electric Company, November 1989. Used with permission.

36. I gratefully acknowledge the influence of Douglas McGregor's thinking; see his analysis of Theory X and Theory Y approaches to management in *The Human Side of Enterprise* (New York: McGraw-Hill, 1960). In many ways, McGregor was ahead of his time. Only now are we seeing evidence that his Theory Y assumptions are being used in the new philosophy of empowerment.

37. See Chris Argyris, "Personality vs. Organization," *Organizational Dynamics*, Fall 1974, pp. 3–6.

38. Quoted in "Major Firms Requiring Less-Bossy Bosses," *Milwaukee Journal*, March 1992, p. D5.

39. Quoted in John P. Kotter, *The General Managers*, p. 114.

40. Savage, *Fifth Generation Management*, Chapter 10; in a similar vein, J. A. Conger cites "lack of networking-forming opportunities" as a major factor leading to powerlessness in organizations. See p. 22 in "Leadership: The Art of Empowering Others," *The Academy of Management Executive*, vol. 3., 1989, pp. 17–24.

41. Fred V. Guterl, "Goodbye, Old Matrix," *Business Month*, February 1989, pp. 32–33.

42. H. Norman Schwarzkopf with Peter Petre, *General H. Norman Schwarzkopf: The Autobiography: It Doesn't Take a Hero* (New York: Linda Gret Bantam, 1992), p. 232.

43. Described in Robert Slater, *The New GE*, p. 73.

44. Karl von Clausewitz, *On War*, translated by M. Howard and P. Paret (Princeton, N.J.: Princeton University Press, 1976).

45. Georg Simmel, *Conflict and the Web of Group-Affiliations*, translated by Kurt H. Wolff and Reinhard Bendix (New York: Free Press, 1955), pp. 130–131.

46. Edward A. Shils and Morris Janowitz, "Cohesion and Disintegration in the Wehrmacht in World War II," *Public Opinion Quarterly*, vol. 12, 1948, pp. 280–315.

47. Charles C. Moskos, Jr., *The American Enlisted Man* (New York: Russell Sage Foundation, 1970), Chapter 6.

48. Douglas McGregor, *The Human Side of Enterprise* (New York: McGraw-Hill, 1960), pp. 33–57.

49. Tracy Kidder, *The Soul of a New Machine* (Boston: Little, Brown, 1981).

50. See Roy A. Bauer, Emilio Collar, and Victor Tang, *The Silverlake Project: Transformation at IBM* (New York: Oxford University Press, 1992).

51. Richard Saul Wurman, *Information Anxiety* (New York: Doubleday, 1989).

Chapter 1

1. Ken Auletta, *Greed and Glory on Wall Street* (New York: Warner Books, 1986), p. 241.

2. The Playco example is based on Calvin Morrill's article, "Conflict Management, Honor, and Organizational Change," *American Journal of Sociology*, vol. 97, 1991, pp. 585–621.

3. Morrill, "Conflict Management," p. 587. All special terms and phrases used by Playco executives are noted by quotation marks.

4. Paul M. Hirsch describes this process in "From Ambushes to Golden Parachutes: Corporate Takeovers as an Instance of Cultural Framing and Institutional Integration, *American Journal of Sociology*, vol. 91, 1986, pp. 800–837; and his *Pack Your Own Parachute* (Reading, Mass.: Addison-Wesley, 1987).

5. Morrill, "Conflict Management," p. 593.

6. James S. Coleman, *Power and the Structure of Society* (New York: W. W. Norton and Co., 1974), pp. 24–25.

7. Andre Shleifer and Lawrence Summers, "Breach of Trust in Hostile Takeovers," in Allan J. Auerbach (ed.), *Corporate Takeovers: Causes and Consequences*, pp. 33–56 (Chicago: University of Chicago Press, 1988).

8. Richard M. Titmuss, *The Gift Relationship: From Human Blood to Social Policy* (New York: Random House, 1971).

9. These paragraphs are based, in part, on Michael Best, *The New Competition* (Cambridge, Mass.: Harvard University Press, 1990), Chapter 5.

10. See, for example, Jolie Solomon, Frank Washington, and Myron Stokes, "GM: It's Rocky in Recovery," *Newsweek*, October 12, 1992, p. 61.

11. Richard Florida and Martin Kenney, "Transplanted Organizations: The Transfer of Japanese Industrial Organization to the U.S.," *American Sociological Review*, vol. 56, 1991, pp. 381–398.

12. Hirsch, *Pack Your Own Parachute*, p. 22.

13. Hirsch, *Pack Your Own Parachute*, p. 23.

14. Neil Fligstein, "The Intraorganizational Power Struggle: The Rise of Finance Presidents in Large Corporations," *American Sociological Review*, vol. 52, 1987, pp. 377–391; and *The Transformation of Corporate Control* (Cambridge, Mass.: Harvard University Press, 1990).

15. See, e.g., Bernard Wysocki, Jr., "American Firms Send Office Work Abroad to Use Cheaper Labor," *Wall Street Journal*, August 14, 1991, pp. 1, A6.

16. Tom Peters, *Thriving on Chaos* (New York: Harper and Row, 1987), pp. 25–28.

17. James D. Squires, *Read All about It* (New York: Times Books, 1993).

18. Wayne E. Baker and Robert R. Faulkner, "Role as Resource in the Hollywood Film Industry," *American Journal of Sociology*, vol. 97, 1991, pp. 279–309.

19. Pauline Kael, "Why Are Movies So Bad? Or, The Numbers," *New Yorker*, June 23, 1980, pp. 132–136.

20. Mark Litwak, *Reel Power: The Struggle for Influence and Success in the New Hollywood* (New York: William Morrow, 1987), p. 155.

21. James Brian Quinn and Christopher Gagnon, "Will Service Follow Manufacturing into Decline?" *Harvard Business Review*, November/December 1986, p. 95.

22. See, for example, *The Good Society* (New York: Alfred A. Knopf, 1991) and *Habits of the Heart* (New York: Harper & Row, 1985) by Robert N. Bellah, Richard Madsen, William M. Sullivan, Ann Swidler, and Steven M. Tipton.

Chapter 2

1. Robert K. Mueller, *Corporate Networking* (New York: Free Press, 1986).

2. John J. Gabarro, *The Dynamics of Taking Charge* (Boston: Harvard Business School Press, 1987), p. 98.

3. For example, see Douglas McGregor, *The Human Side of Enterprise* (New York: McGraw-Hill, 1980).

4. The importance of relationships in business and social life has been documented in numerous sociological and psychological studies. Hundreds of them are cited throughout this book.

5. Jane Hannaway, *Managers Managing* (New York: Oxford University Press, 1989), p. 111.

6. Donald M. Schwartz, "A Study of Interpersonal Problem-Posing," unpublished doctoral dissertation, University of Chicago, Department of Education, 1976, p. 24.

7. On deindividuation, see, for example, P. G. Zimbardo, "The Human Choice: Individuation, Reason and Order Versus Deindividuation, Impulse, and Chaos," in W. J. Arnold and D. Levine (eds.), *Nebraska Symposium on Motivation,* vol. 16 (Lincoln: University of Nebraska Press, 1969).

8. Paul M. Hirsch, "From Ambushes to Golden Parachutes: Corporate Takeovers as an Instance of Cultural Framing and Institutional Integration," *American Journal of Sociology,* vol. 91, 1986, pp. 800–837.

9. From a videotaped interview and employee roundtable, *First Edition X,* March 1990, GE Video Production Center. Used with permission.

10. Attributed to Kurt Lewin.

11. Kurt H. Wolff (trans. and ed.), *The Sociology of Georg Simmel* (New York: The Free Press, 1950).

12. Mihaly Csikszentmihalyi, *Flow: The Psychology of Optimal Experience* (New York: Harper & Row, 1990), p. 164.

13. See, for example, ibid.; E. Diener, "Subjective Well-Being," *Psychological Bulletin,* vol. 95, 1984, pp. 542–575; J. A. House, *Work Stress and Social Support* (Reading, Mass.: Addison-Wesley, 1981); M. Jahoda, *Current Concepts of Positive Mental Health* (New York: Basic, 1958); S. S. Jouard and T. Landsman, *Healthy Personality: An Approach from the Viewpoint of Humanistic Psychology,* 4th ed. (New York: Macmillan, 1980); Charles Kadushin, "Social Density and Mental Health," in Peter V. Marsden and Nan Lin (eds.), *Social Structure and Network Analysis* (Beverly Hills, Calif.: Sage, 1982), pp. 147–158; S. R. Pinneau, "The Effects of Social Support on Psychological and Physiological Stress," unpublished doctoral dissertation, Ann Arbor, University of Michigan; C. Schaefer, J. C. Coyne, and R. S. Lazarus, "The Health-Related Functions of Social Support," *Journal of Behavioral Medicine,* vol. 4, 1981, pp. 381–406; S. E. Taylor and J. Brown, "Illusion and Well-Being: A Social Psychological Perspective on Mental Health," *Psychological Bulletin,* vol. 103, 1988, pp. 193–210; K. A. Wallston and B. S. Wallston, "Who Is Responsible for Your Health? The Construct of Health Locus of Control," in G. Saunders and J. Suls (eds.), *Social Psychology of Health and Illness* (Hillsdale, N.J.: Erlbaum, 1982), pp. 65–95.

14. Numerous studies support this finding, many of which are reviewed in *Doctor-Patient Studies, Newsletter of the University of Chicago Doctor-Patient Relationship Project* (December 1990, nos. 1–5; December 1991, nos. 6–8).

15. For example, see Ed A. W. Boxman, Paul M. De Graaf, and Hendrick D. Flap, "The Impact of Social and Human Capital on the Income Attainment of Dutch Managers," *Social Networks,* vol. 13, 1991, pp. 51–73; Ronald S. Burt, *Structural Holes* (Cambridge, Mass.: Harvard University Press, 1992); John J. Gabarro, *The Dynamics of Taking Charge* (Boston: Harvard Business School Press, 1987); John P. Kotter, *The General Managers* (New York: The Free Press, 1982); Linda A. Hill, *Becoming a Manager* (Boston: Harvard Business School Press, 1992).

16. For example, "[a] U.S. automobile executive estimates that about a quarter of the cost advantage of Japanese firms is due to the superior efficiency of

their supplier networks." These networks are based on strong partnerships. Quoted in John McMillan, "Managing Suppliers: Incentive Systems in Japanese and U.S. Industry," *California Management Review*, vol. 32, 1990, p. 38. See also evidence presented in Chapter 12.

17. Allan Cox, *Straight Talk for Monday Morning* (New York: John Wiley & Sons, 1990).

18. Quoted in Robert Rosenthal and Lenore Jacobson, *Pygmalion in the Classroom* (New York: Holt, Rinehart and Winston, 1968).

19. Rosenthal and Jacobson, *Pygmalion in the Classroom*. Several examples given in this section are from their book. Their study stimulated a stream of research attempting to replicate or refute their findings. Many studies replicated their results, but others did not. Based on my review of this stream of research, I conclude that the Pygmalion expectancy effect is real, but it is not guaranteed in all circumstances and it does not occur as a simple mechanical effect. Interaction quality is the most important determinant of expectancy effects.

20. See also, Dov Eden, *Pygmalion in Management: Productivity as a Self-Fulfilling Prophesy* (Lexington, Mass.: Lexington Books/D.C. Heath, 1990).

21. Robert K. Merton, *Social Theory and Social Structure* (New York: Free Press, 1957), pp. 421–436.

22. B. L. Bushard, "The U.S. Army's Mental Hygiene Consultation Service," in *Symposium on Preventive and Social Psychiatry* (Washington, D.C.: Walter Reed Army Institute of Research, 1957), pp. 431–443.

23. J. Sterling Livingston, "Pygmalion in Management," *Harvard Business Review*, September–October 1988, p. 122.

24. See, for example, A. S. King, "Self-Fulfilling Prophesies in Training the Hard-Core: Supervisory Expectations and the Underprivileged Workers' Performance," *Social Science Quarterly*, vol. 52, 1971, pp. 369–378; William M. Skilbeck and Barry E. Collins also found some support for the Pygmalion effect in supervisor-worker interactions in "Transmission and Compliance with Expectations in a Simulated Supervisor-Worker Interaction," paper presented at the annual meeting of the Western Psychological Association, Los Angeles, Calif., April 8–11, 1976.

25. Jan B. Heide and George John, "Alliances in Industrial Purchasing: The Determinants of Joint Action in Buyer-Supplier Relationships," *Journal of Marketing Research*, vol. 37, 1990, pp. 24–36.

26. Edward E. Jones, "Interpreting Interpersonal Behavior: The Effects of Expectancies," *Science*, vol. 234, 1986, pp. 41–46. In psychology, the Pygmalion effect is incorporated in "expectancy theory."

27. This example was kindly provided by Linda Ginzel, based on her presentation to the Executive MBA fall retreat, University of Chicago Graduate School of Business, Delavan, Wisconsin, September 1992.

28. Eden, *Pygmalion in Management*.

29. Douglas McGregor, *The Human Side of Enterprise* (New York: McGraw-Hill, 1980).

30. J. Sterling Livingston, "Pygmalion in Management," *Harvard Business Review*, September–October 1988, p. 122.

31. Eden, *Pygmalion in Management*, pp. 124–127.

32. For example, see D. Bryne, *The Attraction Paradigm* (New York: Academic Press, 1971); Robert B. Cialdini, *Influence* (Glenview, Ill.: Scott, Foresman and Co., 1985); D. Byrne and J. Lamerth, "Interpersonal Attraction," *Annual Review of Psychology*, vol. 24, 1973, pp. 317–336.

33. Matthijs Kalmijn, "Status Homogamy in the United States," *American Journal of Sociology*, vol. 97, 1991, pp. 496–523.

34. For a classic study of the effects of propinquity on interpersonal attraction, see L. Festinger, S. Schacter, and K. Back, *Social Pressures in Informal Groups: A Study of Human Factors in Housing* (New York: Harper & Row, 1950).

35. This tendency has been noted by many, including Jane Hannaway, *Managers Managing* (New York: Oxford University Press, 1989), Chapter 6.

36. See, for example, Edward E. Jones and Richard E. Nisbett, "The Actor and the Observer: Divergent Perceptions of the Causes of Behavior," in E. E. Jones, D. Kanouse, H. H. Kelley, R. E. Nisbett, S. Valins, and B. Weiner (eds.), *Attribution: Perceiving the Causes of Behavior* (Morristown, N.J.: General Learning Press, 1971), pp. 79–94.

37. For example, see R. B. Zajonc, "The Attitudinal Effects of Mere Exposure," *Journal of Personality and Social Psychology Monographs*, vol. 9, part 2, 1968; R. B. Zajonc, H. M. Markus, W. R. Wilson, "Exposure Effects and Associate Learning," *Journal of Experimental Social Psychology*, vol. 10, 1974, pp. 248–263; R. B. Zajonc, W. C. Swap, A. Harrison, and P. Roberts, "Limiting Conditions of the Exposure Effect: Satiation and Relativity," *Journal of Personality and Social Psychology*, vol. 18, 1971, pp. 384–391.

38. This is a key theme in game theory. For a highly readable account, see Robert Axelrod, *The Evolution of Cooperation* (New York: Basic, 1984).

39. David Sally reviews numerous experiments in his "Conversation and Cooperation in Social Dilemmas: Experimental Evidence from 1958 to 1992," unpublished manuscript, Graduate School of Business, University of Chicago, 1992.

40. See, for example, Mark Granovetter's seminal research, especially "Economic Action and Social Structure: The Problem of Embeddedness," *American Journal of Sociology*, vol. 91, 1985, pp. 481–510, and *Society and Economy* (forthcoming).

41. Psychologists would call my principle 4 the "contact hypothesis." This hypothesis is supported by research, but some studies show that certain relationships, especially race relations, don't improve with repeated interaction. School desegregation, for example, often leads to *less* social integration. One reason is that the traditional academic environment is very com-

petitive and forces students to be rivals. When this environment is changed to encourage and reward cooperation, the results are very positive: more friendship and less prejudice between racial or ethnic groups. For an excellent summary of this research, see Robert B. Cialdini, *Influence: Science and Practice* (Glenview, Ill.: Scott, Foresman and Co., 1985), pp. 149–156.

42. The small-world phenomenon is well known. See, for example, Ithiel de Sola Pool and Manfred Kochen, "Contacts and Influence," *Social Networks*, vol. 1, 1978/79, pp. 5–51.

43. Based on Edward O. Laumann's presentation to the University of Chicago's Vail Management Development Seminar, 1991.

44. Pool and Kochen, "Contacts and Influence," discuss estimates, estimation procedures, and difficulties in measuring network size.

45. Pool and Kochen, ibid., p. 15, provide this estimate, based on the assumptions that (1) acquaintanceship is random, and (2) the average number of acquaintances is 1000.

46. Max Gunther, *The Luck Factor* (New York: Macmillan, 1977).

47. See, for example, Mark S. Granovetter, "The Strength of Weak Ties," *American Journal of Sociology*, vol. 78, 1973, pp. 1360–1380. I made these distinctions in my study of corporate relations with investment banks. See Wayne E. Baker, "Market Networks and Corporate Behavior," *American Journal of Sociology*, vol. 96, 1990, pp. 589–625.

48. See evidence and discussion in Chapters 10 and 12.

49. In "Developing Buyer-Seller Relationships," *Journal of Marketing*, vol. 51, 1987, pp. 11–27, F. Robert Dwyer, Paul H. Schurr, and Sejo Oh use a two-dimensional array to understand the variety of marketing relationships. They array "seller's motivational investment in relationship" against "buyer's motivational investment in relationship." See also Chapter 10, note 31.

50. Conveyed to me by personal letter (November 27, 1991). Used with permission.

51. Douglas McGregor, *The Human Side of Enterprise* (New York: McGraw-Hill, 1980).

52. Based on an extensive cross-cultural study of friendship: Yehudi A. Cohen, "Patterns of Friendship," in Yehudi A. Cohen (ed.), *Social Structure and Personality: A Casebook* (New York: Holt, Rinehart and Winston, 1961), pp. 351–386.

53. Robert B. Cialdini calls such people "compliance professionals" because they are so adept at using social psychological methods to secure compliance with their objectives. See, for example, Chapter 2 in his *Influence: Science and Practice* (Glenview, Ill.: Scott, Foresman, 1985).

54. Stephen R. Covey, "The Taproot of Trust," *Executive Excellence*, vol. 8, 1991, p. 3.

55. D. J. Steffensmeir, *The Fence* (Totowa, N.J., Roman & Littlefield, 1986), p. 157.

56. James B. Stewart, *Den of Thieves* (New York: Simon & Schuster, 1991).

57. Wayne E. Baker and Robert R. Faulkner, "The Social Organization of Price-Fixing Conspiracies," University of Chicago working paper, 1992.

58. See, for example, the research cited in Chapter 4.

59. From a speech given by Carl R. Rogers and taken from his *On Becoming a Person* (Boston: Houghton Mifflin, 1961).

Chapter 3

1. Quoted in Philip Kotler, *Marketing Management*, 6th ed. (Englewood Cliffs, N.J.: Prentice-Hall, 1988), p. 101.

2. Story in *Time*, September 30, 1991, p. 19.

3. H. Edward Wrapp, "Good Managers Don't Make Policy Decisions," *Harvard Business Review*, July–August 1984, pp. 4–11. Quotation from p. 5.

4. From his speech at the Crowell Collier Institute of Continuing Education (New York); reported in *Business Week*, February 18, 1967, p. 202.

5. Richard Neustadt, *Presidential Power: The Politics of Leadership* (New York: John Wiley, 1960).

6. Alvin Toffler, *Powershift* (New York: Bantam Books, 1990).

7. Loy Singleton, *Telecommunications in the Information Age* (New York: Ballinger, 1984).

8. Richard Saul Wurman, *Information Anxiety* (New York: Doubleday, 1989).

9. See, for example, J. Edward Russo and Paul J. H. Schoemaker, *Decision Traps* (New York: Doubleday, 1989).

10. Wrapp, "Good Managers," p. 4.

11. Chapter 3 in Harry Levinson and Stuart Rosenthal, *CEO: Corporate Leadership in Action* (New York: Basic Books, 1984). Quotation from p. 68.

12. Stephen W. Quickel, "Welch on Welch," CEO of the Year, *Financial World*, April 3, 1990, pp. 62–67.

13. Thomas J. Peters and Robert H. Waterman, *In Search of Excellence: Lessons from America's Best-Run Companies* (New York: Harper and Row, 1982).

14. "The CEO Disease/Avoiding the Pitfalls of Power," *Australian Business*, May 1, 1991, pp. 36–41 (which is reprinted from *Business Week*, April 1, 1991).

15. Mitchell Locin, "Little Rock Hops for Local Hero," *Chicago Tribune*, November 4, 1992, sec. 1, p. 5.

16. Ronald S. Burt, *Structural Holes* (Cambridge, Mass.: Harvard University Press, 1992).

17. Henry Mintzberg, "The Manager's Job: Folklore and Fact," *Harvard Business Review*, July–August 1975, pp. 49–61.

18. See, for example, Rosabeth Moss Kanter, "Power Failure in Management Circuits," *Harvard Business Review,* July–August 1979, pp. 65–75.

19. See an excellent discussion of reciprocity in Chapter 2 of Robert B. Cialdini, *Influence: Science and Practice* (Glenview, Ill.: Scott, Foresman, 1985). Anthropologists and sociologists have documented that reciprocity is a rule in *all* cultures and societies.

20. For insights on gossip and decision making, see James G. March and Guje Sevon, "Gossip, Information and Decision-Making," in Lee S. Sproull and J. Patrick Crecine (eds.), *Advances in Information Processing in Organizations,* vol. 1 (Greenwich, Conn.: JAI Press, 1984), pp. 95–107.

21. From interview with Allan Ditchfield, April 23, 1993. Used with permission.

22. "The CEO Disease," p. 40.

23. Described in letter from Kathryn E. Milano, Federal Express, January 18, 1993.

24. Ram Charan, "How Networks Reshape Organizations—for Results," *Harvard Business Review,* September–October 1991, p. 110.

25. Described in Noel M. Tichy and Stratford Sherman, *Control Your Own Destiny or Someone Else Will* (New York: Doubleday, 1993), pp. 156–166.

26. Jane Hannaway, *Managers Managing* (New York: Oxford University Press, 1989), pp. 104–105.

27. See, e.g., "Japan: All in the Family," *Newsweek,* June 10, 1991, pp. 37–39.

28. Kathleen M. Eisenhardt, "Speed and Strategic Choice: How Managers Accelerate Decision Making," *California Management Review,* vol. 32, 1990, pp. 1–16.

29. Eisenhardt, "Speed and Strategic Choice," discusses in detail the concepts of real time information networks and fast decision making.

30. See, for example, Charles Savage, *Fifth Generation Management: Integrating Enterprises through Human Networking* (Digital Press, 1990); and Lee Sproull and Sara Kiesler, *Connections: New Ways of Working in the Networked Organization* (Cambridge, Mass.: MIT Press, 1992).

31. In Brad Schepp, "The 10-Second Commute," *Home Office Computing,* December 1991, pp. 45–48.

32. For example, see Richard L. Nolan, Alex J. Pollock, James P. Ware, "Toward the Design of Network Organizations," *Stage by Stage,* vol. 9, 1989, pp. 1–12, published by Nolan, Norton, & Co.

33. Henry Mintzberg, "The Manager's Job: Folklore and Fact," *Harvard Business Review,* July–August 1975, pp. 49–61.

34. Ibid., p. 167.

35. Ibid.

36. See, for example, Sproull and Kiesler, *Connections,* p. 15, Chapter 2.

37. Ibid., pp. 37, 39.

38. James. L. McKenney, Michael H. Zack, and Victor S. Doherty, "Complementary Communication Media: A Comparison of Electronic Mail and Face-to-Face Communication in a Programming Team," in Nitin Nohria and Robert G. Eccles (eds.), *Networks and Organizations: Structure, Form, and Action* (Boston: Harvard Business School Press, 1992), Chapter 10.

39. Quoted in Sproull and Kiesler, *Connections*, p. 40; originally cited in L. K. Trevino, R. Lengel, and R. L. Daft, "Media Symbolism, Media Richness, and Media Choice in Organizations," *Communication Research*, vol. 14, 1987, pp. 553–574.

40. On the importance of symbols, ceremony, and management, see, for example, Harrison M. Trice, James Belasco, and Joseph A. Alutto, "The Role of Ceremonials in Organizational Behavior," *Industrial Management Review*, vol. 23, 1969, pp. 40–51.

41. Jane Hannaway, *Managers Managing* (New York: Oxford University Press, 1989), p. 144.

42. Joshua Hammer, "The Fall of Frank Mancuso," *Newsweek*, May 6, 1991.

43. On networks in publishing, see Walter W. Powell, *Getting into Print* (Chicago: University of Chicago Press, 1985) and Lewis Coser, Charles Kadushin, and Walter W. Powell, *Books: The Culture and Commerce of Publishing* (New York: Basic, 1982), especially Chapter 3, "Networks, Connections, and Circles."

44. Personal interview, Summer 1991.

45. Tom Peters, *Thriving on Chaos* (New York: Harper & Row, 1987), p. 283.

46. Ibid., p. 184.

47. Described, for example, in James Brian Quinn, Henry Mintzberg, and Robert M. James, *The Strategy Process* (Englewood Cliffs, N.J.: Prentice Hall, 1988), pp. 734–735.

48. Described in "To Our Share Owners," 1992 Annual Report, General Electric Co.

49. Ibid, p. 4.

50. Ibid.

51. Personal interview, Summer 1991.

52. Described to me by one of my Executive MBA students.

53. Estimate of cost savings from Anne B. Fisher, "How to Cut Your Legal Costs," *Fortune*, April 23, 1990, pp. 185–192. Based, in part, on Wayne E. Baker and Robert R. Faulkner, "Strategies for Managing Suppliers of Professional Services," *California Management Review*, vol. 33, 1991, pp. 33–45.

54. Wayne E. Baker, "Market Networks and Corporate Behavior," *American Journal of Sociology*, vol. 96, 1990, pp. 589–625.

55. Gerald F. Davis, "Agents without Principles? The Spread of the Poison Pill through the Intercorporate Network," *Administrative Science Quarterly*, vol. 36, 1991, pp. 583–613.

56. See, for example, Linda Brewster Stearns and Mark S. Mizruchi, "Broken-Tie Reconstitution and the Functions of Interorganizational Interlocks: A Re-Examination," *Administrative Science Quarterly,* vol. 31, 1986, pp. 522–588.

57. Edward O. Laumann and David Knoke, *The Organizational State* (Madison, Wis.: University of Wisconsin Press, 1987).

58. Sociologist Arthur L. Stinchcombe argues in *Information and Organizations* (Berkeley, Calif.: University of California Press, 1990) that the organization's main information task is to manage such uncertainties. The organization must be where the news breaks, whenever it breaks.

59. See, for example, Rosabeth Moss Kanter, "Power Failure in Management Circuits," *Harvard Business Review,* July–August 1979, pp. 65–75.

60. Roger L. Hale, Douglas R. Hoelscher, and Ronald E. Kowal, *Quest for Quality,* 2d ed. (Minneapolis: Tennant Company, 1989), p. 56. Used with permission.

61. Based on Edward O. Laumann and David Knoke, *The Organizational State* (Madison, Wis.: The University of Wisconsin Press, 1987), p. 208.

62. I learned this from an excellent study conducted by one of my MBA students, Kenneth A. Posner (MBA '91), "Using Hedonic Models to Examine the Value of Location" (MBA Honors paper, Graduate School of Business, University of Chicago). In the paper, he summarizes Edwin S. Mills' argument in "Sources of Metropolitan Growth and Development" (*The Institute for Urban Economic Development,* 1991) that firms cluster to exchange ambiguous information via face-to-face interaction.

Chapter 4

1. Robert Fulghum, *It Was on Fire When I Lay Down on It* (New York: Ivy Books, 1989), p. 41.

2. I am grateful to the law firm for permission to share this story.

3. Systematic differences in perception between members of the same organization have been documented for some time. In the early 1960s, for example, Likert documented big differences between supervisors and subordinates. See R. Likert, *New Patterns in Management* (New York: McGraw-Hill, 1961), p. 91.

4. Harry L. Davis, Stephen J. Hoch, and E. K. Easton Ragsdale, "An Anchoring and Adjustment Model of Spousal Predictions," *The Journal of Consumer Research,* vol. 13, 1986, pp. 25–37; Stephen J. Hoch, "Who Do We Know: Predicting the Interests and Opinions of the American Consumer," *The Journal of Consumer Research,* vol. 15, 1988, pp. 315–324; Stephen J. Hoch, "Perceived Consensus and Predictive Accuracy: The Pros and Cons of Projection," *Journal of Personality and Social Psychology,* vol. 53, 1987, pp. 221–234.

5. This is sometimes called the "egocentric bias." See, for example, L. Ross, D. Greene, and P. House, "The 'False Consensus Effect': An Egocentric Bias in

Social Perception Processes," *Journal of Experimental Social Psychology*, vol. 13, 1977, pp. 279–301.

6. Based on Donald M. Schwartz, "A Study of Interpersonal Problem-Posing," unpublished doctoral dissertation, University of Chicago, Department of Education, 1976, p. 24.

7. This tendency has been noted by many, including Jane Hannaway, *Managers Managing* (New York: Oxford University Press, 1989), Chap. 6.

8. Tom Peters, *Thriving on Chaos* (New York: Harper and Row, 1987), p. 538.

9. Allan Cohen and David Bradford, *Influence without Authority* (New York: Wiley, 1990).

10. Robert E. Kaplan, "Trade Routes: The Manager's Network of Relationships," *Organizational Dynamics*, Spring 1984, pp. 37–52.

11. Woody Powell discusses the implicit reciprocity between academic book editors and their informal "scouts" (e.g., senior academics who find and "screen" potential book publications). See Walter W. Powell, *Getting into Print* (Chicago: University of Chicago Press, 1984), pp. 50–51. As Woody points out, Pierre Bourdieu stressed the importance of implicit reciprocity in social exchange. See *Outline of a Theory of Practice*, translated by Richard Nise (New York: Cambridge University Press, 1977).

12. Exchange theory has a long pedigree and many adherents in both sociology and psychology. See, for example, Karen S. Cook, Richard M. Emerson, M. R. G. Gillmore, and Toshio Yamagishi, "The Distributive Power in Exchange Networks: Theory and Experimental Evidence," *American Journal of Sociology*, vol. 89, 1983, pp. 275–305; James Coleman, *Foundations of Social Theory* (Cambridge, Mass.: Harvard University Press, 1990); J. S. Adams, "Inequality in Social Exchange," in L. Berkowitz (ed.), *Advances in Experimental Social Psychology*, vol. 2 (New York: Academic Press, 1965); E. Walster, G. W. Walster, and E. Berscheid, *Equity, Theory and Research* (Boston: Allyn & Bacon, 1978).

13. Peter Blau, *The Dynamics of Bureaucracy* (Chicago: University of Chicago Press, 1955, rev. 1963).

14. Rosabeth Moss Kanter, *Men and Women of the Corporation* (New York: Basic Books, 1977), p. 171.

15. Cohen and Bradford, *Influence without Authority*, pp. 77–92. They use the term *currencies* to describe the types of benefits that can be exchanged in relationships. Currency is a metaphor that fits the notion of exchange or trade in relationships. Some readers of earlier drafts of the book felt that it was too impersonal and implied a cult-of-the-deal approach to relationships. To avoid the potential misinterpretation, I replaced the term *currencies* with the term *benefits*.

16. In addition to the three categories described here, Cohen and Bradford, *Influence without Authority*, also include *position-related* and *personal-related* benefits or currencies (pp. 77–92).

17. The concept of implicit (or implied) contracts has a long history in psychology, marketing, economics, and sociology. I summarize some of this history in my "Market Networks and Corporate Behavior," *American Journal of Sociology*, vol. 96, 1990, pp. 589–625.

18. John Gabarro, "Socialization at the Top—How CEOs and Subordinates Evolve Interpersonal Contracts," *Organizational Dynamics*, Winter 1979, p. 10.

19. Based, in part, on Gabarro, ibid.

20. David McClelland, *Power—Inner Experience* (New York: Irvington, 1979), pp. 183–184. This concept is further developed by Peter Block in *The Empowered Manager* (San Francisco: Jossey-Bass, 1991), Chap. 2.

21. Block, *Empowered Manager*, p. 22.

22. In *The Empowered Manager*, Block lists four assumptions of the patriarchal contract: "submission to authority," "denial of self-expression," "sacrifice for unnamed future rewards," and "belief that the above [the three preceding assumptions] are just" (p. 23).

23. John J. Gabarro and John P. Kotter, "Managing Your Boss," *Harvard Business Review*, January–February 1980, p. 92.

24. Attitudes toward authority or authority figures have been discussed by many, including Cohen and Bradford, *Influence without Authority*, pp. 254–259; Gabarro and Kotter, "Managing Your Boss," pp. 94–95; Eric Berne, *Games People Play* (New York: Ballantine, 1978); Abrahamn Zaleznik, *The Managerial Mystique* (New York: Harper and Row, 1989), Chap. 14. This section is based on my experience, direct observations of managers, and my interpretation of these secondary sources.

25. Based, in part, on my interpretation of Eric Berne's transactional analysis; see his *Games People Play* and related sources. For a longer discussion of attitudes toward people in authority, see, for example, Cohen and Bradford, *Influence without Authority*, pp. 254–259; for a discussion of parent-child carryovers in marriage, see Harville Hendrix, *Getting the Love You Want* (New York: Harper Perennial, 1988).

26. On how organizations infantilize employees, see Chris Argyris, "Personality vs. Organization," *Organizational Dynamics*, Fall 1974, pp. 3–6.

27. Zaleznik, *Managerial Mystique*, p. 236.

28. See, for example, Cohen and Bradford, *Influence without Authority*, pp. 256–257.

29. These terms are in wide use. Gabarro and Kotter, "Managing Your Boss," use the term "mutual dependence" and Cohen and Bradford, *Influence without Authority*, use the term "interdependence."

30. Jeffrey Pfeffer, *Managing with Power* (Boston: Harvard Business School Press, 1992), p. 17.

31. James A. Newman and Roy Alexander, *Climbing the Corporate Matterhorn* (New York: John Wiley & Sons, 1985), p. 124.

32. For example, Linda A. Hill calls it "managerial style" in *Becoming a Manager* (Boston: Harvard Business School Press, 1992), p. 175; and Gabarro and Kotter, "Managing Your Boss," call it simply "style."

33. Hill, *Becoming a Manager*, pp. 175–176. As she points out, these are well known in the management literature.

34. Discussed by Gabarro and Kotter, "Managing Your Boss," p. 98.

35. Sociologists distinguish three general types of resources: material capital (raw materials, equipment, land, etc.), cultural capital (ideas, symbols, reputations, etc.), and social capital (social networks). See, for example, James S. Coleman, "Social Capital in the Creation of Human Capital," *American Journal of Sociology*, vol. 94, 1988, pp. S95–S120 and Randall Collins, *Theoretical Sociology* (San Diego, Calif.: Harcourt Brace Jovanovich, Inc., 1988).

36. Hill, *Becoming a Manager*, pp. 105–111.

37. Described in "The CEO Disease," *Australian Business*, May 1, 1991, pp. 36–41.

38. According to letter from Kathryn E. Milano, Corporate Advertising, Federal Express (January 18, 1993).

39. S. Rosen and A. Tesser, "On the Reluctance to Communicate Undesirable Information: The MUM Effect," *Sociometry*, vol. 33, 1970, pp. 253–263.

40. Allan Cox, *Straight Talk for Monday Morning* (New York: Wiley, 1990), p. 24.

41. See, for example, Linda D. Molm, "Affect and Social Exchange: Satisfaction in Power-Dependence Relations," *American Journal of Sociology*, vol. 56, 1991, pp. 475–493; D. E. Kanouse and L. R. Hansen, "Negativity in Evaluations," in E. E. Jones et al. (eds.), *Attribution: Perceiving the Causes of Behavior* (Morristown, N.J.: General Learning Press, 1972).

42. For example, see research by Stanford University psychologist Felicia Pratto, reported in "What's So Good about Remembering the Bad?" *Newsweek*, November 2, 1992, p. 83.

43. Reported in James M. Kouzes and Barry Z. Posner, *The Leadership Challenge* (San Francisco: Jossey-Bass, 1987), pp. 16–19.

44. Gabarro and Kotter, "Managing Your Boss," p. 100.

45. Richard P. Feynman, *"Surely You're Joking, Mr. Feynman!"* (New York: Bantam, 1985), pp. 148–159.

46. Robert E. Kaplan, "Trade Routes: The Manager's Network of Relationships," *Organizational Dynamics*, Spring 1984, p. 40.

47. Rosabeth Moss Kanter, "The Middle Manager as Innovator," *Harvard Business Review*, July–August 1982, pp. 95–105.

48. Kanter, *Men and Women*, pp. 184–185.

49. Kaplan, "Trade Routes." He discusses functional differences, functional plus level differences, and unequal dependence.

50. Ibid.

51. Kanter, *Men and Women*, p. 185.

52. Kaplan, "Trade Routes," p. 40.

53. See an excellent discussion of reciprocity in Chapter 2 of Robert B. Cialdini, *Influence: Science and Practice* (Glenview, Ill.: Scott, Foresman and Co., 1985). Anthropologists and sociologists have documented that reciprocity is a rule in *all* cultures and societies.

54. Charles Savage, *Fifth Generation Management: Integrating Enterprises through Human Networking* (Digital Press, 1990), p. xii.

55. Based on an extensive cross-cultural study of friendship. Yehudi A. Cohen, "Patterns of Friendship," pp. 351–386 in Yehudi A. Cohen (ed.), *Social Structure and Personality: A Casebook* (New York: Holt, Rinehart and Winston, 1961).

56. These ideas and concepts are explicit in social exchange theory. See, for a recent example, James S. Coleman, *Foundations of Social Theory* (Cambridge, Mass.: Harvard University Press, 1990).

57. Based on interview with industry expert Thomas Caprel, 1993.

58. John P. Kotter, *The General Managers* (New York: The Free Press, 1982), pp. 69–70.

59. Ibid.

60. Described in Carol A. Norman and Robert A. Zawacki, "Team Appraisals—Team Approach," *Personnel Journal*, September 1991, pp. 101–104.

61. Brad Lee Thompson, "An Early Review of Peer Review," *Training*, July 1991, pp. 42–46.

62. Ibid., pp. 42–46.

63. Harry Levinson, "How They Rate the Boss," *Across the Board*, June 1987, pp. 53–57.

Chapter 5

1. Alfred Rosenblatt and George F. Watson, "Concurrent Engineering," *IEEE Spectrum*, vol. 28, 1991, p. 22.

2. This story is based on a research project conducted by my XP 62 Executive MBA students G. D. Collingwood, J. J. Miller, W. A. Canton, and R. P. Jih, "Post Chemical Company: PIM Electronic Polymer Project." I am very grateful for their permission to tell their story.

3. The principles of differentiation and integration are so fundamental that almost any text on organization theory could be cited. The classic reference is Paul R. Lawrence and Jay W. Lorsch, *Organization and Environment* (Boston: Harvard Business School Press, 1986 [1967]). I use the concepts of differentiation and integration in my "The Network Organization in Theory and Practice," a chapter in Nitin Nohria and Robert Eccles (eds.), *Networks and Organizations* (Boston: Harvard Business School Press, 1992).

4. Described in Stephen P. Robbins, *Organization Theory: Structure, Design, and Applications*, 3d. ed. (Englewood Cliffs, N.J.: Prentice-Hall, 1990), p. 86.

5. Lawrence and Lorsch, *Organization and Environment*. This book is now considered a classic. It has been subject to a number of criticisms, but its main message is established doctrine in organization theory. Recent work, particularly in the area of innovation, includes Deborah Dougherty, "Interpretative Barriers to Successful Product Innovation in Large Firms," *Organizational Science*, vol. 3, 1992, pp. 179–202. Paul C. Nystrom found that managers who work in different parts of an organization hold different beliefs, even after controlling for age, status, and differences in promotion opportunities. See his "Comparing Beliefs of Line and Technostructure Managers," *Academy of Management Journal*, vol. 29, 1986, pp. 812–819.

6. Ibid.; Lawrence and Lorsch provide the classic definition of what I call level-one integration: "the quality of the state of collaboration that exists among departments [i.e., horizontal differentiation] that are required to achieve unity of effort by the demands of the environment" (p. 11).

7. Charles Savage, *Fifth Generation Management: Integrating Enterprises through Human Networking* (Digital Press, 1990), p. 79.

8. Ibid., p. 80.

9. Savage, ibid., for example, emphasizes this point. He divides the history of management into five generations (proprietorships, steep hierarchies, matrix, computer networking, and human networking). Fourth-generation organizations are computer-networked but still based on departments and functions. The concept of serial handoffs is characteristic of each of the first four generations (pp. 79–82).

10. Savage, ibid., emphasizes this point (p. 79). See also, Baker, "Network Organization."

11. See, for example, Wayne E. Baker and Robert R. Faulkner, "Role as Resource in the Hollywood Film Industry," *American Journal of Sociology*, vol. 97, 1991, pp. 279–309; Robert R. Faulkner, *Music on Demand: Composers and Careers in the Hollywood Film Industry* (New Brunswick, N.J.: Transaction Books, 1983).

12. See, for example, Lee Sproull and Sara Kiesler, *Connections* (Cambridge, Mass.: MIT Press, 1991) and Savage, *Fifth Generation*, p. 82.

13. Tom Peters, *Thriving on Chaos* (New York: Harper and Row, 1987), p. 424.

14. Ibid., pp. 440–444.

15. Based on Michael Beer, Russell A. Eisenstat, and Bert Spector, *The Critical Path to Corporate Renewal* (Boston: Harvard Business School Press, 1990), pp. 70–100.

16. Savage, *Fifth Generation*, pp. 180–185.

17. Ibid., p. 181.

18. Ram Charan, "How Networks Reshape Organizations—for Results," *Harvard Business Review*, September–October 1991, pp. 104–115.

19. Described in interviews and by Noel M. Tichy and Stratford Sherman, *Control Your Destiny or Someone Else Will* (New York: Doubleday, 1993), Chap. 13.

20. Ibid, p. 158.

21. This section is based on one of my research projects, which was published in Wayne E. Baker, "The Network Organization in Theory and Practice," Chapter 15 in Nitin Nohria and Robert G. Eccles (eds.), *Networks and Organizations: Action, Form, and Structure* (Boston: Harvard Business School Press, 1992) and a teaching case, "Capital Partners," which I wrote with the help of MBA student Pablo Beloff (Graduate School of Business, University of Chicago, 1990). It also draws from related studies of similar organizations, including Tom Burns and G. M. Stalker, *The Management of Innovation* (London: Tavistock Publications, 1961); Wayne E. Baker and Robert R. Faulkner, "Role as Resource in the Hollywood Film Industry," *American Journal of Sociology*, vol. 97, 1991, pp. 279–309; Robert G. Eccles and Dwight B. Crane, "Managing through Networks in Investment Banking," *California Management Review*, vol. 30, 1987, pp. 176–195; and Henry Mintzberg, *The Structuring of Organizations* (Englewood Cliffs, N.J.: Prentice-Hall, 1979).

22. See Baker, "Network Organization."

23. Described in Peter Annin and John Schwartz, "Making PCs, Texas Style," *Newsweek*, January 6, 1992, p. 35.

24. Based on interviews with industry observers. See also, for example, John Schwartz and Bruce Shenitz, "Tighter Times at Big Blue," *Newsweek*, December 9, 1991, p. 50.

25. National Public Radio program, 1992.

26. MBWA comes from Peters and Waterman, *In Search of Excellence.*

27. See Baker, "Network Organization."

28. Based on Michael Beer, Russell A. Eisenstat, and Bert Spector, *The Critical Path to Corporate Renewal* (Boston: Harvard Business School Press, 1990), p. 73.

29. From Fred V. Guterl, "Goodbye, Old Matrix," *Business Month*, February 1989, p. 35.

Chapter 6

1. Theodore G. Remer, *Serendipity and the Three Princes* (Norman, Okla.: University of Oklahoma Press, 1965), p. 170.

2. Based in part on ibid., a treatment of the biography of Horace Walpole, the tale of "The Three Princes," and the history of the term *serendipity*. GE's accidental discovery of Lexan is described in Robert Slater, *The New GE* (Homewood, Ill.: Business One Irwin, 1993), pp. 32–36.

3. Reported in "A Gleam of Light for Solar Energy," *Business Week*, November 30, 1992, pp. 93–94.

4. Remer, *Serendipity*. Definition from the Oxford English Dictionary.

5. Sociologist C. Wright Mills advises writers to induce serendipity by upending file cabinets and mixing files on the floor. Reorganizing stimulates the imagination by creating "accidental" combinations of file contents. See his *The Sociological Imagination* (New York: Oxford University Press, 1959).

6. Max Gunther, *The Luck Factor* (New York: Macmillan, 1977), p. ix.

7. Howard Gardner, *Frames of Mind* (New York: Basic Books, 1983) and *The Unschooled Mind* (New York: Basic Books, 1991). This is also the conclusion of Rogers Peters, *Practical Intelligence* (New York: Harper and Row, 1987).

8. Other ingredients, according to Gunther in *The Luck Factor* are (1) living in a zigzag, not a straight line; (2) using a "ratchet effect" that preserves gains by limiting loss in poor investments (psychologists call this "avoiding the sunk cost fallacy") and letting winnings run; and (3) the "pessimism paradox," which means "nurturing" pessimism to protect oneself and not fall prey to overoptimism (psychologists refer to this as "defensive pessimism" or "avoiding the overconfidence bias"). For an accessible treatment of the psychology of decision making, see J. Edward Russo and Paul J. H. Schoemaker, *Decision Traps* (New York: Doubleday, 1989).

9. Described in Tom Burns and George M. Stalker, *The Management of Innovation* (London: Tavistock, 1962).

10. See Margaret J. Wheatley, *Leadership and the New Science* (San Francisco: Berrett-Koehler, 1992), p. 4.

11. Some ideas in this chapter were stimulated in conversations with my friend and colleague Ananth Iyer. I gratefully acknowledge his input.

12. Quoted in "And Now for Something Completely Different," *Management Review*, May 1991, p. 50, which is excerpted from a speech given by John Cleese to the British-American Chamber of Commerce in New York.

13. All excerpts and paraphrased material from Tennant Company publications are used with permission. I am grateful to Tennant for enabling me to share their story.

14. Roger L. Hale, Douglas R. Hoelscher, and Ronald E. Kowal, *Quest for Quality*, 2d ed. (Minneapolis, Minn.: Tennant Company, 1989), pp. 11–12.

15. Ibid., pp. 26–27, 106–110.

16. Ibid., p. 114. The following paragraphs are gleaned primarily from pp. 97–130.

17. Ibid., pp. 7, 132–158.

18. Alun Anderson, "A Unique Lab Design Fits the British to a Tea," *Science*, vol. 2, July 1991, pp. 377–378. Copyright 1991 by the American Association for the Advancement of Science. Used with permission. Emphasis in quoted material is mine.

19. Allen's proximity results are reported in Thomas J. Peters and Robert H. Waterman, Jr., *In Search of Excellence* (New York: Warner Books, 1982).

20. Wayne E. Baker and Ananth Iyer, "Information Networks and Market Behavior," *Journal of Mathematical Sociology*, vol. 16, 1991, pp. 305–332.

21. Described, for example, in Doron P. Levin, "A Bet Chrysler Can't Afford to Lose," *The New York Times*, August 26, 1991, pp. C1, C3.

22. Described, for example, in John Schwartz, "The Blues at Big Blue," *Newsweek*, December 16, 1991, pp. 44–46.

23. Thomas J. Peters and Robert H. Waterman, Jr., *In Search of Excellence* (New York: Warner Books, 1982).

24. Quoted in Hale, Hoelscher, and Kowal, *Quest for Quality*, p. 120.

25. See, for example, Michael L. Tushman, "Special Boundary Roles in the Innovation Process," *Administrative Science Quarterly*, vol. 22, 1977, pp. 587–605.

26. Ibid.

27. Ibid.

28. See, also, Thomas J. Allen and S. I. Cohen, "Information Flow in Research and Development Laboratories," *Administrative Science Quarterly*, vol. 14, 1969, pp. 12–19.

29. Everett M. Rogers, *Diffusion of Innovations*, 3d ed. (New York: The Free Press, 1983).

30. Hale, Hoelscher, and Kowal, *Quest for Quality*, p. 114.

31. I heard this fish-scale theory directly from Donald Campbell when I was a Ph.D. graduate student at Northwestern University, 1976–1981.

32. "The Arthur D. Little Survey on the Product Innovation Process, Results of the Worldwide Survey" (December 1991).

33. J. R. Kimberly and M. J. Evanisko, "Organizational Innovation: The Influence of Individual, Organizational and Contextual Factors on Hospital Adoption of Technological and Administrative Innovations," *Academy of Management Journal*, vol. 24, 1981, pp. 689–713.

34. Karen A. Bantel and Susan E. Jackson, "Top Management and Innovations in Banking: Does the Composition of the Top Team Make a Difference?" *Strategic Management Journal*, vol. 10, 1989, pp. 107–124.

35. Described in Michael Beer, Russell A. Eisenstat, and Bert Spector, *The Critical Path to Corporate Renewal* (Boston: Harvard Business School Press, 1990), pp. 70–100.

36. Allen and Cohen, "Information Flow."

37. These three fundamental questions (and their implications) are based on a great deal of research on the role of information and information processing in organizations. See, for example, Jay Galbraith, *Designing Complex Organizations* (Reading, Mass.: Addison-Wesley, 1973); W. Richard Scott, *Organizations: Rational, Natural, and Open Systems* (Englewood Cliffs, N.J.: Prentice-Hall, 1981), Chap. 10; Arthur L. Stinchcombe, *Information and Organizations* (Berkeley, Calif.: University of California Press, 1990).

Michael L. Tushman develops these ideas for R&D departments in his "Managing Communication Networks in R&D Laboratories," *Sloan Management Review*, Winter 1979, pp. 37–49. Robert Faulkner and I discuss the role of information processing requirements in the formation of interorganization networks in our "The Social Organization of Conspiracy: Illegal Networks in the Heavy Electrical Equipment Industry," University of Chicago Graduate School of Business working paper, 1993.

38. See Jacob W. Getzels, "The Problem of the Problem," pp. 37–49 in Robin Hogarth (ed.), *New Directions for Methodology of Social and Behavioral Science* (San Francisco: Jossey-Bass, 1982).

39. Tushman, "Managing Communication Networks."

40. See, for example, Tushman, "Managing Communication Networks," Galbraith, *Designing Complex Organizations*; Scott, *Organizations*; Stinchcombe, *Information and Organizations*.

41. The example of investment banks is based on Robert Eccles and Dwight Crane, *Doing Deals: Investment Banks at Work* (Boston: Harvard Business School Press, 1988) and Wayne E. Baker, "Market Networks and Corporate Behavior," *American Journal of Sociology*, vol. 96, 1990, pp. 589–625.

42. For example, see Donald G. Marquis, "The Anatomy of Successful Innovations," *Managing Advancing Technology*, vol. I, 1972, pp. 35–48; Tushman, "Managing Communication Networks." The functional form of organization, which produces the bottleneck problems I discussed in Chapter 5, is often cited as a chief culprit.

43. Getzels, "The Problem of the Problem."

44. Quoted in ibid., p. 37.

45. Marquis, "The Anatomy of Successful Innovations."

46. Hale, Hoelscher, and Kowal, *Quest for Quality*, p. 31.

Chapter 7

1. Based on discussions with authority Raymond Friedman; Ray Friedman and Donna Carter, "African-American Network Groups: Their Impact and Effectiveness" (Boston: Harvard Business School working paper, 1993); Raymond Friedman and Caitlin Deinard, "Black Caucus Groups at Xerox Corporation (A)," (Boston: Harvard Business School working paper, 1991).

2. Ibid.

3. See, for example, Rosabeth Moss Kanter, *Men and Women of the Corporation* (New York: Basic Books, 1977); for an extensive review, see the American Psychological Association's *amicus curiae* brief in support of respondent, Price Waterhouse (petitioner) vs. Ann B. Hopkins (respondent), Supreme Court of the United States, No. 87-1167 (October 1987).

4. American Psychological Association, *amicus curiae* brief, pp. 20–22.

5. Discussed, for example, in Stephen Franklin, "Outplacement Strategies for Diverse Work Force," *Chicago Tribune*, October 15, 1991, sec. 3.

6. Donald R. Katz, *The Big Store: Inside the Crisis and Revolution at Sears* (New York: Viking, 1987).

7. Ibid.

8. Described, for example, in Ronald E. Yates, "Japan Firms in U.S. Make Efforts to Fit In," *Chicago Tribune*, January 13, 1992, sec. 4, pp. 1–2. Hearings were held by the U.S. House Government Operations Subcommittee on Employment and Housing.

9. Reported in Ronald E. Yates, "Japanese Managers Say They're Adopting Some U.S. Ways," *Chicago Tribune*, February 29, 1992, pp. 1–2.

10. Amanda Troy Segal and Wendy Zellner, "Corporate Women," *Business Week*, June 8, 1991, pp. 74–83. See also Ellen A. Fagenson (ed.), *Women in Management*, vol. 4, Women and Work: A Research and Policy Series (Newbury Park, Calif.: Sage, 1993).

11. Louis Harris & Associates Inc. conducted the survey for *Business Week* in 1992. It included 400 female executives at companies with annual sales of $100 million or more. Reported in Segal and Zellner, "Corporate Women," p. 77.

12. Herminia Ibarra, "Homophily and Differential Returns: Sex Differences in Network Structure and Access in an Advertising Firm," *Administrative Science Quarterly*, vol. 37, 1992, pp. 422–447; Daniel J. Brass, "Men's and Women's Networks: A Study of Interaction Patterns and Influence in an Organization," *Academy of Management Journal*, vol. 28, 1985, pp. 518–539.

13. Kanter, *Men and Women*, p. 222.

14. Based on Clayton P. Alderfer, Charleen J. Alderfer, Leota Tucker, and Robert Tucker, "Diagnosing Race Relations in Management," *Journal of Applied Behavioral Science*, vol. 16, 1980, pp. 135–166; Clayton P. Alderfer, "Changing Race Relations Embedded in Organizations: Report on a Long-Term Project with the XYZ Corporation," in Susan E. Jackson (ed.), *Diversity in the Workplace: Human Resources Initiatives* (New York: Guilford Press, 1992), pp. 138–166; Clayton P. Alderfer, Charleen J. Alderfer, Ella L. Bell, and Jimmy Jones, "The Race Relations Competence Workshop: Theory and Results," *Human Relations*, vol. 45, 1992, pp. 1259–1291.

15. Alderfer, Alderfer, Tucker, and Tucker, "Diagnosing Race Relations," p. 140.

16. See, for example, J. P. Fernandez, *Racism and Sexism in Corporate Life* (Lexington, Mass.: Lexington Books, 1981).

17. Described in Alderfer, "Changing Race Relations," and Alderfer, Alderfer, Bell, and Jones, "The Race Relations Competence Workshop."

18. Ibid.

19. *The Sociology of Georg Simmel,* translated and edited by Kurt H. Wolff (Glencoe, Ill.: Free Press, 1950 [1908]).

20. Peter Blau's *Inequality and Heterogeneity: A Primitive Theory of Social Structure* (New York: Free Press, 1977) is one of the seminal works, which was followed by Blau and Joseph E. Schwartz's study of intermarriage in *Crosscutting Social Circles* (New York: Academic Press, 1984), as well as many other studies, such as the chapters in Part III of *Structures of Power and Constraint: Papers in Honor of Peter M. Blau,* edited by Craig Calhoun, Marshall W. Meyer, and W. Richard Scott (Cambridge: Cambridge University Press, 1990).

21. Blau and Schwartz, *Crosscutting.*

22. Joseph E. Schwartz, "Penetrating Differentiation: Linking Macro and Micro Phenomena," pp. 353–374, in Calhoun, Meyer, and Scott, *Structures of Power.*

23. Kanter, *Men and Women,* Chap. 8.

24. Ibid., p. 207.

25. Kanter, *Men and Women,* p. 208; see also, American Psychological Association's *amicus curiae* brief.

26. Segal and Zellner, "Corporate Women," p. 77.

27. Edward W. Jones, "What It's Like to be a Black Manager," *Harvard Business Review,* July–August 1973, pp. 108–116.

28. Kanter, *Men and Women,* p. 209.

29. According to, for example, All the Right Stuff, a study of 1000 men and women middle managers conducted by researchers from Loyola and Northwestern Universities, reported in Segal and Zellner, "Corporate Women," p. 76. Conservative economists like University of Chicago's Gary Becker argue that women are paid less because competing family-work obligations cause them to devote less energy to work. Empirical research by University of California (Berkeley) sociologists Denise Bielby and William Bielby, however, shows that women, in fact, devote *more* energy to work than men do, even those men who lack family or domestic responsibilities.

30. Carol Kleiman, "Demographics Lead Push for Diversity," *Chicago Tribune,* September 15, 1991, section 8, p. 1.

31. See, for example, A. Packer and W. Johnston, *Workforce 2000: Work and Workers for the 21st Century* (Indianapolis, Ind.: Hudson Institute); Carol Kleiman, "Demographics"; U.S. Labor Department projections.

32. Kanter, *Men and Women,* p. 266.

33. Based on discussions with Ray Friedman (1993); Friedman and Carter "African-American Network Groups."

34. Taylor Cox, Jr., "The Multicultural Organization," *Academy of Management Executive,* vol. 5, 1991, pp. 34–47; R. Roosevelt Thomas, Jr., "From Affirmative Action to Affirming Diversity," *Harvard Business Review,* March–April 1990, pp. 107–117.

35. Cox, "Multicultural Organization," p. 40.

36. Nancy J. Adler, *Internal Dimensions of Organizational Behavior* (Kent, 1986), pp. 77–83, cited in Cox, "The Multicultural Organization."

37. Alderfer, "Changing Race Relations."

38. Reported in Laura L. Castro, "More Firms 'Gender Train' to Bridge the Chasms That Still Divide the Sexes," *The Wall Street Journal*, January 2, 1992, pp. 11, 14.

39. Cox, "Multicultural Organization," p. 40.

40. Kanter, *Men and Women*, p. 270.

41. Reported in Carol Kleiman, "Some Firms Breaking Glass Ceiling," *Chicago Tribune*, April 13, 1992, sec. 4, p. 7.

42. Bruce D. Butterfield, "Affirmative Action for White Males at Xerox," *Boston Globe*, October 20, 1991, sec. A, p. 37.

43. Kanter, *Men and Women*, 1977, pp. 281–284.

44. See, for example, Blau and Schwartz, *Crosscutting*, and M. Jahoda, "Race Relations and Mental Health," in *UNESCO Reports* (New York: Columbia, 1961).

45. Kanter, *Men and Women*, p. 282.

46. Ibid., pp. 282–283.

47. Carol Kleiman, *Women's Networks: The Complete Guide to Getting a Better Job, Advancing Your Career and Feeling Great as a Woman through Networking* (New York: Lippincott & Crowell, 1980).

48. Ibarra, "Homophily," and Brass, "Men's and Women's Networks."

49. In *Women's Networks*, Kleiman provides one of the most comprehensive lists around. Because it's from 1980, however, you may have to do some digging to find the successors and descendants of the networks she lists.

50. In addition to Kanter, *Men and Women*, pp. 276–277, see also, for example, Patricia Yancey Martin, Dianne Harrison, and Diana DiNitto, "Advancement for Women in Hierarchical Organizations: A Multilevel Analysis of Problems and Prospects," *The Journal of Behavioral Science*, vol. 19, 1983, pp. 19–33.

51. Gordon Jaremko, "Oilpatch 'driven by fear,'" *Calgary Herald*, November 13, 1992, p. D-1.

52. J. Sterling Livingston, "Pygmalion in Management," *Harvard Business Review*, July–August, 1969, pp. 121–130.

53. Based on Raymond A. Friedman, *The Balanced Workforce at Xerox Corporation* (Boston: Harvard Business School, 1991).

54. Thomas, "From Affirmative Action," pp. 116–117.

55. Ibid., p. 109.

Chapter 8

1. Based, in part, on Howard H. Stevenson and C. Roland Christensen, *Head Ski Company, Inc.* (Boston: Harvard Business School, 1967).

2. The organizational life cycle is well known in organizational theory and research. The field of organizational ecology, for example, examines the birth and death of organizations. For a management discussion, see, for example, Ichak Adizes, *Corporate Lifecycles* (Englewood Cliffs, N.J.: Prentice-Hall, 1988).

3. For the concept of crisis as a positive force, see Tom Peters, *Thriving on Chaos* (New York: Harper and Row, 1987).

4. Larry E. Greiner, "Evolution and Revolution as Organizations Grow," *Harvard Business Review*, July–August 1972, pp. 37–46.

5. Ibid.

6. Ibid., pp. 41–42.

7. Ibid., p. 42.

8. Ibid., p. 42

9. Ibid., p. 42.

10. David Krackhardt and Robert N. Stern, "Informal Networks and Organizational Crises: An Experimental Simulation," *Social Psychology Quarterly*, vol. 51, 1988, pp. 123–140. Reed E. Nelson, "The Strength of Strong Ties: Social Networks and Intergroup Conflict in Organizations," *Academy of Management Journal*, vol. 32, 1989, pp. 377–401.

11. See, for example, Charles F. Herman, "Some Consequences of Crises Which Limit the Viability of Organizations," *Administrative Science Quarterly*, vol. 8, 1963, pp. 61–82.

12. This is a key assumption in Krackhardt and Stern, "Informal Networks."

13. Greiner, "Evolution and Revolution," p. 42.

14. Ibid., pp. 42–43.

15. Alfred D. Chandler, *The Visible Hand: The Managerial Revolution in American Business* (Cambridge, Mass.: Harvard University Press, 1977) and Henry Ogden Armour and David J. Teece, "Organizational Structure and Economic Performance: A Test of the Multidivisional Hypothesis," *Bell Journal of Economics*, vol. 9, 1978, pp. 106–122.

16. Greiner, "Evolution and Revolution," p. 43.

17. See, for example, Chap. 1 in Robert Slater, *The New GE* (Homewood, Ill.: Business One Irwin, 1993).

18. Wayne E. Baker and Robert R. Faulkner, "The Social Organization of Conspiracy: Illegal Networks in the Heavy Electrical Equipment Industry," University of Chicago working paper, 1993.

19. Greiner, "Evolution and Revolution," p. 43.

20. Ibid.

21. Krackhardt and Stern, "Informal Networks," focuses on *friendship* ties as bridges between groups. Nelson, "Strength of Strong Ties," used the more general concept of *strong ties* as bridges in low-conflict organizations. Strong ties are absent in high-conflict organizations.

22. See, for example, Nelson, "Strength of Strong Ties," pp. 378–379.

23. See George C. Homans, *The Human Group* (New York: Harcourt, Brace, 1950) for an early statement of this proposition.

24. Greiner, "Evolution and Revolution," p. 43.

25. Personal communication (September 1992).

26. Robert G. Eccles and Dwight B. Crane, "Managing through Networks in Investment Banking," *California Management Review*, vol. 30, 1987, p. 189.

Chapter 9

1. Paul Hirsch, *Pack Your Own Parachute* (Reading, Mass.: Addison-Wesley, 1987), p. 119.

2. Ibid.

3. My dissertation is "Markets as Networks: A Multimethod Study of Trading Networks in a National Securities Market," Evanston, Ill., Northwestern University, Department of Sociology, 1981. I published two articles based on my dissertation research: "The Social Structure of a National Securities Market," *American Journal of Sociology*, vol. 89, 1984, pp. 775–811, and "Floor Trading and Crowd Dynamics," in Patricia Adler and Peter Adler (eds.), *The Social Dynamics of Financial Markets* (Greenwich, Conn.: JAI Press, 1984). Ananth Iyer and I published a related article, "Information Networks and Market Behavior," *Journal of Mathematical Sociology*, vol. 16, 1992, pp. 305–332.

4. Statistic given in presentation on networking conducted by the Alumni Office of the University of Chicago's Graduate School of Business (1991).

5. The classic study is Mark S. Granovetter, *Getting a Job: A Study of Contacts and Careers* (Cambridge, Mass.: Harvard University Press, 1974).

6. Ibid. Findings are summarized in the introduction.

7. Ibid., p. 18.

8. Ibid., p. 13.

9. Ibid., p. 14.

10. Raymond A. Friedman and Caitlin Deinard, "Black Caucus Groups at Xerox Corporation (A)," Boston: Harvard Business School, 1991.

11. Granovetter, *Getting a Job*, p. 15.

12. Ibid., p. 13.

13. Mark Granovetter's seminal paper "The Strength of Weak Ties," *American Journal of Sociology*, vol. 78, 1973, pp. 1360–1386, stimulated a stream of research, much of which is reviewed by him in his "The Strength of Weak Ties: A Network Theory Revisited," in Peter Marsden and Nan Lin (eds.), *Social Structure and Network Analysis* (Beverly Hills, Calif.: Sage, 1982), pp. 105–130.

14. Ronald S. Burt and Don Ronchi, "Contested Control in a Large Manufacturing Plant," pp. 121–157 in J. Wessie and H. Flap (eds.), *Social*

Networks through Time (Utrecht, Holland: ISOR, University of Holland, 1990).

15. Richard Thain, *Think Twice before You Accept That Job* (Homewood, Ill.: Dow Jones-Irwin, 1986), p. 153.

Chapter 10

1. Philip Kotler, *Marketing Management,* 6th ed. (Englewood Cliffs, N.J.: Prentice-Hall, 1988), p. 9.

2. Based on telephone interview with Adam Aronson, founder and now emeritus chairman of the board of Mark Twain Bancshares, August 10, 1992; the 1991 annual report and 1992 quarterly reports; Richard Ringer, "A Winning Sales Team for a St. Louis Bank," *Bank Marketing,* February 1992, p. 24.

3. Telephone interview, August 10, 1992.

4. Telephone interview, August 10, 1992.

5. Quoted in Ringer, "A Winning Sales Team."

6. According to the 1991 *Sales & Marketing Management* survey of America's best sales forces, reported by William Keenan, "America's Best Sales Forces," *Sales & Marketing Management,* September 1991, pp. 41–57. Dow Chemical, Eli Lilly, and Progressive Corporation are also at the top of their respective categories.

7. Kotler, *Marketing Management;* Theodore Levitt, *The Marketing Imagination* (New York: The Free Press, 1983).

8. Kotler, *Marketing Management,* p. 9.

9. Based, in part, on Ken Partch, "'Partnering': A Win-Win Proposition...Or the Newest Marketing Hula Hoop?" *Supermarket Business,* vol. 46, 1991, pp. 29–34, 165–166.

10. Quoted in ibid., p. 31.

11. Jan B. Heide and George John, "Alliances in Industrial Purchasing: The Determinants of Joint Action in Buyer-Supplier Relationships," *Journal of Marketing Research,* vol. 27, 1990, p. 25.

12. See, for example, statistics cited by Tom Peters, *Thriving on Chaos* (New York: Harper and Row, 1987), p. 112; William H. Davidow and Bro Uttal, *Total Customer Service* (New York: HarperCollins Publishers, 1989), p. 30.

13. Davidow and Uttal, ibid., p. 31.

14. The Bible: Ecclesiastes, 9:10.

15. Donald V. Potter, "Success under Fire: Policies to Prosper in Hostile Times," *California Management Review,* vol. 33, 1991, pp. 1–15. This article won the fifth annual Pacific Telesis Foundation Award.

16. Davidow and Uttal, *Total Customer Service,* p. 165.

17. Davidow and Uttal, ibid., make a similar argument on pp. 42–46.

18. See, for example, Bill Powell, "Japan's Quality Quandary," *Newsweek*, June 15, 1992, p. 48.

19. Mark S. Granovetter, "Economic Action and Social Structure: The Problem of Embeddedness," *American Journal of Sociology*, vol. 91, 1985, pp. 481–510. Antecedents of Granovetter's embeddedness principle include Stewart Macaulay, "Non-contractual Relations in Business: A Preliminary Study," *American Sociological Review*, vol. 28, 1963, pp. 55–67.

20. Jonathan K. Frenzen and Harry L. Davis summarize the economist's position on p. 2 of "Purchasing Behavior in Embedded Markets," *Journal of Consumer Research*, vol. 17, June 1990, p. 1–12. They use the nice term *interpersonal vacuum* on p. 1.

21. Telephone conversation (August 19, 1992) and fax (August 1993). The estimate of employment does not distinguish part-time, short-term employment from long-term. In addition, there is some double counting caused by a person working for two (or more) direct selling organizations.

22. Statistic cited in Nicole Woolsey Biggart, *Charismatic Capitalism: Direct Selling Organizations in America* (Chicago: University of Chicago Press, 1989), pp. 1–2.

23. Ibid., p. 8.

24. Frenzen and Davis, "Purchasing Behavior," pp. 1–12. The description of home parties is paraphrased from p. 4.

25. Ibid.

26. Statistics cited by Aimee L. Stern, "Courting Consumer Loyalty with the Feel-Good Bond," *The New York Times*, January 17, 1993, p. 10.

27. See James S. Coleman, "Social Capital in the Creation of Human Capital," *American Journal of Sociology*, supplement, 1988, pp. S95–S120.

28. Granovetter, "Economic Action," pp. 481–510.

29. See, for example, Mark S. Granovetter, "The Strength of Weak Ties," *American Journal of Sociology*, vol. 78, 1973, pp. 1360–1380. I used these distinctions in my study of how corporations manage their relationships with investment banks. See Wayne E. Baker, "Market Networks and Corporate Behavior," *American Journal of Sociology*, vol. 96, November 1990, pp. 589–625.

30. Based on interviews with industry participants. Company name and other identifying information have been changed.

31. F. Robert Dwyer, Paul H. Schurr, and Sejo Oh, "Developing Buyer-Seller Relationships," *Journal of Marketing*, vol. 51, 1987, pp. 11–27, analyze a variety of marketing relationships by arraying "seller's motivational investment in relationship" against "buyer's motivational investment in relationship." My sociological model is much different from their psychological model (though the two are not incompatible). For example: (1) Overall, the relationship grid applies to *any* type of business or social relationship (see Chapter 2), not just marketing relationships. (2) My *spectrum of relationships*

arrays *type* of relationship (deal-oriented to relationship-oriented), not degree of motivational investment (high to low). In fact, motivation is not a distinguishing feature in my model. A person who is deal-oriented is highly motivated to make deals; a person who is relationship-oriented is highly motivated to build partnerships. (3) One of the important distinguishing features of my model is the degree of *social embeddedness*. At the deal-oriented end of the spectrum, business and social relationships are not intermixed; at the relationship end of the spectrum, multiple business and social ties are intermixed and embedded (what network analysts call multiplex ties).

32. Barbara Bund Jackson, *Winning and Keeping Industrial Customers: The Dynamics of Customer Relationships* (Lexington, Mass.: D. C. Heath, 1985).

33. See Wayne E. Baker and Robert R. Faulkner, "Strategies for Managing Suppliers of Professional Services," *California Management Review*, vol. 33, 1991, pp. 33–45.

34. Based on letter from Kathryn E. Milano, Corporate Advertising, Federal Express (April 26, 1993).

35. A description of ASAP and its evolution is summarized in Jackson, *Winning and Keeping Industrial Customers*, pp. 135–144.

36. Jeffrey Lant, *Money Talks: The Complete Guide to Creating a Profitable Workshop or Seminar in Any Field*, published by JLA Publications, a division of Jeffrey Lant Associates, Inc., 50 Follen Street, Suite 507, Cambridge, MA 02138. Telephone: (617) 547-6372. He discusses developing relationships on pp. 190–191.

37. See, for example, Kotler, *Marketing Management*, pp. 695–696; Davidow and Uttal, *Total Customer Service*, p. 30. See also, Peters, *Thriving on Chaos*, p. 112.

38. See, for example, Kotler, ibid., pp. 695–697; Davidow and Uttal, ibid., p. 31.

39. See, for example, Potter, "Success under Fire."

40. Baker and Faulkner, "Strategies for Managing Suppliers of Professional Services."

41. See, especially, Chap. 7 in Davidow and Uttal, *Total Customer Service*.

42. From "Capital Partners," Wayne E. Baker and Pablo Beloff, Graduate School of Business, University of Chicago, 1990.

43. Davidow and Uttal, *Total Customer Service*, p. 84.

44. Jan B. Heide and George John, "Alliances in Industrial Purchasing: The Determinants of Joint Action in Buyer-Supplier Relationships," *Journal of Marketing Research*, vol. 37, 1990, pp. 24–36.

45. Kathleen M. Eisenhardt, "Speed and Strategic Choice: How Managers Accelerate Decision Making," *California Management Review*, vol. 32, 1990, pp. 1–16.

46. Described in Davidow and Uttal, *Total Customer Service*, p. 161.

47. Described in Peters, *Thriving on Chaos*, p. 183.

48. Davidow and Uttal, *Total Customer Service*, pp. 161–162.

49. Telephone interview with Adam Aronson.

50. Quoted in Partch, "'Partnering,'" p. 46.

51. Described in William Keenan, "America's Best Sales Forces," *Sales & Marketing Management*, September 1991, p. 55.

52. Roger L. Hale, Douglas R. Hoelscher, and Ronald E. Kowal, *Quest for Quality*, 2d ed. (Minneapolis: Tennant Company, 1989), p. 56.

53. Based on personal communication, executive MBA program, University of Chicago Graduate School of Business, Fall 1991.

54. Verified by telephone conversation with Coopers & Lybrand, Chicago office, August 24, 1992.

55. Quoted in Regis McKenna, *The Regis Touch* (Reading, Mass.: Addison-Wesley, 1985), p. 57.

56. Wayne E. Baker, "Market Networks and Corporate Behavior," *American Journal of Sociology*, vol. 96, 1990, pp. 589–625.

57. The 80/20 rule is sometimes called the Pareto rule.

58. Heide and John, "Alliances in Industrial Purchasing.

59. Richard Florida and Martin Kenney, "Transplanted Organizations: The Transfer of Japanese Industrial Organization to the U.S.," *American Sociological Review*, vol. 56, 1991, pp. 381–398.

60. Peters, *Thriving on Chaos*, p. 138.

61. See Baker and Faulkner, "Strategies for Managing Suppliers."

62. Based on interview with and letter from Kathryn E. Milano, Corporate Advertising, Federal Express (April 26, 1993; June 18, 1993).

63. Ibid.

64. See, for example, Roland T. Rust, Bala Subramanian, and Mark Wells, "Making Complaints a Management Tool," *Marketing Management*, vol. 1, 1992, pp. 41–45; Frederick F. Reichheld and W. Earl Sasser, Jr., "Zero Defections: Quality Comes to Services," *Harvard Business Review*, September–October 1990, pp. 105–111.

65. Rust, Subramanian, and Wells, ibid.

66. Ibid, p. 43.

67. Ibid., p. 45.

68. Hale, Hoelscher, and Kowal, *Quest for Quality*, p. 56.

Chapter 11

1. Regis McKenna, *The Regis Touch* (Reading, Mass.: Addison-Wesley, 1985), p. 57.

2. Tom Peters, *Thriving on Chaos*, (New York: Harper & Row, 1987), pp. 293–294.

3. Described by Keith Hooper (personal communication); see also, T. J. Howard, "A Life Set to Double Time," *Chicago Tribune*, October 21, 1992, sec. 5, pp. 1–2.

4. See Philip Kotler, *Marketing Management*, 6th ed. (Englewood Cliffs, N.J.: Prentice-Hall, 1988), p. 602.

5. Based on information kindly provided by Diane Fitzgerald, Director of Corporate Communications, Fruit of the Loom, Inc. William Farley's quote is used by permission.

6. McKenna, *Regis Touch*, p. 58; for a similar conclusions, see Peter H. Reingen and Jerome B. Kernan, "Analysis of Referral Networks in Marketing: Methods and Illustration," *Journal of Marketing Research*, vol. 23, 1986, pp. 370–378.

7. McKenna, *Regis Touch*, p. 59.

8. For a comprehensive review, see Everett M. Rogers, *Diffusion of Innovations*, 3d ed. (New York: The Free Press, 1983). Ananth Iyer and I review some of this research in our study of diffusion in market networks; see Wayne E. Baker and Ananth Iyer, "Information Networks and Market Behavior," *Journal of Mathematical Sociology*, vol. 16, 1992, pp. 305–332.

9. Rogers, *Diffusion of Innovations*, pp. 276–277.

10. McKenna, *Regis Touch*, p. 56.

11. Stephen R. Covey, "The Taproot of Trust," *Executive Excellence*, vol. 8, 1991, p. 3.

12. Rogers, *Diffusion of Innovations*, p. 244.

13. Ibid. See also, other studies cited in this chapter.

14. See, for example, William M. Barr and John M. Conley, *Fortune and Folly: the Wealth of Institutional Investors*, from the Institutional Investor Project at Columbia University (to be published by Irwin). Robert J. Shiller and John Pound, "Survey Evidence on Diffusion of Interest and Information among Investors," *Journal of Economic Behavior and Organization*, vol. 12, 1989, pp. 47–66; Baker and Iyer, "Information Networks and Market Behavior."

15. James S. Coleman, Elihu Katz, and H. Menzel, *Medical Innovation: A Diffusion Study* (New York: Bobbs-Merrill, 1966). See Ronald S. Burt's reanalysis of these data in "Social Contagion and Innovation: Cohesion and Structural Equivalence," *American Journal of Sociology*, vol. 92, 1987, pp. 1287–1335.

16. Bryce Ryan and Neal C. Gross, "The Diffusion of Hybrid Corn in Two Iowa Communities," *Rural Sociology*, vol. 8, 1943, pp. 15–24.

17. Interviews with industry participants.

18. The terms adopter, opinion leader, and change agent have a long pedigree and are widely used. For an accessible introduction, see Rogers, *Diffusion of Innovations*.

19. Kotler, *Marketing Management*, p. 602.

20. Rogers, *Diffusion of Innovations*, p. 28.

21. Ibid., Chap. 7; first proposed by Rogers in *Diffusion of Innovations*, 1962.

22. My discussion of Rogers' five adopter categories and some of their characteristics is based primarily on the third edition of *Diffusion of Innovations*, Chap. 7.

23. Ibid., p. 249.

24. Ibid., Chap. 8.

25. Ibid., pp. 281–288.

26. So conclude Reingen and Kernan, "Analysis of Referral Networks in Marketing," pp. 370–378.

27. Peters, *Thriving on Chaos*, p. 290. His discussion of word-of-mouth marketing is on pp. 290–295.

28. Rogers, *Diffusion of Innovations*, p. 332.

29. McKenna, *Regis Touch*, pp. 60–61. He lists the financial community, industry watchers, customers, the press, the selling chain, the community.

30. Ibid., pp. 62–65.

31. Rogers, *Diffusion of Innovations*, pp. 329–330, points out that commercial salespeople often suffer credibility problems.

32. Ibid., p. 332.

33. McKenna, *Regis Touch*, p. 67.

34. Suggested by Peters, *Thriving on Chaos*, p. 294.

35. Peters' advice, ibid., p. 294, to seek smaller firms is based on solid research, conducted in the 1970s and early 1980s. Research on the organizations of the 1990s shows that big companies *can* be innovative—and thus good targets for word-of-mouth marketing—if they are based on the network organization model (see Chapter 15).

Chapter 12

1. Roger L. Hale, Ronald E. Kowal, Donald D. Carlton, and Tim K. Sehnert, *Made in the USA: Strategic Supplier Quality Management* (Minneapolis: Tennant Company, 1991) p. 7.

2. For an insightful analysis of networks in publishing, see Lewis Coser, Charles Kadushin, and Walter Powell, *Books: The Culture and Commerce of Publishing* (New York: Basic Books, 1982).

3. Michael E. Porter, *Competitive Strategy* (New York: The Free Press, 1980).

4. Robert J. Gaston and Sharon Bell, Applied Economics Group, Inc., "The Informal Supply of Capital," final report, U.S. Small Business Administration, Office of Advocacy, January 29, 1988.

5. Robert J. Shiller and John Pound, "Survey Evidence on Diffusion of Interest and Information Among Investors," *Journal of Economic Behavior and Organization*, vol. 12, 1989, pp. 47–66.

6. The facts here are based on Michael Best, *The New Competition: Institutions of Industrial Restructuring* (Cambridge, Mass.: Harvard University Press, 1990), Chap. 5.

7. See, for example, John McMillan, "Managing Suppliers: Incentive Systems in Japanese and U.S. Industry," *California Management Review,* vol. 32, 1990, pp. 38–55.

8. Based on interviews with industry participants.

9. McMillan, "Managing Suppliers," p. 39.

10. Rosabeth Moss Kanter, *When Giants Learn to Dance* (New York: Simon and Schuster, 1989), p. 137.

11. Hale, Kowal, Carlton, and Sehnert, *Made in the USA.* Ford example summarized on pp. 31–34; quote from p. 33. Used with permission.

12. For example, "[a] U.S. automobile executive estimates that about a quarter of the cost advantage of Japanese firms is due to the superior efficiency of their supplier networks." McMillan, "Managing Suppliers," p. 38.

13. Kanter, *When Giants Learn to Dance,* pp. 127–140. The DEC example and quotations are from this section on stakeholder alliances.

14. Ibid.

15. Quoted in Hale, Kowal, Carlton, and Sehnert, *Made in the USA,* p. 8. Used with permission.

16. See, for example, Jolie Solomon, Frank Washington, and Myron Stokes, "GM: It's Rocky in Recovery," *Newsweek,* October 12, 1992, p. 61.

17. Based, in part, on "Clout! More and More, Retail Giants Rule the Marketplace," *Business Week,* December 21, 1992, pp. 66–73.

18. Ibid.

19. Retailing would, therefore, become a classic oligopoly.

20. McMillan, "Managing Suppliers," p. 47. Toyota, for example, uses sole-source for 28 percent of a sample of 80 parts.

21. Statistics from Russell Johnston and Paul R. Lawrence, "Beyond Vertical Integration—the Rise of the Value-Adding Partnership," *Harvard Business Review,* July–August 1988, p. 98.

22. McMillan, "Managing Suppliers," p. 42. Emphasis added.

23. Based on Richard Florida and Martin Kenney, "Transplanted Organizations: The Transfer of Japanese Industrial Organization to the U.S.," *American Sociological Review,* vol. 56, 1991, pp. 381–398. I emphasize the transplanting of supplier practices, but many *intra*organizational practices also have been successfully transplanted (e.g., work teams, rotation of workers among tasks, flat hierarchies, and worker participation).

24. Ibid., pp. 393–394.

25. JIT is not used completely throughout the Japanese transplant supplier pyramids, which Florida and Kenney speculate is due to the fact that they're still under development (ibid., p. 393).

26. In the beginning, many original U.S. suppliers of Japanese transplants were unable to adapt to Japanese supplier practices, so the transplants encouraged their suppliers from Japan to locate facilities in the United States. Now, however, almost half of transplant suppliers are U.S.-owned, and Japanese management practices are diffusing throughout the U.S. system, ibid.

27. Ibid., p. 389.

28. Published by Tennant Company, Minneapolis, Minnesota (1991). My discussion in this section is based on this book. I am grateful to Tennant for allowing me to share their story and for permission to paraphrase and quote from their book.

29. Hale et al. summarize the seven points on pp. 27–28. I've repeated the points verbatim here, with discussion of them in my own words. They devote a specific chapter to each point (pp. 29–120).

30. Quoted in Hale, Kowal, Carlton, and Sehnert, *Made in the USA*, p. 125.

31. See, e.g., McMillan, "Managing Suppliers," p. 42.

32. Hale, Kowal, Carlton, and Sehnert, *Made in the USA*, p. 100.

33. Richard Saul Wurman, *Information Anxiety* (New York: Doubleday, 1989).

34. J. Edward Russo and Paul J. H. Schoemaker, *Decision Traps* (New York: Doubleday, 1989).

35. Hale, Kowal, Carlton, and Sehnert, *Made in the USA*, p. 28.

36. This section is based, in part, on my article with Rob Faulkner. Wayne E. Baker and Robert R. Faulkner, "Strategies for Managing Suppliers of Professional Services," *California Management Review*, vol. 33, 1991; interviews with industry observers and participants.

37. Baker and Faulkner, "Managing Suppliers of Professional Services," p. 34.

38. Based on personal letter, 1991.

39. Baker and Faulkner, "Managing Suppliers of Professional Services."

40. See, for example, "Are investment banks double-crossing clients?" *Business Week*, August 8, 1988.

41. Based on telephone conversation with and information provided by Joseph Silberman, Corporate Affairs, Leo Burnett U.S.A. (June 21, 1993).

42. Based on Baker and Faulkner, "Managing Suppliers of Professional Services," pp. 41–43.

43. See, for example, Wayne E. Baker, "Market Networks and Corporate Behavior," *American Journal of Sociology*, vol. 96, 1990, pp. 589–625.

44. Hale, Kowal, Carlton, and Sehnert, *Made in the USA*, p. 27.

45. Hale, Kowal, Carlton, and Sehnert, *Made in the USA*, p. 117.

46. "Clout!" *Business Week*, p. 71.

47. Jan B. Heide and George John, "Alliances in Industrial Purchasing: The Determinants of Joint Action in Buyer-Supplier Relationships," *Journal of Marketing Research*, vol. 37, February 1990, pp. 24–36.

48. This great idea was introduced to me by a team of my executive MBA students from XP '62: Mike Carruthers, Steve Harrison, Mark Lingofelt, Lyle Masimore, John Onopchenko.

49. Hale, Kowal, Carlton, and Sehnert, *Made in the USA*, p. 135.

Chapter 13

1. From telephone interview, January 26, 1993.

2. Interview with Mac McDowell, September 2, 1992.

3. Regis McKenna, *The Regis Touch* (Reading, Mass.: Addison Wesley, 1986), p. 56.

4. Howard G. Haas with Bob Tamarkin, *The Leader Within* (New York: Harper Business, 1992), p. 91.

5. This group is described in detail by Nitin Nohria, "Information and Search in the Creation of New Business Ventures: The Case of the 128 Venture Group," Chapter 9 in Nitin Nohria and Robert G. Eccles (eds.), *Networks and Organizations: Structure, Form, and Action* (Boston: Harvard Business School Press, 1992).

6. Ibid., p. 245.

7. From NSACI Networkers materials kindly provided by vice president of programs Carol Pape.

8. Interview with Carol Pape, January 7, 1992.

9. Bob Burg, "Begin Your Own Profitable Networking Group," *Insurance Sales*, July 1991, pp. 34–35.

Chapter 14

1. Rosabeth Moss Kanter, *When Giants Learn to Dance* (New York: Simon and Schuster, 1989), p. 118.

2. This section is based on interviews with industry participants and on published materials. Bill Powell and Joanna Stone, "The Deal of the Decade," *Newsweek*, July 15, 1991, p. 40; Andrew Pollack, "I.B.M. Now Apple's Main Ally," *The New York Times*, October 3, 1991, p. D1; Andrew Kupfer, "Apple's Plan to Survive and Grow," *Fortune*, May 4, 1992, pp. 68–72; Robert McGough, "The Grand Alliance," *Finance World*, December 10, 1991, pp. 40–46. Prior to the alliance, Apple began to create hardware and software that permitted Apples to talk with IBMs, as Rosabeth Moss Kanter documents in *When Giants Learn to Dance*, p. 49.

3. Term used by IBM President Jack Kuehler, quoted in McGough, ibid., p. 45.

4. See, for example, "Digital Pact Will Move Microsoft Further from IBM," *Chicago Tribune*, November 12, 1991, sec. 3, p. 3.

5. Statistic cited in Stratford Sherman, "Are Strategic Alliances Working?" *Fortune*, September 21, 1992, p. 77.

6. McGough, "The Grand Alliance," p. 44.

7. The compete-acquire binary view comes in many guises. One of the most popular is the *market versus hierarchy* distinction made by economists such as Oliver E. Williamson. See, for example, his "The Economics of Organization: The Transaction Cost Approach," *American Journal of Sociology*, vol. 87, 1985, pp. 548–577. In his view, a company either competes aggressively in the market or absorbs a competitor into its hierarchy. This bipolar view has been roundly criticized, most notably by Mark S. Granovetter in his "Economic Action and Social Structure: The Problem of Embeddedness," *American Journal of Sociology*, vol. 91, 1985, pp. 481–510.

8. Three chapters in *Networks and Organizations: Structure, Form, and Action* (Boston: Harvard Business School Press, 1992), a book edited by Nitin Nohria and Robert G. Eccles, analyze biotechnology networks: Walter W. Powell and Peter Brantley, "Competitive Cooperation in Biotechnology: Learning through Networks?" (Chapter 14); Stephen R. Barley, John Freeman, and Ralph C. Hybels, "Strategic Alliances in Commercial Biotechnology" (Chapter 12); Bruce Kogut, Weijan Shan, and Gordon Walker, "The Make-or-Cooperate Decision in the Context of an Industry Network" (Chapter 13).

9. Powell and Brantley, ibid.

10. As of the mid-1980s, according to *Wards Automotive International*.

11. Based on Robert B. Reich, *The Work of Nations* (New York: Random, 1992), pp. 126–131; Jordan D. Lewis, *Partnerships for Profit: Structuring and Managing Strategic Alliances* (New York: Free Press, 1990), p. 70.

12. Based on Powell and Brantley, "Competitive Cooperation"; Kogut, Shan, and Walker, "The Make-or-Cooperate Decision"; and Barley, Freeman, and Hybels, "Strategic Alliances." Here, of course, I'm talking about the "new" biotechnology. Traditional biotechnology (fermentation of beer, wine, antibiotics) has been around for a long time, but the groundwork for the new biotechnology wasn't until the 1970s when Cohen and Boyer figured out how to cut and paste DNA, Millstein and Kohler produced monoclonal antibodies, DNA sequencing was worked out, and the first synthetic gene was produced.

13. Powell and Brantley, ibid., p. 369.

14. Nitin Nohria and Carlos Garcia-Pont, "Global Strategic Linkages and Industry Structure," Boston, Harvard Business School Working Paper, November 1990.

15. Ibid.

16. See Kogut, Shan, and Walker, "The Make-or-Cooperate Decision."

17. Kanter, *When Giants Learn to Dance*, pp. 123–125.

18. David A. Burnett, Michael J. Kelly, Nancy A. Kutz, and Dean R. Nelson, "Developing a Dispersed, Multi-institutional Liaison Network," Executive Program, Graduate School of Business, University of Chicago, 1992.

19. From telephone conversation with Dr. David Burnett, January 10, 1993.

20. See, for example, Edward O. Laumann and David Knoke, *The Organizational State* (Madison, Wis.: University of Wisconsin Press, 1987).

21. Ibid. These authors provide a superb analysis of informal political networking among organizations. On patterns of PAC contributions, see Mark S. Mizruchi, "Similarity of Political Behavior among Large American Corporations," *American Journal of Sociology*, vol. 95, 1989, pp. 401–424. Sociologists often use the term *action set* to describe a coalition of organizations that pool resources for the purpose of carrying out specific activities. See, for example, Howard E. Aldrich, *Organizations and Environments* (Englewood Cliffs, N.J.: Prentice-Hall, 1979) and Howard E. Aldrich and Peter Marsden, "Environments and Organizations," pp. 361–392 in Neil J. Smelser (ed.), *Handbook of Sociology* (Beverly Hills, Calif.: Sage, 1988). Robert Faulkner and I explore *illegal* action sets in our network study of a famous price-fixing conspiracy ("The Social Organization of Conspiracy: Illegal Action Sets in the Heavy Electrical Equipment Industry," University of Chicago manuscript, 1992).

22. Powell and Brantley, "Competitive Cooperation," p. 368.

23. Roger L. Hale, Douglas R. Hoelscher, and Ronald E. Kowal, *Quest for Quality*, 2d ed., (Minneapolis: Tennant Company, 1989), p. 120.

24. Harry L. Davis, Stephen J. Hoch, and E. K. Easton Ragsdale, "An Anchoring and Adjustment Model of Spousal Predictions," *The Journal of Consumer Research*, vol. 13, 1986, pp. 25–37; Stephen J. Hoch, "Who Do We Know: Predicting the Interests and Opinions of the American Consumer," *The Journal of Consumer Research*, vol. 15, 1988, pp. 315–324; Stephen J. Hoch, "Perceived Consensus and Predictive Accuracy: The Pros and Cons of Projection," *Journal of Personality and Social Psychology*, vol. 53, pp. 221–234.

25. I presented some of my research on alliances at the joint annual meeting of the Public Choice Society and the Economic Science Association in a talk entitled "Competition, Cooperation, and Collusion: Three Faces of Economic Behavior," March 20–22, 1992, New Orleans, Louisiana. Other sources include interviews with alliance participants, and Kanter, *When Giants Learn to Dance*; Jordan D. Lewis, *Partnerships for Profit: Structuring and Managing Strategic Alliances* (New York: Free Press, 1990); Kathryn Rudie Harrigan, *Strategies for Joint Ventures* (Lexington, Mass.: D. C. Heath, 1985).

26. On the role of continuity expectations in supplier relationships, see Jan B. Heide and George John, "Alliances in Industrial Purchasing: The Determinants of Joint Action in Buyer-Supplier Relationships," *Journal of Marketing Research*, vol. 37, 1990, pp. 24–36.

27. Lewis, *Partnerships for Profit*, p. 222.

28. Ibid., p. 223.

29. From telephone interviews and letters from the CFO of a large joint venture (November 1992; June 1993).

30. Ashish Nanda and Christopher A. Bartlett, "Corning Incorporated: A Network of Alliances," Harvard Business School, 1990/1991.

31. Harrigan, "Strategies for Joint Ventures," Chapter 2.

32. Letter from the CFO of a joint venture (November 1992).

33. Nanda and Bartlett, "Corning Incorporated."

34. Letter from CFO (November 1992).

35. Harrigan, "Strategies for Joint Ventures," p. 57.

36. Quoted in Thomas McCarroll, "Love at First Byte," *Time,* July 15, 1991, p. 46.

37. McGough, "Grand Alliance," p. 40.

38. Tom Peters, *Thriving on Chaos* (New York: Harper and Row, 1987), p. 474.

39. Organizational ecologists have shown that the forces of legitimation and competition influence the birth and death rates of organizations. For a recent treatment, see Michael T. Hannan and Glenn R. Carroll, *The Dynamics of Organizational Populations* (New York: Oxford University Press, 1992). Kogut, Shan, and Walker, "Make-or-Cooperate Decision," and Barley, Freeman, and Hybels, "Strategic Alliances in Commercial Biotechnology," present analyses of the history of biotech alliances that support my three-stage model of alliances.

40. See, for example, discussion of this point in Powell and Brantley, "Competitive Cooperation."

41. Ibid., pp. 369+.

42. According to Barley, Freeman, and Hybels, "Strategic Alliances in Commercial Biotechnology," p. 324.

43. Nohria and Garcia-Pont, "Global Strategic Linkages."

44. Robert B. Reich, *The Work of Nations: Preparing Ourselves for 21st-Century Capitalism* (New York: Random/Vintage, 1992). See, especially, Part Two.

45. Ibid., p. 110.

46. Lewis, "Partnerships for Profit," pp. 203–214.

47. The Bible: Ecclesiastes, 9:10.

48. See, for example, Kogut, Shan, and Walker, "Make-or-Cooperate Decision," on the effect of prior alliances on future alliances in biotechnology.

49. These arguments incorporate "balance theory," one of the well-known approaches in modern network analysis. The focus is the *triad,* three-person (or three-organization) groups. A triad is "balanced" when, for example, "a friend of a friend is a friend." It's imbalanced when "a friend of a friend is an enemy." I develop these ideas for strategic alliances in my "Competition, Cooperation, and Collusion."

50. The concept of organizational learning is used by Peter M. Senge, *The Fifth Discipline: The Art and Practice of the Learning Organization* (New York: Doubleday, 1990). See, also, Chris Argyris and Donald A. Schon, *Organizational Learning* (Reading, Mass.: Addison-Wesley, 1978).

51. Based on Ranjay Gulati, "The Dynamics of Alliance Formation," Ph.D. dissertation, Department of Sociology, Harvard University, 1993.

Chapter 15

1. From John F. Welch, Jr., "Soft Values for a Hard Decade: A View of Winning in the '90s," General Electric Executive Speech Reprint, 1989. All GE materials are used with permission.

2. General Electric, *Annual Report*, 1989, p. 5. In the original text, "boundary-less" is hyphenated as "boundary-less." I have deleted the hyphen to make the term consistent with current usage at GE.

3. The GE story is based on public information, including GE's 1989, 1990, 1991, and 1992 *Annual Reports*; Noel M. Tichy and Stratford Sherman, *Control Your Own Destiny or Someone Else Will* (New York: Currency/ Doubleday, 1993); Robert Slater, *The New GE: How Jack Welch Revived an American Institution* (Homewood, Ill.: Business One Irwin, 1993); reprints of various GE executive speeches; Thomas A. Stewart, "GE Keeps Those Ideas Coming," *Fortune*, August 12, 1991, p. 41; personal interviews with GE managers; and other published articles (references are provided throughout the chapter).

4. The phrase "white-knuckle decade" comes from a speech given by John F. Welch, Jr., "Managing for the Nineties," at the GE *Annual Meeting of Share Owners*, Waukesha, Wisconsin, April 27, 1988.

5. From "To Our Share Owners," General Electric Company, *Annual Report 1991*, pp. 1–5, in which Welch and Vice Chairman Edward E. Hood, Jr., reviewed and commented on changes in the past decade.

6. Statistic cited in John F. Welch, Jr., "Managing for the Nineties," presented at the General Electric Annual Meeting of Share Owners, Waukesha, Wisconsin, April 27, 1988.

7. Quoted on p. 114 by Noel Tichy and Ram Charan, "Speed, Simplicity, Self-Confidence: An Interview with Jack Welch," *Harvard Business Review*, September–October, 1989, pp. 112–120.

8. John F. Welch, Jr., "Soft Values for a Hard Decade: A View of Winning in the '90s," General Electric, Executive Speech Reprint, 1989.

9. Ibid.

10. Described in Slater, *The New GE*, Chap. 13; Tichy and Sherman, *Control Your Destiny*, Chap. 16.

11. Slater, ibid., p. 212.

12. Ibid., p. 214.

13. Tichy and Sherman, *Control Your Destiny*, pp. 200–201.

14. "To Our Share Owners," General Electric, *Annual Report*, 1990, p. 3.

15. Tichy and Sherman, *Control Your Destiny*, p. 201.

16. For example, as I mentioned in Chapter 1, the rise of the hostile takeover culture was accompanied with its own colorful terms and phrases. See Paul M. Hirsch, "From Ambushes to Golden Parachutes: Corporate Takeovers as an Instance of Cultural Framing and Institutional Integration," *American Journal of Sociology*, vol. 91, 1986, pp. 800–837. I discuss linguistic usage in the context of the money culture in Wayne E. Baker and Jason B. Jimerson, "The Sociology of Money," *American Behavioral Scientist*, vol. 35, 1992, pp. 678–693.

17. Slater, *The New GE*, p. 214; Tichy and Sherman, *Control Your Destiny*, p. 202.

18. Described in "To Our Share Owners," General Electric Company, *Annual Report*, 1991, pp. 1–5.

19. Slater, *The New GE*, p. 215; GE 1991 *Annual Report*; Stewart, "GE Keeps Those Ideas Coming," pp. 44–48; Tichy and Sherman, *Control Your Destiny*, p. 205.

20. "Letter to Our Share Owners," General Electric 1991 *Annual Report*, p. 3.

21. Described in "To Our Share Owners," General Electric 1992 *Annual Report*, p. 4.

22. Ibid., p. 4.

23. Tichy and Sherman, *Control Your Destiny*, p. 205.

24. Michael Hammer and James Champy, *Reengineering the Corporation* (New York: Harper Business, 1993).

25. Slater, *The New GE*, p. 230.

26. Ibid., p. 230.

27. Based on interviews with industry users, and on Geary A. Rummler and Alan P. Brache, "Managing the White Space," *Training*, January 1991, pp. 55–70.

28. Some people break the technique into more steps, such as the 11-step plan in Rummler and Brache, "Managing the White Space."

29. Slater, *The New GE*, pp. 230–234; Stewart, "GE Keeps Those Ideas Coming," pp. 48–49; GE *Annual Report*, 1992, p. 3.

30. "To Our Share Owners," GE 1992 *Annual Report*, p. 3.

31. See Chris Argyris, "Personality vs. Organization," AMACOM: *Organizational Dynamics*, Fall 1974, pp. 3–6.

32. "To Our Share Owners," GE 1991 *Annual Report*, p. 5.

33. Ibid.

34. From a speech given by Carl R. Rogers and taken from his *On Becoming a Person* (Boston: Houghton Mifflin, 1961).

35. Tichy and Sherman, *Control Your Destiny*, present a detailed description of Crotonville in Chap. 11.

36. I discuss these issues in Wayne E. Baker, "The Network Organization in Theory and Practice," Chapter 15 in Nitin Nohria and Robert G. Eccles (eds.), *Networks and Organizations: Action, Form, and Structure* (Boston: Harvard Business School Press, 1992).

37. This section is based, in part, on ibid.

38. Ibid., p. 398.

39. Rummler and Brache, "Managing the White Space."

40. Ibid., p. 56.

41. I asked him to do this exercise when I was researching a teaching case, "Capital Partners," which I wrote with the help of MBA student Pablo Beloff, Graduate School of Business, University of Chicago, 1990. I analyzed networks formally in my "The Network Organization in Theory and Practice," Chapter 15 in Nohria and Eccles, *Networks and Organizations.*

42. John F. Welch, Jr., "A Boundary-less Company in a Decade of Change," presented at General Electric, *Annual Meeting of Share Owners,* Erie, Pennsylvania, April 23, 1990.

43. Howard G. Haas with Bob Tamarkin, *The Leader Within* (New York: Harper Business, 1992), p. 85.

44. E. M. Forster, *Howards End* (New York: Bantam, 1985).

Index

Note: An *n* after a page number refers to a note.

About the Author

Wayne E. Baker is associate professor of business policy and sociology at the University of Chicago's Graduate School of Business. There, he teaches the innovative MBA course he developed, called "Managing Organizations Through Networks." He also is a consultant to and conducts executive training for major corporations, financial institutions, and professional service firms.